KU-795-044

The Cambridge Companion to the

ORCHESTRA

....

EDITED BY
Colin Lawson
Thames Valley University

WITHDRAWN
FROM STOCK

CAMBRIDGE
UNIVERSITY PRESS

PUBLISHED BY THE PRESS SYNDICATE OF THE UNIVERSITY OF CAMBRIDGE
The Pitt Building, Trumpington Street, Cambridge, United Kingdom

CAMBRIDGE UNIVERSITY PRESS
The Edinburgh Building, Cambridge CB2 2RU, UK
40 West 20th Street, New York, NY 10011-4211, USA
477 Williamstown Road, Port Melbourne, VIC 3207, Australia
Ruiz de Alarcón 13, 28014 Madrid, Spain
Dock House, The Waterfront, Cape Town 8001, South Africa

http://www.cambridge.org

© Cambridge University Press 2003

This book is in copyright. Subject to statutory exception
and to the provisions of relevant collective licensing agreements,
no reproduction of any part may take place without
the written permission of Cambridge University Press.

First published 2003

Printed in the United Kingdom at the University Press, Cambridge

Typeface Minion 10.75/14 pt   *System* LaTeX 2$_\varepsilon$ [TB]

A catalogue record for this book is available from the British Library

ISBN 0 521 80658 5 hardback
ISBN 0 521 00132 3 paperback

014037710

The Cambridge Companion to the Orchestra

This guide to the orchestra and orchestral life is unique in the breadth of its coverage. It combines orchestral history and orchestral repertory with a practical bias offering critical thought about the past, present and future of the orchestra as a sociological and as an artistic phenomenon. This approach reflects many of the current global discussions about the orchestra's continued role in a changing society. Other topics discussed include the art of orchestration, score-reading, conductors and conducting, international orchestras, and recording, as well as consideration of what it means to be an orchestral musician, an educator, or an informed listener. Written by experts in the field, the book will be of academic and practical interest to a wide-ranging readership of music historians and professional or amateur musicians as well as an invaluable resource for all those contemplating a career in the performing arts.

Colin Lawson is a Pro Vice-Chancellor of Thames Valley University, having previously been Professor of Music at Goldsmiths College, University of London. He has an international profile as a solo clarinettist and plays with The Hanover Band, The English Concert and The King's Consort. His publications for Cambridge University Press include *The Cambridge Companion to the Clarinet* (1995), *Mozart: Clarinet Concerto* (1996), *Brahms: Clarinet Quintet* (1998), *The Historical Performance of Music* (with Robin Stowell) (1999) and *The Early Clarinet* (2000).

Cambridge Companions to Music

Contents

Illustrations

The contributors

Robert Barclay has a certificate in Science Laboratory Technology from the City and Guilds of London. He graduated from the University of Toronto with an Honours Degree in Fine Arts, and has a PhD from the Open University in the United Kingdom. He has worked at the Canadian Conservation Institute of the Department of Canadian Heritage since 1975, specialising in the care and preservation of wooden objects, historic and technical artefacts and musical instruments. He lectures extensively on the conservation of historic collections, for Canadian and overseas audiences, and has travelled to several African countries to give courses and consultations on collections care.

Tim Carter is the author of the Cambridge Opera Handbook on Mozart's *Le nozze di Figaro* (1997), *Jacopo Peri (1561–1633): his Life and Works* (1989), *Music in Late Renaissance and Early Baroque Italy* (1992) and *Monteverdi's Musical Theatre* (forthcoming). He has just moved from Royal Holloway, University of London, to become David G. Frey Distinguished Professor of Music at the University of North Carolina, Chapel Hill.

Simon Channing is currently Head of Performance Planning at the Royal College of Music, where he also runs the Postgraduate Orchestral Pathway and is a Professor of flute. After reading English at Cambridge, he studied at the Guildhall School of Music and Drama in London before starting his professional life as a freelance flautist. In 1988 he joined the London Philharmonic Orchestra, becoming its chairman in 1991. In 1997, he spent a year at the Academy of Performing Arts in Hong Kong as Head of Woodwind, Brass and Percussion, before joining the RCM in 1998.

Stephen Cottrell is a Lecturer in Music at Goldsmiths College in London. His academic research is particularly concerned with ethnomusicological approaches to Western art music, and a monograph, *Professional Music-Making in London* (Ashgate Press), is forthcoming. Other publications include 'Smoking and all that Jazz' in *Smoking: a cultural history* (2003); and 'Music as Capital' in the *British Journal of Ethnomusicology* (2002). He also works professionally as a saxophonist specialising in contemporary music, and has released numerous CDs, both as a soloist and as the leader of the Delta Saxophone Quartet.

Clive Gillinson CBE has been Managing Director of the London Symphony Orchestra since 1984, having played in the cello sections of the Philharmonia and the LSO. In recent years he has initiated the development of the UBS and LSO Music Education Centre at St Luke's, the LSO's annual residency in New York and the Orchestra's innovative own CD label LSO Live. He has also been Chairman of the Association of British Orchestras and is currently a Governor and member of the Executive Committee of the National Youth Orchestra of Great Britain. He was one of the founding Trustees of the National Endowment for Science, Technology and the Arts.

Sue Knussen has enjoyed a varied career in music and the media. Her experience spans work with Leonard Bernstein on his lecture series *The Unanswered Question* through editorial and production work with composers and conductors including Michael Tilson Thomas, Esa-Pekka Salonen and Sir Simon Rattle. She was the Education Director for the Los Angeles Philharmonic and has been a director and producer of television documentaries about music, including *The Art of Conducting* and *Leaving Home*, a seven-part series about twentieth-century music featuring Sir Simon Rattle, for which she was awarded the BAFTA for best arts series of its year.

Peter Laki is a native of Budapest, Hungary, where he studied musicology at the Franz Liszt Conservatory. He earned his PhD at the University of Pennsylvania in 1989. Since 1990, he has served as Programme Annotator for the Cleveland Orchestra, and since 1992 he has also been Visiting Lecturer at Case Western Reserve University. He is the editor of *Bartók and His World* (1995). He contributed the chapter on Bartók's violin works to *The Cambridge Companion to Bartók* (2001).

Colin Lawson has an international profile as a period clarinettist, notably as a member of The English Concert, The Hanover Band and the London Classical Players, with which he has recorded extensively and toured world-wide. He has appeared as concerto soloist at many international venues, including Carnegie Hall and the Lincoln Center, New York. He is editor of *The Cambridge Companion to the Clarinet* (1995), author of two Cambridge Handbooks (1996, 1998) and co-author of *The Historical Performance of Music* (1999). He taught at the Universities of Aberdeen, Sheffield and London prior to his current appointment as Pro Vice-Chancellor at Thames Valley University.

Erik Levi is currently Senior Lecturer in Music and Director of Performance at Royal Holloway, University of London. He is author of *Music in the Third Reich* (1994) and several chapters and articles on German music of the 1920s and 1930s. An experienced journalist, broadcaster and critic, he has contributed reviews to *BBC Music Magazine*, *Classic CD*, *The Strad* and *International Piano Quarterly* and works regularly as a professional accompanist and chamber musician.

Robert Philip is a Lecturer in Music at the Open University. His work on historical recordings first became widely known through his many programmes for BBC Radio 3 and the World Service. In 1992 he published *Early Recordings and Musical Style: Changing Tastes in Instrumental Performance 1900–1950* (Cambridge University Press), described in *Early Music* as 'a monumental work at the cutting edge of a new face of musicology'. His most recent writings are chapters for *The Cambridge Companion to the Piano* (1998) and *Performing Brahms* (forthcoming). He is currently writing a second book on twentieth-century performing trends, *A Hundred Years of Performance* (Yale University Press).

Richard Rastall read Music at Cambridge, with postgraduate work in musicology and composition, before taking a doctorate at Manchester University on minstrelsy in medieval England. He is the author of *The Notation of Western Music* (1983, rev. 1998) and many works on early music sources, minstrelsy, and music in early English drama. He is currently Reader in Historical Musicology at the University of Leeds, and Dean of the Faculty of Music, Visual and Performing Arts. He is a Fellow of the Society of Antiquaries.

John Rushby-Smith is a freelance record producer and composer. He worked as a Senior Music Studio Manager for BBC Radio for twenty-eight years, much of the time with the BBC Symphony Orchestra. He was the technical director for the 1985 BBC/Barbican retrospective *Stockhausen – Music and Machines* and oversaw the broadcasting of more than 500 Promenade Concerts from London's Royal Albert Hall. He conducted an acoustic appraisal of concert halls around the world for the BBC and delivered a paper on his findings at the 1988 Cambridge Conference of the Institute of Acoustics. His recordings have won several major awards, including Gramophone Awards and, on two occasions, the coveted *Grand Prix du Disque Charles Cros.*

Julian Rushton lectured at the Universities of East Anglia and Cambridge before becoming West Riding Professor of Music at the University of Leeds from 1982. His books include opera handbooks on Mozart; *Classical Music: A Concise History*; studies of Berlioz including *The Music of Berlioz* (2001); and a handbook on Elgar's 'Enigma' variations. He has also published editions of music by Berlioz and Potter, and numerous articles. He was President of the Royal Musical Association from 1994 to 1999, and is currently Chairman of the Editorial Committee of *Musica Britannica.* In 2000 he was elected Corresponding Member of the American Musicological Society.

Robert Saxton was born in London. After advice from Britten, he studied with Elisabeth Lutyens, at Cambridge with Robin Holloway, as a postgraduate at Oxford with Robert Sherlaw Johnson and with Luciano Berio. Formerly Head of Composition at the Royal Academy of Music, he is now a University Lecturer and Tutorial Fellow in Music at Worcester College, Oxford. Selected commissions include works for the BBC (radio and TV), Opera North/Huddersfield Festival, LSO and Rostropovich, London Sinfonietta, the Fires of London, ECO, Teresa Cahill, Steven Isserlis and others. He is currently writing an opera, *The Legend of the Wandering Jew*, for BBC Radio 3.

Jeremy Siepmann, formerly Head of Music at BBC World Service, is a musician, author, teacher and broadcaster, whose pupils include pianists of world-wide repute. His books and audiobooks include biographies of Chopin, Brahms, Beethoven, Liszt, Mozart and Bach, two volumes on the history of the piano, and a 7-CD set on the Instruments of the Orchestra. He is the editor of *Piano* magazine and author/narrator of two major CD series for Naxos records, one biographical, the other analytical. He has contributed articles, reviews and interviews to numerous journals and reference works, some of them being reprinted in book form for Oxford University Press and Robson Books.

Jon Tolanski was formerly a musician with the Royal Opera at Covent Garden as well as many of London's major symphony orchestras. He is an award-winning international broadcaster and lecturer on music performers and a writer and archivist of music performance. He was the co-founder of the Music Performance Research Centre (MPRC) at the Barbican Centre, an innovative audio-visual organisation for the archival recording, preservation and study of public performances of music. He now specialises in making documentary features on musicians for world-wide radio and internet organisations.

Jonathan Vaughan studied double bass with Rodney Slatford and Bill Webster at the Royal College of Music. He freelanced with most of the UK's orchestras and opera companies before joining the London Symphony Orchestra in 1992. He immediately became secretary of the orchestra's Sickness and Benevolent Association, was elected to the Board of Directors, and became Finance Liaison Director in 1997, and two years later the orchestra's Chairman. In 2002 he was appointed Director of the National Youth Orchestra of Great Britain.

Preface

The chapters that make up this book were commissioned from various friends and colleagues, all specialists in their respective fields. Our purpose has been to stimulate constructive, critical thought about the past, present and future of the orchestra, as both a sociological and artistic phenomenon. In this respect we are reflecting many of the discussions that are currently taking place on a global basis about the orchestra's continued role as a musical entity in an ever-changing social environment. We have also included within these pages a great deal that combines practice with theory, including discussions of what it means to be an orchestral musician, informed listener or educator.

As Tim Carter points out at the beginning of chapter 1, the orchestra can be defined as both an institution and a corporate musical instrument, histories that are contiguous yet not necessarily congruent, since corporations of instruments existed for some time before the orchestra came into being. The social history of the orchestra has been characterised by elements of continuity alongside the inexorable shift from private to public patronage. During the nineteenth century the middle classes became major arbiters of musical taste, while conductors were increasingly professional entrepreneurs and interpreters who used the orchestra as a vehicle for their own virtuosity. The organisational structures of the modern symphony orchestra can be traced back to the late nineteenth century and have been shaped by different political traditions. The twentieth century has seen a rich variety of developments, including the rise of the chamber orchestra and the revival of historical instruments. At the same time, within an increasing globalisation of orchestral culture, some significant attempts have been made to bridge the gulf that has at times existed between contemporary composers, orchestras and audiences. Yet the immediate future of the orchestra remains an important thread running through many of the contributions to this book. A substantial body of musical opinion undoubtedly sees the orchestra as a nineteenth-century relic, cumbersome and riddled with bureaucracy, more comfortable in the territory of 'Mozart to Mahler' than in the challenges of post-modernism. Yet the body of authors represented within these pages finds considerable optimism in the orchestra's ability to adapt and, as Erik Levi observes at the end of chapter 1, 'it would surely be premature to proclaim that the orchestra is in the grip of a slow death'. This resonates with Stephen Cottrell's assertion later in the book: 'The orchestra is too important to be allowed to subside into a cultural antiquity for an ever-diminishing group of interested historians.'

Although wide-ranging in its scope, this volume is intended as a true 'companion'. It is not, however, a 'compendium'. Comprehensiveness would require a volume many times the size of this. My contributors and I have therefore had to be selective in our essays and overall scheme, and in our illustrations, musical examples and bibliographical references. But this has been balanced by the opportunity for each of us to address our subjects from a personal viewpoint, and this policy has been actively encouraged, subject to reasonable editorial constraints. I have been especially fortunate in persuading individual colleagues to bring into focus within single chapters such vast topics as the development of orchestral instruments, the nature of orchestral repertory, notation, orchestration and the history of conducting and directing. Complementing these surveys are chapters addressing the art of recording the orchestra, from the viewpoints of both performance historian and sound engineer. Contemporary concerns lie at the heart of chapters on training the orchestral player, the development of educational programmes and the orchestral composer.

In their glimpse of the life of an orchestral musician, Clive Gillinson and Jonathan Vaughan take us behind the scenes for an appraisal that is characterised by realism, yet offers a genuine sense of why it is that the profession of orchestral player remains an aspiration for so many conservatoire students. Undoubtedly, some of these eventually find themselves in agreement with the sentiments expressed by the American writer Henry Pleasants a generation ago: the orchestral musician 'has no music of his own, nor can he play anyone else's music with the immediacy that it had for those to whom it was originally addressed, or expect from his listeners the same immediacy of response . . . Given such constraints as these, compounded by the stagnation of the repertory, it is a tribute to the serious musician's skills, diligence and patience that he is not a duller fellow than he is, especially the orchestral musician, playing more or less the same notes in more or less the same way under the daily supervision of a variety of opinionated conductors year in and year out.'[1] Yet the orchestra retains an appeal for a huge range of musicians and audience and it is for such an extended circle that this book is intended. I believe that our authorship's special combination of historical perspective and professional experience has not been attempted on such a scale in any previous book relating to the orchestra.

It is a pleasure to acknowledge the help given so willingly by so many in the preparation of this book. I am indebted to all my contributors for their co-operative attitude and prompt response to various problems and queries. As can readily be imagined, the circle of performers and writers whose advice has been sought is much more substantial than the mere list of contributors might imply and this book would have been much poorer without their unstinting help. My academic colleagues at Goldsmiths College and latterly at Thames Valley University have been a constant source of inspiration. My wife Hilary and son Oliver have offered considerable encouragement to the whole project, even though the book's gestation has coincided with a busy period involving new academic challenges and a demanding concert schedule. I must also extend my sincere thanks to Penny Souster and her team at Cambridge University Press for their helpful advice and for creating a characteristic and fundamentally helpful sense of urgency.

Colin Lawson

Acknowledgements

Acknowledgement for kind permission to reproduce illustrations and music examples is due to the following:

Illustrations

BBC Symphony Orchestra: Figs. 1.1, 2.1, 9.1, 12.1, 12.2
The Hanover Band: Figs. 8.1, 13.1
London Symphony Orchestra: Fig. 7.1
Royal College of Music, London: Fig. 10.1

Fig. 7.1 is a photograph by Keith Saunders; 8.2 by Bill Cooper; 8.1, 9.1 by Alex von Koettlitz; 10.1 by Sisi Burn

Music examples

4.2, 4.3 reproduced by permission of Ernst Eulenberg Ltd
4.4 © Copyright 1947 by Hawkes & Son (London) Ltd
reproduced by permission of Boosey & Hawkes Music Publishers Ltd
4.5, 5.6 reproduced by permission of Peters Edition Ltd
4.6 reproduced by permission of Chester Music Ltd
13.1 reproduced by permission of Novello & Company Ltd
13.2, 13.11, 13.12 reproduced by permission of Universal Edition,
A. G. Wien

1 The history of the orchestra

TIM CARTER AND ERIK LEVI

The orchestra before 1800

Any history of the 'orchestra' will depend significantly on how the term is defined. One can start from two quite different premises: that an orchestra is a corporation of instrumental musicians; and that an orchestra is a corporate musical instrument. The distinction is, in effect, that of the orchestra as an institution and as a sounding body. The history of the institution is a matter for economic, social and other historians dealing with the musical profession and its broader place in Western (or Westernised) art traditions. The history of the 'instrument' is more inherently musical, concerning how composers have been motivated by, and have motivated, changes in the constitution of the orchestra in different genres, forms and styles through the ages. These histories are contiguous – one cannot have the instrument without the body of instrumentalists – and yet not necessarily congruent: corporations of instrumentalists existed long before the orchestra as such came into being. For example, it is a moot point whether one can use the term 'orchestra' for a group of ceremonial trumpeters at a medieval court, for a Renaissance string or wind band, or even for the *24 violons du Roi* in the Versailles of Louis XIV of France. It is no less moot whether one can speak of orchestration, as distinct from the use of instruments, in the works of Monteverdi, Lully, Bach and Handel or even, perhaps, early Haydn.

Most would probably agree that the history of the orchestra – whether as an institution or as an instrument – in any useful sense of the term begins somewhere in the seventeenth century, for all the important precedents in, say, the instrumental bands in late Renaissance churches such as St Mark's, Venice, or in the North Italian courts. The Renaissance had already seen established the notion of instrumental consorts – instruments of the same or similar family covering more or less the equivalent of the four 'voice' ranges of soprano, alto, tenor and bass – that allowed for independent instrumental ensembles. Mostly these consorts were kept distinct, not least in terms of where they might perform: hence the distinction between 'indoor'/*bas* and 'outdoor'/*haut* instruments (respectively, strings and brass, with various wind families somewhere in between), or between consorts of viols (*viole da gamba*) in the chamber and 'violins' (the *viole da braccio* that developed into the modern violin, viola and cello) in the ballroom.

However, such groupings could be combined for larger entertainments. Renaissance theatrical works involving music, such as the Florentine *intermedi*, also established associations of instrumental colouring – strings for heaven-scenes, soft winds for the pastoral, trombones for the Underworld – that would last in opera through the centuries. But two issues come together in the Baroque period, one concerning mechanisms of production and the other concerning their product. Both had a profound effect on the changing status of instrumental music and its performers.

Crucial in terms of production was the expected or intended mobility of musical repertories within and across national boundaries. In this case, the composer must be able to assume the presence of a reasonably standard-ised body of instrumentalists wherever his music might be performed, be it Venice, Rome, Vienna, Paris, London or even the New World. The standard-isation of musical resources prompted by music-printing is clearly one issue here, just as it was for vocal repertories during the sixteenth century: for print to be a commercial proposition (not that it always was), musical works must be performable outside the narrow confines of the composer's imme-diate circle. But the most mobile repertory in the seventeenth, eighteenth and perhaps even early nineteenth centuries was (Italian) opera, which did not primarily rely on print for its dissemination. Here, rather, the mecha-nism of transmission was initially by way of performers and impresarios, whether singly or, more often, in companies modelled on the touring groups of theatrical *commedia dell'arte* players. Opera also became implicated in emerging notions of the canon, the work standing of and for itself, repro-ducible in time and for all time. But if a Venetian opera by Monteverdi was to be performed in Naples (*L'incoronazione di Poppea* in 1651), if Cavalli wrote an opera for Paris (*Ercole amante*, for the celebrations of the marriage of Louis XIV in 1660, although it was performed only in 1662), or if Lully's *Cadmus et Hermione* could be staged in London in 1686, that presumes at least the expectation of reasonably consistent instrumental resources, for all that some adaptation might be needed to suit local circumstances. Thus the early history of the orchestra is closely tied to the opera house; the same applies to the early history of orchestral music, not least the symphony. In-deed, the influence of the opera orchestra whether as an institution or as an instrument remained powerful long after we prefer to focus our attention elsewhere in the late eighteenth and nineteenth centuries. Our reluctance to accept that point arises from ingrained prejudices against opera and its modes of production in favour of more 'abstract', and therefore less com-mercially tainted, instrumental genres. Second in importance was probably the instrumental groupings encouraged in churches and similar institutions both Catholic and Protestant; but then, sacred music, too, tends not to come high up in our musical canons.

In terms of product, at least two specific aspects of the musical Baroque demand consideration. One is the duality of styles normally, if inaccurately, expressed as the *stile antico* versus the *stile moderno* : the *stile antico* involves the interaction of contrapuntal lines of relatively equal status (as in Renaissance counterpoint and its Baroque extensions, chiefly fugue); the *stile moderno* instead relies on melody and accompaniment. The role of instruments within the *stile antico* is necessarily limited to doubling (or substituting for) a vocal line, although in polychoral writing one or more of the separate choirs might be entirely instrumental. The *stile moderno* offered more possibilities. Although its melody was usually vocal, the accompaniment was instrumental, whether notated in full (as in lute- or keyboard-tablatures) or by way of the shorthand known as 'figured bass', comprising a bass line – the basso continuo – with explicit or implied figures revealing the harmony. The basso continuo may be realised by one instrument (say, a harpsichord) or by several (say, harpsichords, organs, chitarroni and bass viol(in)s), such that it has become common to talk about the continuo 'band' or even orchestra in this period; even in Monteverdi's first opera, *Orfeo* (1607), the constitution of the large continuo group changes according to dramatic circumstance. But that accompaniment can also, and increasingly does, involve upper instrumental parts that both support and interact with the voice, whether to colour the vocal utterance (as in, say, tone-painting) or to place it within a formal frame (as with instrumental ritornellos).

Granting instrumental music coloristic or structural roles involves perhaps the most significant shift of the Baroque period: conceding aesthetic status and semiotic power to wordless music. True, the Renaissance had its instrumental preludes, fantasias and dances, but such music was low down the pecking-order of Renaissance styles because it appealed to the senses rather than (by way of the text) to the intellect; it was but an imperfect representation of some harmony of the spheres. It was also largely functional, whether to create a moment of respite between one action and another (an interlude between chamber madrigals; an organ fantasia within the Mass), or to create the time and space for an action to take place (a dance; the consecration of the Host). But new notions of musical rhetoric emerging in the Baroque period granted music *per se* a communicative power independent of its text. They did so by adding to a semiotic system based on symbols (somehow resembling the meaning to be conveyed) one based on signs (somehow representing that meaning). These signs could be interpreted by the competent listener thanks to their conventional association: for example, a descending chromatic tetrachord represents 'lament' even without a lamenting text. At that point, wordless music conveys meaning; a sonata can be 'read' much as one might read a painting. Add to that the principles of tonal patterning that also emerged in the Baroque, and instrumental music thus gained both structural force and expressive power to determine the shape and flow of a musical argument.

The processes were neither swift nor straightforward. Instrumental music only slowly escaped the limits of functionality: most purely instrumental items in most operas have a specific function, if only to cover changes of scenery or allow for stage movement, while even in the nineteenth-century concert hall the symphony (or its separate movements) was often preludial to some other musical act, be it vocal (a virtuoso opera aria) or an instrumental equivalent (a concerto). Likewise, the orchestra as in effect a single musical instrument did not emerge fully formed. The notion of the strings as core became apparent early on, chiefly, one assumes, because of the range (whether of pitch or of dynamic), flexibility (also in terms of temperament) and cohesiveness of the *viole da braccio* family, but also, perhaps, because of the core role of the string band in late Renaissance dance. The early model in Italy, which lasted much longer in France, was a five-part scoring (one soprano, two altos, one tenor and one bass). However, this gradually changed to a standard four parts (in effect, SATB), with or without an additional 16′ instrument on the bass line sounding an octave lower (Monteverdi's specification of a 'contrabasso di viola' for the *Combattimento di Tancredi e Clorinda* of 1624 is an early example).

By the mid-seventeenth century, any opera house had to have on hand a string band and a continuo group – plus occasional wind players as needed – but in the case of the strings it might get away with just one to a part and perhaps no viola, assuming that the theatre was on the small side. It is probably pointless to argue over whether such instrumental groups were an 'ensemble' or an 'orchestra'. Having more than one player per (string) part – often considered a defining feature of an orchestra – was not a *sine qua non*. The string parts in Monteverdi's *Orfeo* seem to have been doubled (ten players for five parts), but this was essentially a matter of increasing the sound rather than to create a specific sonority; thus Monteverdi claimed in the performance notes for his *Ballo delle ingrate* printed in 1638 that the five instrumental parts 'can be doubled according to the needs of the size of place in which it is to be performed'. However, by the second half of the century genres such as the concerto grosso became predicated upon the contrast between one-to-a-part soloists (the concertino) and a larger group (the ripieno). Other instruments were optional and essentially coloristic; they were also usually played by individuals with a range of responsibilities. A very early example is, again, Monteverdi's *Orfeo*, where even two of the violin players (Giovanni and Oratio Rubini) also probably each played the chittarone. Such multi-tasking remained common in the profession through the eighteenth century (wind players shifting from flute through oboe to clarinet; a situation not unknown in modern pit orchestras) and to the present day (clarinettists playing saxophone), even as rising standards of instrumental performance forced increased specialisation just on specific instruments rather than their families. However, in the early Baroque period instrumental parts were not always so idiomatic that they could not be scored differently: the dance music in Monteverdi's *Ballo delle ingrate* was originally performed (in 1608) by 'a large number of musicians playing both string and wind instruments', and not just the strings presumed indicated in the 1638 print.

'Orchestra' as a term for a body of instrumentalists – as distinct from the area in the theatre where they played – was in use in France and Italy by the 1670s, and in Germany and England by the first quarter of the eighteenth century. By the 1730s there were numerous orchestras across Europe recognisable in the modern sense of the term. Charting their changing composition through time, as in Appendix 1, permits one to see quite clearly the gradual establishing of a standard orchestral constitution starting with the strings, to which were added individual wind and brass (plus associated percussion) instruments, and then their complete families. Some of the apparent oddities in the number and distribution of instruments may just be quirks of taste, but they also no doubt reflect both function (the greater the number of players, the grander the occasion) and environment. For the latter, the tendencies towards large groups of oboes and bassoons in the late Baroque and pre-Classical periods, or towards a bottom-heavy string section with surprising numbers of double basses later in the eighteenth century, presumably derive from attempts to cope with acoustic realities: even indoors, performance spaces constructed in wood, and the tendency for audiences to wear heavy clothing, would dampen the sound (hence the penetrating double-reed instruments) and would also favour the upper frequencies (hence the bass reinforcement). Such statistics as those in Appendix 1, however, mask quite striking variations across time and place, and also a tendency to preserve older performing and other practices, whether out of preference or just because of an innate resistance to change. The Paris Opéra retained the distinction between the *petit choeur* (the continuo group, plus some obbligato instruments) and the *grand choeur* (for the larger-scale instrumental items such as overtures and dances) until 1778; even Haydn directed his 'London' symphonies from the keyboard in the manner of a Baroque continuo player, adding improvisatory flourishes in the process; and most orchestral music was published and sold in single parts, requiring further copying for larger-scale performance.

The rise of the orchestra was further supported by, and prompted, changes in instrument design and manufacture, newly emerging systems of musical training (for example, the conservatoires established in Naples and Venice in the seventeenth century), and even the development of standard tunings and temperaments, although absolute pitch standards continued to vary quite widely. It also reflected emerging notions of a corporate orchestral 'sound' produced by a disciplined body of musicians, and necessitated new modes of musical direction, whether from the continuo player, the principal violinist, or a conductor. Both Lully in France and Corelli in Italy were famed for their abilities in co-ordinating large ensembles – in Corelli's case often up to sixty instrumentalists, and at times more – by way of unison bowing, careful intonation and a clear beat. Lully also did much to establish a standard orchestral scoring in his operas – strings plus two oboe and two bassoon parts (to which other wind and brass instruments might be added as required) – which by virtue of its transmission across Europe by his pupils and admirers provided the basis for the orchestra of the Classical period; the majority of symphonies by Haydn and Mozart are for this scoring, with the addition only of two horns. The French, too, made orchestral colour an integral part of their style, such that the orchestration of, say, Rameau or Gluck (in his Paris operas) was invariably more subtle and more varied than the music of most Italians.

The majority of the 'orchestras' before 1800 listed in Appendix 1 are, in effect, house ensembles, be that 'house' a royal or noble patron's, a church or a theatre, for all that such an ensemble might perform different music in a variety of places. The emergence of the independent orchestra as a more or less permanent professional, even self-governing, body is quite a late phenomenon, and one tied to the rise of the concert hall and related institutions (e.g., pleasure gardens) as a viable – later, perhaps the chief – space for musical performance: important early examples from the second half of the eighteenth century are the *Concert spirituel* in Paris, the Grosse Konzert in Leipzig, and in London the Bach–Abel and the Salomon concerts (the latter famously involving Haydn). Inevitably, this is an urban phenomenon involving the rising taste for musical entertainment within a civic middle class, and the new possibilities arising thereby for composers and performers to embrace freelance professional careers. The mechanisms of the opera house (for both composer and consumer) were thus transferred to equivalent non-operatic environments. But such concerts became fixed as a primary mode of musical production only when various former roles of individual patrons or institutions were subsumed by the city (in the nineteenth century) or by the state (in the twentieth), and only when musical art achieved aesthetic independence from its more immediate purposes.

Composers have always been influenced by the performers for whom they have written, and Bach's obbligato instrumental parts in his cantatas, or Haydn's in his early symphonies, were clearly motivated by specific musicians available to them. The emancipation of orchestral wind and brass instruments so noticeable in the second half of the eighteenth century – where they could take part in the thematic presentation rather than just playing a supporting role – also reflects the increasing virtuosity of (often German or Bohemian) players. But an orchestra is more than just a collection of soloists, and by the mid-eighteenth century, one can detect the notion of the orchestra itself as a single virtuoso body, indeed one for which 'concertos' might be written. The specific ensembles for which Handel wrote his orchestral concertos, or Bach his orchestral suites, remain obscure, but by the second half of the eighteenth century orchestras in Mannheim and Paris had distinctive reputations as highly disciplined musical bodies. The famous 'Mannheim style' adopted by the Stamitz family, Mozart's excitement over the performance of his 'Paris' symphony, or the rich variety of Haydn's 'London' works mark a new relationship between composers and the medium. They also establish the point where the symphony becomes high art, and good orchestral writing a *sine qua non* of the composer's profession.

The orchestra after 1800

Political and social upheavals at the end of the eighteenth century had a profound impact on almost every aspect of music. Yet the orchestra after 1800 evinces features of continuity as much as change. For example, the sustained growth of public concerts and concert societies and the inexorable shift from private to public patronage of orchestral activities had already started in the eighteenth century. The success of public ventures such as the Hanover Square Concerts in London (1775) or the Gewandhaus Concerts in Leipzig (1781) in effect therefore provided the prototype for the formation of numerous orchestral societies in the nineteenth century. Yet during this process the middle classes began to exercise an increasing influence over the aristocracy as arbiters of musical taste, even if a number of major composers still worked for princely patrons. Thus, circumstances varied considerably depending on political contexts, whether 'absolute' monarchy, or a tendency in theory or practice towards republicanism, or in cases where the power of the monarch was constitutionally limited.

Many aspects of the orchestra that changed after 1800 are explored more thoroughly later in this volume. They include such important issues as the incorporation of more woodwind, brass and percussion instruments into the orchestral fabric, as well as the evolution of sophisticated technological designs that enhanced these and other instruments' capacities for greater tonal power, range and agility. The growing influence of the conductor was no less significant in shaping the future character of the orchestra. In the eighteenth century, the conductor's role was normally taken by the leader of the orchestra or by the keyboard continuo player and limited to that of maintaining the pulse, indicating cues and ensuring co-ordination of ensemble. Yet by the 1850s, the conductor wielded a baton, and rarely if ever directed from an instrument. This change was certainly initiated in the opera house, primarily because of the increasing complexity and size of the orchestral forces that were required for nineteenth-century operatic works. Moreover, conductors were no longer exclusively composers, as they had been before. While composer-conductors continued to demand the right to control performances of their music, in part for pragmatic reasons and in part because of their vision and romantic self-imaging, their work could also be exploited by a professional entrepreneur such as Habeneck who regarded himself as a performer and interpreter in his own right, utilising the orchestra as a vehicle for demonstrating his own virtuosity.

The venues and social contexts in which orchestras performed were far more varied than before. This makes it difficult to generalise about the size of an orchestra, particularly in the earlier part of the century, where orchestral players were not contracted exclusively to one ensemble, and records of personnel have not fully survived. None the less the statistics provided in the Appendices illustrate a pattern of growth that is reasonably consistent throughout most countries in Europe, and also a move towards greater standardisation. This was particularly the case after the emergence of large and independently constituted concert orchestras such as the Berlin Philharmonic and the Boston Symphony Orchestra towards the end of the nineteenth century.

As well as expanding in size, orchestras were disseminated across wider geographical areas than before. Whereas in the Baroque and Classical eras orchestral activity had been largely restricted to provincial courts and long-established musical centres, economic growth and population movement saw the establishment of orchestral societies in newly industrialised urban towns. In England, for example, the flourishing textile industries of the North-West created a burgeoning demand for regular musical activity which was realised in Liverpool through the creation of the Philharmonic Society in 1840, and in Manchester through the efforts of Karl (later Charles) Hallé who in 1857 founded the orchestra that bears his name. Likewise, the flood of European immigrants to the larger cities in the United States provided the cultural backdrop to the formation of the New York Philharmonic Society in 1842 and the Boston Symphony Orchestra in 1881. In all these examples, the creation of a new orchestra becomes a matter of civic pride and even obligation. It is a case not just of the democratisation of the arts, but also of the notion that the arts serve a civilising function. Significantly neither Britain nor the United States adopted the German model of creating an opera house in every city, and one can argue that the emergence of large symphony orchestras in these countries represents one further example of the downgrading of opera in the artistic canon.

Yet despite developments in Britain and the United States, it should be emphasised that the opera house remained the focal point for much orchestral activity. Orchestral musicians contracted to opera houses in large urban centres such as Paris, Vienna and Berlin continued to work primarily in the theatre, venturing relatively infrequently into the concert hall before 1850. Attempts to correct this imbalance met with varying degrees of success. In Dresden, for example, regular subscription orchestral concerts were only established as late as 1858 despite the valiant efforts of a succession of dynamic court opera directors including Weber and Wagner. In Vienna the Philharmonic Orchestra established by Otto Nicolai in 1842 drew its membership from the orchestra of the court opera. But in its early years the ensemble gave only two concerts per season, increasing this number to six by 1861.

One explanation for opera's continued prominence related to the greater commercial opportunities it afforded to composers. By and large composers were able to experiment more creatively with orchestral sonority in the theatre than in the concert hall. Opera orchestras employed a larger number of personnel and were able to accommodate novel or unusual instruments, many of which only gradually gained acceptance in purely orchestral works. It is therefore not surprising that some of the earliest nineteenth-century treatises on orchestration draw most of their examples of scoring and instrumental potentiality from operatic literature. For example in Kastner's *Cours d'instrumentation* (Paris, 1839, rev. 1844), the chosen musical excerpts derive from operas by Mozart, Gluck, Meyerbeer, Beethoven, Winter, Boieldieu, Weber, Halévy, Méhul and Berlioz, with only two references to Beethoven's symphonies. Admittedly Beethoven's orchestral works are featured more frequently in Berlioz's widely disseminated *Traité d'instrumentation* (Paris, 1844). But it should also be noted that of the sixty-six extended music extracts, thirty-nine are taken from operas by Gluck, Weber, Halévy, Meyerbeer, Rossini, Mozart and Beethoven.

Despite the wider ramifications of the French Revolution and the Napoleonic Wars, the court maintained some degree of influence over orchestral matters. Yet its power to harness the cultural environment had certainly declined. In Germany and Austria, for example, the position remained variable. Although court orchestras in larger cities survived periods of financial and political turbulence through realising a fruitful partnership between private and public enterprise, those in the provinces were less fortunate. Indeed, many court orchestras that had established an international reputation during the eighteenth century, such as those at Bonn and Trier, were disbanded, often on financial grounds. Yet aristocratic patronage of orchestral activities in the provinces by no means collapsed. One remarkable feature of musical life in the first half of the nineteenth century is the extent to which a number of the leading composers of the period secured employment as directors of provincial court orchestras. One thinks in particular of the work of Louis Spohr, employed as court Kapellmeister in Kassel, and later in the century of Brahms, whose brief tenure with the court orchestra in Detmold in the 1850s sharpened his gifts as a composer of orchestral music. Perhaps the most tangible demonstration of the flourishing relationship between the aristocracy and the composer was realised in the small town of Weimar where the piano virtuoso Johann Nepomuk Hummel was appointed court Kapellmeister in 1819, considerably enhancing the repertory and standards of performance over the next twenty years. The most important of Hummel's successors was Franz Liszt, who abandoned his career as an itinerant virtuoso in 1848 to take charge of the orchestra with the objective of making Weimar one of the most enlightened cultural centres in Europe, promoting operas by Wagner and Berlioz as well as his own symphonic poems.

Remarkably, aristocratic patronage of orchestral activity did not entirely subside even after the unification of Germany in 1871. Despite limited numbers of players, the Weimar Staatskapelle prospered at the end of the nineteenth century, thanks partly to the founding in 1872 of the Großherzoglichen Musikschule for the training of instrumental musicians. Thus when Richard Strauss became court Kapellmeister in 1889, the orchestra had the technical capability to give the first performances of such challenging works as the composer's tone poems *Don Juan* and *Macbeth*. No less remarkable were the standards of execution achieved at the court orchestra of Meiningen, where Duke George II supported a court orchestra which under the directorship of Hans von Bülow (1880–4), Richard Strauss (1885–6) and later Max Reger (1911–15) attained a reputation for excellence that was recognised and admired throughout Europe.

Yet in the increasingly industrialised environment of the mid-nineteenth century, the achievements at Weimar and Meiningen were exceptional. By and large, orchestral enterprise became synonymous with musical activity in metropolitan centres where it was supported by a mixture of civic initiative and individual entrepreneurial skill. Arguably one of the earliest concert orchestras to establish itself on this basis was the Société des Concerts du Conservatoire in Paris. Founded in 1828 by the violinist François Antoine Habeneck, it drew its initial membership from the finest instrumentalists from Paris's orchestras, received a generous subsidy from the government of Charles X, and rehearsed with sufficient frequency to attain an unrivalled precision of ensemble. Although Habeneck led the orchestra with an iron grip, its charter was established along democratic principles so that it was run essentially by the members of the orchestra.

While the Grande Salle at the Conservatoire had an audience capacity of nearly a thousand, the relative expense of concert tickets, coupled with the difficulty of obtaining season subscriptions, gave the orchestra a reputation for exclusivity. But with the wider dissemination of music, in which publishing played a vital role, came a burgeoning desire to bring orchestral works to a less affluent public. In Paris in 1861 this objective was accomplished by Jules Pasdeloup, who initiated a series of Concerts Populaires which took place in a far less salubrious district of the French capital. Pasdeloup charged ticket prices that were almost half those of the Conservatoire and enjoyed success with the public until 1884, when his efforts in this direction were superseded by those of two further orchestral entrepreneurs, Eduard Colonne and Charles Lamoureux. The success of Pasdeloup, Colonne and Lamoureux challenged the exclusivity and conservatism of certain sectors of French musical life. Apart from establishing a high personal profile for these particular conductors, their particular enthusiasm for new French music changed the very nature of musical developments in the country, helping to establish a cultural environment that prompted a strong national awareness amongst audiences.

Similar contrasts between social exclusivity and populism, determined to a certain extent by the performance venue, were also manifested in London, where several concert societies thrived during the nineteenth century. The oldest and best known, the Philharmonic Society founded in 1813, sustained its reputation through engaging high-profile soloists and commissioning important new works such as Beethoven's Ninth Symphony. Performing in the relatively confined Hanover Square Rooms, with a capacity of 900, it charged high ticket prices and maintained a reputation for exclusivity which only changed after 1869 with a move to the much larger St James's Hall. Conversely, the New Philharmonic Society, which was founded in 1852 but survived only until 1879, evolved in the opposite direction, beginning its existence in the spacious Exeter Hall, but moving four years later to the Hanover Square Rooms, where higher admission prices were charged. Both organisations were however challenged by the entrepreneurial skills of the Frenchman Louis Jullien, whose promenade concerts drew enormous and socially diverse audiences between 1840 and 1859, and later by the equally successful German-born August Manns, who established the Crystal Palace Concerts series after 1854.

The repertory of the orchestra after 1800 underwent considerable changes from that of previous eras. During the latter part of the eighteenth century, concert programmes in the majority of European cities were tied to conventions that normally required the alternation of short vocal and instrumental items and the avoidance of performing two pieces in the same genre consecutively. A typical sequence of works adopted in such places as Leipzig between 1780 and 1800 would open with an overture followed by an aria, a concerto or a solo number, and concluded with a vocal or choral finale drawn from an opera or oratorio – a pattern that was almost exactly replicated in the second half of a concert. This mould was gradually broken, however, through a combination of factors. In particular the increasing length and significance of the symphony, as represented in the works of Beethoven and later composers, made it much more difficult to retain such rigid principles of programming. Thus, during the first decades of the nineteenth century Beethoven's 'Eroica' Symphony, for example, was often featured as the opening work of the second half of a concert, sometimes being followed by an operatic aria.

Although concert programmes up to the end of the nineteenth century often continued to feature a mixture of operatic, vocal and instrumental material, the elevation of the symphony as the most important orchestral genre also served to hasten the emergence of a museum repertory based upon the musical canon of the great German composers from Haydn to Brahms. The American musicologist William Weber describes this development as beginning in the 1840s when orchestras generally stood outside the mainstream of musical taste. During this period, critics and theorists, as well as a number of composers, reacted against the intense commercialisation of music as reflected in the wide dissemination of simplified editions of popular operatic arias and piano works. Within this context the symphonies of Mozart and Beethoven were regarded as emblematic of loftier musical principles, and such works increasingly formed the backbone of orchestral programmes. After 1848 when many orchestras had moved from being private concert societies into civic cultural institutions, the taste for commercial musical entertainment was better satisfied by emerging salon and café orchestras whose repertory focused on light instrumental music and operetta.[1] Meanwhile the orchestral concert attained a much more hallowed status, commemorating high art and the new social order through the works of great masters. As Weber remarks, 'the canon of great works emerged among the most important bastions of high culture in the new industrial society, providing high-minded art as a counterpoise to the increasingly aggressive profit-seeking in the market place.'[2]

To substantiate this argument, Weber examines concert programmes in four European cities in some detail. In Leipzig, for example, the repertory of the Gewandhaus concerts during the period 1780 to 1870 demonstrates an increase in the proportion of repertory by dead composers from 13 to 76 per cent. This manifestation of extreme conservatism was only challenged temporarily in the 1860s by the Euterpe series which favoured the progressive music of Liszt, Wagner and their disciples. The programmes of the Philharmonic Society in London, although adhering more closely to the conventions established in the eighteenth century, also reflect similar tendencies to those at the Gewandhaus, with music by living composers constituting only a quarter of the repertory presented in the 1870s. In Vienna, the Philharmonic concerts, firmly established in the 1860s, provided even greater focus on symphonic repertory than in those cities. Although music by living composers such as Brahms, Bruckner, Dvořák and Smetana appeared on its programmes during the 1880s, the organisers maintained a strong reliance upon the symphonies of Mozart, Beethoven, Schubert and Mendelssohn. This purist and conservative approach to programming may have been modelled on that of the concerts presented by Habeneck at the Conservatoire in Paris between 1828 and 1847, where salon music and popular *bel canto* arias were studiously avoided, and the performance of music by living composers was restricted to one piece at every other of the dozen concerts presented each season. The popular concerts presented by Pasdeloup and Colonne between 1860 and 1880 offered audiences much more opportunity to hear new French music and works by Wagner, although in the case of Colonne's programmes, over 70 per cent of the repertory still remained rooted in the past, and much of the new music was made up of operatic extracts.

The end of the nineteenth century marks the birth of the modern symphony orchestra. It was during this period that many of the major European and American symphony orchestras were formed, and with this development came an increasing standardisation in terms of size, instrumentation, employment structures, and repertorial policy. For example, the membership of the Boston Symphony Orchestra in 1906 and 1970 numbered 96 and 104 players respectively, while statistics for other orchestras throughout the twentieth century have demonstrated a membership averaging around 100.[3] In terms of the disposition of instruments in the modern symphony orchestra, the tendency towards providing greater strength in the first violins over the seconds was prevalent at the turn of the century, while the augmented numbers of wind and brass players, and even harps, were already in place to cope with the extravagant orchestral demands made by composers such as Richard Strauss and Mahler. The only major change to the instrumental balance of the orchestra since 1900 has been the considerable augmentation in the percussion section. But while the symphony orchestra has readily accommodated the percussion (and to some extent also the piano as an orchestral instrument), it has remained notoriously conservative with regard to accepting wind and brass instruments such as saxophones or Wagner tubas that were invented during the nineteenth century. This may be as much for economic reasons as for artistic ones.

While there are tangible connections between the size and instrumental make-up of an early and late twentieth-century symphony orchestra, it should be pointed out that the modern symphony orchestra sounds rather different from its predecessors. Changes in instrumental design and the raw material used for instruments, coupled with the increased employment of vibrato in the strings and woodwind, have served to create a tonal quality that is far stronger in volume, offering greater brilliance to the listener. Performance styles have also changed, but more significantly, the advent of broadcasting and recording has served to fix a standard and idealised orchestral sound. An inevitable consequence of these developments is that many orchestras have lost the distinctive elements of timbre that remained unique to certain countries before the First World War.

The organisational structures of the modern symphony orchestra can be traced back to the late nineteenth century and have been shaped by different political traditions. For many European orchestras, the state or municipality has taken over their financial stewardship much in the way that the court fulfilled such a role in earlier eras. The members of the orchestra are therefore employed as civil servants, and their managers assume positions as government or civic functionaries. In the free-market economy of the United States, orchestras are generally organised in a different manner. Following the structures that were established in some of the country's older orchestras, many operate as independent non-profit corporations that are controlled by a lay board of directors and business managers. Government subsidies remain at a modest premium, making the orchestra reliant upon industry or commerce to provide necessary funding. A third system of organisation, adopted by such orchestras as the Vienna Philharmonic, Berlin Philharmonic and London Symphony Orchestra, is that of the co-operative in which the orchestra is owned and organised by the musicians with the help of a professional administrator, and financed through a mixture of state and private sponsorship. These structures are discussed further by Stephen Cottrell in chapter 15 of this book.

Although opportunities for employment in orchestras have been open in theory to both genders, in practice the symphony orchestra has remained strongly resistant to engaging women until relatively recently. Although the Second World War radically changed women's position in the workplace, be it on the factory floor or on the farm, the only female instrumentalist who was almost guaranteed employment in an orchestra was the harpist. Some orchestras in the United States employed a few women in the string sections, but rarely if ever in the wind and brass. Even after 1945, when many countries ostensibly outlawed sexual discrimination in the workplace, the percentage of female orchestral members has risen very slowly. A study by Julia All-mendinger and J. Richard Hackman published by the University of North Carolina Press in 1995 suggested that in 1994, the representation of women in US and UK orchestras stood at 36 per cent and 30 per cent respectively, while those in Germany and Austria were much lower at 16 per cent.[4] Further investigation revealed that women continued to be poorly represented in the major orchestras, where in many instances they counted for far less than 7 per cent of the personnel. Amongst the most chauvinist institutions was the Vienna Philharmonic, which only admitted a few women into its ranks in 1997, but continues to oppose any dilution of the sexes on the grounds that women might endanger the unique sound quality and performing traditions of the orchestra.

No discussion of the orchestra in the twentieth century can ignore the impact of modern technology on its activities. The invention of broadcasting, film and recording not only opened up new possibilities for the wider dissemination of orchestral music, but also enhanced opportunities for employment. From the 1920s radio stations in Europe began to establish their own orchestras which broadcast regular concert programmes over the airwaves, and occasionally provided background music for plays. Although transmission was initially rather primitive, special studios were built which enabled sound engineers to experiment with recording techniques and to avail themselves of increasingly sophisticated equipment. Since most national broadcasting systems are financed by the state, radio orchestras are in essence public institutions working both in the studio and the concert hall. From the outset, generous subsidies enabled them to explore more enterprising repertory than the conventional symphony orchestra. For example, British musical life during the 1930s would have remained parochial and conservative had it not been for the BBC Symphony Orchestra's active promotion of contemporary music. Likewise, the rebuilding of German music, and also Italian, after the Second World War could not have been accomplished without the dynamic contribution of the radio orchestra.

The relationship between the orchestra and the cinema has been more turbulent. During the silent-film era, cinema orchestras of varying sizes were established in picture houses throughout Europe, either performing originally composed scores or providing a pot-pourri of familiar musical extracts as directed by the conductor. Their function was both aesthetic, in that they attempted to heighten the emotional impact of events taking place on the screen, and practical, in that their sounds drowned out the whirr of the projector. In Germany cinema orchestras became especially popular and by 1929 employed over 6,000 musicians.

After the advent of the soundtrack in 1930, the cinema orchestra became obsolete almost overnight, with obvious catastrophic consequences for many musicians. But in America, the booming film industry began to draw instrumentalists to Hollywood where competing studios formed their own orchestras to perform synchronised background music. Since many of the composers who were contracted to compose film scores were influenced by the Austro-German late romanticism, studio orchestras were generously endowed with large instrumental personnel, their extravagant and opulent sonorities providing audiences with the necessary means of escape from the disturbing political realities of the period.

By the 1970s changes in public taste and commercial pressures had sounded the death-knell for many American studio orchestras, such as those at MGM and Warner Brothers. Since the cinema was now competing with television for mass audiences, film companies could no longer afford to sustain orchestral ensembles on the same scale as before. Besides, the late-romantic film score was out of fashion, having been superseded by a wide-spread use of pop music. Yet orchestral music has by no means disappeared from the film world. High-profile composers such as John Williams and James Horner continue to write scores following the traditions established by Steiner, Korngold and Waxman in the 1930s, the major difference being that symphony orchestras are more regularly employed to perform their music. Moreover, in today's pluralist environment, some film music has entered the standard orchestral repertory and features regularly in concert programmes.

Although recording soundtracks for the latest blockbuster films un-doubtedly provides a lucrative source of income for an orchestra, its profile in the music world is more enhanced by regular work in the recording studio. Indeed, throughout the twentieth century, commercial recording has proved to be a vital component of orchestral activity. Its importance can be mea-sured in many ways. On a purely historical level, it has provided orchestras with the opportunity to give a degree of permanency to certain performing traditions. It has also acted as a useful documentary means for chronicling orchestral achievements over a period of years. Some ensembles such as London's Philharmonia Orchestra were initially formed by the EMI record company in the mid-1940s for the sole purpose of serving a burgeoning consumer demand for high quality long-playing records. This connection between commercial enterprise and orchestral activity has strengthened in recent years to the extent that recording has become an essential marketing tool for establishing an orchestra's identity, bringing its work to the widest public, and thereby attracting greater financial sponsorship.

More than in any other century, the orchestra has been utilised as a pro-paganda tool, particularly by politically repressive regimes. During the Third Reich, for example, the NS Reichs Sinfonie Orchester was created as the or-chestra of the Führer, drawing its membership from musicians who had lost their jobs during the financial crisis of the early 1930s. The orchestra was based in Munich but spent most of its time touring the country. Propaganda speeches from local Nazi officials accompanied its concerts, which were given mainly in local town halls or schools. Long-established German orchestras also served to bolster the regime, participating in concerts organised by the 'Strength through Joy' movement, or honouring special days in the Nazi calendar. During the Second World War, orchestras such as the Berlin Philharmonic made regular tours to the occupied territories and politically friendly countries to enhance morale and emphasise the supposed superiority of German culture. At the same time, many musicians were forcibly transferred to occupied Poland where local gauleiters pursued a resolutely imperialist policy in establishing their own German orchestras. While the Ministry of Propaganda nominally handled cultural issues, it is interesting to note that during the 1940s Hitler played a leading role in the creation of the Linz-Bruckner Orchestra – an ensemble of 140 players designed to confirm the Austrian city's position as the capital of the Greater German Reich. Much the same could also happen on the opposite side of the political coin. In the Soviet Union, the regime may not have appeared to pursue such an overtly aggressive policy towards its orchestras, yet from the 1930s onwards it operated a rigorous censorship of their programmes. Also, after the Second World War, Soviet orchestras regularly appeared in Eastern European countries with the purpose of solidifying political ties. The cultural ministry supervised orchestral tours to the West after the mid-1950s in which orchestras such as the Leningrad Philharmonic or the USSR Symphony Orchestra likewise acted as ambassadors for Soviet musical life.

1.1 Rudolf Kempe conducting the BBC Symphony Orchestra at the Royal Albert Hall, London, 29 August 1975

It is somewhat ironic that the conservative policies towards repertory upheld by repressive regimes such as Nazi Germany and the Soviet Union have also been replicated in many orchestral programmes in democratic countries. Outside the special conditions of the radio station and the recording studio, the symphony orchestra has remained one of the most implacable guardians of a museum culture, its programmes increasingly orientated towards music of the past.[5] This situation has arisen largely as a result of the increasing dislocation between the modern composer and his public. Audiences have remained notoriously conservative, vehemently rejecting the composer's desire to extend the boundaries of orchestral technique and sonority. As a consequence, relatively few stylistically advanced twentieth-century works have established a secure place on the concert platform, and during periods of financial uncertainty, concert promoters have proved even more reluctant to support music that was not readily accessible.

Some impresarios and conductors have been sufficiently enlightened to try to bridge the gulf created between contemporary composers, orchestras and audiences. Utilising the orchestra's potential for financial patronage – and the tendency for rich Americans to see such patronage both as an obligation and as a convenience – Serge Koussevitsky commissioned several leading composers, including Stravinsky, Hindemith, Roussel and Prokofiev, to write works in celebration of the fiftieth anniversary of the Boston Symphony in 1930. During the 1960s the BBC Promenade Concerts under Sir William Glock pursued aggressive policies of programming modern, new or otherwise 'difficult' music. Similar opportunities were afforded to composers in the New York Philharmonic's 125th anniversary series in 1967. A more recent trend, espoused particularly in the United States and Great Britain, is the appointment of composers-in-residence whose function is to provide new repertory for the orchestra. The scheme has enjoyed some success, although it remains to be seen whether such an arrangement will ultimately affect the monochrome nature of many concert programmes.

One remarkable feature of the modern symphony orchestra has been its dissemination over a much wider geographical sphere than the metropolitan centres of Europe and the United States. Since the beginning of the twentieth century innumerable orchestras have been established in many regions of the world, including Latin America, Australia and the Far East (see Appendix 3). Initially such orchestras drew their membership, conductors and audiences from immigrants who desired to retain a connection between European culture and their new environments. But this trend changed with the development of national music conservatories which were able to train native musicians to the same high standards as their European and American counterparts. Inevitably a certain degree of cross-fertilisation between indigenous musical traditions and those of the West took place in

Latin America and the Far East, though the European musical canon still occupies hallowed status in concert programmes.

Perhaps the most dramatic expansion of orchestral activity took place in Asia in the aftermath of the Second World War. In Japan, for example, concerts and recordings of Western classical music have attracted huge audiences. Regular appearances by European and American orchestras stimulated local interest and encouraged talented Japanese instrumentalists to study at European and American conservatories with government support. In order to satisfy a growing market for orchestral music, the number of orchestras in the country since 1945 has risen from two to twenty-five, of which eight are based in Tokyo. One cannot of course ignore the darker side of this process, since Japan was aggressively and explicitly Westernised by the allies after its defeat in the Second World War. And in general, the marketing of Western music in Asia comes close to a form of cultural or colonial imperialism. Nonetheless a similar intensification of orchestral activity has been experienced in other countries of the Far East such as South Korea and Taiwan, and in China orchestras survived the Maoist Cultural Revolution to flourish in many of the larger cities by the 1980s.

While the increasing globalisation of orchestral culture has been a very distinctive feature of the twentieth century, an equally important component of musical life during this period has been its fragmentation and increasing tendency towards specialisation. Although symphony orchestras continue to thrive, albeit by offering programmes that are often confined to a rather limited repertory, their pre-eminence has been challenged by the chamber orchestra, which provides audiences with an alternative instrumental ensemble of greater flexibility and stylistic diversity, and also, more recently, by the move towards period performance. Chamber orchestras emerged during the period after the First World War partly as a result of an aesthetic desire to counter the bloated sonorities of the late-Romantic orchestra, and partly in response to a more unstable economic climate that could no longer support large performing bodies. With its limited instrumentation and reduced running costs, the chamber orchestra could afford to promote contemporary music more wholeheartedly than its symphonic counterparts. In 1926 for example the conductor Paul Sacher founded the Basle Chamber Orchestra with this purpose and over the next fifty years forged close working relationships with many leading composers, including Bartók, Stravinsky, Strauss, Honegger, Henze and Lutoslawski, all of whom contributed major works for the ensemble.

Another important feature of the chamber orchestra repertory was its focus on music of the eighteenth century – an area that, with the exception of a few classical symphonies and a number of Bach's Brandenburg Concertos, had largely been overlooked by the symphony orchestra. Once again the desire to rediscover music of the Baroque and Classical eras was emblematic of the reaction against Romanticism and a growing frustration with the symphony orchestra's tendency to promote a limited number of canonic works. The chamber orchestra therefore provided the perfect forum for reappraising the music of such forgotten masters as Vivaldi, Telemann and Johann Christian Bach, while allowing much wider access to the early symphonies and concertos of Haydn and Mozart.

Although orchestras modelled on the pattern of the Basle Chamber Orchestra have continued to play an important role in musical life up to the present day, their influence has been considerably diminished by the rise of ensembles that have specialised almost exclusively in one area of the repertory. For example some specialist ensembles began to concentrate their attention almost exclusively on contemporary music. Since the 1950s many avant-garde composers have adopted complex performance techniques and utilised extravagant combinations of instruments that could not be easily accommodated by the conventional chamber orchestra. To rehearse and perform such repertory in a commercially viable situation requires musicians of commitment with superb reading skills and unusual instrumental dexterity – talents that were absorbed into orchestras such as the London Sinfonietta which was founded in 1968 to establish the rapport with living composers that was largely absent from the symphony orchestra.

A further threat to the standard chamber orchestra came in the 1970s when early music increasingly became the sole province of orchestras which employed period instruments and adopted performing conventions drawn from Baroque or Classical treatises. This phenomenon is explored in chapter 8 of this book. Initially such ensembles confined their exploration to music composed before 1800, but in the 1990s increasing attention was paid to nineteenth-century repertory, often with stimulating and provocative results. These developments are interesting in that they suggest a reaction in certain sectors of the musical world against standardisation and conglomerate cultural enterprise, and a concern with the preservation or reclamation of a past heritage that has much in common with the late twentieth-century environmental movements.

As we move into a new century, the future survival of the orchestra continues to arouse much heated debate, whose substance is reflected within the following chapters of this book. The orchestra faces serious challenges on a number of fronts, not least the problem of securing sufficient sponsorship either from the state or from commerce, to support its activities. Since an increasingly ageing population attends orchestral concerts, it has to find new ways of presenting its repertory and making it more accessible to younger people. To overcome these problems, many symphony orchestras have established educational programmes, at least partly in an attempt to justify their place in the world (see Sue Knussen's chapter later in this book). Yet, as observed by several contributors to this book, the success of such schemes is highly dependent upon orchestral musicians being sufficiently gregarious and accessible to be able to reach out to the community at large. Adapting to a changing cultural environment will no doubt require a degree of flexibility that is perhaps alien to the conventions which have sustained the orchestra for so long. But given the tremendous amount of orchestral music that is currently available on compact disc, not to mention the continual formation of new orchestras in the furthest reaches of the world, it would surely be premature to proclaim that the orchestra is in the grip of a slow death.

2 The development of musical instruments: national trends and musical implications

ROBERT BARCLAY

Development in context

Discussion of the development of musical instruments inevitably raises questions of cause and effect: did composers demand changes to instruments, were these encouraged by performers, or were the instrument makers responsible? A popularly held belief since the rise of organology as a discipline in the nineteenth century is that of a progressive and essentially evolutionary process. European citizens were surrounded by mechanical development, social engineering, and the maturation of scientific thought, while the theory of human evolution itself became formalised. Furthermore, in the processes of colonisation, European civilisation had encountered and subsumed 'primitive' cultures, while at the same time the artefacts and practices of these cultures started to be systematically catalogued and preserved. It was not difficult to draw general conclusions on the evolution of musical instruments by making direct comparisons between items collected from undeveloped cultures and those made and used within the Western sphere. Evolution of form and function seemed obvious. It is scarcely surprising that nineteenth-century organologists, embedded in their culture of progress and development, would theorise such a harmonious explanation.

An evolutionary theory of musical instrument development required a driving force. Given the lowly status of the artisan in the nineteenth-century social structure, it was unthinkable that developments which might influence higher intellectual pursuits could be driven from below.[1] It was therefore necessary that the composer be charged with initiating invention. This is epitomised by the often-quoted words of Philipp Spitta, when commenting upon the use of the late nineteenth-century pianoforte in playing Johann Sebastian Bach's keyboard music:

> No instrument but one which should combine the volume of tone of the organ with the expressive quality of the clavichord, in due proportion, could be capable of reproducing the image which dwelt in the master's imagination when he composed for the clavier. Everyone sees at once that the modern pianoforte is in fact just such an instrument.[2]

Spitta appears to be arguing that Bach is precognisant in being able to compose for an instrument that would not exist until long after his death. He is also suggesting that it was incumbent upon musical instrument makers to discern what it was the composer imagined, and then to catch up technically with such forward-looking composition. From a twentieth-century perspective this appears little short of nonsensical. However, before we relegate this theory to its historical context, it is interesting to examine some recent assertions. As one example of many, a well-known modern musician has said that 'musicians like Mozart and Beethoven were ... enormously ahead of their time. Beethoven certainly didn't compose for the fortepiano: he imagined the sound of the modern grand piano.'[3] This thinking is a clear lineal descendant of that quoted above, and although anachronistic is by no means an unusual feature of present-day thought.

A more liberal and less class-structured examination of the role of the artisan shows that invention and development of instruments rarely arise through the needs of the composer. In a wide-ranging examination of the progress, adaptation and evolution of musical instruments, Laurence Libin argues that the composer is, in fact, the least probable driver of change.[4] Composers work generally within the framework provided by the instrumentation at their disposal. It is performers who search for easier ways of following the composers' wishes, and artisans who then work to solve the performers' problems. As Stewart Carter has remarked in a study of Georges Kastner's treatise on instrumentation: 'Technology influenced instrument construction, which in turn influenced orchestration, which in turn influenced composition.'[5] It is important to emphasise that the famous dialogues between Johann Sebastian Bach and Gottfried Silbermann, or between Ludwig van Beethoven and John Broadwood, are dialogues between the artisans and these musicians as *performers*, not as composers.

Another complicating factor is that, since at least the nineteenth century, industrial production has been driven by market forces that emphasise improvement and fairly rapid obsolescence.[6] In this scenario, the instrument maker and dealer are placed firmly in the driver's seat. The application of keywork and valves to wind instruments at the beginning of the nineteenth century, and the plethora of variations on these themes, is evidence of an industry-driven market.[7] Also, it is notable that many of these innovations were aimed at the amateur player, and not at the seasoned professional whose training was more often based upon less cutting-edge equipment. The resistance of composers and the music establishment to innovations in design is seen in their persistence with orchestras of relatively conservative instrumentation. The market was thus very much ahead of the composer and the professional player, which is actually the inverse of the contemporary organological stance captured in the above quotation from Spitta.

In summary, there are two points to be made. First, although it is very easy to assume that musical instrument development in a Western, orchestral context has been founded on the needs of composers, there is much evidence that innovation is actually driven more by the needs of music performance and commercial gain. In a rigidly layered nineteenth-century social structure, innovation would be seen as driven from above. Modern views that support this contention are out of step with our current understanding of historical cause and effect. The hands are tutor to the intellect – not the other way around – and the bank account is also a key factor.

Secondly, there is a false assumption that innovation and evolution of design necessarily result in improvement. In fact, innovation does not replace that which went before it; consumer and user cultures overlap. As an example, in the late nineteenth century the trumpet players at Covent Garden used slide trumpets for the first English performances of Wagner operas. They had no need to use valves because they already had perfectly usable chromatic instruments and the skills to play them. Clearly, the contention that the modern grand piano is essential for the music of Beethoven and Bach makes the assumption that Broadwood's pianos and the various keyboards used by Bach are inferior for their own music. That design and innovation have been progressive and evolutionary is, at one level, scarcely challenged. Nevertheless, a modern contextual reading of the situation shows musical instruments fitting into their time and place as part of a seamless lived culture. As an example, no amount of adaptation of the natural trumpet within the twentieth century resulted in an instrument more capable of reflecting the dynamic, intricate and idiomatic compositions of earlier centuries. The music of these periods played upon modern instruments is not better (because, of course, there can never be a standard of comparison) but it is easier for the modern player. The contention that 'they would have if they could' is a music-historical non sequitur that betrays a lack of appreciation and understanding of context.[8]

Introduction

Although it is unwise to generalise too far in terms of instrument manufacture, one can discern three rough geographical regions of Europe: Mediterranean, middle European, and British. Italy, being bounded to the north by the Alps, tended to produce instruments of a particular character quite distinct from the part of Europe north of the mountains. Then, instrument making in the British Isles, isolated to some extent by the English

Channel, also showed certain unique characteristics. In addition to these three general regions, the Iberian Peninsula and Scandinavia can be viewed as having some distinct qualities. Increasing commerce between manufacturing and artistic centres tended to blur distinctions during the seventeenth century and those following. However, regional differences persisted, and to this day there is no true homogeneity among the instruments of the world's orchestras.

While the orchestra as a distinct body was coalescing, certain kinds of instruments not adaptable for such new roles either fell out of use altogether, or became instruments for solo use, or for playing in smaller ensembles. This chapter deals with those instruments that were adaptable enough to fit into their new roles, and which therefore had a continuing place in the developing orchestra. It must also be borne in mind that, until the modern era, the concept of the orchestra as a distinct and defined body was highly flexible. Composers and performers alike used the forces that were available, or could be mustered as circumstances demanded, for individual performances.

The instruments of the orchestra did not develop steadily and uniformly, but rather in sudden leaps forward, followed by periods of what might be referred to as consolidation. In the middle of the seventeenth century the first of two waves of orchestral instrument development took place. The second wave coincided with the political and social upheavals in Europe during the high tide of late eighteenth-century industrialisation. After both these phases there were periods of consolidation, where the new practices and tools were refined and developed to exploit their fuller potential.

The first wave, 1650–1700

The first wave of development of the instruments of the orchestra coincided with a vogue in Italian fashions in architecture, painting, costume and, of course, music. In France, the advent of Louis XIV, *Le Roi Soleil*, heralded a period of glory (at least for that class who could avail themselves of it). In England the Restoration, a period of artistic expansion, followed the Civil War and Puritanism, while the incessant squabbling with the French had just started on a new phase. And in the German countries, the end of the Thirty Years War signalled a period of some peace and prosperity. The stage was set for musical experiment.

Strings
Discussion of the development of orchestral instruments rightly begins with the violin family. This ensemble was so familiar at the beginning of the seventeenth century that as notable a commentator as Michael Praetorius

stated: 'This is common knowledge and does not need to be discussed here.'[9] This is a pity, as we lack some details of this early period that Praetorius could very ably have provided. Nevertheless, an ensemble of bowed string instruments provided the matrix around which the orchestra came to be formed. The *24 violons du Roi* of the French court provided a typical fashion model for others to emulate. In view of the strong influx of Italian musical fashion north of the Alps, it is highly likely that all the instruments used in the French court were made in Italy. It is already possible to discern the developments in violin-making in Italy, particularly Cremona, that would eventually have such a profound effect in the nineteenth century. As the popularity of the core string section spread throughout Europe, other schools of violin-making prospered.

The final forms of violin, viola and cello that we know today began to be established throughout the century, although there were many variations in dimensions. Tenor-size violins, larger cellos, and small violins are all encountered. A tendency towards 'standard' models is seen in the violins, for example, with the smaller dimensions of the Amatis giving way to the more robust forms of Stradivari and Guarneri. Instruments of the violin family were generally not very highly arched in the belly, and the neck lay on the same plane as the body. The bridge was therefore low. The finger-board was wedge-shaped in profile and extended only a short distance over the top of the belly. Gut strings were used throughout.

The instruments of the viol family were displaced by those of the violin, with the result that few changes of any importance to this discussion were made to them. The exception was the violone, the bass of the family, which had been adopted as a continuo instrument and continued in that role. The sloping shoulders of the modern double bass, unique among the unfretted bowed strings, are an echo of that old viol tradition.

The role of the lute in providing basso continuo parts had necessitated great changes in compass and size. The chittarone was equipped with extra open strings on the bass side, and a much extended and widened neck. These developments were the last that the lute would see in this context, as its role in the orchestra became supplanted by other more versatile instruments, particularly the harpsichord.

Woodwinds

The oboe, along with other orchestral wind instruments, made its appearance quite suddenly in the 1660s. Jean Hotteterre and the instrument makers and musicians of the *Grande Écurie* are generally credited with its development and introduction. It deviated from its forebear, the shawm, in many ways important to its orchestral role. It was made in separable joints, had a narrower bore, and had smaller finger holes. Unlike the shawm, there was no pirouette upon which the player's lips were placed, and the thinner and finer reed was mounted on a detachable staple. Initially, there was one flat sheet metal key, a C lying open. To this was added an E♭ lying closed. There were actually two upper keys; the E♭ was doubled so that a hole could be opened using either hand (use of the left hand for the upper section and the right for the lower had not yet been standardised). The touch of the lower key was split so that the small finger of either hand could reach it. Padding was either thin felt or leather glued in place. All these changes gave greater flexibility and control of volume, producing a much refined sound more suitable for blending with and complementing string instruments. The rapid spread in the oboe's popularity is seen in excellent instruments by Stanesby of London, Grenser in Dresden and many other makers of equal merit throughout Europe.[10]

The bassoon provided the bass voice to the oboe. In its modern form it also arose from the Hotteterre circle of artisans, by adaptation of the curtal. Because of its pitch, the lengthy bore of the bassoon is folded upon itself so as to place the finger holes in a comfortable position. Keys were provided for the right hand. Nevertheless, in order to accommodate the fingers, transverse drillings are necessary where the vents pass through the wood at an acute angle from the surface to the bore. From an acoustic point of view the result is hardly ideal, but it does contribute to the bassoon's characteristic mellow tone-colour. The skill necessary to drill these holes at the correct angle, and then to provide a clean entry into the bore, is not often appreciated.

The transverse flute proved to be more adaptable to orchestral use than the recorder, primarily because of its wide dynamic range and the degree of control offered by its method of tone formation. Its development was also driven by the same circle of French artisans, and like the other wind instruments its popularity spread quickly to the other centres. Initially, it had one key on the foot joint, but to avoid awkward cross-fingerings in more complex compositions, further keys were added.

It is a pity we know so little about Hotteterre and his contemporaries. They are the epitome of the artisan/musicians who created essentially new instruments in anticipation of musical demand. This meant, in effect, that all technical parameters of a range of well-established wind instruments needed to be reassessed. The delicate adjustments to bore sizes required complete re-tooling, including in particular the manufacture of special and extremely accurate tapered reamers. Indeed, the entire effort required an enormous confidence in the viability of the finished product. The achievements of such craftsmen are all too often lost in the glare of the music composed for their products.

Brasswinds

Around the middle of the seventeenth century a major change in the trumpet occurred. Hitherto, the bell profile had been relatively shallow and the throat fairly wide, but in a short space of time bells with a sharper flare and narrower throat began to appear. Also, the average size of the bore decreased. These changes coincided with the appearance of more demanding music for the instrument's upper register. Such works as Maurizio Cazzati's compositions for San Petronio in Bologna, Pavel Vejvanovsky's sonatas, and the various trumpet scorings by Jean-Baptiste Lully indicate a new idiomatic treatment of the instrument. Although the trend had been developing since the trumpet corps first played with other musicians in the first decades of the century (e.g. Schütz's 'Danket dem Herren...', from *Psalmen Davids* of 1619, SWV 45), expressive work for the instrument blossomed fully in the 1660s.

At this time the trumpet was a natural instrument. There were no vents, valves or other devices to modify pitch; tone formation rested entirely with the player's lips and airways. Such is the prevalence of the vented trumpet in the modern baroque orchestra that audiences are too often led to believe that it has some historical precedent.[11] The Imperial German city of Nuremberg produced the lion's share of Europe's brass instruments during this period, but an English school arose in the mid-seventeenth century whose instruments bore very characteristic elements of design and style.

The bell profiles of trombones mirrored the changes in the trumpets. In addition, the action of the slide was greatly facilitated by the application of a 'stocking' at the end of each slide leg, which minimised friction and kept it constant in all positions. Tuning of brass instruments was done by inserting short tuning bits, longer straight shanks, or coiled crooks. Instruments would be supplied with a range of such pieces to allow for pitch adjustments and changes of key. At this period, brass instruments were easily dismountable so that changes in the length of wind-ways were possible, and damaged parts could also be replaced.

Percussion

Drums, predominantly timpani, found their way into the orchestra with the introduction of the trumpet corps. Two timpani, made of shells of beaten sheet metal and tuned to C and G, provided a harmonic bass to the trumpets. The integration with strings and woodwinds of such martial and ceremonial noise-makers necessitated swift and effective refinement. The chief technical refinement to the drum itself was in the tuning, where screw devices to give finer and quicker adjustments had already been employed since the previous century. These screws bore on an iron band that pulled the skin of the head tight over the edge of the shell. Legs were sometimes attached to the body of the tympanum, or two instruments could be placed on an iron or wooden stand. Drumsticks underwent rapid change. The percussive effect of wood and other hard substances was moderated with the gradual introduction of felt, leather and similar resilient but softer padding materials.

Keyboards

Plucked string keyboards had been developing as versatile solo instruments since the sixteenth century, and the harpsichord eventually became the chosen continuo instrument for the orchestra. Harpsichords and other plucked string keyboard instruments of similar design show wide regional variations; Italy, the Lowlands and England all produced distinctive and highly individual versions. The chief developments in the seventeenth century, as they relate to orchestral use, were in compass and versatility.[12] Many of the technical developments of the harpsichord were in response to the instrument's absence of volume control. Double manual keyboards paralleled the normal 8′ register with another which had different plucking points, providing an 'edgier' complementary tone. A 4′ register was also used to add brilliance.

While the whole class of instruments was undergoing redesign, treasured old instruments were reworked to comply with current practice. The changes made to Flemish harpsichords, for example, included the removal of the 4′ register and its substitution with one of 8′ pitch, while *petit ravalement* increased the compass of the instrument by inserting more but narrower keys. These changes allowed valuable instruments to be used for playing contemporary keyboard compositions that required the greater compass. The Edinburgh keyboard instrument scholar Grant O'Brien provides details of the transformations undertaken on harpsichords from the workshop of the Flemish makers, Ioannes and Andreas Ruckers.[13]

Gradual consolidation, 1700–1780

It was in the eighteenth century that the orchestra really began to come together as a homogeneous body. This cohesion had implications for the balance between instruments, not only in playing style and technique, but also in technical development. However, with a few notable exceptions, the existing instruments saw adaptation and alteration to suit changing musical fashions, but underwent no major structural changes. The first flush of development was followed inevitably by a plateau of systematic refinement and exploitation.

Strings

The instruments of the violin family became established in the general forms in which we find them today, although anomalous instruments such as the violino piccolo were still in use. The neck angle of all instruments was still low, the fingerboard was still relatively short, and gut strings were used. These instruments lacked the power that was to be demanded of them in the near future.

The chief and enduring development of this period was in string instrument bows. Tartini is credited with starting the modification around 1730. The old outward-facing curve was turned inwards, allowing the player control over the tension of the horsehair. At the same time the mechanism for tensioning the hair was refined by adding a fine screw adjustment. Pernambuco wood began to be used. These changes provided players with enormously superior control. From around 1775 onwards, under the leadership of François Tourte of Mirecourt, the design of the bow reached its peak. Bows by Tourte, and his contemporaries Adam and Sirjean, are in great demand by string players to this day. Although often taken for granted, the violin bow is an intricate and highly complex construction. The best of violins is useless without a bow of matching quality.

Woodwinds

A multitude of refinements to the established designs of all woodwinds continued to be made, primarily in the addition of more keys. The clarinet was the notable addition to the woodwind instrument forces. Hitherto, single beating reeds of the clarinet type had been limited to folk instruments, but in a relatively short space of time, around 1700, the new instrument became a part of the developing orchestra. The invention of the clarinet is ascribed to J. C. Denner of Nuremberg, the pre-eminent German woodwind maker of the late seventeenth century.[14] The oboe d'amore, the oboe da caccia, and the basset horn also arose as variations on themes during this period.

Brasswinds

Trumpets and trombones saw a general increase in the degree of flare of their bells, coupled with a narrowing of their tubing. Mechanical manufacturing methods, such as spinning of bells and machine-drawing of tubing, spelled an end to the old-established workshops of Nuremberg, and new centres of production gained prominence. Vienna, Prague, Leipzig and many other cities became known for their brass instruments.

The horn was a newcomer during this period. When hunting horns were introduced into the orchestra around the turn of the seventeenth century it was to provide a bucolic effect. However, the strong French horn-making tradition typified by the work of Chrétien produced instruments quite unsuited for orchestral use. Their products arose from the hunting tradition and were not considered art musical instruments. In order for the horn to become an orchestral instrument, rather than a colourful curiosity, much redesign was necessary. Many of the advances in horn design appear to have arisen from the Leichamschneider workshop in Vienna.[15] Horns began to be produced with ranges of crooks, they were made smaller and more compact, their tubing became much narrower and more conical, and mouthpiece design evolved radically. All of these changes were aimed at integrating the instrument, and also giving it a distinct character, quite unlike the trumpet with which its sound had been associated.

Percussion

Timpani continued to be the predominant percussion instrument of the orchestra. Their size and number increased, and their tuning mechanisms became more sophisticated. The subtle use of timpani in Mozart's *Serenata Notturna* is an example of how refined they had now become. Side-drums began to make an appearance, and towards the end of the century the bass drum was introduced from the East. Unlike hammered metal kettledrums, the frames of these drums were made of wood, steamed and bent into shape. The heads were held in place by wooden bands tensioned with ropes, a practice that had been common for centuries in military drums. Stands and supports made the instruments easier to use in the orchestral setting.

Keyboards

The harpsichord's limited dynamic palette was somewhat ameliorated by the use of the harp stop, with the strings muted by a mechanically introduced felt or leather band, and by using leather instead of quill in the jacks of some registers. Machine stops provided quick changes of timbre or dynamic by the use of levers which withdrew or engaged registers. The mechanical sophistication of these instruments is impressive. Further changes to old and treasured harpsichords which had been made in the seventeenth century, termed the *grand ravalement*, included extending the casework to increase the compass further, and the removal and substitution of many parts.

Although the pianoforte mechanism had been developed around 1700 by Bartolomeo Cristofori, it was not until the 1760s that such makers as Johannes Zumpe began making marketable instruments. These and the many others that followed did not, however, supplant the harpsichord in its orchestral role, but rather assumed solo and accompaniment duties.

The second wave, 1780–1840

The turn of the eighteenth century saw the second major wave of changes in the design, construction and manufacture of musical instruments. These changes are, of course, reflections of the huge social upheavals of the period, characterised by the rise of industrialism, the American and French revolutions, and Napoleon's pan-European perestroika. The collapse of court sponsorship of music composition and performance, enhanced commerce between previously insulated centres, and the new popular appeal of music, all contributed to the reworking of every instrument of the orchestra, and the invention of many others. This accelerated development was aided and driven by far-reaching changes in consumer patterns, as seen in the rise of the relatively new commercial concepts of commodification and obsolescence.

Strings

It is during this period that the bowed string instruments of the violin family took the detailed form that they maintain to the present. The development of these instruments lay in the hands of a cadre of violin makers and restorers, chief among whom was Jean-Baptiste Vuillaume. As with all other instruments of the orchestra, new sonority and carrying power were necessary to fill larger concert halls. It so happened that the bowed instruments of the Italian schools (principally Cremona) responded far better than those from other regions to the many changes that were considered necessary. Among the changes were a larger and stiffer bass bar, higher arching, a longer neck which was angled back, a longer fingerboard, a higher bridge, and tougher strings to withstand the greater tension. Such changes produced instruments with profoundly different acoustic and playing characteristics. During this period bowed string instruments, primarily based upon Italian dimensions, were manufactured in large quantities in many parts of Europe by workshops that soon became factories. The towns of Mittenwald, Markneukirchen and Mirecourt gained particular prominence.

At the same time that new, redesigned instruments were being sold in quantity, the classic Cremona violins of the seventeenth and eighteenth centuries were also being reworked for those violinists and connoisseurs who could afford their upkeep. The instruments of other European centres did not respond so well to the changes, with the result that nowadays they are much more likely to be encountered in their original state. It is during this period that the full development of the Cremona violin took place. It is not much of an exaggeration to refer to this development, from a social and historical perspective, as an 'invention' because the changes made to the original instruments were so profound and far-reaching.[16] Old instruments were re-necked, new bass bars were fitted, and many other intrusive internal changes made. It is not commonly known that only one Stradivari violin in existence has its original neck, and that the inner workings of all have been changed repeatedly and quite dramatically over their centuries of use.[17] In all mechanical and acoustic essentials, the classic Cremona instruments date from the nineteenth century. The wood of the bellies and backs of most instruments has been carved away and added to, and steamed and reshaped repeatedly, while the bass bar, sound post and other components have been changed beyond the makers' recognition. In spite of much argument to the contrary, their appeal is not related in any way to the sound that they now produce, but to their pedigrees and the enormous musical impetus that intimate knowledge of their history provides. It has been remarked recently that people have the capacity to delude themselves about the sounds of their instruments, 'and that is why the sound is so subjective and susceptible to suggestion, belief, and myth'.[18]

Plucked string instruments had now fallen out of favour in an orchestral context, primarily because of their lack of penetrating power when in competition with other instruments having wider dynamic ranges. Far from falling out of use, these instruments were transferred to the salon, small halls, and other locations of more intimate music performance. The exception was the harp, which under the developmental skills of such French makers as Sebastian Erard, achieved limited use in the orchestra. Intricate pedal mechanisms, wonders of the mechanical technology of their time, had been developed at the end of the eighteenth century by Cousineau and others.

Woodwinds

The keywork and bore profiles of all woodwind instruments underwent massive revision in response to the needs for projection, volume and versatility. The Munich craftsman Theobald Boehm radically redesigned the transverse flute, and his innovations spread quickly to other instruments. His redesign involved having the keys standing normally open, rather than closed as was the common earlier practice. To this end he used his ring keys (which had appeared sporadically earlier) with which the finger can close the hole while also depressing a key, and long axles to transfer the motion elsewhere. Another important innovation was the use of pairs of metal pillars to support the key fulcrums. Previously, the wood turner had left raised rings on the outer surface of the instrument body wherever a key fulcrum would be needed. The wood would need to be carefully carved away, leaving the pair of pillars raised at each side of the key, and the rest of the profile cylindrical. This was very time-consuming compared with producing quickly a plain cylinder of wood on the lathe, and then screwing the pillars into it. The padding between the keys and the body of the instrument underwent development. Keys were made cup-shaped and employed multiple layers of fish skin, felts, leathers and, later, synthetic materials. Metal bodies were used on some instruments, notably the flute and later the saxophones, but on others they proved less effective.

All these rapid developments required accurate and reproducible machining, reliable spring steel (which was first introduced in wire form by Buffet), and fine soldering techniques. The development of gas flame soldering, replacing the charcoal hearth, had profound effects on assembly techniques. Also, the development of reproducing lathes, turning out one kind of component in quantity, made mass manufacture feasible. A Boehm-system flute, for example, requires over twenty identical pillars, each with a screw thread at the base and a transverse hole drilled through the head.

The plethora of key systems and other inventions that make this period in musical instrument history so confusing – and so fascinating – eventually settled down to a form of standardisation. However, preferences tended to be split along national lines. As Anthony Baines has put it: 'Whenever something new has appeared in the woodwind world, if it pleases the French, then it is likely to be viewed with suspicion in Germany, and vice versa.'[19] Different key systems (Boehm and non-Boehm), reed types and playing styles persist to the present.

Brasswinds

The same need for projection and volume noted above with the string and woodwind instruments also drove the development of brasswind instruments. Other factors were the need to fill in notes missing from the natural harmonic series, and the elimination of out-of-tune harmonics. Two innovations in brass instrument design ran in parallel from the end of the eighteenth and into the nineteenth century: the air column could be split by opening apertures in the sides, or its length could be modified using valves and additional tubing.

The first method entailed covering and uncovering vents in the side of the air column, usually with a system of pads attached to keys as in woodwind practice. This method had, of course, been employed in the instruments of the cornetto family for centuries, primarily using just the fingers, but only at the beginning of the nineteenth century did it come to be applied to lip vibrated instruments of metal. Its function was both the correction of out-of-tune harmonics, and the addition of missing notes in the lower register. William Shaw's so-called harmonic trumpet of 1787 is an example of the former application,[20] and the later keyed trumpets, such as the instrument used in Haydn's famous trumpet concerto, were intended to explore a fuller compass for brass instruments. A good example of the latter type is an instrument by Johann Jakob Frank, now in Leipzig.[21] Such designs proved to be ephemeral in the context of the symphony orchestra; only the ophicleide gained any kind of foothold, first in France and then in England.[22]

It was discovered by brass instrument makers that the addition of crooks to lengthen or shorten the vibrating length of an air column could also be accomplished by diverting the air flow by means of valves. Thus, a crook could be 'inserted' mechanically, rather than by hand, as pauses in the music allowed. The valve, itself, was not an innovation (such devices can be found, for example, in the spigots of fire engines from the early eighteenth century) but its application to musical instruments was the breakthrough. Although there is evidence for the invention of such a valve system for instruments in 1788, the first practical application was by the Prussian Heinrich Stölzel in 1814.[23] Many other designs followed, most of which were concerned with minimising sharp bends and edges in the wind-way, while allowing rapid, friction-free operation. As mechanical production became more reliable, these developments became adopted for use on trumpets and horns. The arrival of the tuba in 1835 addressed many of the problems of bass lines in symphonic and opera scores.[24] And as confidence in valved systems grew among composers and orchestral players, many other innovations were introduced. Among the many manufacturers and innovators, the prolific work of the Belgian instrument maker Adolphe Sax must be especially recognised.[25]

Slide brass instruments of the trombone family supplied the bass line in the orchestra, and occasionally were also made in the higher register. Regional differences are mostly seen in the diameter of trombone tubing, the English favouring narrower tubes than those used on the Continent. Slide trumpets, having a U-shaped bow facing backwards which was tensioned by a clock spring or elastic, became a particular speciality of English orchestras, and lasted in some cases into the twentieth century.

Percussion

The tuning systems applied to timpani became mechanically more sophisticated. Initially, the T-shaped handles distributed evenly around the rim had to be turned individually and incrementally. Uneven tension of the head from inaccurate turning resulted in stresses and problems in tuning, especially when the edge of the head was struck near the rim. To counter this problem, gear-driven or pulley-linked mechanisms were designed, so that by turning one handle the whole head could be tensioned evenly. Even so, the more conventional design with individual handles continued, and is still in use today. The orchestra's range of percussive sound was widened progressively by the introduction of cymbals, gongs, the triangle and similar devices.

Keyboards

The primary keyboard of the nineteenth century (aside from the organ) was the piano, although not integrated into the orchestra but appearing as a solo, concerto and accompaniment instrument. Pianos of the late eighteenth and early nineteenth centuries tell the continuing story of the craftsmen's struggle with string tension and distortion of wood. Doubling of strings, improved string alloys, and rising pitch standards caused enormous stresses on conventional wooden structures, with the result that frames twisted and tuning became unreliable. Another seldom mentioned factor is the effect of more efficient home heating among a new bourgeois class who could afford such luxuries. Heating a house in most temperate climates results in a lowering of relative humidity, while seasonal fluctuations would be much more pronounced. This lack of atmospheric stability has deleterious effects on wood, causing shrinkage, swelling and cracking. Complaints were undoubtedly relayed to makers, who were probably both frustrated and stimulated. Solutions included additional bracing, iron and brass compensation bars, and several forms of metal reinforcement. The key advance in design was the one-piece cast iron frame introduced by Alpheus Babcock of Boston, Massachusetts in 1825.[26] Although it was commonly felt that metal components would affect tone adversely, this proved to be unfounded. The iron frame soon became universal, and the problem of wayward tuning was alleviated.

Mechanical actions of pianos became increasingly intricate. Once the piano had begun to supplant the harpsichord as a solo instrument, there were continuing demands for a quicker, more sensitive, and more reliable action. The double escapement, or repetition, action produced by Erard in the 1820s, for example, has over fifty individually crafted parts per key. The social implications of this development on factory conditions, tooling, and production methods are often not appreciated. Long gone were the days when one individual craftsman followed the production of the instrument from start to finish. Each area of production now had its specialist who, in some factories, knew no other task.

Gradual consolidation, 1840–present

The first part of the nineteenth century had seen the maximum development and proliferation of orchestral instrumentation. It is not easy to grasp that since then instrument development in an orchestral context has actually maintained a plateau. As Simon Wills has observed: 'The thing that we call the modern orchestra is not really modern at all. It existed more or less in its present form in the early nineteenth century – even its seating arrangements were fixed by 1860.'[27] Even though this is a generalisation, and variations continued to be made, it remains true that from this time a certain stasis was setting in. When one examines the plethora of new materials and mechanisms, and the wide gamut of variations on themes bestowed by the nineteenth and twentieth centuries, the opposite appears to be the case. From a technical point of view, though, few fundamental changes have been made to any instrument of the orchestra for a century and a half. And few, if any, of the many instruments invented since the middle of the nineteenth century have achieved a permanent place in the symphony orchestra.

Technological advances in the twentieth century, particularly in electronics, produced such instruments as the theremin, the ondes martenot and the celeste, and later the many varieties of electronic keyboard derived from Hugh Le Caine's method of voltage control.[28] Diversification of musical ensembles has ensured the viability and further development of most of these instruments, but none have found more than a small and transient role in an orchestral setting.

In one area, the nineteenth and twentieth centuries saw vast changes. No more was musical instrument manufacture and development a solely European province. Particularly notable among many manufacturers of the range of orchestral instruments are the piano companies of Steinway and Chickering in New York and Boston respectively, the brass instrument manufacturers concentrated in Elkhart, Indiana, and later the vast industrial complex that allowed such companies as Yamaha to prosper in Japan.

Within a well-established and quite conservative overall technical pattern there have been, of course, many variations and incremental changes in instruments, some of which will be outlined below. Development has not stood still, but there is certainly a recognition that the established pattern functions extremely well, and that no profound change of technical direction is desirable, necessary, or even possible.

Strings

Conservatism in design and development in this period is most evident in the forms of the bowed string instruments. Classic violins, violas, cellos and basses of Cremona and other centres, which were reworked for the most part early in the nineteenth century, are still in use today. The fact that these instruments are still perfectly usable in the orchestra while into the third century of their present iteration says much for their shallow gradient of development, and the relative stability of their forms. New instruments made during this period follow the nineteenth-century patterns very closely, and demonstrate the stability of the craft, and the satisfaction of the users of its products with the status quo. Developments in synthetic stringing materials, on the other hand, show a distinct lack of conservatism. The vast majority of players use strings made from a wide variety of modern materials produced by a highly competitive industry. Greater reliability, musical power and durability are the result, and gut strings have become a comparative rarity outside period performance.

Woodwinds

The conical Boehm flute has been described as 'the greatest of all landmarks in the history of woodwind design'.[29] Although Theobald Boehm later developed the cylindrical bore still in use today, the radical redesigns of the early to mid-nineteenth century have seen no further broad development. It is a testament to the stability of orchestral instrumentation that flutes by such nineteenth-century makers as Lot, Godefroy and Bonneville are still highly desired by orchestral players.[30] Although reworked over their hundred and more years of use, they at least still remain amenable to adaptation and updating as use demands.

Developments in the other woodwind instruments of the orchestra show a similar plateau, with changes in detail of design, but not in basic character. As with other instruments in the twentieth century, wide ranges of styles, materials and technical details have been made available. Outside period orchestras there is nowadays little demand for vintage instruments among woodwinds, and many believe that historic instruments 'play out' in time. The grand exception is vintage saxophones, which are highly prized.

Pitch standards have changed over the years, and only in the last century was international consensus achieved. In the eighteenth century, for example, a pitch of around $a' = 422Hz$, almost half a tone lower than today's, was the most common, though by no means universal. It was not until 1939 that a conference in London established $a' = 440Hz$ as the International Standard Pitch, a pitch which the English had been favouring for some time. Previously there had been a Continental pitch, set at $a' = 435Hz$, while the Berlin conservatory had prescribed $a' = 437.5Hz$. In nineteenth-century England, Philharmonic pitch was high, at $a' = 452Hz$.[31] Indeed, long after 1939 some smaller musical organisations continued with the pitches they had used previously, so a wind instrument player might need more than one instrument, depending upon the occasion.

The variations in key-work, layout and pitch among reed instruments alluded to in the previous section, which grew out of national and regional competitiveness in the nineteenth century, persist to this day. Choice of reed shape and construction is also very important in establishing tone-colour. Players of such instruments as the German clarinet and the Viennese oboe maintain a distinct sound and style. The French versus German flavour is most pronounced in the bassoon.

The application of synthetic materials has resulted in greater reliability and cheaper cost of manufacture. Ebonite, a highly vulcanised natural rubber, was introduced in the later nineteenth century as an alternative

2.1 Flute, oboe and bassoon sections of the BBC Symphony Orchestra at the Royal Festival Hall, London (1970s)

to wood, and met with some success. Other synthetic materials have been adopted since. With supplies dwindling of the exotic tropical hardwoods so desired by woodwind makers and players, the future will see much further experimentation with synthetic products.

Brasswinds

'More power still' has been the call since the 1960s, and the big sound required of all brasses resulted in a general increase in dimensions. For example, until the 1950s horn players, especially in England, still preferred nineteenth-century horns by makers such as Raoux, Courtois and Labbaye. These were originally natural horns which had had valves added later in the century. Since the last half of the twentieth century increasingly more power has been demanded of brass players, particularly by recording engineers and a new breed of eminent conductors. The old horns, with their narrow bores and smaller bells, could not compete. In a similar way, the narrow-bored 'peashooter' trombones favoured by English players inevitably lost their competitive edge. Also, advances in acoustics had provided evenness of response and better centring of notes for all the brasses. The modern orchestral horn, the so-called double horn, has a fourth valve operated by the thumb that will change the open horn from F to Bb. The player generally plays on the F configuration of the horn in the lower range, and on the Bb in the upper. This provides security of note placement, and the cleanness and projection the modern player needs.[32] There is now a triple horn, but many players consider it too cumbersome for general use.

The piccolo trumpet arose from the desire to play the high register works characteristic of the Baroque period within the dynamics of the modern orchestra. The so-called Bach trumpet by Besson was the orchestral precursor.[33] The shorter tube length, at two-foot pitch, provides a set of high notes relatively low in the harmonic series. In this way accuracy of attack can be coupled with the necessary dynamic balance. The bass trumpet represents the other end of the scale. Wagner had encountered such instruments in band use, and he adopted one, probably in 8′ C, for his operatic scores. Nowadays, a four-valve model is most often used, and played by a trombonist because of the large size of the mouthpiece.[34]

Advances in alloys, spring components and lubricants have all contributed to ease of playing and reliability. The choice of valve systems and layouts for brass instruments is wide. Some players prefer rotary valves, while others use pistons. Most instruments have settled down to using one system or the other exclusively, but in others such as the trumpet a choice is available. There are comprehensive arguments for both systems. While choice really comes down to personal preference, it is sometimes derailed by the waves of fashion that pass through the symphony industry.

Percussion

The slate of tone-colours and effects in percussion was progressively increased with the introduction of such instruments as wood blocks, cymbals, tubular bells and the larger gongs. The xylophone, whose tones are produced by the resonance of wood, and the glockenspiel, which uses metal, also appear. It is interesting that the tone-colours of resonant hardwoods became of interest to musical instrument developers at this period, stimulated no doubt by the collection and study of such instruments from colonised cultures elsewhere in the world. The glockenspiel, as its name suggests, used the principle of striking metal plates with hammers that had been used in chiming clocks for a considerable period.

Keyboards

Mechanical changes to the piano were incremental and relatively minor throughout the later nineteenth century and the whole of the twentieth century. However, piano manufacture entered an enhanced international phase, and manufacturers of great craftsmanly and commercial reputation now span the globe, from Steinway in the United States, to Yamaha in Japan, and Bosendorfer in Germany. The celeste, or celesta, was introduced in 1886 by Auguste Mustel. He applied a keyboard and hammer mechanism to the glockenspiel. Struck metal resonates in such a way that the higher frequencies often dominate, hence the bright sound. Following Javanese practice, Mustel added wooden resonator boxes that emphasised the fundamental tones of the metal slabs, thus producing a mellow and reliable tone quality. The instrument was first used in the orchestra by Tchaikovsky in 1892 in the 'Dance of the sugar plum fairy' from the *Nutcracker*, and has seen sporadic use since then. The ondes martenot appeared in 1928. This was an electronic instrument that took the capacitance principle of the theremin and applied it to a keyboard, combining the ethereal sound of the latter with secure tuning. Olivier Messiaen made particular use of the instrument in his *Turangalîla Symphony* of 1948, where it featured with piano and percussion instruments reminiscent of the gamelan.

Conclusion

Naturally, the orchestra did not develop uniformly, either geographically or historically. The whole of Europe, and later other parts of the world, was covered with intersecting networks of musical ideas, craft developments and practical experiments. Developments moved in fits and starts; those destined to be successful spread and colonised, others were born and died in swift succession. One can visualise individual waves of ideas and practices, situated in both time and space, flowering, spreading outwards, intersecting and coalescing. Within such an intricate series of developments, it is clearly impossible to provide more than a general view of this complex series of social and technical interactions. It is hoped that this chapter at least provides a starting point for further exploration.

3 The orchestral repertory

PETER LAKI

Beginnings

When musicians were first assembled in numbers surpassing the usual small consort of wind and string players, it was not to play by themselves but always to accompany singers and dancers at the theatre. The Florentine *intermedi* of the sixteenth century and Monteverdi's *Orfeo* in Mantua (1607) required considerable instrumental forces, and in the case of *Orfeo*, these were listed in the score, with specific assignments indicated throughout the piece. Yet the musicians in *Orfeo* are more an ensemble of soloists than a real orchestra; there was probably no more than a single player to the part. Louis XIII's *24 violons du Roi* were apparently the first group in which the strings played in sections, but they still performed theatrical music, as did their English followers, King Charles's *Four and Twenty Fiddlers*. Jean-Baptiste Lully left a few marches and other short pieces for orchestra that seem not to belong to any of his operas or *comédies-ballets*, but they do not differ appreciably from his theatrical music.

Paradoxically, while the repertory of these 'pre- and proto-orchestras'[1] did not comprise much autonomous orchestral music, the words that would designate the orchestral genres of the future did not, originally, refer to orchestral music at all. In the first instance, the terms 'symphony' and 'concerto' designated vocal genres (as in Giovanni Gabrieli's *Sacrae symphoniae* of 1597 or Lodovico Viadana's *Concerti ecclesiastici* of 1602). Even in the early eighteenth century, when a 'symphony' was definitely an instrumental piece, it was not consistently distinguished from genres that today would fall under the category of chamber music: the names 'symphony', 'sonata', 'trio', 'quartet' etc. were often used interchangeably. Johann Sebastian Bach (1685–1750), George Frideric Handel (1685–1759), and many of their contemporaries wrote works for large instrumental forces that were either suite-type compositions (as Bach's Overtures) or concertos of different kinds (as Bach's Brandenburg Concertos or Handel's concerti grossi). Eventually, the symphony (*sinfonia*) emerged as the leading orchestral genre, and the term and the performing medium became permanently linked to one another.

From the *sinfonia* to the symphony

Originally serving as the instrumental introduction to performances of Italian opera, the *sinfonia* gradually established itself outside the theatre by the middle of the eighteenth century. The production of symphonies during that century was enormous: Jan LaRue's catalogue contains no fewer than 16,558 entries.[2] This proliferation can be explained by the wide variety of functions fulfilled by the genre. It continued to serve the theatre, in addition to being used in church and at important official functions as well as, increasingly, in the new type of venue known as the concert, which could be either private or public.[3]

The first composer to make a name for himself as a writer of concert symphonies was Giovanni Battista Sammartini of Milan (1700/1–76). Sammartini wrote about seventy symphonies. The earlier ones are for strings alone and are written in what is essentially a chamber-music style. Some of his later works include oboes, horns or trumpets, indicating a change to a more orchestral way of thinking. Concurrently, Sammartini made significant moves in the direction of expanding the earlier bipartite sonata form into a tripartite structure, with some motivic development taking place in the middle sections.

The demand for symphonic music performed in concert rather than in a theatrical setting was much greater outside Italy, or in the parts of Italy occupied by the Austrians, like Milan, where Sammartini spent his career. The concert symphony gradually spread to almost all European countries, including France, England, Sweden, and, in particular, the German lands.[4] A group of composers working in Mannheim had a decisive influence on the further evolution of symphonic music. Johann Stamitz (1717–1757) was one of the first to increase the number of movements from three to four, inserting a minuet between the slow movement and the finale. (The minuet could also stand at the end of a three-movement symphony, replacing the Gigue-inspired fast dance or a short Presto in duple meter, which were the most frequent finale types.)[5]

Contemporaries of the Mannheim school, Johann Sebastian Bach's sons Carl Philipp Emanuel Bach (1714–88) and Johann Christian Bach (1735–82) were two of the most important symphony writers of their time. Carl Philipp Emanuel, who worked in Berlin and later in Hamburg, developed one of the most personal styles of any eighteenth-century composer; his harmonic experiments and his intense *Empfindsamkeit* ('sensitivity') set him apart from everyone else. He never visited Italy, and his eighteen symphonies are quite independent from any Italian models.[6] His younger half-brother Johann Christian, by contrast, went to Italy early in his life and eventually established himself in London, where he became one of the primary exponents of the so-called 'galant' style. As music master to the Queen, J. C. Bach moved in a court environment, but through the publication of his scores and through performances at public concerts, he reached a rather wide audience. He became one of the most influential orchestral composers of his time; the young Mozart in particular learned a great deal from him.

Haydn, Mozart and Beethoven

J. C. Bach was born three years later than Joseph Haydn (1732–1809), universally recognised as the 'father of the symphony'. What makes Haydn such a central figure in the history of the symphony is – beyond that hard-to-define but easy-to-feel quality that is genius – the remarkable stylistic evolution that took place during the thirty-odd years separating his Symphony No. 1 (1761) from No. 104 (1795). Haydn had studied with one of the leading representatives of the Neapolitan opera school, Nicola Porpora (1686–1768), who handed him the tradition of the Italian theatrical symphony. During his career, Haydn turned the genre from the relatively simple Italianate model to levels of structural and emotional complexity that the symphony had never attained before. The vast majority of the symphonies are in four movements with a minuet in third (sometimes second) place; important deviations from this norm may be found only in the early works, some of which lack a minuet, others beginning with an Adagio.

In his so-called 'Sturm und Drang' symphonies written around 1770 (many of them in minor keys: No. 44 ('Mourning') in E minor, No. 45 ('Farewell') in F♯ minor, No. 52 in C minor) Haydn struck a proto-romantic tone that was unprecedented in the history of the genre. Haydn gradually increased the length of the works, and expanded the instrumentation, adding a flute to the standard grouping of two oboes, two horns and strings. In certain works, especially the ones written in the festive key of C major, a pair of trumpets and timpani were also added. The wind instruments became increasingly independent from the strings, especially in the later symphonies; not only do their parts diverge more and more but they also get important solos to play, initiating a practice that will become standard later on. On the other hand, solos for the concertmaster or the first cellist, as found for instance in the early Symphony No. 7 ('Le midi'), or the solo string quartet that opens the slow movement of No. 93, did not find immediate continuation.

Like several of his contemporaries such as Carl Ditters von Dittersdorf (1739–99), Haydn began some of his symphonies with slow introductions. This practice, found in only a few of the early symphonies, gradually became the norm by the mid-1780s. Slow introductions quickly acquired a special dramatic meaning: they raised the expectations of the audience for the allegro tempo, creating an atmosphere of suspense. Especially in Haydn's late symphonies, they often included modulations into distant keys, posing tonal 'questions' to which the arrival of the tonic in the Allegro was the answer.

Many of the early symphonies have only one significant thematic group in their first-movement expositions. Gradually, a second thematic group (the so-called secondary theme) emerged, but in some of the late symphonies, Haydn uses a 'monothematic' construction in which the secondary theme is derived from the first theme. This is by no means a return to the earlier state of affairs since the two thematic groups are clearly separated in function, even though they share the same melodic material. Monothematic writing was one of several ways in which the symphonic idiom was individualised in Haydn's hands. With boundless musical imagination, he invested each one of his works, especially the later ones, with singular characteristics not found in the others.[7]

Such stylistic developments went hand in hand with the change in the way the symphonies were disseminated. At first Haydn worked exclusively for the local venues provided by his aristocratic employers (Count Morzin and then, for many years, Prince Esterházy). Later he had more and more outside commissions to fulfil and a growing publishing market to satisfy. Finally, in the London symphonies, he encountered the sophisticated new audience of the public subscription concerts.

It is surely no coincidence that Haydn's symphonies were the first to acquire nicknames – this is an indication not only of their unrivalled popularity but also a recognition of their individual character. While the titles of the early programmatic cycle 'Le matin' – 'Le midi' – 'Le soir' (Nos. 6–8) originate with the composer, many of the others do not. Yet the very fact that posterity felt compelled to attach nicknames to so many of the symphonies tells us something important about how some of them were perceived by the discriminating listeners for whom they were written. Whether the nicknames refer to actual musical features ('Bear', 'Hen', 'Surprise', 'Clock'), anecdotes ('Miracle') or anecdotes reflected in musical features ('Farewell'), their very presence is an indication that an orchestral repertory was born that was appreciated by an ever-widening audience.

Few composers remained exempt from Haydn's influence, and that includes Wolfgang Amadeus Mozart (1756–91), whose first mature efforts in the genre fall into the early 1770s and show familiarity with the new musical style his future friend was developing just then. Works like the 'little' G minor Symphony (K183) exemplify the new trend towards the individualisation of the genre. Its good fortune was that at this early juncture, it was taken up by two masters who were able to invest it with equally strong, though very different, personal characteristics.

As mentioned above, Haydn had studied with an Italian master in Vienna. Mozart, on the other hand, acquired the Italian style on site during his early travels, visiting London (where Italian opera was a significant presence) as a boy of eight, and spending time in Italy on three occasions as a teenager. His operas *Mitridate* and *Lucio Silla* received performances at the Regio Ducal theatre in Milan (which, it should be remembered, was then ruled by the Austrians). Both have three-movement Italian *sinfonie* as their overtures, as do some of Haydn's operas as well (for instance, *Lo speziale*). Yet the operatic overture and the symphony soon began to develop along divergent lines. The third movement of the overture began to merge with the first scene of the opera; overtures therefore lost their finales and eventually their slow movements, too. Mozart adopted the four-movement symphonic form with minuet as early as 1768, although one of the earliest such works, K45, was recycled, with its minuet omitted, as a three-movement *sinfonia* for the comic opera *La finta semplice*.[8]

Mozart wrote approximately forty symphonies (it is hard to give an exact number since some works have been lost and others are of questionable authorship). Quantitatively, the majority of the symphonies were written while the composer was still living in his native Salzburg. Between his move to Vienna in 1781 and his death a decade later, he produced only six symphonies (as opposed to, among a profusion of other works, seventeen piano concertos) – possibly because of a lack of demand. The uniqueness of these works lies less in formal features than it does in Mozart's entirely personal approach to melody and instrumentation. No. 39 in E♭ (K543), No. 40 in G minor (K550), and No. 41 in C (K551), written in close succession during the summer of 1788, represent three different musical characters – gentle, tragic, and grandiose, respectively. Mozart's harmonic language contains advanced modulations into distant keys, and his rhythmic vocabulary can become unusually complex, as in the minuet of the G minor Symphony. His writing for woodwind is often independent from the string parts, and the symphonies contain many examples of soloistic writing for flute, oboes and clarinets. The influence of these works may be felt in the London symphonies of Haydn, written after Mozart's death, and even more in the music of Beethoven. Mozart's G minor Symphony in particular can be said to have opened the door to musical romanticism.

This spectacular development of the orchestral idiom naturally affected all the genres in which an orchestra was used, including concertos and music for the stage as well as for the church. Earlier concertos, from the Baroque era and even most of Haydn's works, tended to use a small orchestra (often strings only) to accompany instrumental soloists. Mozart, especially in the mature piano concertos written for his own concert series in Vienna, uses the same orchestral forces as he does in his symphonies, with as much – or possibly even more – solo writing for woodwind instruments. A similar orchestral expansion takes place, for instance, in Haydn's late masses and oratorios as well. Serenades and divertimenti, often scored for just a few players during the early Classical era, also came to be more orchestrally conceived in many works of Mozart.

The nine symphonies of Ludwig van Beethoven (1770–1827) represent a dramatic decrease in quantity from Haydn and Mozart that can be attributed to a process of individualisation carried to extremes. Having been used once, no musical character and no structural model could ever be repeated in Beethoven's music; therefore, each work is a singular manifestation of a given stage in the most spectacular stylistic evolution ever undergone by a composer. It is said that in his First Symphony (1800), Beethoven was still indebted to the styles of Haydn and Mozart; yet this opinion seems coloured by our knowledge of Beethoven's later, more radical works. Actually, there is hardly a phrase in the First Symphony that could have been written by an older composer; not only the famous out-of-key opening but hundreds of other details proclaim the emergence of an unmistakably new voice on the musical scene.

With each subsequent symphony, Beethoven conquered new worlds of musical expression. The odd-numbered symphonies have traditionally been singled out as the most revolutionary works. Undoubtedly the Third (the 'Eroica', 1805) represents an immense quantum leap in terms of sheer length, concentration of expression and the appearance of programmatic elements that seek to portray abstract ideas rather than concrete objects. The story of the torn-up dedication to Napoleon is only an external indication of the presence of such elements. The enormous dramatic contrasts in the first movement, the funeral march in the second and the finale's thematic links to the *Prometheus* ballet (music about a mythological hero!) are internal signs indicating the work's heroic character. Likewise, the Fifth Symphony portrays heroism, although in a different way than the Third. If the 'Eroica' is a monument to heroism, the Fifth is an enactment of a heroic struggle from tragedy to victory. The Seventh turns the idea of a rhythmic ostinato into a means of transcendent expression, while the Ninth breaks all the rules by introducing singers (soloists and chorus) into the four-movement symphonic scheme, creating what was surely the most ambitious orchestral work written to date. The recall of the themes of the first three movements at the beginning of the fourth was the first instance of explicit motivic links among different parts of a symphony – a device that many later composers seized upon in a multiplicity of ways.

Yet however spectacular the innovations of the odd-numbered symphonies, the even-numbered ones are no less expressive of Beethoven's genius, and one must beware of the common distortion that places the 'struggling' Beethoven above the more peaceful or even humorous manifestations of his personality. The uncommon intensity of the slow introductions to the Second and Fourth Symphonies, the strong dramatic accents in the allegedly 'backward-looking' Eighth, and, in particular, the poetic evocation of nature in the Sixth (the 'Pastoral'), are features that make each of these works equally important to our understanding of this extraordinary musical creator.

The size of the orchestra gradually increased in Beethoven's symphonies. Already in the First, we find two flutes whereas most of Haydn's and Mozart's works have only one if any at all; a third horn is added in the 'Eroica'; a piccolo, a contrabassoon and three trombones join the group in the last movement of the Fifth; the Ninth contains a fourth horn and – for the first time – percussion instruments other than the timpani (triangle, cymbals, bass drum). The soloistic use of the woodwind and brass – and even the timpani, as in the Eighth and Ninth Symphonies – is more advanced than ever before, and the introduction of string solos (the two solo cellos in the second movement of the Sixth) is noteworthy.[9]

Besides his symphonies, concertos and choral works, Beethoven also cultivated the 'concert overture' in which an important stylistic evolution came full circle. The concert symphony, as we have seen, had evolved from the Italian operatic overture; in a later stage the first movement of the concert symphony returned to the theatre as a new type of overture. The introductions to Mozart's *Le nozze di Figaro* and *Don Giovanni* are examples of the one-movement sonata Allegro, often without development section; this form became the preferred one for overtures. Beethoven used it in works like *Prometheus* and later, with various modifications, in the overtures to *Leonore* and *Egmont*, which include significant programmatic elements. The overture to *Coriolan* (1807), although inspired by Heinrich Joseph von Collin's drama, is only tenuously linked to that drama; it is in fact one of the first true *concert* overtures.

From Schubert to the end of the nineteenth century

The symphonic output of Franz Schubert (1797–1828) is contemporaneous with that of Beethoven, his last symphony (the 'Great C major') coming only a year after Beethoven's Ninth. Even though the first six of his symphonies are usually considered to be overly dependent on Haydn, Mozart, and early Beethoven, Schubert's contribution to the genre is crucial.[10] Especially in the 'Unfinished' Symphony and in the 'Great C major', Schubert found an original artistic response to Beethoven's symphonies – a response that would match Beethoven in scope and dramatic energy, yet remain free from any direct stylistic influence. Unlike Beethoven, who tended to construct his symphonic movements of short melodic gestures, Schubert often started with full-fledged melodic statements that he would later break up into smaller units but not before allowing the entire melody to unfold like a song. The opening theme of the 'Unfinished', played in unison by the first oboe and the first clarinet, is a case in point. This difference generates a whole new approach to musical time, one that is less goal-oriented and more expansive, emphasising the moment rather than the process.

If Schubert, a contemporary, defined his symphonic achievement in relation to Beethoven, the same was true of orchestral composers of subsequent generations, from Berlioz to Mahler and possibly beyond. The history of symphonic music in the nineteenth century is largely a history of different interpretations of, and reactions to, the work of Beethoven on the part of composers whose upbringings, artistic outlooks, and personalities were as diverse as could be. It was a stylistic evolution that went hand in hand with some fundamental changes in the make-up and the function of the orchestra itself: ensembles grew in size and the role of the conductor became indispensable. At the same time, the public concert replaced private venues as the primary medium for the presentation of orchestral music.

A point of departure for Hector Berlioz (1803–69) was the Beethoven who, in his 'Pastoral' Symphony, had discovered new ways for music to express emotional programmes. This is not to deny other fundamental influences on Berlioz's music; yet the *Symphonie fantastique*, written only three years after Beethoven's death, is the first work that successfully takes up the challenge of programme music. Schubert, who lived in the same city as Beethoven, struck out on an alternative path in his last symphony; Berlioz the Frenchman, on the other hand, went further in the same direction. The *Symphonie fantastique* has a programme like the 'Pastoral', but much more elaborate: in addition to the descriptive titles of the individual movements, Berlioz offered a lengthy literary text that he insisted should be distributed to audiences whenever the symphony was played. Significantly, however, in the place of 'happy thoughts upon arriving in the countryside' and 'thanksgiving after the storm', we have images such as the 'March to the Scaffold' and the 'Witches' Sabbath' – the Ode to Joy from Beethoven's Ninth is replaced by the *Dies irae* from the Mass of the Dead. The protagonist of the *Fantastique*, intoxicated by opium, is a real 'anti-hero', yet his progress from initial reverie through two lyrical intermezzos to the tragic dénouement is a scenario that would be unthinkable without Beethoven's Third and Fifth Symphonies – even though Berlioz turned Beethoven's dramaturgy completely on its head. Furthermore, the presence of an *idée fixe* (a recurrent musical theme), beyond its programmatic significance, for the first time creates a motivic connection among all the movements in a symphony. In addition to the instruments used by Beethoven, Berlioz's score contains an English horn, two cornets, two ophicleides (ancestors of the tuba) and two harps – a considerable increase in the orchestral forces.

If, for Beethoven, each symphony presented a new artistic problem that demanded an individual solution, Berlioz carried this process of individual-isation so far that the very boundaries of the genre became blurred. The next work he called a symphony after the *Fantastique* was *Harold in Italy*, which is half symphony, half viola concerto; the *Symphonie funèbre et triomphale* was written for a political function which determined its unique musical form. The fourth and last work he called a symphony was *Roméo et Juliette*, which is part opera or oratorio even though the outlines of symphonic form (with traditional movement types such as slow movement and scherzo) are still recognisable. The inclusion of voices in a symphony was obviously inspired by Beethoven's Ninth. Yet the use of a unique, half-vocal and half-instrumental medium as an artistic response to Shakespeare opened a new chapter not only in the history of orchestral music but in the history of the relationship between music and literature as well.[11]

Berlioz continued to develop the programmatic concert overture (*Le corsaire, Roman Carnival*, etc.) as did his German contemporary Felix Mendelssohn (*Hebrides*). Mendelssohn (1809–47) is in some sense Berlioz's antithesis, yet it is significant that they were two of the first major composers who were equally successful as conductors. Their compositional worlds, too, occasionally intersect (compare the slow movements of *Harold in Italy* and the *Italian Symphony*). Like Berlioz, Mendelssohn claimed to be a spiri-tual descendant of Beethoven, but whereas Berlioz took his cue from the programmatic tendencies in Beethoven's music as well as the introduction of voices, Mendelssohn responded above all to Beethoven's classicism, his commitment to triumphant endings and his use of counterpoint. Since the music of the Baroque was so important to Mendelssohn, it stands to reason that he was particularly sensitive to the baroque influences in Beethoven. His choral symphony (*Lobgesang*) is an 'Ode to Joy' without the preced-ing turmoil; his 'Reformation' Symphony pays tribute to the past without falling into conservatism; and his 'Italian' and 'Scottish' Symphonies evoke their respective locales as well as the composer's own unmistakable person-ality. Mendelssohn was fond of eliminating the breaks between symphonic movements – a significant initiative that served to reinforce the unity of the works.[12]

Mendelssohn's friend Robert Schumann (1810–56), in his four sym-phonies, combined Beethovenian and Schubertian impulses; in fact, he was probably the first major composer to include in his work what seem to be explicit allusions to the music of his predecessors. The transition be-tween the third and fourth movements of the Fourth Symphony recreates the analogous 'from darkness to light' passage from Beethoven's Fifth. The Second Symphony is particularly rich in such references, from its opening fanfare, often compared to the beginning of Haydn's No. 104, to the finale, where a quote from Beethoven's song cycle *An die ferne Geliebte* becomes the turning point that changes the course of the movement.

Schumann handled the instruments of the orchestra with more sensitivity than he is usually given credit for. The slow movement of the Fourth Symphony contains a beautiful violin solo, something not found in the works of Beethoven and Schubert; during the later nineteenth century, symphonies would contain many prominent solos for the concertmaster. Schumann also acknowledged programmatic elements to some extent: the solemn procession music in the Symphony No. 3 ('Rhenish'), occurring in the 'extra' fourth movement in the five-movement structure, supposedly represents an actual ceremony Schumann had witnessed near Cologne cathedral.[13]

Thus the idea that music could evoke specific places, portray individual characters or depict concrete events appears in the symphonic works of several composers of different stylistic orientations. When this concept became the governing element of a piece, rather than a passing episode or an added colour, it was bound to explode the framework of the traditional multi-movement symphony. This important step was taken by Franz Liszt (1811–86) in his series of one-movement symphonic poems. There is a significant difference between Berlioz's approach to the issue of programme music and that of Liszt. Berlioz wanted to express his programme 'to the extent that it had musical quality';[14] his programme is filled with the names of musical forms or names of melodies (waltz, *ranz des vaches*, *Dies irae*), producing a certain circularity as the music refers to a programme which in turn refers back to the music. Liszt, on the other hand, sought to represent literary works and abstract philosophical ideas that did not have any inherent 'musical quality' in them. The tragic fate of Mazeppa, the suffering and triumph of Tasso, the hesitations of Hamlet, or the abstract contemplations in *Les Préludes* and *Ce qu'on entend sur la montagne*, are non-musical ideas that are largely responsible for the musical form the pieces assume.

Liszt also wrote two large-scale programmatic symphonies in three movements, based on Goethe's *Faust* and Dante's *Divine Comedy*, respectively. These works manage to express their programme while observing the traditional outline of a three-movement symphony. In his treatment of the Faust theme, Liszt followed a different path than had Berlioz in *La Damnation de Faust*. The French composer, using several soloists and a choir, often focused on the scenes that were associated with music even in Goethe's drama (song of the flea, ballad of the King of Thule), or created closed musical numbers along equally traditional lines (Hungarian march, song of the students and soldiers). Liszt, in his *Faust* Symphony (which was dedicated to Berlioz), sought to address the central characters of the drama (Faust, Gretchen, Mephistopheles) without referring to any particular episodes. The work is purely instrumental except for the optional epilogue, which was added several years later and brings in a tenor solo and men's chorus.

Liszt was fond of using a particular method of thematic character variation that has come to be associated with his name. In the symphonic poems and the *Faust* Symphony, this method is placed directly in the service of the programme. Faust's themes become distorted in the Mephistopheles movement, suggesting that the devil has no themes of his own; he is only a spirit of negation that feeds on the positive spirit of Faust. The two main themes of *Les Préludes* undergo a series of transformations that are consistent with the underlying poetic idea, namely – as Liszt put it in the preface to the score – that life is 'but a series of preludes to that unknown hymn, the first solemn note of which is intoned by Death'. Lamartine's poem includes amorous, dramatic, pastoral, and warlike sections, and these are mirrored in Liszt's music while the thematic unity drives home the fact that all these different characters are merely variations on the large theme of life itself.

Liszt's symphonic poems may have had antecedents in the programmatic concert overtures of Berlioz, Mendelssohn and Schumann, as well as in Liszt's own earlier programmatic works for piano. Yet the symphonic poem, established by Liszt as a major new genre, represented an important innovation as it broke loose from conventional sonata form and followed its subject matter in a remarkably flexible and expressive way. It soon found followers all over Europe.[15]

Orchestral writing developed by leaps and bounds during the 1850s and 60s, thanks to the music dramas of Richard Wagner (1813–83), whose innovations (not least his introduction of a new brass instrument known as the Wagner tuba) had far-reaching effects on orchestral sound. The concert symphony as a genre, however, was not enriched by significant new contributions until Anton Bruckner (1824–96) and Johannes Brahms (1833–97) appeared on the scene almost simultaneously. For different reasons, both waited a long time before making their débuts as symphonic composers: both were in their forties when their respective First Symphonies received their premières. Bruckner was seen as an adherent of the Wagnerian camp, vehemently opposed by the Brahms faction. Yet for all their important stylistic differences, both Brahms and Bruckner made explicit references to Beethoven's Ninth which continued to be the ultimate point of reference for all symphonic endeavours. The theme of the finale in Brahms's First Symphony clearly alludes to the 'Ode to Joy' theme ('every jackass can see that', commented the composer); and several of Bruckner's symphonies open with the same kind of mysterious string tremolo that is heard at the beginning of Beethoven's Ninth. In addition, both composers also drew on Schubert's more lyrical approach to the symphony. Bruckner's expansive forms owe more than a little to the example of Schubert's Ninth, and Brahms's long-standing editorial labours on Schubert's work left their mark on his melodic style. In other respects, however, the works of Brahms and Bruckner show a divergence of artistic paths more fundamental than any differences that may have existed between two contemporaries in earlier times.

Bruckner's path was essentially a solitary one. His symphonies have been popularly described as musical 'cathedrals' in the sense that the architectonic aspect – the construction of large thematic areas, the transitions between them, motivic development and especially counterpoint – seemed to interest him more than the melodic material in itself. This tendency is already tangible in the large orchestral surges in the first movement of the First. The basic movement characters – a passionately dramatic Allegro, a hymn-like Adagio, a Scherzo built from extremely terse thematic material, with a trio in slower tempo, and a dramatic finale with a triumphant ending – remained essentially unchanged during Bruckner's entire life (so did their order, with the scherzo always in third place, except for the Eighth and Ninth Symphonies). The complexity of the realisation and the depth of expression, however, increased with each work, culminating in the monumental Adagio of the Ninth Symphony (the last symphonic movement Bruckner ever completed), whose intense chromaticism points beyond Wagner and anticipates early Schoenberg. (Only five years separate this Adagio, written in 1894, from Schoenberg's *Verklärte Nacht* of 1899.[16])

Brahms's style, by contrast, seems to flow more directly from the music of his predecessors. In addition to the Beethovenian and Schubertian connections already mentioned, Brahms in his symphonies pays homage to Schumann (the opening and the second movement of the Third Symphony allude to Schumann's Third). And in the closing passacaglia of the Fourth Symphony, Brahms appropriated a model borrowed from Bach's Cantata No. 150 and made it the basis for an entirely new approach to the symphonic finale. (The uniqueness of this movement is not diminished by the fact that the finale of the *Haydn Variations* had also ended with a passacaglia-like treatment of the theme.[17])Brahms's uniqueness as a symphonic composer has less to do with quantifiable technical innovations (though certainly his harmonies and rhythms contain important advances over his predecessors) than with a significant deepening of the emotional content, and a new combination of majesty and lyricism that defies analysis yet may have turned out, in the long run, to influence later composers more strongly than did the concrete techniques he had introduced.

Brahms's innovations do not lie in an increase in the size of the symphony as is the case with Bruckner, and he remained free, in particular, of any significant influence from the new German school. Instead, he renewed the symphony 'from within'. He preserved the external framework of the classical symphony but endowed his themes with a rhythmic physiognomy that was all his own. He also made orchestration a much more integral part of his concept (it is enough to think of the role of the horn in the finale of the First Symphony). Brahms replaced the Beethovenian scherzo, which had lived on, albeit much transformed, in the symphonies of Schumann, Mendelssohn and Bruckner, with a type of intermezzo that was peculiar to him. The third movements of the First and Second Symphonies strongly modify the traditional ABA form; the third movement of the Fourth is essentially in sonata form (what appears to be the 'Trio' section is little more than a passing episode). Only the third movement of the Third Symphony has a regular trio, but the character of that movement is as far removed from a scherzo as can be.

The field of orchestral composition was long dominated by the German-speaking countries. With the exception of Berlioz, very few composers from the rest of Europe made lasting contributions to the symphonic literature during the first half of the nineteenth century. The feat of 'internationalising' the symphony was largely accomplished by two younger contemporaries of Brahms, the Russian Piotr Ilyich Tchaikovsky (1840–93) and the Czech Antonín Dvořák (1841–1904). Tchaikovsky's seven symphonies (Nos. 1–6 and the 'Manfred', after Byron) and Dvořák's nine represent decades of intense preoccupation with the genre, in the course of which both composers succeeded, each in his own way, in adapting the Germanic models to their own individual expressive needs. They also incorporated musical elements from their respective home countries. The chronology of their symphonies runs roughly parallel: Dvořák's First ('The Bells of Zlonice') dates from 1865, Tchaikovsky's First ('Winter Daydreams') from 1866. Each composer reached the peak of his creative powers with a final set of four symphonies: Tchaikovsky with the Fourth (1877), the 'Manfred' (1885), the Fifth (1888) and the Sixth ('Pathétique', 1893), Dvořák with Nos. 6 (1880), 7 (1885), 8 (1888) and 9 ('From the New World', 1893).[18] Both composers achieved wide popularity by virtue of their exceptional melodic gifts, yet they are equally admirable as orchestrators and masters of musical structure.[19] In his 'Pathétique', Tchaikovsky in particular introduced innovations (third movement in 5/4 time, last movement in slow tempo) that were radically modern at the time and found echoes in many compositions of more recent date. It should also be remembered that Tchaikovsky was the first major composer to use the newly invented celesta in his *Voyevoda* and the *Nutcracker* ballet.

Unlike their German colleagues who felt the need to choose between 'programme' and 'absolute' music, all the important non-German composers of symphonic music in the second half of the nineteenth century devoted themselves in equal measure to the symphony and the symphonic poem. This is true of Tchaikovsky (who called his programmatic works 'fantasy overtures', as *Romeo and Juliet*, simply 'fantasies', as *Francesca da Rimini*, or 'symphonic ballads', as *The Voyevoda*), Dvořák (whose late works include the symphonic poems *The Water Goblin*, *The Noonday Witch*, *The Golden Spinning-Wheel* and *The Wild Dove*), and also, in France, both César Franck (1822–90) and Camille Saint-Saëns (1835–1921). The diversification of symphonic genres continued with the development of other one-movement forms such as the free-standing scherzo or variation set (Dvořák), the symphonic suite (Dvořák, Tchaikovsky), and the concert overture (Dvořák). The extent to which some of the symphonies themselves should be considered programmatic has been hotly debated. Tchaikovsky's programme to his Fourth Symphony is well known, as are Dvořák's comments about Longfellow's *Hiawatha* as a source of inspiration for the 'New World' Symphony. Yet both have to be taken with a grain of salt: Tchaikovsky confided his programme to his confidante Mme von Meck, only to declare immediately that he felt it to be woefully inadequate. As for the exact nature of the relationship between Longfellow's poem and Dvořák's music, it has always remained something of a mystery. Among Tchaikovsky's Russian contemporaries, Nikolai Rimsky-Korsakov (1844–1908) became one of the most brilliant orchestral writers of his time, who introduced a new sense of colour that influenced younger composers as different as Ravel and Respighi.

Between the nineteenth and the twentieth centuries

Of the great composers born around 1860, Gustav Mahler (1860–1911) and Richard Strauss (1864–1949) continued to consider the symphony and the symphonic poem all but mutually exclusive: Mahler is associated only with the former and Strauss primarily with the latter. Strauss's mature multi-movement works[20] (*Symphonia domestica*, *Alpensinfonie*) are as overtly programmatic as are the symphonic poems, and while some of Mahler's symphonies are undoubtedly based on literary sources (several even have sung texts), the composer repeatedly guarded against narrowly programmatic interpretations. As for the non-Germans Edward Elgar (1857–1934), Jean Sibelius (1865–1957) and Carl Nielsen (1865–1931), they recognised no ideological divide between the two kinds of compositions. Alongside their symphonies (two by Elgar, seven by Sibelius, and six – often bearing programmatic subtitles – by Nielsen), these composers wrote 'symphonic studies' (Elgar's *Falstaff*), programmatic overtures (Elgar's *Froissart* and *In the South*), and tone poems (Sibelius's *Tapiola* and Nielsen's *Pan og Syrinx*).

The first of these composers to achieve international fame was Richard Strauss, who stunned the world with his first tone poems (*Don Juan, Tod und Verklärung*) in the late 1880s, that is, years before the final symphonies of Dvořák and Tchaikovsky were written. Strauss took the concept of the symphonic poem, as first formulated by Liszt, a major step further. For one thing, the programmes became more detailed and more specific. Each one of Till Eulenspiegel's 'merry pranks' or Don Quixote's extraordinary adventures is given highly illustrative musical treatment. Even Nietzsche's philosophy in *Also sprach Zarathustra* is represented in a rather concrete form, 'insofar as it contains musical possibilities' – to quote Berlioz's phrase from the programme to *Symphonie fantastique* which applies admirably to the case of *Zarathustra*. In order to achieve maximum flexibility in rendering his programme, Strauss abandoned most symphony-like elements that were still present in Liszt's symphonic poems (although analysts have still discerned the outlines of sonata form in *Ein Heldenleben*). It is significant in this context that Strauss preferred the term 'tone poem' (*Tondichtung*) to 'symphonic poem' (*symphonische Dichtung*).

Strauss often used a post-*Tristan* harmonic idiom with extreme chromaticism, and revolutionised the art of orchestration. He continued to enlarge the orchestra, requiring six horns in several of the symphonic poems and as many as eight in *Ein Heldenleben*, and special percussion instruments such as the wind machine in *Don Quixote*. He also frequently asked for extremely high registers, extended techniques such as fluttertonguing on the brass instruments to portray the bleating sheep in *Don Quixote* and individual parts for all twelve violas in the same passage.[21]

There is no doubt that Strauss's friend and rival Gustav Mahler also *thought* programmatically: he responded to literature and philosophy even more deeply than did Strauss. Yet for Mahler the relationship between the conceptual sources and the music was far more complex; it resisted verbalisation and forced him to withdraw all programmatic titles and subtitles that he had previously considered using. The movements of the First and Third Symphonies all had such titles in their earlier versions. The literary inspiration becomes explicit only in cases where Mahler resorted to the human voice, as he did in his Symphonies Nos. 2, 3, 4 and 8, as well as *Das Lied von der Erde*. The latter is a six-movement song cycle for two soloists and orchestra that displays clear signs of symphonic structure. These texted works show the range of Mahler's literary sources, from German folk or folk-like poetry to Nietzsche, Goethe, the Latin hymn *Veni creator spiritus* and Chinese poems in German adaptation. Philosophically, all these texts revolve around the same universal questions about the mortal condition, about confronting death and afterlife, about the human and the divine. Interestingly, the Third Symphony, which includes an alto solo singing an excerpt from *Also sprach Zarathustra*, was written in the very same year (1896) Strauss composed his own tone poem on the subject.

Unlike Strauss, Mahler was committed to the idea of the multi-movement symphony with its traditional Allegro, Adagio, Scherzo and Finale characters, but he expanded upon these far beyond Bruckner or any other of his predecessors. Mahler once remarked that 'the symphony [had] to embrace the entire world'. Accordingly, his symphonies are among the longest ever written; but even more important are the emotional extremes they all contain. The Second Symphony employs soloists and chorus in its last movement like Beethoven's Ninth – but it also has a movement for solo voice and orchestra, a practice Mahler followed in his Third and Fourth Symphonies as well. The Eighth is a choral symphony in the true sense of the word, the singers participating throughout the gigantic composition. In all of his works, Mahler was fond of juxtaposing the extremely simple and the extremely complex, the trivial and the transcendent. This startled the contemporaries, but Mahler soon became as universal a point of reference for symphonic composers of the twentieth century as Beethoven had been for the nineteenth.[22] The offstage instruments in the Second Symphony and the special percussion instruments (cowbell, hammer) employed to stunning dramatic effect in the Sixth are just two of Mahler's most striking innovations in the field of instrumentation.

Among the contemporaries of Mahler and Strauss, there were several whose contribution lay less in radical innovation than in strikingly personal styles more or less within the framework of tradition. Both Elgar and Sibelius broke new ground without conspicuous departures from the inherited norms. Both wrote music that became symbolic of their respective countries, as neither England nor Finland had previously produced symphonic works of international significance. Elgar achieved this by a certain dignified, yet passionate, character in his music that was identified with Edwardian England, while Sibelius was inspired by the folk traditions of his native country (its music, but even more significantly, its traditional epic *Kalevala*). Elgar's First Symphony in 1908 was hailed as 'England's First'; Sibelius's Second, six years earlier, was similarly considered a national event of the highest order in Finland.

Sibelius's First Symphony, written in 1899, was still somewhat influenced by Tchaikovsky. In his subsequent works he perfected a technique of motivic development all his own, in which large structures grow directly from small motivic cells, often skipping the intermediate level of classical periods. This makes the stages in the music's growth – from soft openings to great climactic moments – almost imperceptible. The Fourth Symphony (1911), with its dark orchestral colours and dissonant harmonic language, is Sibelius's most 'modern' work. In the later symphonies, traditional form continues to be treated in a strikingly personal way – an evolution that reaches its peak in the one-movement Seventh Symphony (1924). This work is based on the contrast between some material subjected to constant variation and an unchanging theme, both spread across sections in different tempos so there is considerable thematic overlap among the various sections.[23]

Elgar's music is a combination of a very private sensibility (often described as 'nostalgic', 'brooding', and 'noble') with a public, even official exterior. Elgar strove for, and gained, recognition by the political establishment; he rose from relatively humble origins to be elevated to knighthood and even baronetcy – and it seems that his musical style was singularly suited for the achievement of such high political status.[24]

A contemporary of Elgar and Sibelius, Carl Nielsen in Denmark created a style that was neither 'modernistic' nor 'traditional'. The break with the past is not as dramatic as in the case of Mahler or Strauss; yet his quintessentially romantic urge for self-expression impelled Nielsen to introduce innovations that were as bold as any at the time ('progressive', or constantly changing, tonality, and highly original timpani writing, to mention only two particularly striking features).[25]

Strauss and Mahler consciously carried the nineteenth-century Austro-German tradition into the new era; Elgar, Sibelius and Nielsen each gave his own answer to the question of traditionalism vs. modernism and national vs. universal styles. Claude Debussy (1862–1918), on the other hand, owes little to nineteenth-century French music, and, even though in later years he considered himself as a *musicien français* (i.e. a composer representing the essence of his country), his concerns were never nationalistic in any sense of the word. The composer who most influenced Debussy was probably Richard Wagner, but in his mature works, Debussy consciously strove to achieve the opposite of what Wagner had done. Debussy sought to conquer for music that elusive line between dream and awakening that the symbolist poets Paul Verlaine and Stéphane Mallarmé had captured in their works. His early masterpiece *Prélude à l'après-midi d'un faune*, after Mallarmé's eclogue (1894), uses chromaticism in a more subdued and less goal-oriented way than Wagner, and his instrumentation expresses sensuality not in the manner of *Tristan und Isolde* but at a certain remove, consistent with Mallarmé's description of the *syrinx* as an *instrument des fuites* ('elusive instrument'). A solo flute plays the part of the antique syrinx, opening the piece with a languid theme that has become famous as an example of a melodic style independent from any traditional models.

Debussy almost completely dispensed with thematic development of the kind universally practised since the time of Beethoven; he also showed little interest in either the symphony or the symphonic poem that had dominated orchestral music for so many years. Rather than expressing concrete literary programmes, his later orchestral works – especially *Three Nocturnes, La Mer, Images*, and the ballet *Jeux* – are based on visual 'images' defined much more vaguely. Those images are transformed into music through a whole array of orchestral colours never heard before, using musical structures that, instead of moving inexorably forward, are happy to linger and to explore specific sensations or 'impressions' in great depth.

The 1870s gave the musical world such profoundly different figures as Ralph Vaughan Williams (1872–1958), Alexander Scriabin (1873–1915), Sergei Rachmaninov (1873–1943), Charles Ives (1874–1954), Arnold Schoenberg (1874–1951), Maurice Ravel (1875–1937) and Ottorino Respighi (1879–1936). Their artistic goals, and the means used to achieve them, are possibly even more diverse than those of the composers born in the 1860s.

Rachmaninov is usually considered to be the most conservative member of his generation and in fact, he held on to a vocabulary inherited from his elders, especially Tchaikovsky, though he expressed his own thoughts and feelings using that vocabulary. Influenced by theosophic mysticism, his former classmate Scriabin brought post-Wagnerian chromaticism to the brink of atonality in a series of dramatic-passionate symphonies (*The Divine Poem, The Poem of Ecstasy* and *Prometheus: Poem of Fire*). Yet it was Schoenberg who actually crossed that line: his first fully atonal work, *Three Pieces for Piano*, Op. 11, was soon followed by the epoch-making *Five Pieces for Orchestra*, Op. 16 (1909). Schoenberg started his career as an orchestral composer with the lush post-romantic scores of *Gurrelieder* and *Pelleas und Melisande*, after which the vastly reduced textures and compressed musical forms of the First Chamber Symphony (1906) represented a major breakthrough. Introducing a radically new sound balance (single strings against single winds), the Chamber Symphony made history with harmonic innovations (chords based on fourths instead of thirds) as well. Since Schoenberg completely avoided tonal centres in the *Five Pieces*, traditional formal patterns such as the sonata or the rondo became irrelevant, since these had been entirely predicated on tonal progressions. Nor did Schoenberg have to rely on a literary or philosophical programme to justify an unorthodox musical form: as 'pieces', rather than symphonic movements or tone poems, the music achieved total autonomy. Instrumentation is a defining factor in the *Five Pieces*, possibly to an even greater extent than in the works of Debussy. An a' played by the flute is a completely different entity than an a' played by the violin, and – especially in the famous 'Farben' ('Colours') movement (see Ex. 5.6, p. 108), the consequences of this principle (known as the *Klangfarbentechnik*, or *Klangfarbenmelodie*) are quite consistently thought through. As Schoenberg developed his twelve-tone method in the 1920s, imposing fixed rules on a previously free atonal style, fixed formal structures returned to his music as well, as in the *Variations*, Op. 31.

While Schoenberg focused on formulating new approaches to harmony and sound colour, Charles Ives was pursuing a quest in an entirely different, though equally new, direction. His main concern was not the reorganisation of the twelve chromatic pitches but rather a new relationship to *his* musical sources which were not Brahms, Wagner and Mahler (although he was familiar with these masters) but the church hymnody of his native United States. The melodic material was not necessarily new, but the extremely complicated polymeters and multiple simultaneous tempos (which in some cases require two conductors) were quite unprecedented. No other composer found so many innovative ways of transforming pre-existent, traditional material, and no one could draw such far-reaching consequences of what has been repeatedly shown to be an essentially romantic aesthetic, influenced mainly by Ralph Waldo Emerson and other American transcendentalists. In his shorter orchestral works (*The Unanswered Question*) as well as the symphonies and orchestral 'sets', the placement of familiar material in unexpected and strikingly unfamiliar contexts results in the unmistakable Ivesian character. Ives reached the peak of his art in the Fourth Symphony, a complex and multifaceted masterpiece completed in 1916 but not performed in its entirety until 1965.

One year younger than Schoenberg and Ives, Maurice Ravel started his career under Debussy's influence, but soon asserted his original voice. A brilliant orchestrator and a sensitive musical poet, Ravel devoted most of his orchestral music to dance forms. From his early *Pavane for a Dead Princess* to many moments of his opera *L'enfant et les sortilèges*, he invested those forms with a plethora of different meanings. In the ballet *Daphnis and Chloé* he celebrated sensual love and beauty in an imaginary world of ancient Greek shepherds. In *La Valse* and *Boléro*, he revealed the innermost essence of the respective dance rhythms. And in *Le Tombeau de Couperin* – a six-movement suite for piano, four of whose movements he orchestrated – he became one of the pioneers of neo-classicism.[26]

Although Vaughan Williams was three years older than Ravel, he took lessons from his French contemporary, adding a French impressionistic touch to his background, whose defining elements were sixteenth-century English church music and English folksong. Reacting against Elgar's passionate romanticism, he perfected in his nine symphonies a simpler and calmer style, using techniques of early music such as modality and counterpoint, yet contemporary precisely in its avoidance of elements from the era immediately preceding.[27]

Early music was also a defining experience for the Italian Ottorino Respighi, but he combined that interest with exotic orchestral colours learned from his teacher Rimsky-Korsakov and brought to fruition in his popular triptych of symphonic poems about Rome.

The generation of the 1880s

Slightly younger than the composers mentioned above are Béla Bartók (1881–1945), Igor Stravinsky (1882–1971), Anton Webern (1883–1945), Edgard Varèse (1883–1965) and Alban Berg (1885–1935). Historians have been unanimous in calling these composers 'modernist', 'revolutionary' or 'radical', but each carried out his own 'revolution' in a strikingly different way. Contrary to earlier opinions asserting that Bartók's modernism was compromised by his commitment to materials derived from the folk music of his native Hungary and neighbouring ethnic groups, it was precisely through those materials that Bartók carried out his modernist revolution. As a scholar of folk music, he was able to distil, from the songs he had collected, some abstract characteristics (rhythmic patterns, melodic contours) that could not be found in Western music of the nineteenth century. It was those characteristics, rather than the original songs themselves, that he used in many of his works. This distinguishes his folklorism from its earlier manifestations and also gives his greatest orchestral works, from the *Dance Suite* (1923) to *Music for Strings, Percussion and Celesta* (1936) and the *Concerto for Orchestra* (1943) their unmistakable identity. In the last two works, one may still observe modified sonata-form structures, but the recapitulations are varied to such an extent that the variation principle becomes at least as important to the understanding of the works as the sonata principle which was their original conceptual basis.[28]

The majority of Igor Stravinsky's orchestral output consists of ballet scores, and it was in these that his personal idiom, and more particularly his orchestral idiom, were formed. Stravinsky's first ballet written for Serge Diaghilev's Paris-based Ballets Russes was *The Firebird*, which, although still heavily influenced by Stravinsky's teacher Rimsky-Korsakov, makes use of the ostinato technique found in so many of Stravinsky's later works. In the field of orchestration, the string arpeggios on harmonics in the introduction and the innovative writing for the D clarinet are just a few of Stravinsky's striking effects. *Petrushka*, with its collage-like incorporation of a nineteenth-century waltz by Lanner and a contemporary Parisian street song, expands the stylistic breadth of the music; the hero's bi-tonal *Leitmotiv* inaugurates a technique for which an illustrious future lay ahead. Yet the Russian element still predominates. The work's extensive piano solo – a trace of its original conception as a *Konzertstück* – is highly unusual for 1911.

Two years later, Stravinsky produced *The Rite of Spring*, which changed the course of twentieth-century music as no other work has done. *The Rite* raised the issue of national identity in an entirely new way, introduced fundamentally new approaches to melody, harmony, and rhythm, and replaced a conventional ballet plot with a more abstract subject matter. The power of these innovations was so great that no composer coming after Stravinsky could avoid the challenge of taking a stand, in one way or another, on these issues.

Stravinsky's neo-classical orchestral works were again often ballets (*Apollon musagète, Jeu de cartes, Le baiser de la fée*). Interestingly, however, he was the only member of the 'modernist' generation to be interested in traditional symphonic form. In the *Symphony of Psalms* (1930), settings of three excerpts from the Book of Psalms are arranged in a three-movement form, although the connections with traditional symphony are rather tenuous. The case is different in the *Symphony in C* (1940) and the *Symphony in Three Movements* (1945); these were, significantly, commissions from the United States, where interest in the symphony had never waned as it had in Europe after Mahler's death. Their style is eclectic like a lot of middle-period Stravinsky, including echoes of not only classical and romantic origin but of Stravinsky's own *Rite of Spring* as well. Stravinsky's late serial period consists mostly of vocal and choral works. His short *Variations in memoriam Aldous Huxley* is not only a homage to the British novelist who became Stravinsky's friend in California, but also a belated tribute to the method of Schoenberg and his two most famous pupils Berg and Webern, all by then deceased.[29]

Alban Berg wrote only one major work for orchestra alone, though he of course used the orchestra in his two operas and two concertos (Chamber Concerto and Violin Concerto). In this context, only the Three Pieces, Op. 6, need be considered, which unite the influences of Mahler and Schoenberg in a personal and powerful way. Mahlerian ländlers and marches are put through Schoenbergian atonality, resulting in an extremely dramatic (indeed, almost operatic) musical narrative, calling for a huge orchestra with quadruple woodwinds. The percussion battery includes a hammer: Mahler had used it in his Sixth Symphony where he ultimately removed the third hammer blow, apparently out of superstition; in Berg's piece, the third hammer blow is there, ending the work in a way that has been likened to 'a door slamming shut on the past'.[30]

Having undergone the same Mahler and Schoenberg influences as his friend Berg, Webern arrived at totally different conclusions. His orchestral oeuvre is larger than Berg's, and ranges from the early, largely tonal, *Passacaglia*, Op. 1, to sets of six and five atonal pieces (Op. 6 and 10, respectively) and finally to the serial *Symphony*, Op. 21 and *Variations*, Op. 30. For the *Six Pieces* (1909), we have a letter from Webern to Schoenberg explaining the music in programmatic terms. This work in its original version employed a huge orchestra, although there are very few tutti passages. (Webern later made a second version for reduced instrumental forces.) The *Five Pieces* (1911–13) are scored for a chamber-size orchestra (solo strings and winds, as in Schoenberg's *Chamber Symphony*, with plucked instruments, percussion

and harmonium added). The extreme brevity of these pieces (the five movements together run just about six minutes in performance) is typical of this
period in Webern's career and allows only for fleeting glimpses at what are
in fact five character studies in miniature. The instant effects are realised
thanks to the *Klangfarbenmelodie*, expanding upon Schoenberg's 'Farben'
from his *Five Pieces*.

With the solidification of the twelve-tone method in the 1920s, Webern,
like Schoenberg, was able to overcome the epigrammatic brevity of previous
works; the ten-minute, two-movement *Symphony*, Op. 21, is a large-scale
composition by Webern's standards. Scored for only four winds, harp, and
strings, this is an extremely delicate piece in which the twelve-tone structure
allows for the creation of something along the lines of sonata form. Dynamic
and textural changes take place at junctures that parallel the major division
points of sonata movements, but the driving impulse of sonata form is
replaced by a more contemplative attitude, and the themes by single pitches
or two-note 'sigh' motives that compress whole worlds of expression into
tiny cells.[31]

Of all the composers born in the 1880s, Edgard Varèse is certainly the
one with the fewest apparent links to any music previously written. He
felt that composers had made use of only a fraction of the sounds that
were available, and he consciously strove to throw open the whole world
of sound to music. While many of his ideas could only be realised with the
advent of electronic music (and Varèse lived long enough to write a *Poème
électronique* in 1958), his vision is embodied with uncommon imaginative
power in his first surviving work, *Amériques* (1921). (Varèse's early works,
composed before his emigration from France to the United States in 1915,
are all lost.) The orchestral forces of *Amériques* are among the largest ever
assembled for a symphonic composition, and sounds with and without fixed
pitch are treated as absolute equals throughout. Of particular importance
to Varèse was the siren, which provided a continuum of pitch going beyond
the twelve-tone system. Varèse meant the title *Amériques* – significantly in
the plural – as 'symbolic of discoveries – new worlds on earth, in the sky, or
in the minds of men'.

Composers born between 1890 and 1906

Many of the composers discussed under the previous heading extended the
sounds, the genres, and the philosophical underpinnings in a number of different ways. Many of those coming immediately after them leaned – to the
extent such generalisations are possible at all – toward finding new possibilities within the existing frameworks rather than changing the frameworks

themselves. Some of the most important new careers starting around and just after World War I were those of Bohuslav Martinů (1890–1959), Sergei Prokofiev (1891–1953), Arthur Honegger (1892–1955), Paul Hindemith (1895–1963), Aaron Copland (1900–90) and Dmitri Shostakovich (1906–75).

While these composers have little in common stylistically, each wrote symphonies along more or less traditional lines – a type of composition most of the leading composers born twenty or thirty years earlier (with the significant exception of Stravinsky) tended to avoid. The generation of the 1890s and early 1900s embraced aspects of the past around the same time as did their elders Ravel and Stravinsky. The young Prokofiev's *Classical Symphony* (1917), the first of his seven symphonies, dates from the same year as Ravel's *Tombeau de Couperin* and predates Stravinsky's *Pulcinella* by three years. Prokofiev's later symphonies encompass modernistic works written during the fifteen years spent in the West, before a turn to traditionalism set in with the Fifth Symphony, composed back in Russia during World War II.[32]

Prokofiev's contemporaries Hindemith and Martinů explored the past from aspects quite different from those seen in the *Classical Symphony*. In the symphony *Mathis der Maler*, Hindemith integrated centuries of musical history in a coherent style of his own, while Martinů was inspired by the baroque concerto grosso idea to create one of the many authentic voices of the 1930s.

The composer who, more than any other, defined the term 'symphony' for the twentieth century was Dmitri Shostakovich. Deeply aware that the symphony was loaded with historic connotations that no composer embracing the genre could escape, he built upon each stage of its development from Beethoven to Tchaikovsky and Mahler. Adherence to classical form was a requirement of Soviet 'socialist realism' from the 1930s onwards; but within this officially sanctioned framework Shostakovich managed to tell an intensely personal story, widely understood as a response to the vicissitudes of life under the Soviet regime, before, during, and after World War II.

Shostakovich's First Symphony, written at the age of nineteen, shows not only uncommon melodic and orchestrational mastery but also many of the stylistic traits (irony, march and dance *topoi* inherited from Mahler, etc.) that would characterise much of his mature work. After the experimental Second and Third Symphonies and the uncompromisingly avant-garde Fourth, Shostakovich the classical artist appears in the much-performed and much-discussed Fifth. If it is not exactly a 'Soviet artist's response to just criticism' as Shostakovich was probably instructed to declare, it is certainly a response to a political situation. The fast, slow, and scherzo-like movement characters are mandated by a tradition from which Shostakovich would not deviate; but their actual realisations allow, and even invite, interpretations along programmatic lines with an ambiguity almost certainly intended in the last movement (real triumph or make-believe?).[33] Shostakovich's symphonies Nos. 6–8 and 10, written between 1939 and 1953, continue to grapple with complex issues of tragedy and its resolution. The Ninth, of all the symphonies, is a shorter, light-hearted work that brings a respite from the emotionally supercharged atmospheres of its companions. Nos. 11 and 12 have politically motivated subtitles (*The Year 1905* and *October 1917*, respectively), but the music transcends mere political expediencies. Nos. 13 and 14, which continue the Mahlerian tradition of including voices, are special cases: the first movement of No. 13 sets Yevgeni Yevtushenko's poem about Babi Yar, the site where thousands of Jews were murdered during World War II. No. 14, Shostakovich's *Lied von der Erde*, as it were, is a poignant song cycle about death. No. 15, the most enigmatic of the symphonies, hovers between playfulness and tragedy like some of the earlier works, but its highly unusual last movement brings the symphony to a transcendent conclusion, in what almost seems like Shostakovich's *Tod und Verklärung*. The Russian master's scoring is noted for the many extended chamber-music-like passages and extended instrumental solos; this economy of means turns the appearance of the full orchestra into a major event, both structurally and dramatically.

Although many composers attempted to write classical symphonies in the twentieth century, only a few succeeded, as Shostakovich did, in giving new meaning to the old form. The greatest interest in the genre was displayed in the United States, where commissions coming from major symphony orchestras (above all, the Boston Symphony under Serge Koussevitsky) ensured a constant demand for new works (Aaron Copland, Roy Harris, Walter Piston, Roger Sessions).[34] In Europe, the cultivation of the symphony by Arthur Honegger, Karl Amadeus Hartmann and others did not seem to represent a general trend.

The last fifty years

By the 1950s, many younger Europeans had embraced the advanced experimental directions of total serialism, electronic music, and *musique concrète*. This did not, at first, bode well for orchestral music, as some began to declare the orchestra to have become obsolete. Nevertheless, even the most revolutionary composers found their way to orchestral composition, even if they eschewed the symphony as a genre.

Many of the crucial figures of the post-World War II avant-garde had studied with Olivier Messiaen (1908–92) in Paris. In his own works, Messiaen brought to orchestral writing some experiences unlike those of any other composers: on one hand, his background as a virtuoso organist and a musical improviser of genius, on the other, his theoretical studies of Greek and Indian rhythmic systems as well as – later – birdsong.

Even in his first works, Messiaen displays an unmistakably personal harmonic language. In 1948, he finished his ten-movement *Turangalîla Symphony*, his largest orchestral work to date and crowning achievement of his early period. (The title is a combination of two Sanskrit words that could be rendered approximately as 'Movement' and 'Cosmic Love', respectively.) Messiaen was inspired by the Tristan legend, especially the motif of the love-death, but his representation is far from programmatic in a nineteenth-century sense. Rather, it conveys an ecstatic vision of love through a specially devised structure of interlocking movement types, with three strongly rhythmical 'Turangalîla' movements and four ecstatic 'Amours' developing the same theme, all framed by an introduction and a finale, with the self-contained 'Joie du sang des étoiles' in the middle. As with nearly all of Messiaen's later works, *Turangalîla* contains a virtuoso piano solo, written for Yvonne Loriod, as well as extensive parts for tuned percussion and celesta. In addition, Messiaen makes ample use of the electronic instrument ondes martenot in *Turangalîla*. The idea of interlocking movements was retained in later works such as *Chronochromie* (1959–60) with its alternating, musically contrasted strophes and antistrophes, even though in the intervening years, Messiaen's style had become much more rigorous and eliminated what some had seen as romantic excesses in the earlier work. Messiaen continued to compose large-scale orchestral works right to the end of his life, now always incorporating transcriptions of birdsong. In *Des canyons aux étoiles* (1971–4), a piece inspired by Messiaen's visit to the national parks of Utah, the horn is one of the solo instruments with many innovative playing techniques (including playing on the mouthpiece alone). Some moments in *Eclairs sur l'au-delà* (1988–92) reconnect with the expansive melodic writing of Messiaen's early years.[35]

If Messiaen explored harmonies based on personally developed theories and perfected a special combination of woodwind, keyboard and percussion colours, his contemporary Elliott Carter (b. 1908) proceeded in a different direction. After an early period marked by neo-classicism, he turned his attention to a radical rethinking of the notion of tempo: by means of the so-called 'metric modulation', a proportional tempo change in which, for instance, a quaver triplet can become a regular quaver in the new tempo. These procedures and a serially derived but not quite serial harmony become components in Carter's multi-layered structures, as found in such works as the *Variations for Orchestra* (1953–5), the *Concerto for Orchestra* (1968–9) and the *Symphony of Three Orchestras* (1976). The 1997 *Symphonia*, whose three movements had been commissioned and premièred separately, show that Carter's music has retained all its rhythmic edge and formal complexity.[36]

Like Carter, Witold Lutoslawski (1911–94) underwent a profound stylistic change during his mid-forties from a more traditional style to innovation and experiment. His early *Concerto for Orchestra* (1954) is close to Bartók in its orientation, but in *Jeux vénitiens*, written only seven years later, the Polish composer had not only caught up with Western avant-garde but emerged as one of its leaders. Through a 'creative misreading' of John Cage's ideas on indeterminacy, Lutoslawski introduced aleatoric elements into his score, allowing each player to determine the number of times they repeated a given passage during an allotted period of time. This procedure, employed at strategic formal junctures in the piece, becomes an important form-generating factor, as the texture and intensity of such passages is audibly different from the rest of the work. This trend continues in many other works, most notably *Livre pour orchestre* (1968).

Lutoslawski was one of the few composers in the second half of the twentieth century to be able to give symphonic form a genuine new meaning. With its two movements, 'Hésitant' and 'Direct', the Second Symphony (1965–6) created a structure that was independent from the classical tradition yet equally clear and meaningful. The Third Symphony (1983), according to Lutoslawski's own analysis, also has to be viewed as a bipartite form, even though the work also has an introduction, an epilogue and a coda. Yet the principal idea, namely that a 'preparatory' section is followed by a 'main statement', has been preserved from the earlier work, while the musical style becomes markedly more melodic, without sounding backward-looking or derivative in the least. The Fourth Symphony (1993), another 'Introduction and Allegro', contains even more *cantando* lines and fewer aleatoric passages as the composer continued to admit new stylistic elements into his artistic world.[37]

Unlike Lutoslawski, most composers born in the 1920s or later have either written symphonies that embraced at least some aspects of traditional symphonic form, or avoided symphony as a genre altogether. One of the most influential musical minds of the last half-century, Pierre Boulez (b. 1925), who is also one of the great conductors of our time, considers orchestral music not as a self-contained genre but rather as a vehicle that allows him to develop ideas independent from the notion of genre; new approaches to pitch and rhythm, as well as the rearrangement of the instruments in space (*Pli selon pli*, *Rituel*, *Répons*).[38] Orchestral music, in other words, can no longer be considered as an entity separate from other forms of music but is just one possible manifestation of more general compositional ideas. The same seems to be true of other avant-gardists of the Boulez generation such as György Ligeti (b. 1923) and Iannis Xenakis (1922–2001), both of whom have written prolifically for orchestra. Ligeti's *Atmosphères* (1961) and *Lontano* (1967) are examples of his concept of micro-polyphony, the use of a large number of individual lines woven together in textures of unprecedented complexity; yet here, too, the orchestra is more a means to an end than a vehicle that is able to impose its own demands on the composer. Similarly, in the 'formalised music' of Xenakis, the orchestra serves to realise the composer's procedures based on probability theory rather than functioning as a traditional orchestra would. Works such as *Terretektorh* (1966) and *Polytope* (1967), where the instrumentalists are scattered among the audience, invent a radically new way of using the orchestra. The piece, in Xenakis's own words, is 'an accelerator of sonorous particles, a disintegrator of sonorous masses, a synthesizer',[39] but hardly an orchestral work in the usual sense of the word.

Yet other members of the same generation have successfully reconciled musical progress with the demands of orchestral music – even the symphony – as a genre. Henri Dutilleux (b. 1916) distances himself from the neo-classical tradition, juxtaposing larger and smaller instrumental groups in a definitely non-concerto-grosso-like manner in works such as Symphony No. 2 (1955) and *Timbres, espace, mouvement* (1978, rev. 1990). The latter work, whose innovative *timbres* include an opposition of high woodwinds and low strings (violins and violas are omitted), alludes to a Van Gogh painting (*The starry night*) in its subtitle, but avoids impressionistic techniques in connecting visual and auditory experiences. In *Métaboles* (1965) he devised a new approach to form by an open chain of gradual motivic transformations. In all these instances, the innovations take effect without exploding the orchestral medium as such, or orchestral music as a genre.

In two major works for full orchestra, *The Triumph of Time* (1972) and *Earth Dances* (1986), Harrison Birtwistle (b. 1934) builds upon the modernist tradition of the first half of the century. In the latter work, he uses the possibilities of the orchestra to create a new kind of polyphony, one characterised by the superimposition of various 'layers' that are entirely independent from one another in their melodic and rhythmic shape. To these 'vertical' layers corresponds a 'horizontal' organisation in sections whose succession does not follow a linear logic but instead evolves in an 'open', labyrinthine manner. The composer evoked the image of a traveller wandering in an unfamiliar city to describe the form of the piece. Even reference to old music (Dowland's 'In darkness let me dwell') does not lead Birtwistle in a post-modern direction in *The Shadow of Night* (2001). Birtwistle alludes to his source in a covert way, expanding on it by means of some novel musical content of his own.

A number of composers flourishing in the post-World War II period have come close to, and in some cases reached or even exceeded, the magical number of nine symphonies. Aside from marginal figures such as the Swedish Allan Pettersson (1911–80, seventeen symphonies), these include such diverse musical personalities as the German Hans-Werner Henze (b. 1926, nine symphonies), the English Peter Maxwell Davies (b. 1934, six symphonies and ten 'Strathclyde Concertos'), and the Russian-German Alfred Schnittke (1934–98, nine symphonies). This renewed interest in a genre previously thought to be moribund must be considered a 'post-modern' phenomenon, especially since many of these works – for all their differences – utilise, or make allusion to, the musical past in various ways. This may happen by means of reconnecting with the previously disparaged 'golden era' of the symphony: Henze's Seventh (1984) embraces not only the four-movement symphonic structure but also something of its traditional ethos. Others intentionally, and sometimes dramatically, contrast old and new elements: in Schnittke's Seventh (1993), a simple waltz melody is cut down to bare bones as it is presented, totally alienated, in the deepest registers of the tuba, contrabassoon, and double bass.

For composers such as the Americans George Rochberg (b. 1918) or David Del Tredici (b. 1937), who re-embraced tonality and re-introduced elements of a late-romantic harmonic style, the traditional orchestra is a natural means of expression. One of the most prominent avant-gardists of the sixties, the Polish Krzysztof Penderecki (b. 1933), also joined (or perhaps inaugurated) the neo-romantic movement with his works written since the mid-seventies. From the generation born after the end of the war, the American John Adams (b. 1947) has rebelled against serialism and abstract experimentation, but without admitting too many nineteenth-century elements in his vocabulary. Combining the rhythmic drive of 1960s minimalism with a more adventurous harmonic idiom and a high degree of instrumental virtuosity, Adams has written a series of highly influential orchestral works from *Harmonielehre* (1985) to *Naïve and Sentimental Music* (1998).

Born in 1958, the Finnish Magnus Lindberg probably spoke for many of his contemporaries when he repudiated the notion that music had to 'start over from square one', an opinion held by several members of the previous generation. Comfortable with the most modern compositional techniques including electronic and spectral music, Lindberg nevertheless refuses to give up the expressive aspects of the classical tradition; yet at the same time he does not opt for an overt return to tonality.[40] Instead, in orchestral works like *Corrente* (1992), *Feria* (1997) and *Cantigas* (1999), he manages to combine the search for uncharted territory with a natural desire to include elements of traditional thinking. He seems to share this dual objective with other composers of the present generation, whose works prove that the symphony orchestra continues to be a viable musical medium. The recent international success of *Asyla* (1997) by the English Thomas Adès (b. 1971) – a work in which elements as disparate as a baroque passacaglia and a passage with two unrelated tempos are united in a coherent four-movement quasi-symphonic structure – raises our hopes that the symphony orchestra will continue to inspire works of great originality for years to come.

4 From notation to sound

RICHARD RASTALL

Introduction

Why does one try to 'read a score', and what does it mean to do so? Conductors have two main reasons for undertaking this activity. The first is that the written or printed score is the key to understanding what happens in the music. As a conductor's principal task is to rehearse the music for performance, knowledge of the forces involved, the style, structure, and main features of the piece are vital in planning the various practical tasks that make up the rehearsal.

The second is to find out in detail what the piece sounds like, creating an aural image – 'hearing the music in one's head' – so that the conductor knows in advance what sounds the orchestra should make and, more specifically, the required details of balance, articulation, rhythm, tempo, and so on that distinguish a performance from a mere play-through of the notes. Some conductors go through this process of auralising the score entirely from the musical notation, while others use the piano to create the actual sound of the melodic and harmonic content of the piece.

Composers undertake this second process in reverse, trying to put on paper instructions for recreating the sounds that they have imagined. Some composers, too, use the piano in this process, generating ideas and fixing the main outlines of harmonic and rhythmic content in their minds. For the great majority, whose main active interest is in listening to orchestral music rather than creating or recreating it, the reasons for learning to read a score are less ambitious but more varied. A knowledge of essentials will allow the listener to follow the music in performance, both to see what is happening while it is happening and, perhaps, to gather details of the music that are not immediately audible; with more detailed knowledge of scores the structural, timbral, rhythmic or other outlines of a piece become evident; and with rather more expertise we can find out, in considerable detail and even without hearing a performance, what the music sounds like and what effect it might have on us.

These skills are worth learning to any level. Auralising a score – that is, hearing the written music in one's head – is a skill that takes very considerable experience and practice, but any achievement in score-reading helps one's appreciation of the music. The extent to which one can internally 'hear' the music is, however, questionable. Many musicians can auralise a simple score with considerable accuracy, but as the complexity of the score increases the process demands increasing mental concentration and understanding of the implications of the written score. Most would probably admit that with very complex scores a precise auralisation is not possible, and that the most one can achieve – although well worthwhile and often sufficient for the musician's purpose – is to know what the music *feels* like, itself a difficult experience to define. It has to be said, too, that the more difficult it is to auralise a score accurately the less chance one has of discovering the emotional impact of the music by this means.

This chapter starts with relatively simple examples and works up to more complex scores in order to show what are the principles and problems involved in creating an aural image of a piece of orchestral music. The reader will find that intense concentration is necessary to improve the current level of ability. Most people who can sing a fairly simple vocal line at sight will be able to auralise such material without actually singing it; putting two or more lines together, as in a hymn-tune or simple part song, is considerably more difficult; taking account of different orchestral sounds, rhythmic counterpoints between instruments, and the various special effects that instruments are capable of will all make the process of auralisation more problematic. In auralising an orchestral score, the immediate difficulty is to find one's way around the notation and layout.

The layout of the orchestral score

There has never been a completely standard layout for an orchestral score, but in most periods composers have evidently had a clear understanding of what could be considered 'normal'. There has been some divergence of 'house style' among publishers, but apart from that layout depends on three main factors. The first of these is the genre of the music: the presence of solo instruments makes extra and specific notational demands, for instance, and the resulting situations are too varied for generalisations to be useful here. Second, there have been some fairly standard changes over time. These affect even what might be regarded as 'modern' publications in general circulation. There are certain respects in which a nineteenth-century score of a Schubert symphony differs from a twentieth-century score of the same work, and yet both might be in current use. Both might also be different from what the composer wrote, but that is another issue altogether. Third, geography has some influence on layout, for different places have slightly different conventions. Thus a score published in Germany may be laid out rather differently from one published in the same year in England.

Ex. 4.1 J. S. Bach, Third Orchestral Suite (Bach Gesellschaft edition): p. 54, opening of the Air

As an illustration of a score for string orchestra, Ex. 4.1 shows the start of the famous Air from Bach's third orchestral suite. Although the instrumental designations at the beginning of the system (that is, the array of staves performed simultaneously) suggest solo instruments, this is an orchestral piece usually played by two or more instruments on each line. 'Violino I' is not to be taken to mean a single player, therefore, but two or three violinists playing the line together. 'Continuo' is a bass line played by the low stringed instruments – cellos and double bass, presumably – together with any keyboard instrument used in the performance. No keyboard instrument is specified, but a harpsichord would be appropriate. We should normally expect some figuring on this bass line, indicating the harmonies to the harpsichordist, but there is no figuring anywhere in this suite.

Among the various vertical lines that start the system itself is a thin line that joins all of the staves, but before that there is a thicker straight bracket with end-pieces at top and bottom that define the extent of the system on the page. This bracket later came to have a more precise function, but in nineteenth-century and earlier scores this is its main purpose. In the course of each system the extent of the system is also defined by the bar lines, which are drawn straight through from the top of the 'Violino I' staff to the bottom of the 'Continuo' staff. Finally, there is a bow-shaped bracket, called a 'brace', that comes first of all and affects only the two violin staves. Its purpose is to define the staves on which instruments of the same sort can be found.

Were the cellos to divide and take up two staves, for instance, those staves also would be given a brace at the start of each relevant system.

The C-clef on the viola line remains less generally familiar than treble or bass clefs. Gaining facility at reading C-clefs is really a matter of practice, whether the alto clef (with middle c' on the middle line of the staff) or the tenor clef (with middle c' on the fourth line) encountered in high cello, bassoon and trombone parts. A cursory glance shows that the violas have only a subsidiary, harmony-filling role; the main theme is clearly in the first violins, with the second violins alternately filling in and taking a more active melodic role. The bass line, if one strips away the quaver octaves, outlines a harmonic bass that moves sometimes by step and sometimes by larger intervals. In trying to auralise the sound of this texture we soon discover that the top and bass lines are the crucial ones.

The strings in the score are ordered with the highest at the top and the lowest at the bottom. This is a general rule in any orchestral score, not just for the strings: but it holds only within each instrumental family group and there are some exceptions. Ex. 4.2, the opening of the finale of Schubert's 'Great' C major Symphony, shows how this works. Schubert's orchestra consists of double woodwind (two each of flutes, oboes, clarinets and bassoons) with two horns, two trumpets, three trombones, timpani and strings. In this case each pair of instruments shares a staff, and the designation 'zu 2' shows when they play in unison. (This is hardly necessary for the bassoons – 'fagotti' – here, which are playing in octaves, and it is probably an error.) Of the three trombones, the top two share a staff and the bass trombone has a staff to itself. The woodwind are in order of pitch, with the flutes at the top and the bassoons at the bottom; and the strings are in pitch order, as before. In this case, the double basses play with the cellos only for very brief phrases, and it is therefore convenient for them to have a separate staff.

The trumpets and trombones are also in pitch order, but the position of the horns, at the top of the brass section rather than in the middle, might be considered inconsistent. In fact, the horns are often thought of as members of the woodwind family, musically speaking: so, although they do join the other brass instruments in the score, they are always placed at the top, next to the woodwind instruments.[1]

This score also shows the normal arrangement of instrumental families: woodwind at the top, then brass, percussion (here only two timpani, sharing a staff because they are played by a single performer) and strings. With the exception of the percussion, each family is defined by a bracket at the start of each system, effectively encouraging the eye to consider the score in terms of these family groupings. It does not take any experience to recognise the alternation of two gestures, both in octaves: one, very loud, played by the whole orchestra except timpani, and the other, soft, played by the strings

Ex. 4.2 Franz Schubert, Symphony No. 7 (the 'Great' C Major Symphony) (Eulenburg): p. 164, opening of finale

without double bass (*contrabasso*). It is worth noting at this point that much of the power of this passage comes from the articulation that Schubert marks so precisely: the accents on each second bar and the staccato marking of the quiet string gestures. As in Ex. 4.1, the two violin parts are joined by a brace; so are the two trombone staves, for the same reason. In this case the cello and *contrabasso* staves are also joined by a brace: this is not invariably done, and acts as a warning here that the cellos and double basses share a staff for most of this symphony.

In orchestral works with chorus, the voices may take one of two positions in the score. The older placing, which can be seen in Beethoven's 'Choral' Symphony, for example, places the voices above the strings, between the timpani and the first violins. In a later disposition, the strings are split and the voices inserted between the violas and the cellos. Especially for any rehearsal pianist working from the full score, this has the advantage of showing the two main bass lines – the vocal and string basses – in juxtaposition at the bottom of the page. Ex. 4.3 shows this layout in the section 'Denn es wird die Posaune schallen' ('The trumpet shall sound') from Brahms's *German Requiem*.

This score reverts to an older use of a single bracket for the whole system, rather than using several brackets for instrumental families: only the chorus has such a bracket as a family, and that is necessarily written on top of the primary bracket. Braces are used, as before, for the trombones (here joined by a tuba), for the violins, and for the cellos and double basses; and they are needed also for the flutes and piccolo, which take up two staves. The families are however distinguished by another relatively late feature of orchestral scores, the breaking of bar lines between family groups. The bar lines are drawn right through the woodwind staves, for instance, but break before the horns and again after the timpani. The continuing importance of the strings is indicated by the repetition of the tempo marking 'Vivace' over the top of the first violins. The bar lines are nevertheless broken between violas and cellos, because the voices make their appearance there. In later scores there is also a break above the timpani, but it was evidently considered that the one staff for the timpani does not constitute a separate section for the percussion family.

Examining the musical functions of the various families in this score, it is immediately clear that the woodwind instruments double the voices, including transpositions in the flutes and piccolo to the higher octave. The trombones and tuba double the voices too, but an octave lower: and the trombones fade out before the end of the phrase in order to re-enter with renewed percussive effect. The horns, trumpets and timpani strengthen the rhythmic effects of the passage without confirming the melodic and harmonic outlines to any extent. Brahms was rather old-fashioned in his use of horns and trumpets, which in earlier times had only a very restricted

Ex. 4.3 Johannes Brahms, *Ein deutsches Requiem*, op. 45 (Eulenburg): p. 181, opening of Vivace section from movement VI

repertory of notes. By the time of the *German Requiem* they could certainly have been given a more actively melodic role. Equally, he could have given the timpani an enhanced role by using more of them, but he chose to keep them in a subsidiary, rhythmic, role by using only a pair, with the traditional tonic and dominant tuning.

Against this texture, which is basically tied to the vocal lines and rhythms, the strings offer a real counterpoint. This single line in octaves is based on the harmonies of the vocal texture: in fact, it is a decorated version of the vocal bass line. The primary object of this string writing is to provide an exciting fast-moving background in short note-values; the secondary object is to offer a melodic counterpoint to the rather four-square and repetitive vocal texture and its instrumental doublings.

Much of the character of this passage is due to the dynamics and articulation that Brahms gave it. It is basically a *fortissimo* passage, but the dynamic is immediately modified in two ways. The *sforzando* marking on the third beat of the first bar, and again in the second bar, effectively throws the main accent on to that beat, apparently contradicting the basic metre. The timpani trills on those third beats support the sforzandos. Second, the staccato markings in the string bass lines, and also the semiquaver bowing in the upper string parts (notated in an abbreviated form), demand more energy from the players than would legato quavers, and this helps to give a decidedly outgoing and even aggressive feeling to the music. Although the staccato dots are omitted from the third bar onwards, bars 3–5 should surely be performed similarly, as the punched-out brass staccato crotchet chords of bars 3 and 6 suggest. This percussive use of brass has to be experienced to be understood: trombones can be percussive in a way that is quite impossible even on trumpets, and passages like this one should be listened to carefully for the effect to be identified.[2]

As already noted, a pair of timpani did not count as a separate instrumental family in the score, but were joined with the brass in having the bar line ruled right through from horns to timpani (Ex. 4.2). This was no doubt for historical reasons: trumpets and drums having worked as a team for so long, composers continued to think of the timpani as belonging with the extended brass group. Attaching the timpani to the brass remained an option for many composers, and this was even extended to include other percussion instruments. An alternative was to separate the timpani from the brass, and if other percussion instruments were present they, too, could be given their own staves. Composers tended to be flexible about their treatment of percussion, partly depending on what instruments were involved. Carl Nielsen used both types of layout in his Sixth Symphony, attaching timpani, triangle, side-drum and bass drum to the brass in the finale, but elsewhere notating brass and percussion under separate brackets.

In this second situation Nielsen needed more than a single bracket for the percussion group. As a family, the percussion are anomalous: they tend to function without brackets at all, which often makes them look like a miscellaneous collection of individual instruments rather than a coherent group; they are sometimes divided into more than one group, one or both of these having its own bracket; and the percussion in any case includes a number of individual instruments – harp, piano, organ, celesta, and so on – that must be bracketed (and/or braced) and bar-lined separately.[3] (The organ also requires its pedal staff to be bar-lined separately from the two manual staves.) Reading a percussion score demands some preparatory work and considerable concentration. It does help that untuned instruments are usually given only a one-line staff (although the score of Stravinsky's *The Rite of Spring* uses 5-line staves throughout).

Ex. 4.4 shows the first page of Benjamin Britten's *The Young Person's Guide to the Orchestra*, subtitled *Variations and Fugue on a Theme of Purcell*. Not all of the percussion instruments are in action on this page, but all of the players certainly are: Britten asks for at least three percussion players (that is, apart from the timpanist and harpist, who do not count as 'percussion' in this specialised sense), and in this passage they must play xylophone, side-drum, cymbals and bass drum between them. (The score also includes parts for castanets, gong, tambourine, chinese block and whip, to be played by the same performers.) The timpani and percussion are joined by a bracket in the score, and each staff or line is barred separately; the 'percussion' instruments proper are joined also by a brace; and the harp, which is barred separately through both staves, has its own brace.[4]

The Young Person's Guide to the Orchestra is an excellent introduction to the art of score-reading, since the presentation of instrumental families and individual members provides a clear aural parallel to what is written in the score. Ex. 4.4 can be read and understood in the light of what has been said about earlier examples, with the exception that the transposing instruments (clarinets and horns, in this case) demand some additional explanation.

Transposing instruments

A number of instruments transpose by an octave, either up or down. The piccolo, for instance, sounds an octave higher than it is written: or rather, it is conventionally written an octave lower than it sounds, since notating it at pitch would demand the use of too many leger lines above the staff. A piccolo part looks much the same as an ordinary flute part, therefore, and the reader must make a mental note that it actually sounds rather different. This mental adjustment is easier if the piccolo is written on the top staff of

Ex. **4.4** Benjamin Britten, *The Young Person's Guide to the Orchestra*, op. 34 (Boosey & Hawkes): p. 5, opening of Theme A

the system. In some scores, however, the piccolo is notated below the flutes, on the staff otherwise occupied by the third flute, because the third flautist plays both instruments, changing from one to the other as necessary.

Other instruments transpose down an octave, such as bass clarinet, contrabassoon and double bass. These are not normally difficult to auralise, except that sometimes the double basses share a staff with the cellos. The bass clarinet raises the main problem of transposing instruments, however.

A number of instruments, for various reasons, have a key other than C major as their 'open' key – that is, the key which they play with the normal fingering. The convention began with the horns, which originally had a very limited series of notes. They therefore used various crooks which fitted into the instrument and changed the overall length of the tubing and therefore the pitch of the harmonics used to produce musical notes. The convention of transposition is also used for trumpets, clarinets and the cor anglais. Playing an 'open' scale – that is, a scale with no chromatic notes and therefore conventionally notated as C major – on a clarinet in B♭ will produce the sound of the scale of B♭ major; playing the same C major scale on a clarinet in A will produce the sound of a scale in A major. It follows that a clarinet or trumpet in B♭ must be notated a tone higher than the sounds to be produced, a horn in F or a cor anglais (which is also in F) a fifth higher. Horns in D are notated a minor seventh higher than the sound to be produced, and so on for other intervals. All these instruments transpose downwards, but trumpets and clarinets in D and E♭ transpose upwards, and must therefore be notated lower than the sound to be produced.[5]

The transposing instruments in Ex. 4.2 are, as it happens, all instruments in C, so that they do not present any problem (the horns in C sound an octave lower than written when in treble clef). In Ex. 4.3 there are clarinets in B♭ (in German H = B♮ and B = B♭), and their parts should be compared particularly with those of the flutes, playing an octave higher than the clarinets. Ex. 4.4 shows not only clarinets in B♭ but also horns in F, sounding a fifth lower than the notation.

The examples shown so far have been of music in which the individual instrument families each have a complete harmonic and melodic texture. In such a case listening to any one family, such as the woodwind alone or the strings alone, will provide a musical texture in which no vital melodic or harmonic element is obviously missing. This is not the only way of writing for an orchestra, however, and at this stage it may be helpful to consider a score that uses the instruments rather differently.

Ex. 4.5 shows part of 'Jupiter' from Holst's *The Planets*. Violins, violas and cellos play the tune in octaves, doubled by B♭ clarinets notated a tone higher. At rehearsal number IX the flutes, oboes and cor anglais (sounding a fifth lower than written) join in. The bass line is played by the double basses

Ex. 4.5 Gustav Holst, *The Planets* (Peters Edition): p. 93, from movement IV, 'Jupiter, the Bringer of Jollity'

(an octave lower than written), the bassoons, double bassoon (sounding an octave lower than written) and the bass clarinet (which is in B♭ and sounds a major ninth below written pitch). We should note, too, that the two timpani players, with six drums between them, are able to double not only the rhythms but also most of the notes of the bass line, starting at the bar before rehearsal number IX.

In this passage, the tune and the bass are the only important melodic lines. Between these is a harmonic filling which can most easily be read in the part for the two harps. The harps partly follow the tune in the top and largely follow the bass line in their own bottom notes, but neither of these is their primary function. The six horns in F (sounding a fifth lower than written) play a version of these same chords, this role being taken on by trumpets and bass trombone at rehearsal number IX. The horns and tenor tuba are added to this chordal filling in the last bar of the page. (The three trumpet notes at the beginning of this page are the end of a trumpet solo, now degenerated into harmonic filling that doubles notes in the horn parts.)

It will be seen that Holst strengthened all three elements of the musical texture – melody, bass line and harmonic filling – at rehearsal number IX, thus keeping the balance between these elements during the approach to a climax a few bars later. Although this is not immediately obvious from the score, it becomes clear once the reader sorts out the different musical elements.

Some matters of layout and special effects

Now follows a miscellaneous (and far from comprehensive) collection of matters that fall within the broad areas of layout and instrumental usage. Further examples may be found in standard orchestration treatises such as those by Jacob, Berlioz, Forsyth, Piston and Rimsky-Korsakov.[6]

In terms of layout, the reader will already be aware of the wide diversity of practice in such matters as the use of bar lines to distinguish (or not) the instrumental families in a score. Historical period, place of publication and the individual publisher may all have a hand in these variations. By way of a specific example of such diversity I shall discuss a particular usage, the treatment of a complete bar's rest, by a particular publisher, Oxford University Press. The standard notation for a whole bar's silence, whatever the actual length of the bar, is a semibreve rest. In a full score, or any photographic reduction of a full score, this results in many bars of semibreve rests while particular instruments are silent. In a miniature score, where any instrument not in current use tends to be absent from the page, this is much less of a problem; but in full scores, where it is normal for every instrumental staff to appear throughout, there is huge wastage of space and, it may be argued, a large wastage of time, ink and human effort in printing many bars of semibreve rests. In the period *c.* 1935 to *c.* 1970 Oxford University Press attempted to solve the second of these problems by leaving unused bars blank rather than printing semibreve rests in them. An incidental result of this is that the score is a little easier on the eye, although the inclusion of bar lines still clutters the page. The Press used this notation in many (but by no means all) of the works of Ralph Vaughan Williams and William Walton. I am not aware that any other composer was involved, and I do not know if these two composers were active in persuading the Press to try the experiment. The Press must have thought it worthwhile, since the experiment continued for so long; but no other publishing house took it up, and Oxford University Press did not continue it beyond *c.* 1970.

A similar kind of experiment has become more widespread and is now normal practice: the omission of any staff from a page or part of a page in which the relevant instrument is not in use. This gives a quite different look to the page, but it is a great help to the conductor and indeed to any reader of the score. The advantage is that there is nothing at all for the eye to look at in any part of the page where there is no musical activity: so the eye is not drawn to any print of no musical significance, such as bars' rest. This solves the more important of the two problems mentioned above; and I stress that the instrument concerned retains its space on the page, so that the overall layout of the orchestral system does not change from page to page. By contrast, the compression of systems in miniature scores can be a considerable problem to the inexperienced reader. The practice of simply omitting an instrument not in current use was not in fact a new one, since it can be seen in the finale of Haydn's 'Farewell' Symphony. Haydn did not, however, retain the space for each instrument as its staff disappeared – it would have been pointless to do so at the end of the work – and this is the real innovation of the twentieth-century procedure. We can see this principle in action in Ex. 4.6, discussed below.

The other area to be discussed in this section concerns instrumental usages in which the visual impact of the notation does not match the aural impact of the musical effect. In some cases the musical effect is immediately audible, although the notation seems to show nothing much; in others, the notation catches the eye much more than the aural effect demands attention from the ear. Such effects modify the 'feel' of the score (to return to the point made earlier about not being able to auralise everything). One obvious example is the kind of accompanying string passage-work that looks very black on the page but has little thematic significance.

Another example is the use of string harmonics. These are not particularly noticeable in a score, but they modify the sound of the music considerably. String harmonics are obtained by touching the string lightly while it is being bowed, in such a way as to inhibit one or more of the lower harmonics. For instance, touching a vibrating string one third of the way along its length will make it impossible for the fundamental (first harmonic) and second harmonics to sound. The lowest harmonic having a node (point of rest in the vibration) at that place is the third, so that the third harmonic is the note sounded. The modern notation for a string harmonic is a normal note-head at the pitch of the note fingered, together with an open diamond note-head for the note at the position in which the string must be lightly touched. (The point of 'lightly' is that the lower harmonics must be inhibited, but not the note as a whole: this is quite different from fingering an actual pitch by stopping the string against the fingerboard.) One of the most common string harmonics is the fourth, obtained by touching the string at a nodal point a perfect fourth above the main, fingered, note.[7] Illustrations of this can be seen in Ex. 4.6. Harmonics can also be played on the harp, usually the second harmonic, sounding an octave above the string played. Here, too, the notation is not particularly noticeable – a small open circle above the note-head – but the bell-like sound of harp harmonics is unmistakable.

The brass, too, have a range of special effects that sound more noticeable than they look on the score. The instruction to fit mutes, for instance, signals a radical change in the sound of a brass instrument, and the effect is even more radical when a whole group of instruments is muted. There are now many different types of mute, and although most of them are mainly confined to jazz and other popular musics, they are increasingly used in the orchestra.[8] One effect of any mute is, of course, to make the sound quieter: but mutes also tend to strengthen or weaken individual harmonics, and so to modify the sound as a whole. The most commonly used mute on trumpets and trombones – the straight mute – generally makes the sound sharper and better-defined because it strengthens certain dissonant harmonics.

One way of muting a brass instrument is for the player to put a hand in the bell. This is known as 'stopping', an impossible technique on a trombone and difficult on a trumpet: but it is a common effect on horns, where the bell is held by the right hand in any case. The most common use of stopping a horn is now the 'brassy' or *cuivré* effect, notated by placing a cross above the note-head. This instructs the player to stop the horn fully (i.e. put the hand right down the bell) and to blow hard. The effect can be very exciting, and can cut through a thick orchestral texture.[9]

This is not the place for a general discussion of the composer's instructions to the performers, which take many forms and are for a variety of purposes. What they largely have in common is that they are verbal instructions, usually in Italian in earlier centuries, but increasingly from the late eighteenth century in the composer's native language. Many of these instructions affect the sound of the music: but, while they have their own vocabularies, forms of abbreviation and conventional interpretations, their meanings are usually to be found in a music dictionary and do not need further interpretation. An instruction to the timpanist to play with wooden sticks, for example, is not open to alternative explanations, and the listener mainly needs to experience the sound produced and to remember it for future occasions. Such instructions are to a large extent generic, but there is one type of instruction, peculiar to the instrument itself, that can usefully be discussed here because it is in no sense self-explanatory: the tuning instructions for the harp.

The orchestral harp is tuned to the diatonic scale of C♭.[10] Its seven pedals modify the tuning of the seven notes of the scale, raising them either a semitone or a whole tone. In each case the pedal can be fixed in the two 'lower' positions – that is, physically lower, although they produce higher sounds. Thus the C pedal gives the note C♭ in the top position, C♮ in the intermediate position, and C♯ in the bottom position: the pedal affects all octaves, so that every C on the instrument is affected in the same way. This mechanism makes available any scale that uses not more than seven different pitches. Additional pitches can be made available by changing the pedals during the music, but then the original inflexion is lost. For instance, if the harp is tuned to the diatonic scale of C major, a C♯ can be introduced in the course of the music by means of the relevant pedal. This means, however, that every C on the instrument is raised to C♯, so that C♮ is unavailable until the process is reversed. An alternative strategy might be to keep C♮ but to lower the D♮ to D♭ : then C♮ and C♯ (= D♭) are available simultaneously, but D♮ is no longer available. A second alternative would be to raise B♮ to B♯ (= C) and C♮ to C♯: then C♮, C♯ and D♮ are all available, although B♮ is not.

It follows that the disposition of individual pitch-classes on the harp may require considerable thought on the part of the composer, and also that the composer's indications to the harpist may look decidedly strange, as may the selection of pitches notated.[11] For example, the series C♯, D♯, E♭, F♮, G♮, A♮, B♮ would give a whole-tone scale starting on C♯. The fact that one pitch is doubled – D♯ equals E♭ – means that a glissando could be played in this scale; the doubled pitch would not be noticed unless the glissando were a slow one. Equally, the E♭ could be changed to E♯ (= F♮) without, in this case, changing the pitch-resources in use. This flexibility when enharmonic equivalents are used sometimes leads to very strange-looking chords that actually sound perfectly normal.

A late twentieth-century score: Lutoslawski's Cello Concerto

In the nineteenth century, broadly speaking, composers tended to think of the orchestral woodwind, brass and string families as homogeneous choruses. This technique can be seen in Ex. 4.4, where each of these families has a complete melodic and harmonic texture. Exx. 4.3 and 4.5 show this approach being modified but not radically changed. Brahms's use of the whole string family to provide a rhythmically independent melodic line hardly changes the general approach: and Holst's attitude is essentially a nineteenth-century one, applied to tune, bass and chords separately rather than to a homogeneous quasi-contrapuntal texture (as in 'four-part harmony'). Twentieth-century composers were able to take a more flexible view of orchestral resources, in which individual members of a family – including the strings – could act independently and with an unlimited interaction with members of other families as well as their own. In this situation doublings may be much less conventional than those observed in earlier examples, and various solo instruments or groups of various sizes may interact with one another in combinations that would not be found in a nineteenth-century score.

Another twentieth-century innovation has been the introduction of imprecision of various types. Most obviously, these include the aleatoric sections in which a composer exercises reduced control over the details of the musical texture by asking the performers to undertake certain tasks – for instance – at their own speed, or with pitches chosen by them. Usually the element of control is still considerable, with the composer demanding that such a section be started and ended by all the players simultaneously, that pitches be chosen from a given selection or within a certain pitch-range, and so on. This is perhaps a reaction against other styles in which all the main parameters of the music – pitch, duration, intensity (dynamics) and articulation – are very closely specified.

However the composer exercises control over the music, and to whatever degree, the notation must to some extent be modified. This causes problems to the reader, who must learn what the various signs and instructions mean. Often this requires the reader to take note of written explanations at the beginning of the score, explanations that are often common to several works, and even to the works of several composers, or alternatively may refer only to the one work in question. These changes are allied to some changes in the notation itself, and to ways of writing down orchestral and other music. Finally, therefore, I turn to a work of the late twentieth century in order to illustrate some of the features, and some of the changes, that we can now regard as standard for the immediate future.

Ex. 4.6 shows a page from the Cello Concerto (1970) by Witold Lutoslawski. The work uses a large orchestra, with triple woodwind, four horns and triple brass plus tuba; and it includes a large array of percussion played by three performers, in addition to celesta, harp and piano. The layout of the score is much as expected, with the solo cello placed immediately above the strings and the percussion also in the usual position; the only surprise is that the horns appear between the trumpets and the trombones.

Ex. 4.6 Witold Lutoslawski, Concerto for the Cello and Orchestra (Chester/Hansen): p. 54

54

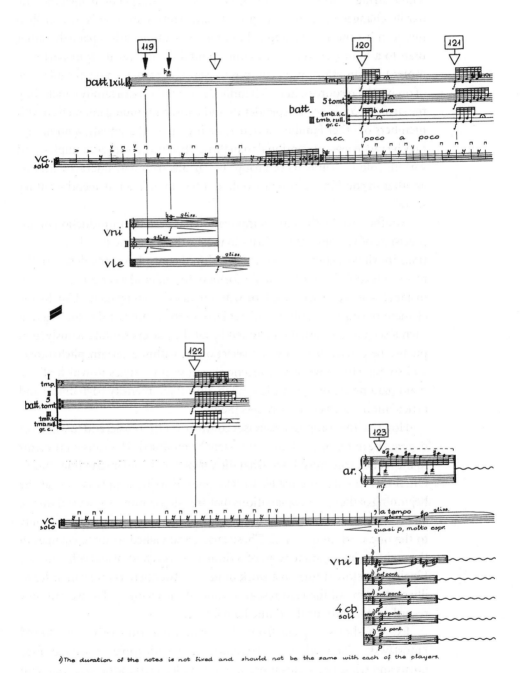

The score does not show all of the instrumental lines on every page, however, and does not show the instrumental families by means of brackets or bar lines. Instead, all instruments are identified at the start of every system or, if they begin part-way through a system, on their reappearance. At the beginning of the score is a series of explanations of the notation, the relationship between measured and unmeasured sections of the music, and the role of the conductor in these different sections. Additional explanations are given throughout the work in the form of footnotes: notes appear on 26 of the 66 pages of music, often with more than one footnote on a page.

Page 54 shows a passage in which the solo cello is accompanied only by percussion (including timpani and harp) and strings. There are two systems on the page, separated by the conventional thick double line: each system includes only those instruments that play in the course of it. Moreover, no instrument is shown where it does not play, so that individual staves begin or end in mid-system. The page is part of a long passage of unmeasured music in which there are no regular stresses. The conductor's downbeats are indicated by the large white arrow-heads, on most of which the composer has placed a rehearsal number. The conductor does not otherwise beat time in this passage: the prefatory notes state that vertical alignment in the unmeasured passages does not indicate simultaneous sounds, and indeed the footnote on this page is designed to make the individual string players independent in the repeated section at the bottom of the page. On the other hand, the downbeats shown by the white arrows presumably mean that all players start the sections concerned together, so the vertical lines through the system at those places must indicate simultaneity there. The prefatory notes do not mention the black arrows, which are also accompanied by vertical lines. These seem to be subsidiary beats – 'upbeats' – and likewise to imply simultaneity.

For most of the page the rate at which events occur is decided by the solo cello, to whose part the other instruments' music is attached: in turn, xylophone, violins and violas; timpani and other percussion; and harp, second violins and four solo double basses. At the very end of the page, at rehearsal number 123, a passage starts in which this last group plays brief repeated sections for as long as the solo cello requires. The passage continues on to the next page (not shown in Ex. 4.6) and is ended by another downbeat from the conductor. This is the section in which the footnote asks the performers not to play together.

This page offers much for the reader to think about, starting with the information contained in the prefatory notes. The headless stems and beams of the solo cello part, for instance, indicate the repetition of a pitch or chord: the pitch in operation at the start of the page (a harmonic sounding f″) is given on the previous page. Because the cello's rhythm controls the flow of the music on this page up to rehearsal number 123 it is unnecessary for the accompaniment at rehearsal number 119 to be given durations: those notes are played to the conductor's beat, following the cello part. Another important element for the reader is the precision and care with which such matters as bowing, accents, dynamics and tempo (albeit in an unmeasured section) are specified. These elements need to be auralised with care when the reader comes to imagine the sound of this page.

In the accompaniment at rehearsal number 119 the xylophone and strings play in octaves, although this is not immediately apparent. The main (black) notes of the strings are an octave below the xylophone's notes: but the harmonics a perfect fourth above the fingered notes (that is, the fourth harmonics) sound two octaves above the main notes and therefore an octave above the xylophone. Observe the curious effect on these notes of the dynamic (loud, with an immediate *decrescendo*) together with a downward *glissando*. This is a precisely heard effect that is difficult to read into the score at first sight.

The cello's double-stopped demisemiquaver passage that follows this includes some unusual chromatic alterations: the single upright with a cross-piece is a half-sharp, raising the note d by a quarter-tone; and the triple upright with cross-pieces raises the note by three-quarters of a tone. These notations for quarter-tones are explained in the prefatory notes. While the cello's lower note is a pedal on bottom G, therefore, the upper notes rise by quarter-tones from d to f♯. The prefatory notes explain that accidentals apply to only one note, which is why the accidental is repeated for the second f♯.

The solo cello's next note is a fourth harmonic, sounding two octaves above the main written note f'. The cello's next passage, up to rehearsal number 123, is accompanied by three bursts of activity by the percussion. On the top staff, the first percussion player moves from xylophone to timpani, playing three drums. The next staff down is used by the second percussionist, playing the five tom-toms. As these instruments are roughly pitched relative to one another, they occupy the five lines of the staff, as shown by the black squares where one would expect a clef at the beginning of the staff. On the third staff, which has only three lines, are a side-drum without snares (*tamburo senza corda*), a tenor drum (*tamburo rullante*) and a bass drum (*gran cassa*). Again, each drum is given one of the lines, as shown by the squares in the clef space. The player is directed to use hard sticks (one would normally use a felt-covered stick for a bass drum). In this passage there is a gradual acceleration up to rehearsal number 123, where the music returns to the earlier speed. Again, this acceleration is controlled by the cellist: as before, the percussionists do not play in strict time, either with each other or with the cellist, but the beginning of each burst of activity is timed with the solo cello's part.

At rehearsal number 123 the solo cello takes up the slow *glissando* movement. The second violins' glissandos are again made with harmonics sounding two octaves higher than the main note: here the pitch at the end of each *glissando* is specified. The double basses, too, have glissandos – not, however, with harmonics but *sul ponticello* (on the bridge), which creates a weird unsettling sound. Finally, the harp's repeated figuration demands both B♮ and B♭: the latter is supplied as an A♯, since A♮ and A♭ are not needed.

It is a far cry, in both historical and musical terms, from Bach's Third Suite to Lutoslawski's Cello Concerto. The details of the problems for the score-reader vary, and so do their difficulty: but the basic problems remain the same. The only road to finding score-reading easier is practice, and all of the works cited here are good examples for the reader to use. In addition, I would cite the best-known work by that consummate orchestrator Rimsky-Korsakov – *Scheherazade* – as a score using a full Romantic orchestra with an unrivalled clarity of purpose.

5 The art of orchestration

JULIAN RUSHTON

Introduction

Instrumentation and orchestration have been defined as 'the art of combining the sounds of a complex of instruments (an orchestra or other ensemble) to form a satisfactory blend and balance'.[1] If the two terms are separable, 'instrumentation' concerns selection of the ensemble, including the study of the technical aspects which determine the choice of instruments for a particular purpose, while 'orchestration' is used for the application of skills in an artistic fashion. Thus an orchestral realisation of a musical conception may be an original work, without any existence prior to its orchestral realisation; or it may be a transcription for orchestra of music by the person orchestrating it, or by someone else.

Orchestration is thus more than the effective disposition of pitches (not to mention rhythms) among the instruments of the orchestra; but this skill remains indispensable, and advice on the craft of instrumentation forms a substantial literature. The first celebrated example, though not the first publication of its kind, was by the French composer Hector Berlioz, and was for many years incomparably the most influential and most widely used in teaching.[2] Orchestration treatises concentrate mainly on technical details, including some description of instrument mechanisms and a comprehensive listing of the possibilities and impossibilities of the various instruments, with examples of recent usage. The creative, aesthetic dimension of orchestration is less open to explanation in a textbook, but more vital to the composer and listener. Orchestral sonorities form an integral part of musical thinking in the European traditions of concert music, and a vital element of its expressive language and rhetoric. Berlioz, indeed, had a wider aim than mere instruction; his treatise contains some of his most telling aesthetic and critical observations, relating to the practice of past and contemporary composers as well as to his own. Subsequent treatises vary in their relative emphasis on instruction and aesthetic advice, but most were not written by musicians independently significant as original composers, and lack their especial insights, but also their idiosyncrasies.

Around 1900, when the orchestra was at the height of its cultural significance and musical glory, a provocative view was expressed by the musician and critic Frederick Corder.[3] For the second edition of *Grove's Dictionary*, after eliminating much of the historical material supplied in its predecessor, he revealingly combined a progressive view of technical means with a pained conservatism as to aesthetic ends. For Corder, orchestral colour was essentially decorative, and dependent on solid structural principles.

> [A]n attempt is now being made to produce still greater emotional effect by a style of orchestral writing which defies analysis, and in which the music *per se* has but a weak structure and material of the utmost degree of tenuity . . . there are very few of the musical works we now allude to which will bear the simple but infallible test of being played upon the piano.

If orchestral music failed this 'black-and-white' test, the fault lay with inadequate harmonic and contrapuntal technique; the symphony and symphonic poem (Corder refers to Liszt and Strauss), as much as music for homogeneous sonorities such as a string quartet or solo piano, should be subject to harmonic, contrapuntal, or voice-leading laws. From the viewpoint of the early twenty-first century, such a restriction may appear not so much pedantic as absurd; but our view of music is radically altered not only by twentieth-century musical innovation in pitch, rhythm, and timbre, but also by the existence of recordings. The music now available for fully-coloured reproduction in our homes makes redundant a whole literature of music adapted to keyboard – transcriptions of orchestral and chamber music for solo piano, duet, two pianos, organ – that was once indispensable to the dissemination of the repertory.

For some composers, musical thought does apparently proceed with sufficient abstraction for piano reductions to sound meaningful. Instrumentation is sometimes determined at a relatively late stage in the compositional process, and original intentions in instrumentation are subject to radical change. Brahms's first attempt at a symphony became the Piano Concerto in D minor, with the interesting result that the tunes sound better on the orchestra than on the solo instrument. Elgar converted music drafted for string quartet into the superbly coloured central movements of his First Symphony. Both these composers, however, were keyboard players whose music would seldom, if ever, fail Corder's piano test. On the other hand, Berlioz's orchestral songs, *Les Nuits d'été*, were published with a piano accompaniment which feels like a transcription; nevertheless, orchestrating them years later was a new creative action, almost as if the composer were orchestrating music by someone else (as Berlioz orchestrated Schubert's *Erlkönig*). Orchestration of keyboard music has a recognised place in teaching, including scoring for the monochrome string ensemble; Riemann produced exemplary transcriptions of Haydn piano sonatas for strings, and Strauss advocated preliminary training by writing for string quartet.[4]

Attempts at formulating eternal laws for orchestration are no more successful than for any other aspect of musical creativity. The earliest treatise dealing with modern instrumentation, not listed in bibliographies of orchestration, occupies forty-odd pages in the composition treatise of Antonín Reicha. After detailing the nature, capabilities, and disposition of orchestral instruments and voices, he rules without equivocation that the wind group 'should make good harmony, without the aid of the strings'.[5] This precept is reiterated by Charles-Marie Widor in his largely practical manual; in his conclusion, Widor writes, 'Each separate group must give the sense of harmonic completeness, with the true bass.'[6] Combinatorial rules whereby separate sections of the orchestra should agree polyphonically, sharing or respecting the principal melody line and bass, were an aspect of the common-practice tonal music of the eighteenth and nineteenth centuries, and took on the aspect of universal law. Hence the 'black-and-white' test was used to damn Mahler and Strauss, who were both expert pianists, as well as Berlioz, who was not. The history of thinking about the orchestra in more recent years is connected to the liberation of timbre, or orchestral colour, as an expressive element in its own right. In what follows, I shall trace the historical thread of orchestration over two and a half centuries, pointing mainly to this aesthetic dimension.

Orchestrational development to the time of Mozart

Prior to the eighteenth century, while the concept of instrumentation clearly existed, that of orchestration was embryonic; as *The New Grove* puts it, 'Orchestration is a difficult concept to apply to medieval and Renaissance music.' Orchestral ensembles in the seventeenth century were founded upon the practice of continuo, a bass instrument and a keyboard or other instrument with chordal potential. Baroque ensembles tended to use instruments in isolation, throughout musical sections, rather than varying combinations within musical sections. While the string group was already the foundation of an orchestral sonority, it could still, thanks to the continuo, be omitted from movements with a prominent solo. Baroque instrumentation is directly associated with meaning. Wind instruments in particular acquired specific connotations: French Baroque aesthetics made the oboe pastoral, while the flutes (recorders) were suited to scenes of mourning. The *philosophe* d'Alembert asserted that the flute should not play concertos since rapid passage-work contradicted its natural function and its aesthetic role in the imitation of human passions. Most associations of instruments were by no means so restrictive. If the trumpet of the last judgement, in Handel's *Messiah*, appears literal, in Bach's B minor Mass and Christmas

Oratorio trumpets are used with exhilarating virtuosity for the praise of God. It was only when the skill in melodic playing on the highest harmonics was eroded, by the late eighteenth century, that trumpets, confined to rhythmic blasts on the few available pitches, acquired an almost invariable military connotation.

J. S. Bach, who so frequently transcribed his music for other instruments, has sometimes been assumed to be superior to considerations of mere sonority. Stravinsky viewed him differently: 'What incomparable instrumental writing is Bach's! You can smell the resin in his violin parts, taste the reeds in the oboe.'[7] Never more so, one might add, than when the music is performed by a period-instrument ensemble. Bach's choice of instruments is often determined by symbolism, but not by fixed associations, as in French aesthetics, so much as by the musical idea which, aided by appropriate colouring, acts as a symbol. In Cantata No. 78 ('Jesu, der du meine Seele'), for instance, wave-motions are confided to strings, but drops of Christ's blood are depicted by an obbligato flute, exploiting staccato articulation. Sometimes Bach's instrumentation may seem eccentric, but some of his stranger combinations are emotionally compelling in a sensitive performance; consider the incomparable melancholy of the aria 'Aus Liebe will mein Heiland sterben' (St Matthew Passion), which dispenses with continuo and confides the accompaniment to a flute and two oboes da caccia (cors anglais).

Continuo practice particularly enraged Corder, who, disregarding the dramatic instrumentation of Handel and, especially, Rameau, claimed that orchestration only began when the continuo died. The late eighteenth-century liberation from the continuo had mixed causes, including the practice of performing ensemble music out of doors, both on strings or wind. For one reason or another, composers began to prefer a filled-out texture. Keyboard parts in small ensembles were written out in full in works by Bach and Rameau, and this practice became normal. Ensembles like the string quartet and wind (Harmonie) required no keyboard support, and whereas full orchestration had been a special effect in the operas of Lully, Gluck completed the orchestral texture throughout his French operas, even in recitative.[8] Instead of the continuo, the classical orchestra is founded on string tone, usually in four parts (French terminology for the string section is 'quatuor'); sometimes there were divided violas, or an independent double bass. Horns progressed in the opposite direction to the trumpets, becoming more versatile and escaping routine associations with hunting. In the late Classical and early Romantic orchestra they could be used as foundation instruments, subject to the limitations of the harmonic series, and their melodic potential was developed even before they became fully chromatic, by the use of hand-stopping.

Another source of the Classical orchestra was the ensemble of virtuosi, associated both with the theatre and with concert life. The Mannheim
orchestra was described by Dr Burney as 'an army of generals' because
so many of its members were also composers. But Mannheim, while outstanding, was not unique. Elaborate and expressive orchestration tended to
distinguish German and French opera from Italian, and it was in Germany
and Paris that the symphony developed a life independent of the theatre. The
implied division of taste between Italy and the rest was not uniform, however, in that many French and Austrian audiences preferred something more
typically Italian, whereas some of the most elaborate orchestration of the period originated from composers of the Italian diaspora, such as Jommelli in
Stuttgart or Piccinni in Paris. Most institutions could not afford enormous
orchestras, and even the houses of the nobility, such as Haydn's Eszterháza,
founded their orchestras on a standard ensemble (pairs of oboes and horns
plus strings, with the occasional addition of trumpets and drums). Unusual
ensembles, as in the Haydn symphonies with four horns (Nos. 13 and 31,
'The Hornsignal'), betoken some special occasion, or exceptional availability
of the instruments. A standard ensemble encouraged widespread publication of the repertory, including hundreds of symphonies. Public concerts in
larger cities eventually supported larger orchestras, notably Paris where the
inclusion of clarinets alongside oboes, rather than instead of them, delighted
Mozart in 1778. Paris was strongly associated with the Mannheim personnel
and one of its orchestras commissioned Haydn symphonies before London;
considerably later, the Société des Concerts du Conservatoire was to give the
first regular and fully rehearsed performances of Beethoven's symphonies.
London's Philharmonic Society could also boast virtuosi in its ranks; and
the late Classical and Romantic orchestra, especially when severed from its
theatrical roots, became one of Europe's supreme cultural manifestations
in the age of the industrial revolution.

It was for the Mannheim orchestra, transferred with their employer
to Munich, that Mozart wrote his most elaborately orchestrated opera,
Idomeneo, in 1781. As a composer for orchestra, Mozart like Haydn recognised codes of instrumental association, and since he could rely upon their
being understood by audiences, he turned them to dramatic advantage. In
Idomeneo he followed Gluck's lead in *Alceste* (1767) by demanding trombones for the oracle (he probably did not get them). Trombones were widely
used in church and seldom elsewhere; they thus acquired sacred associations,
which in the theatre evoked the supernatural and inspired awe – nowhere
more than in the statue music of *Don Giovanni* (1787). Mozart made ironic
use of trumpets, without timpani or horns, in *Così fan tutte*. In Fiordiligi's
majestic aria 'Come scoglio' this military sonority reflects her determination
not to be seduced from her departed soldier-lover. The humorous association of hunting horns with cuckoldry is a feature of the aria 'Aprite un po'

quegli occhi' in *Le nozze di Figaro*. Some critical caution is appropriate in reading such signals, however; it is not the instruments as such, but the way they are used, that may signify something. In Fiordiligi's second aria, 'Per pietà', the challenging horn parts belong to a tradition of virtuoso chamber music, and cannot imply sexual inconstancy. This style of writing recurs in the aria 'Komm, Hoffnung' sung by Beethoven's Leonora, who is constancy personified (*Fidelio*, first version 1805); both operas were premièred in Vienna, and a fixed association with infidelity could not have been lost in a mere fifteen years. The associations of woodwind were certainly weaker by this stage, especially with their numbers swollen by the clarinet, an instrument with too short an orchestral history to have acquired specific associations within a baroque aesthetic.

The instrumental palette of *Idomeneo* is of striking richness, and Mozart used it for expressiveness as well as for force and brilliance. At the crucial moment when Idomeneo admits that the sacrificial victim demanded by the gods is his own son (Ex. 5.1A), he does not recall Gluck's sighing oboe (*Iphigénie en Aulide*), but contrives an uncanny impact without any motive, but through colour alone: imagine the low oboes, rich in upper partials, replaced by high bassoons, or by the hollow medium of clarinets, or complacent horns. These bars uncannily anticipate the sound-world of early Romanticism, notably Weber and Berlioz. In a symphony for the standard orchestra, Mozart can invite interpretation by the complexity of texture as well as harmony. The incomparable slow introduction to the 'Prague' Symphony gropes through perturbed shadows to an extended dominant pedal (Ex. 5.1B), on horns and throbbing basses, surmounted by sighs – strings descending, solo woodwind rising, the chromatic scale conveying depth by doubling at the fifteenth. Remnants of a motive are passed among the violins over a skeletal bassoon arpeggio; the trumpet and timpani punctuation suggests that the battle is not over, but has merely moved away.

The Romantic orchestra: sound as meaning

The development of orchestral colour as an element in the meaning of music was mainly the work of theatre composers. The story of the orchestra could be told in terms of novel effects which become assimilated, normal. During the late eighteenth and early nineteenth centuries, the associative language of instrumentation which is part of the life-blood of eighteenth-century musical signification was progressively weakened, the price paid for constant use of a richer orchestral palette. The trombone lost its intrinsic supernatural association to become a routine member of theatre orchestras, and it entered the symphony with Beethoven, Schubert, and Berlioz. The developing clarinet lost the trumpet-like quality of the upper register which

Ex. 5.1 A Mozart, *Idomeneo*, from Act III

gave it its name, and was valued for its perceived vocal qualities and its range and flexibility, including striking contrasts between registers: hearing it sing in the overture to *Der Freischütz* Berlioz, in his treatise, was reduced to exclaiming 'O Weber!'

The early nineteenth century is the foundation period of the modern orchestra, and it is no accident that many orchestration treatises, notably

Ex. 5.1B Mozart, 'Prague' Symphony, slow introduction, bars 28-32

François-Auguste Gevaert's two massive volumes, use examples from Beethoven more than from his predecessors or successors.[9] Riemann distinguished the Classical from the Romantic orchestra because the former was founded on a kind of equality between instrumental sounds which can alternate material within a single movement, whereas the latter looked for special effects from tone colours. The larger contrast is between the Baroque and Classical; the Romantic conception was essentially a continuation of the Classical rather than a contradiction, as Riemann makes clear by exemplifying both tendencies from the music of Beethoven. The example from *Idomeneo* also suggests a considerable overlap in sensitivity to sound as an expressive element in itself.

Beethoven followed Mozart's example even as he developed his idiosyncratic orchestral language. The tenor hero of *Fidelio* is immured in a dank dungeon, which Beethoven evokes more by gesture and colour than themes (Ex. 5.2A). The orchestral score-reader needs to know that the horns' E♭ is not a golden note from its singing register (as it would be on a valve horn) but a baleful cry, produced by hand stopping, undoubtedly meant to sound terrifying, and beautiful only within the romantic aesthetic formulated by Victor Hugo, which embraced the grotesque and ugly in the search for the sublime. A few bars later a sinister throb of timpani distorts the perfect fourth to which these instruments are usually confined by sounding the tritone (diminished fifth).[10] In the first movement of his Ninth Symphony (Ex. 5.2B), emboldened by his theatrical experience, Beethoven has the timpani, and sometimes trumpets, play the normal tonic and dominant perfect fourths, A and D, but subverting the prevailing tonality, B♭. Such anti-functional instrumentation was eagerly seized upon by Berlioz, whose style was formed before the entire brass section acquired its chromatic capability. When such instrumental limitations ceased to exist, composers lost a resource and had to find other means to create comparable effects of alienation.

By around 1830, the four horns of the Ninth Symphony became standard, and the other brass were sometimes supported by a bass instrument, the keyed ophicleide or valved tuba.[11] The growing numbers, as well as melodic capability, of the powerful brass forced other sections to modify their roles. String numbers swelled to fifty or more, and the instruments acquired greater force and brilliance, complemented by the general rise in pitch-standard to about a tone higher than in the early eighteenth century. Expanded woodwind families, unable to compete in power, remained an unrivalled resource for colour variation. Beethoven added piccolo and double bassoon to the symphony orchestra. The cor anglais became the voice of romantic melancholy in Berlioz (*Huit scènes de Faust*, 1829), a usage followed by Meyerbeer and Wagner, notably in Act III of *Tristan und Isolde*. Meyerbeer offered the sombre bass clarinet a fine solo in *Les Huguenots*

Ex. 5.2A Beethoven, *Fidelio*, opening of Act II

(1836), a lead also followed in *Tristan*. Berlioz brought the high clarinet in Eb into the concert hall for a grotesque effect in *Symphonie fantastique* (1830), anticipating Mahler and Strauss. But in opera, commercial houses less well endowed than Paris (or Bayreuth) managed with smaller forces without preventing the later Verdi and Puccini, among others, from orchestrating with a superb sense of colour and rhetorical aptness.

A significant element in contemporary decorum excluded non-standard instruments from the concert hall, including the harp, except in programmatic or vocal music. The standard symphony orchestra became double woodwind, four horns, two trumpets, three trombones, perhaps a tuba, timpani but little or no other percussion, and strings. This was considered fit for what were regarded as purely musical genres, symphony and concerto; Schumann, Bruckner and Brahms required few additional colours in their symphonies and choral music. Mendelssohn's orchestral genius evoked the seascape of *The Hebrides*, the fairies of *A Midsummer Night's Dream*, with little else. Berlioz's colouristic innovations were also sometimes

Ex. 5.2B Beethoven, Ninth Symphony, first movement

associated with the supernatural, but usually required unusual combinations. Mephistopheles summons the will-o'-the-wisps in *La Damnation de Faust* with three piccolos; their Minuet (Ex. 5.3) transforms the stately classical dance into something other-worldly, as much by colouristic and textural as by harmonic or melodic means. Setting off the higher woodwind with bass clarinet and strikingly low pitches from trumpets and cornets, an effect unobtainable in piano transcription, creates a curiously eerie saturation of musical space. Carl Dahlhaus's remark, 'Instrumentation first acquired an essential significance in the music of Berlioz, where the writing is often incomprehensible when abstracted from the tone colour,' may seem exaggerated, but only because the same is true of certain passages in Weber, such as a passage for two low flutes in the Wolf's Glen scene in *Der Freischütz*.[12]

Orchestral pedagogy: from romantic to modern

Berlioz proposed that orchestration should be studied at the Conservatoire as an adjunct to composition studies. Nevertheless, his treatise, in common with most others, presents examples from the literature which are inspired

Ex. 5.3 Berlioz: 'Menuet des follets' from *La Damnation de Faust*

exceptions rather than representations of normal practice; they could hardly be used as models without plagiarism. They range from Gluck (whom Gevaert also quoted extensively, calling him 'the father of the dramatic orchestra') through Méhul and Weber to himself. A notorious passage in Berlioz's Requiem has eight trombones playing the bass to chords on flutes, with the orchestral middle entirely empty. The passage is essentially without rhythm or melody; the musical message lies in the sound, rather than in the harmony. Hugh Macdonald suggested that this idea might have been confined to the treatise; Cecil Forsyth said that 'it probably sounds very nasty'; Norman Del Mar called it 'wholly convincing' in the right acoustic.[13] Because of his individuality, Berlioz features only a little in Gevaert and Widor, far less than Wagner, whose musical standing in the late nineteenth century matched that of Beethoven at the beginning. Wagner's instrumentation, founded on expanded families of instruments and on a musical style which translates surprisingly well on to the monochrome of the keyboard, was more susceptible to analysis, and hence to imitation.

The editorial comments in Strauss's edition of Berlioz's treatise produce a fascinating dialogue between the two masters. Scrupulously reproducing the original, Strauss supplemented it with examples from music Berlioz might have cited (Mozart, Méhul, Meyerbeer), and also more recent music; and as with Gevaert, whose thesis Strauss cordially recommends, it is Wagner whose works in full score dominate the pages.[14] Rimsky-Korsakov's treatise, on the other hand, is illustrated only by his own music, perhaps less through egotism than a need for confidence in connecting intentions with outcomes.[15] He deals more with compositional than with technical or even aesthetic issues, treating melody and harmony separately, and assessing balance and the effect of articulation rather than musical signification. His advice on scoring chords by interlocking the woodwind became an orthodoxy and eventually a cliché. Unfortunately the limited currency of Rimsky-Korsakov's operas makes it difficult to compare the written examples with their sound. The same could be said of the most thoroughgoing of treatises originally in English, by Cecil Forsyth, whose illustrations show a penchant for Joseph Holbrooke. Some more recent treatises, such as Walter Piston's, offer advice on instrumental combinations and effects, surely more useful to the run-of-the-mill arranger than the composer. Originality emerges without such aids, and can be heard in the distinctive sounds of simple chords when scored by Bruckner, Brahms, Elgar, Mahler, Sibelius, or Stravinsky.

Wagner's blend of heterogeneous themes into a harmonically directed whole remains paradigmatic in orchestral tuttis. At the end of *Die Walküre*, the balm of the repeated melody (woodwinds) is coupled with string and harp figurations which touch the same pitches, ensuring harmonic coherence and warmth, and signifying the magic fire which Wotan conjures to protect Brünnhilde; meanwhile the brass sing the melody of his farewell (Ex. 5.4). The rich polyphony of Strauss is spiced by conflicting harmonic combinations, notably in *Elektra*, or counterpoint indifferent to its harmonic context: in *Ein Heldenleben* (1898), the music for critics and for the battle conspicuously, perhaps deliberately, fails the 'black-and-white test'. Mahler's music anticipates modernist instrumentation in its implied conflict between sections of the orchestra; his scoring is a polyphony of equal voices rather like expanded chamber music, an aspect which particularly appealed to his Viennese admirer Schoenberg. Wagner's legacy was differently interpreted in France, where it became a more potent example than Berlioz. The delicate patina of sound in Debussy's orchestral music may be obtained by offering the instrumental groups slightly different materials, creating a depth in the sonic field that is particularly successful for all kinds of evocation. In the example shown, from *Ibéria*, the streets and alleys of a Spanish town, their bustle, their heat, light and shade, are miraculously limned: with a different topic – in the same set of orchestral *Images* Debussy evokes Northern England (*Gigues*) and rural France (*Rondes de Printemps*) – the colours change, but the method remains constant.

Ex. 5.4 Wagner: near the end of Act III of *Die Walküre*

Ex. 5.4 (*cont.*)

Ex. 5.5 Debussy, *Ibéria*, from the first movement

A more radical treatment of the orchestra as a source of evocative sounds, isolated within the composer's work but profoundly influential, is Schoenberg's experiment in the third of his *Five Orchestral Pieces*, Op. 16 (1909). Beginning with a single sustained chord, he achieves a sense of musical movement by articulation of colour alone: the only element of

Ex. 5.6

change is the instrumentation (Ex. 5.6). This piece was published with the title 'Farben' ('Colours'), but also with the more literally evocative 'Summer morning by a lake'. Although the chord does change, almost imperceptibly, the colouristic element remains integral to the conception; yet Schoenberg sanctioned versions for smaller orchestra, chamber ensemble, and two pianos.

The aesthetics of orchestration is bound intimately with composition itself, and the new colours of the twentieth century reflect new creative preoccupations. Additions to the instrumental families provided an occasional rather than a routine resource in the period of greatest orchestral expansiveness. The contrabass clarinet appears in the first piece of Schoenberg's Op. 16, the bass oboe (heckelphone) in Holst's *The Planets* (completed 1916). The saxophone had an intermittent life from the 1860s as a new orchestral voice, mainly in French music, such as Bizet's *L'Arlésienne*. Its growing association with popular dance music made its routine orchestral use problematic, but precisely this reference could be exploited by Alban Berg in *Lulu* (1935). There were notable revivals of virtually obsolete instruments: by Strauss, the oboe d'amore (*Symphonia Domestica*, 1903) and basset-horn (*Elektra*, 1909), and by Berg, the alto trombone (*Three Orchestral Pieces*, Op. 6, 1915). But far more significant was the addition and development of keyboard and percussion sections. The organ is a soloist in Saint-Saëns's Third Symphony (1886); its reinforcing role in large-scale choral works was transferred by Elgar to a purely orchestral context ('Enigma' variations, 1899). The celesta and piano, together with pitched percussion (glockenspiel, xylophone, later marimba and vibraphone), create the possibility of newly brilliant but evanescent fields of orchestral sonority, almost entirely lacking in the nineteenth century, although Berlioz evoked the magic island in *La Tempête* (1830) with a piano duet (he also experimented with a glass harmonica), and Tchaikovsky introduced the celesta in *The Nutcracker* (1892). Stravinsky used the piano as an instrument of tuned percussion (*Symphony of Psalms*, 1930), but also as an individual character with a concertante-like role, notably in *Petrushka* (1911) and *Symphony in Three Movements* (1945).

Percussion especially assists the orchestral composers eager to develop timbre as a means of musical articulation independent of pitch. Despite the use of percussion in some popular musics as a 'rhythm section', the orchestral value of unpitched percussion is primarily colouristic and dynamic; these instruments are not rhythmically subtle. In the first movement of Mahler's Third Symphony (1896), the orchestra is halted by a passage for percussion alone, a disintegration of the musical and rhetorical fabric which is overcome by the strenuous efforts of the pitched instruments; the conflict of Nielsen's Fifth Symphony (1922), in which the side-drum is pitted against the rest of the ensemble, descends from this idea. Development of percussion as an integrated orchestral section might seem to belong less to modernism (given its absorption in pitch and rhythm) than to the post-modernism, whether minimalist or stylistically pluralist, of the late twentieth century. But Varèse's *Ionisation*, for percussion only, was written in 1931. It struggles to achieve sustained musical interest without pitch; the finest moment in this extraordinary piece comes near the end, when pitched percussion finally intervenes.

The present and future of orchestration

The orchestra as the nineteenth century conceived it is essentially a harmonic instrument. The breakdown in harmonically orientated tonality (even in music which retains a tonal centre) marks the end of the art of orchestral composition as traditionally understood. The art of instrumentation remains a force, with the harnessing of electrical and electronic technologies, adumbrated in such inventions as the ondes martenot and a major factor in developments since about 1950. But while many composers continue to write for orchestra, the 'full band' has appeared anachronistic since about 1920. Each reconsideration of the orchestral ensemble is stylistically governed, a series of 'one-off' orchestras: Schoenberg's 'section' of six clarinets in his Op. 22 songs, Stravinsky's *Symphony of Psalms*, without clarinets, violins or violas, multiplying flutes and oboes, and with pianos and harp. In any case, where the music is not harmonically based, the concept 'orchestration', as distinct from 'composing for an orchestral ensemble', becomes dubious. Parallel to this compositional development, however, is an art of orchestration which leads to the orchestrator (sometimes called 'arranger') as an identifiable member of the musical profession. This art has two strands: orchestration may be applied to something already existing as an artefact (like Berlioz's orchestration of Schubert), or to something new but functionally dependent on something outside music, such as a film. Through sheer pressure of time film music, and some musical theatre, requires teamwork, and the orchestrator whose role is really too creative to be called 'arrangement' is often not the composer. Paradoxically, therefore, while orchestration innovations used to emerge from the theatre, more recent film and theatre music has been dependent on the innovations of concert music by (for example) Strauss, Debussy, or Ravel. Exceptions to the use of a highly coloured orchestra, such as Herrmann's string music in *Psycho*, tend to underline the normality of post-romantic lushness, so that for much of its heyday the new art of motion pictures was underpinned by a regressive view of music – a tendency brought to a climax, or nadir, in *Star Wars*.

At their best, orchestral transcriptions for the concert hall are not tied to the palette the original composer might have used, but intriguingly mingle the personalities of the original and arranging composer, as in Tchaikovsky's fourth orchestral suite *Mozartiana*, or Stravinsky's scoring of Bach's chorale variations 'Vom Himmel hoch', although Stravinsky typically added pitches and lines which mark the arrangement as his own. This austere re-composition of Bach is fundamentally different from the brilliantly coloured transcriptions of Elgar, Schoenberg, or Stokowski. Unlike piano music, organ music was never monochrome; even with unchanged registration, the vivid overtone content of combination stops produces a polychromatic effect. The justification for orchestral transcription is to gain dynamic subtlety and clarity, because separate textural strands, for instance in a fugue, can be differently coloured. The outcome is a ripe post-romantic hybrid Bach, calculated to revolt or delight different listeners. There need be no sense of moral superiority for music in which colour is demonstrably a fundamental compositional thought; this would merely be to invert Corder's piano test into an equal and opposite restriction. Some collision between the musical styles of composer and orchestrator may even be considered an aesthetic advantage. Ravel's orchestration of *Pictures in an Exhibition*, despite the attractions of Musorgsky's solo piano original and several alternative arrangements, is a masterpiece which deserves its prominent position in the repertory.[16]

In the pluralistic musical scene of the early twenty-first century, we continue to enjoy music by composers who use orchestration functionally, as a way of presenting their independently conceived *idea*. Composers who have chosen this path are not necessarily lacking in inventiveness where orchestration is concerned. Brahms's handling of orchestral forces serves the structural requirements of his music admirably; the delicacy of the central movements of his symphonies testifies to the assurance of his orchestral ear. The same applies to composers like Vaughan Williams, Copland, Tippett and Carter, who cultivate linear clarity in orchestral colouring to present the complexities of their musical thought with pristine honesty.

In the above ruminations, which have left out far more than they include, I hope to have conveyed the independent value of orchestration as an art which can vitalise music and render it immediately expressive. While twentieth-century composers working for concert audiences tended towards the abolition of orchestration as such, through their use of select ensembles whose instrumental characteristics are integral to the musical conception, others have maintained and developed the traditional definition of orchestration as 'the art of combining the sounds of a large complex of instruments to form a satisfactory blend and balance'. This chapter should have shown the inadequacies of this definition; blend and balance may be the exact opposite of what is intended in the realisation of a musical conception designed for the orchestra. The lonely strands at the cadenza-like close of the first movement of Mahler's Ninth Symphony are as much the product of orchestrational skill as the awesomely expressive climaxes in Strauss's operas, or the miraculous reconciliation of richness with linear independence in the mature work of Alban Berg, or in Nicholas Maw's symphonic *Odyssey* (1987); while the orchestral ensemble can be dismantled and reassembled to convey new musical ideas in music as widely disparate as that of Carl Ruggles, Harrison Birtwistle, or Poul Ruders. The orchestra as an entity survived the twentieth century remarkably well. If its growth in size and colouristic variety is approaching its end, and composers find alternative means of expression, the 'modern' orchestra deserves to maintain an honourable role as an active museum for musical art.

6 The history of direction and conducting

JEREMY SIEPMANN

The mentality of the conductor is a dark, abysmal chapter in the history of music. His profession is by its very nature calculated to corrupt the character. When all is said and done, it is the only musical activity in which a dash of charlatanism is not only harmless but absolutely necessary. CARL FLESCH[1]

You conductors, who are so proud of your powers! When a new man faces the orchestra – from the way he walks up the steps to the rostrum and opens his score – before he even picks up his baton – we know whether *he* is the master or *we*. FRANZ STRAUSS (FATHER OF RICHARD STRAUSS)[2]

A conductor should reconcile himself to the realization that regardless of his approach or temperament the eventual result is the same – the orchestra will hate him. OSCAR LEVANT[3]

Introduction

The conductor is many things to many people, now more than ever. Until well into the twentieth century, for instance, the profession, with few exceptions, was an exclusively male preserve. Today, women conductors, while still a minority, are increasingly familiar. Ethel Leginska (1886–1970) and Nadia Boulanger (1887–1979) were the great pioneers. Their successors include Veronika Dudarova, Iona Brown, Marin Alsop, Jane Glover, Odaline de la Martinez, Sian Edwards, Andrea Quinn and JoAnn Falletta, although at the time of writing, the principal conductors of all the world's major symphony orchestras remain resolutely male, and there is little evidence that this is likely to change in the immediately foreseeable future. And while the conductor still represents the very apex of glamour in the musical world, the profession itself has never been more seriously questioned. While the Soviet experiment with a conductorless orchestra, 'Persimfans', survived for barely a decade (1922–32), the example of the Italian orchestra I Musici and, more recently, the Orpheus Chamber Orchestra in the United States (founded in 1972 and still going strong at the time of writing), has demonstrated that even in some notably complex twentieth-century scores the conductor is entirely expendable. At one well-remembered Promenade Concert in London in the late 1970s, the conductor, Daniel Barenboim, during one of the encores by the Paris Orchestra, walked offstage after only a few bars and left the orchestra to get on with it, which they triumphantly did, to a thunderous ovation at the end. Had he done the same thing in the midst of Mahler's Eighth Symphony or Stravinsky's *The Rite of Spring*, however, any hint of triumph would soon have degenerated into chaos. At one level, then, the conductor serves as a glorified traffic policeman. His first duty is to keep order, and the larger the orchestra, the greater his authority must be. This has always been the case. His present celebrity, on the other hand, is a surprisingly recent phenomenon. The story told by the orchestral historian Adam Carse makes for startling reading:

> In the middle of the [nineteenth] century the conductor was no box-office draw, and he got no headlines; his name did not usually appear on theatrical bills which gave in full the name of every singer and dancer, as well as the names of the scene-painter, costumier and stage-manager. The conductor's name appeared in small letters on concert announcements, and if a performance was reported and criticised, more likely than not the conductor's name was not even mentioned. Notices of hundreds of operatic performances in the first half of the [nineteenth] century can be read without once coming across the name of the conductor, and orchestral concerts were often reported without any mention of the man who shouldered the heaviest responsibility. In two columns about a Philharmonic concert in London in 1842 the conductor's name is the only one missing.[4]

Before proceeding further, it might be useful to clarify one or two important transatlantic discrepancies in terminology which could lead to confusion. In Britain, the term 'director', in an orchestral context, specifically denotes an active player, be it the principal violinist, the resident harpsichordist, or the soloist in a concerto, who may be a string, wind, brass or keyboard player (interestingly, few singers in modern times have opted for this dual role). The term 'leader' refers to the principal violinist, who in Europe generally makes a separate entrance, and receives the applause of the audience, before the arrival on the platform of the conductor (and soloists when there are any). Thus in British usage a performance can be 'led' or 'directed' only by a participating player. The conductor, by definition, stands silently apart, 'speaking' only through gestures. In America, where the principal violinist is called the 'concertmaster', as in Germany, the conductor is often referred to as 'leading' the orchestra.

The story of conducting as we understand it today begins centuries before the modern notion of an orchestra had even dawned. The first conductors were choral directors, invariably the principal singers in monastery, chapel, church and cathedral choirs. Particularly in the days before written notation, their importance was vital, and was only slightly lessened with the introduction of 'neumes' in the Middle Ages. These gave precise indications of pitch but highly imprecise guidance as to rhythm. By the time of the early Renaissance, notation had advanced to something like its later sophistication, and music, outside the monasteries (where it retained the freedom of natural 'speech rhythms'), was now regularly organised into recurrent metrical units, visually indicated by the use of vertical bar lines. To many brought up on the subtle inflections of liturgical chant, this development, necessitated by the advent of polyphony, seemed to portend the end of music. With the interweaving of self-sufficient melodic lines, however, particularly when married to a verbal text, the temporal freedom of ecclesiastical traditions became an unaffordable luxury. Thus the choral director now began to flourish in the secular world, while retaining his importance in the church. In 1517, we find the delightfully named Ornithoparchus describing the technique most commonly employed as 'a certain motion made by the hand of the chief singer, according to the nature of the marks, which motion directs a song according to measure'.[5] Eighty years on, the great Tudor composer Thomas Morley describes 'a successive motion of the hand, directing the quantitie of every note & rest in the song, with equall measure, according to the varietie of signs and proportions'.[6] Interestingly, both men refer only to movements of the hand, never to an external, baton-like implement, although we know that as early as the fifteenth century a roll of paper was regularly used to beat time at the services of the Sistine Chapel in Rome.

Throughout the seventeenth and most of the eighteenth century, no distinction was generally made between a conductor and a composer. With few exceptions, he was one and the same – a man employed to compose music for church, theatre, palace or other musical establishment, and to take charge of its performance. He was an active player – a kind of 'first among equals' – who led his band either from the first violinist's chair or from the harpsichord. Only in exceptional circumstances did he conduct music other than his own. Nor did this pattern change significantly until the last third of the nineteenth century. The greatest conductors were almost without exception great composers, from Lully and Monteverdi in the seventeenth century onwards: in the eighteenth, they included Vivaldi, Bach, Handel, Telemann, Haydn, Mozart and Beethoven; in the nineteenth: Weber, Spohr, Mendelssohn, Liszt, Berlioz, Spontini, Wagner, Tchaikovsky and, straddling the nineteenth and twentieth centuries, Mahler and Strauss. And though they changed with the times, their function remained essentially the same. Johann Gesner's much published account of Bach rehearsing in 1738 can suffice as a job description for the next three centuries, though the personnel have multiplied beyond Bach's wildest dreams.

> If you could only see him, not only singing and playing at the same time
> his own parts, but presiding over thirty or forty musicians all at once,
> controlling this one with a nod, another by a stamp of the foot, a third
> with a warning finger, keeping time and tune, giving a high note to one, a
> low one to another, and notes in between to some. This one man, standing

alone in the midst of loud sounds, having the hardest task of *all* can yet discern at every moment if anyone goes astray and can keep all the musicians in order, restore any waverer to certainty and prevent him from going wrong. Rhythm is in his every limb, he takes in all the harmonies by his subtle ear and utters all the different parts through the medium of his own voice. Great admirer as I am of antiquity in other respects, I yet deem this Bach to comprise in himself many Orpheuses and twenty Arions.[7]

Of all eighteenth-century conductors, none was more modern in outlook and range of activity than Haydn. For much of his long service at the Palace of Eszterháza, on the Austro-Hungarian border, his main preoccupations, apart from pioneering the classical symphony and the string quartet, were with opera. In 1786 alone he not only conducted but produced and directed more than 125 operatic performances, comprising some seventeen different productions, eight of them new to the repertory. In a single decade (1780–90) he supervised well over a thousand operatic productions, in the course of which he added many improvements of his own to works by other men. He made cuts, re-orchestrated, and in several cases actually replaced arias which he found wanting with others composed by himself. In this he anticipated the great interpretative conductors of the Romantic era.

While it took centuries for the conductor to advance much beyond the role of musical policeman, the implements of his trade have undergone considerable refinement since the days of ancient Greece, when he was required to keep time by stamping vigorously on the ground with his right foot, to which was attached a heavy piece of iron. Foot-stamping itself, however, remained a time-honoured technique in Europe well into the nineteenth century, especially in Italy, where it continued, in some places, even into the recording era. But it had always had its rivals. The idea that an orchestra could respond to silent, symbolic gestures traced in the air was a long time dawning, and from the middle of the seventeenth century to the beginning of the nineteenth, players and listeners alike were regularly subjected to a highly audible thumping, often administered with a long and heavy wooden staff. The disadvantages of this system were summarised by the Abbé Raguenet in 1705:

> Some years since, the Master of the Musique at the Opéra in Paris had an elbow chair and desk placed on the stage, where, with the score in one hand and the stick in the other, he beat time on a table put there for that purpose – and so loud that he made a greater noise than the whole band.[8]

Little can the Abbé have imagined that in parts of Europe the practice would survive for another 200 years. The constitution of the beater and the beaten, however, underwent numerous changes, from a roll of paper to a cumbersome leather truncheon stuffed with calf's hair (Bernhard Anselm

Weber, Berlin, *c.* 1810). The custom was not only disagreeable to the ear and a distraction for the mind. On one occasion it proved fatal to the conductor. On 22 March 1687 it claimed its first and only martyr in the form of the composer-director Jean-Baptiste Lully at the court of Louis XIV. Accustomed to keeping time by banging the floor with a long hardwood cane, he missed his aim and struck his foot. In the following days the resultant wound developed gangrene and he died, aged fifty-three.

Lully was in many ways the father of modern conducting. His ruthlessly disciplined band became the model on which the modern orchestra, particularly the opera orchestra, was to be based. He was the first conductor to impose uniform bowing on his string players (this remained a Parisian speciality for generations after his death), he was a pioneer in the dramatic use of orchestration, and he was the first great musician to mould and develop an integrated group of players who regularly rehearsed and performed together as a unit (in London, by contrast, such consistency was considered a luxury well into the twentieth century). His example, however, seems not to have resulted in any great improvement of orchestral standards generally, least of all, apparently, in his native Italy. More than a hundred years after Lully's death, a correspondent sent the following report to a German newspaper:

> The Italian orchestras are in a far from admirable condition. While in Paris every player is on the alert to catch the conductor's indications, in Italy it is a matter of every man for himself. They tune their instruments while a singer is negotiating an aria, talk while they are playing, put their instruments down whenever the notion strikes them to rest or scratch their heads. When the leader gives the sign to begin, he strikes the brass candleholder of his desk with all his might, without giving the musicians the slightest hint. He then immediately draws his bow for the first stroke, quite unconcerned whether all the rest, or only a few, or in fact anybody at all, begins with him. During recitatives, the other players creep under the seats of the orchestra, to chat with one another, take a pinch of snuff, or even to play practical jokes on one of their colleagues. On their return to their seats, two-thirds of them usually arrive too late because one has knocked over a stand, another a candleholder, another the music, or has stepped on a colleague's corn and stops to argue with him. On one occasion, the trumpeter put the bell of his instrument in a neighbour's pocket and blew through the clothing. In Paris, the players are not allowed to leave their seats except in cases of the utmost necessity.[9]

With the advent of opera in the early seventeenth century and of the public concert in the eighteenth, orchestras grew in size, as did the venues in which they played. During this period, as in the sixteenth-century Sistine Chapel, the most commonly favoured aid to efficient conducting was a roll of paper or parchment, held in one hand, and occasionally in both. What this custom may have lacked in grace and precision it made up for in visibility, and along with the principal violinist's bow (decreasingly used for actual playing, especially in Paris), it was the immediate precursor of the modern baton. Other, earlier methods, advocated in the late seventeenth century, included a large white handkerchief held in the hand, and even the use of a mechanical arm, controlled by a pedal and used by an improbably large number of choirmasters.

Meanwhile, the progress of the baton was slow and often far from steady. As early as 1776, in Berlin, Johann Friedrich Reichardt had adopted the baton, rearranged the orchestra, banished the piano and conducted both singers and players from a separate desk. His example, however, remained an isolated instance for two generations and more. It was not until the 1820s that the baton gained anything like widespread currency, and then thanks largely to the influence of one man, the German composer-violinist Louis Spohr (1784–1859). One of the most admired musicians of his time, Spohr first used the purpose-built baton in Hamburg in 1817. But it was his use of it in London, in 1820, according to Spohr's own testimony, that seems to have been decisive (though it was still some years before its use became standard, even in England).

The use of the baton, which had already been adopted by Reichardt and Anselm Weber late in the eighteenth century, gained ground most steadily in Germany. Mendelssohn (1809–47) used it from the beginning. Even after the baton had triumphed over all its rivals as the conductor's implement of choice, however, it eluded standardisation for several decades. While Spohr's epoch-making stick was small and light enough to carry in his pocket, that used by Gasparo Spontini (whose operas are reputed to be the loudest ever written) was expressly designed to intimidate. A fearsome disciplinarian, he brandished an elongated ebony cudgel, tipped at each end with ivory knobs and grasped in the middle by his fist. Mendelssohn, perhaps the first great master of the baton, used a slender, tapered wand of whalebone, delicately encased in soft white leather, to match the gloves which were then *de rigeur* amongst conductors in most European countries. Berlioz eventually followed Mendelssohn's example, recommending an optimum length of twenty-two inches, but at the outset of his distinguished conducting career he used what he described, probably with characteristic exaggeration, as 'a heavy oaken staff' ('with the bark still on it', according to his friend Sebastian Herschel).

For many decades, there was hardly greater standardisation when it came to the positioning of the conductor. In the last quarter of the eighteenth century, and the first of the nineteenth, it was not uncommon in operatic productions to find him stationed between the singers and the orchestra, facing the stage, with his back to the players. Carl Maria von Weber, like numerous conductors after him, often compounded the dangers inherent in this practice by facing the audience, with his back to both orchestra *and* singers. Improbably, this became standard practice in Russia until the late 1860s. In 1776, in Berlin, Reichardt took up his position at the centre of the orchestra, as did the great showman Jullien in the middle of the nineteenth century, while at the Paris Opéra, Jean-Jacques Grasset sat sideways, at the far left of the orchestra, his right side to the audience.

Nor was it only implements and placement that underwent radical change. The method of beating also evolved. The simple up-down movements which had generally sufficed throughout the Renaissance proved inadequate to the varied metres of the Baroque and yielded increasingly, though not rapidly, to the use of a distinct and separate gesture for each beat of the prevailing metre, thus 'down-left-right-up' for a bar in 4/4 time and 'down-right-up' for a bar in 3/4. It was not until the nineteenth century, however, that continuous, let alone expressive, gesturing became the norm (pioneered by Beethoven, who was in other respects among the clumsiest conductors who ever lived, and after him, by Berlioz).

Of all eighteenth-century performance practices, none was more intrinsically counterproductive, or more surprisingly durable, than the custom of 'divided leadership'. Whereas performances in the Baroque era, as mentioned above, had been directed either by the principal violinist or the man at the harpsichord (in either case this was usually the composer himself), in the Classical era and beyond, they were commonly entrusted to both, though the harpsichord was increasingly replaced by the piano, long after the Baroque continuo tradition had become obsolete. As late as the 1840s (which saw the deaths of Chopin, Mendelssohn and Donizetti), we find the following lament by an English critic, following a high-profile concert in London:

> At the commencement of one chorus at a recent concert by the Sacred Harmonic Society, the leader and conductor were so palpably at issue that for a moment a halt and a fresh start appeared inevitable. Mr. Surman, in his accustomed fashion, was minded to bestow his tediousness on the brilliant conception that lay at his mercy, while Mr. Perry was equally resolved that it should have the benefit of a rational degree of speed; and in consequence, the band presently gained a bar on the chorus. Worse yet, a soloist with the Philharmonic was lately fettered with the discordant beatings of no less than three individuals: Sir George Smart, who wielded the baton; Mr. Loder, the leader of the evening; and Mr. T. Cooke, *not* the leader of the evening. These gentlemen were all beating different times, with the result that the band was bewildered. We regard this Gothic practice as an intolerable absurdity.[10]

The conductor as an arbiter of public taste

For much of the eighteenth century, the conductor wore a servant's livery and did as he was told. It was not until the nineteenth, when the public concert and the commercial opera house finally ousted the courts of the nobility as the principal venue for orchestral music-making, that he became a powerful figure in his own right, and an arbiter of public taste. Thus it was that the twenty-year-old Felix Mendelssohn (who had been conducting his own private orchestra from the age of twelve) effected a sea-change in public attitudes to Bach when he mounted the first performance of the *St Matthew Passion* since the composer himself had conducted it. Thus it was that François Habeneck converted the Parisians to the symphonies of Beethoven, as Wagner was later to do internationally. And thus that Liszt, in Weimar, became a tireless and influential champion of new music, as did his sometime son-in-law Hans von Bülow (whose wife Cosima, Liszt's daughter, later left him for Wagner, who became the dominant conductor of the nineteenth century, as he was also its most influential composer).

Wagner was an egotist of such monumental proportions as to render almost irrelevant the fact that he played no orchestral instrument (and the piano only badly) and that despite his unsurpassed genius as an orchestral composer he was an indifferent score-reader at best. More surprising still, given his generally contemptible behaviour in private life, is the testimony of one prominent orchestral musician that 'when Wagner conducted, the players had no feeling of being led. Each believed himself to be expressing himself freely, yet they all worked together in perfect ensemble.'[11] The aura of mystery surrounding the truly charismatic conductor is soundly based. As more than one player has attested, Wilhelm Furtwängler (in many ways the Wagner of the twentieth century) had only to enter a hall during someone else's rehearsal and the whole orchestra's sound seemed to change as if by magic. But Wagner never relied on magic for his results. He was probably the most exhaustive stickler for detail in the annals of conducting. The number and subtlety of his demands were boundless, as was his capacity for rehearsals. As he put it himself, 'Nothing is so worth the utmost study as the attempt to clarify the meaning of a phrase, a bar, nay more, a single note.' To this end, however, for all his professed reverence, Wagner would often come to the composer's aid, even Beethoven's, by 'correcting' passages and details which he felt had been erroneously conceived or notated. Mahler did the same for Schubert and Schumann. In their defence it should be noted that throughout the Romantic era, performers were commonly regarded as being on a par with the composer. Fidelity to the text was the least of their concerns.

Wagner's greatest legacy as a conductor was threefold, and extended far beyond his own interpretations, and far beyond the specifically orchestral.

One was to hear, think, feel and gesture in terms not of individual beats, nor even of bar lines, but of whole phrases, banishing metric angularity in favour of melodic continuity at the highest level. Closely allied to this was a then-unprecedented flexibility of tempo, favouring both structural integrity and a diversity of emotional and dramatic expression, with no loss of rhythmic cohesion. And last but by no means least was the keenest attention to polyphonic clarity. Like Bach's, Wagner's basic mind-set was contrapuntal, and his ear for orchestral balances was matched amongst contemporary conductors only by Berlioz, who approached this, as he approached most things, from a very different point of view.

Both men wrote important treatises on the art of conducting, and their differences are evident on almost every page. Berlioz, no less a romantic, was nevertheless more classical in his approach. He deplored Wagner's conducting, describing his molten rhythmic style as being 'like dancing on a slack wire'. Wagner, untypically, was more generous on the subject of Berlioz's conducting, which he found revelatory and inspiring, citing

> the fantastic daring, the sharp precision with which the boldest
> combinations – almost tangible in their clarity – impressed me, driving
> back with brutal violence my own ideas about the poetry of music, back
> into the very depths of my soul. I was simply all ears for things of which I
> had never dreamed until then, and which I felt I must try to realize.[12]

Unlike Wagner, who required the most exhaustive preparation by all concerned, Berlioz was such a master of the baton that when necessary he could coax magnificent performances from orchestras without a single rehearsal (as happened once with his own, notably tricky, *Roman Carnival* Overture). Like Beethoven, he was an almost recklessly choreographic conductor whose musical intellect co-existed with an intensity of feeling that could overwhelm his players. His rhythms were by no means rigidly metronomic, indeed they were a model of poetic suppleness, but he kept them on a tighter rein than Wagner. What both men shared was a positively voluptuous indulgence of instrumental tone-colour and an insatiable love of the large. Berlioz's ideal orchestra, never realised, included 120 violins, 40 violas, 45 cellos, 18 double basses, 30 harps, 30 pianos, 12 cymbals, 16 French horns, 17 drums, plus a battery of other instruments bringing the total to 465, not including a supplementary chorus of 360. What grievous envy he would have felt had he been alive in 1872, when Johann Strauss II conducted an orchestra of 2,000 instrumentalists with a choir of 20,000 voices for the World Peace Jubilee at Boston, Massachusetts.

Among the most significant developments in the story of conducting was the rise of the specialist conductor – men like Bülow, whose professional life was devoted exclusively to championing the music of others (like many great conductors of the modern age, he was a competent but negligible composer). Others of his era included Arthur Nikisch, Hans Richter, Hermann Levi, Felix Mottl and Theodore Thomas, succeeded in the twentieth century by such major figures as Toscanini, Weingartner, Furtwängler, Walter, Mengelberg, Beecham, Klemperer, Stokowski, Koussevitsky and Monteux. Some, however, were more specialist than others. Conductors such as Mottl, Seidl and Levi are remembered today almost exclusively for their single-minded championing of Wagner. Others, most notably Bülow and Richter, began as Wagner acolytes but later spread their nets, and influence, more widely. It was perhaps only in the twentieth century, however, that the specialist conductor could really be said to have come of age – and at both ends of the stylistic-historical spectrum. After the twelve-tone revolution spearheaded by Schoenberg, new music became a 'problem' to an unprecedented degree. Conductors like Nicolas Slonimsky and, later, Robert Craft, both well-rounded musicians of exceptional sophistication, decided to devote most of their energies to giving it a fair hearing. Later still, Pierre Boulez, himself one of the most significant of twentieth-century composers, raised its profile still further, while bringing his great gifts to bear on much of the mainstream repertory as well. Other composer-conductors of similar determination and skill have included Sir Peter Maxwell Davies and Oliver Knussen.

More pervasive in their influence have been the champions of historical authenticity, especially those active from the mid-century onwards. These include Gustav Leonhardt, Ton Koopman and Frans Brüggen in the Netherlands, August Wenzinger in Switzerland, Nikolaus Harnoncourt in Austria, Charles Mackerras, David Munrow, Christopher Hogwood, Trevor Pinnock, John Eliot Gardiner and Roger Norrington in the United Kingdom, and Noah Greenberg, Joshua Rifkin and Nicholas McGegan in the USA. The scholarship of these and many others is unprecedented in both depth and scope, and the range of repertory conducted by Mackerras, Harnoncourt, Hogwood, Gardiner and Norrington embraces music of all eras. The more extreme 'authenticists' have attempted to substitute scholarship for interpretation altogether, but for most musicians, listeners, philosophers and psychologists this is in fact an impossibility. The very choosing of a tempo is already an act of interpretation. Even today, musical notation remains in many respects a highly inexact art and no amount of history is adequate to its fully artistic realisation in sound. It should also be noted that even the greatest composer-conductors have often disagreed with their own markings, particularly where the metronome is concerned. As no single performance can possibly realise every aspect of even the simplest work, every interpretation must be regarded, at best, as a particular cross-section of the musical possibilities inherent in the score.

The conductor as evangelist

For all their significant and sometimes extreme differences in musical outlook, most of the great nineteenth-century conductors had one thing over-
whelmingly in common: they spent most of their professional lives preach-
ing to the converted. They were high priests of an art which laid unique
claims to universality while traditionally addressing itself to the privileged
few. It is a matter of historical fact that 'art' music has for centuries lent
an often spurious dignity to a class system rooted in the principled per-
petuation of inequality. Those who have attempted to 'democratise' it have
commonly earned the rebuke of their peers. None more so than the French-
born Louis Antoine Jullien, whose thirty-six Christian names, bestowed on
him by his seventy-two godparents, suggested at the very outset that he was
destined for a career of unexampled extravagance. If his career was slow
to get off the ground, the same cannot be said of his person. In childhood
he was ostensibly abducted from a mountain path by a passing eagle, who
later dropped him, considerately, on to soft ground. On another occasion
he went missing, so the story goes, and was eventually found reclining in the
bell of a huge brass instrument from which he had been unable to extricate
himself. As suggested in an item in *The Musical World* of 5 August 1836,
Jullien would stop at nothing to capture the ears of the public: 'M. Jullien
conceived the happy idea on this occasion of setting fire to the four quarters
of the garden, in the midst of which was heard the discharge of musketry
and the clanging of alarm bells; all of this was grounded upon motives from
Les Huguenots by Meyerbeer.'[13] His orchestra sported a double bass which
was almost fifteen feet in height, a monstrous drum, a double-bass saxophone, and other exotica luxuriating in names such as the *serpentcleide*, the
bombardon and the *clavicor*. Jullien was not a man, however, to rest content
with nourishing the ear alone. He laid on a feast for the eyes as well: 'Exactly in the *middle* of his vast orchestra was a crimson platform edged with
gold, and upon this was a music stand formed by a fantastic gilt figure supporting a desk; and *behind* the stand a carved armchair decorated in white
and gold and tapestried crimson velvet – a sort of throne for the musical
monarch.'[14]

As befits such regal trappings, Jullien's baton was no ordinary stick of
wood but a jewel-studded implement, almost two feet in length, which was
handed to him on a silver platter. But beneath the antics and the spectacular
displays he nursed a higher purpose. His aim, simply stated but not simply
achieved, was to find a new and ever-larger audience for the music which
he genuinely admired. He followed a carefully worked-out strategy, and it
worked. But was he a good conductor? And does it matter? Perhaps not, but
the testimony of a noted orchestral player, written forty years after Jullien's

death, should be taken seriously:

> I may say that I have never heard finer performances of many classical
> Overtures and Symphonies than those directed by Jullien, and I have
> played them under all the great conductors for over fifty years. Jullien, of
> course, was considered a charlatan by all those who did not, or would not,
> understand him; but the twenty or thirty classical works he had made a
> study of, no-one I have known has ever made go so well.[15]

Extravagance, showmanship and sartorial splendour have seldom hurt a conductor's career, especially an evangelical conductor's career, but they were not prerequisites for success. In his many years as the unflaggingly energetic master of the now world-famous Promenade Concerts in London, Sir Henry Wood, who was never remotely a matinée idol, brought music, and new music, what's more, to massive audiences, year after year, first at the Queen's Hall, later (after the destruction of the Queen's Hall by a German bomb in 1941) at the Royal Albert Hall, where they continue to this day, now reaching worldwide audiences of many millions, far beyond even the wildest dreams of Jullien. Today, the Proms feature many conductors and orchestras, of many nationalities. From 1895 to 1940 they had one: Henry Wood. A thoroughgoing professional (as pianist, violinist, organist and lifelong singing teacher), he commanded an immaculate stick technique, a formidable memory and an incorruptible artistic integrity, winning the affection of audiences and the admiration of such towering musicians as Sergei Rachmaninov (himself a great if self-effacing conductor, who appeared on the podium only occasionally). Wood was also a tireless champion of up-and-coming young performers, and it was he, almost single-handedly, who first won English audiences for the new and avant-garde compositions of Debussy, Sibelius, Strauss, Scriabin, Bartók and Schoenberg. As an interpreter, he was never ranked, even in England, with the likes of Mahler, Toscanini, Furtwängler, Walter and Klemperer, nor was he ever a major figure outside Britain, but his impact on British musical life remains greater than that of any other conductor, before or since. Of Wood's contemporaries and immediate successors, the best known, Sir John Barbirolli, Sir Adrian Boult, Sir Malcolm Sargent and Sir Thomas Beecham, all enjoyed greater international renown than Wood, but only Beecham is commonly accepted worldwide as one of the greatest conductors of the twentieth century.

Comparable to Wood and Jullien in their evangelical zeal were the German-born Theodore Thomas (1835–1905), the Russian-born Serge Koussevitsky (1874–1951) and the London-born Leopold Stokowski (1882–1977), all of whom found their greatest celebrity in the United States. A child prodigy on the violin, Thomas made his concert début at the age of six, four years before emigrating with his family to the United States. In 1853 he joined Jullien's orchestra on its visit to New York, and it was during this period, though he despised Jullien's flamboyance, that he conceived the determination to do for music in America what Jullien had done for it in France and Britain – a tall order, given the paucity of American musical culture at that time. In 1862 he organised an orchestra for 'Symphony Soirees' in New York which continued uninterrupted for the next sixteen years, and in 1866 began a trailblazing series of outdoor summer concerts which had an incalculable effect on musical life in New York. In 1869 he began his annual tours of the East and Midwest, and in 1873 founded both the Cincinnati Biennial Festival and the Cincinnati College of Music. In 1891 he settled permanently in Chicago as conductor of the Chicago Symphony Orchestra, which he transformed into an ensemble rivalling any in Europe. A determined advocate of Wagner, Liszt, and Brahms (often in the teeth of considerable opposition from orchestras and audiences alike), he also gave the American premières of many works by Tchaikovsky, Dvořák, Rubinstein, Bruckner, Goldmark, Saint-Saëns, Stanford, Raff, and Richard Strauss, to name only some. Unlovable and largely unloved, he transformed the musical life of a nation while never remotely achieving or courting personal popularity.

Prior to his emigration from Russia in 1921, the independently wealthy Serge Koussevitsky had his own private orchestra, which he took on tours, aboard a chartered steamer, down the 1,200 miles of the River Volga, stopping at villages and towns all along the way and playing great music to communities which had never before encountered a symphony orchestra. The annals of musical history have few more stirring tales to tell than this. In 1924, Koussevitsky crossed the Atlantic to begin what turned out to be his quarter-century-long tenure at the head of the Boston Symphony Orchestra, where he championed (and steadfastly commissioned) many new composers and scores. In addition to the staple repertory, he did more for Russian and American music, both old and new, than any other conductor of his time. Despite the catholicity of his tastes, however, he could never warm to the dodecaphonic music of Schoenberg and his school (a characteristic shared, it must be said, by many conductors of our own time).

There is perhaps no conductor in history who combined a zealous championing of the new, and initially unpalatable, with more practised and calculating showmanship than Leopold Stokowski. Despite a persistent rumour to the contrary, the name was genuine. The bizarre and non-specific foreign accent which he affected for most of his long career ('my madda, my fodda, or*kester*' etc.) was not. He was a Londoner born and bred (which did not stop him, so the story goes, from asking a taxi driver as they crossed Westminster Bridge toward the Houses of Parliament, 'Please can you tell, vod is name big clock?'). The degree of fakery and vanity in Stokowski's persona may have helped both his popularity with the public (most of whom were taken in) and the success of his musical evangelism, which is what mattered most to him, but there were many pious and dedicated musicians who could scarcely speak his name without embarrassment or downright contempt. By many, he was ostracised. Yet he was a great conductor – even such polar-opposites as Glenn Gould and Sergei Rachmaninov were agreed on that. And his high-profile collaboration with Walt Disney in the cartoon feature *Fantasia* (in which he can be seen conversing and shaking hands with Mickey Mouse) brought great music – including Stravinsky's *The Rite of Spring*, admittedly much condensed and touched-up – into the lives of many millions who had never even heard the name of Koussevitsky, much less of Bach. There are worse epitaphs.

7 International case studies

JON TOLANSKI

Introduction

In recent years there has been an increasing amount of comment about changes in national orchestral performing styles and sonorities during the second half of the twentieth century. It has been argued that in the last few decades traditionally individual sounds and stylistic characteristics of orchestras from specific different countries have been all but eroded and replaced by a more internationally uniform sonority and approach that has gradually but steadily arisen. That is a generalised claim, but nevertheless recordings definitely do illustrate how some very distinctive traits that formerly existed in certain orchestras have now largely disappeared. For instance, fifty years ago there were striking differences between many of the colours, timbres and also styles of phrasing that could be heard in French, Italian, German, Russian, English and American orchestras. And as recently as only a quarter of a century ago this was still very much the case with four of the world's leading orchestras from different parts: the Berlin Philharmonic, Leningrad (now St Petersburg) Philharmonic, London Symphony and New York Philharmonic. Their individually recognisable qualities, such as the Leningrad brass players' stridently strong vibrato and often, though not always, very marcato style (similar in most Russian orchestras) and the darker, richer and more generally blending sounds in Berlin existed to a greater or lesser extent, regardless of who was conducting.

There have been debates as to whether such marked differences existed a long time earlier, before the time of recordings, but there is no debate about the situation today. There has in recent decades been a noticeable international tendency for orchestras to aspire increasingly to the kinds of generally rich, sophisticated and homogeneous sounds of leading German orchestras such as the Berlin Philharmonic. For instance, the St Petersburg Philharmonic brass, and indeed most Russian brass sections, now play with much less vibrato, indeed sometimes none at all, and less characteristically strong staccato, altogether blending in a more rounded way like the brass of most English, German or American orchestras. Woodwind playing, too, generally sounds more internationally similar than before. For example, the more rustic sounds of the clarinet in many East European orchestras of earlier times, also formerly heard in some French orchestras in particular, have largely disappeared and been replaced by the more mellow and rounder sonorities that are generally expected of entire woodwind sections today. Even the long celebrated traditional sound of the Vienna Philharmonic oboe, which for all its outstanding flexibility was sometimes criticised in some quarters for its 'dryness', has been transformed into a more resonant and mellifluous sonority in line with international trends. There are numerous separate reasons for all these and other developments, and they are all part of the substantial changes that have been affecting the make-up and operations of symphony orchestras in recent times. Those reasons will not be investigated in depth here; nevertheless an awareness of the changes themselves is important in the studies of international orchestras. It helps to illustrate how in some significant ways orchestras used to be more directly related to the environment from which they had originally evolved than they are now, and how latter-day operational developments have to an extent affected their sonorities and performing styles.

1 Berlin Philharmonic Orchestra

Of the four orchestras compared in this study, the Berlin Philharmonic has throughout most of its existence enjoyed a unique degree of international prestige and local financial backing and has most noticeably maintained the original nature of its relationship to its home environment. It was created in 1882 as a group of secessionists from the Bilsesche Kapelle, which was one of a number of private orchestras that had been born in mid-nineteenth-century Germany as prosperous bourgeois music-lovers increasingly supported the financing and organisation of concerts. Benjamin Bilse had formed his orchestra in 1867 and by 1882 it was numbering seventy professional players. That year fifty-four members, discontented with Bilse's dictatorial and thrifty ways, left to form the Philharmonic Orchestra and Franz Wüllner was engaged as the Principal Conductor. The orchestra, which was self-governed, soon became known as the Berlin Philharmonic, but in its early days the city was not supportive, despite the presence of Joseph Joachim as Principal Conductor in 1884. It was in 1887 when the orchestra's promoting impresario Hermann Wolf engaged the celebrated and greatly demanding Hans von Bülow that the Berlin Philharmonic Orchestra first began to attract strong interest. By all accounts Bülow was a fearsome disciplinarian whose interpretations nevertheless could be highly wayward, but he was a flamboyant and virtuoso conductor and in his hands the Berlin Philharmonic rose to fame. During his tenure, which lasted until his death in 1894, the orchestra's Society was able to promote an increasing number of concerts, and they attracted guest visits by leading German conductors of the time, including Hermann Levi, Hans Richter, Felix Mottl and Felix Weingartner. Some particularly prestigious and historic events were the concerts when Brahms, Grieg and Tchaikovsky conducted their music.

On Bülow's death the young Richard Strauss was appointed Principal Conductor, but his position lasted just a year, as in 1895 he was superseded by the charismatic Hungarian Arthur Nikisch. He began a hugely successful twenty-seven-year period during which he exerted a powerful stylistic influence that begot the foundation of an on-going tradition in the Berlin Philharmonic Orchestra. Nikisch fastidiously sought elegance, warmth and refinement and he had a mesmeric effect on the players with his serene and yet intensely concentrated bearing and his outstandingly supple and yet economical baton technique. A short silent film of Nikisch conducting the Berlin Philharmonic Orchestra in 1913, issued on Teldec's *The Art of Conducting* (Teldec 4509 9503 8-3) gives a token suggestion of the technical control and artistic expressiveness in his conducting. The same year he and the Berlin Philharmonic made their first recording (DG 453 8042) performing the 5th Symphony of Beethoven, and it suggests that accounts of Nikisch's somewhat cavalier impetuosity as an interpreter were accurate. About thirty years later Arturo Toscanini is reported to have dismissed the value of Nikisch's recordings, claiming that they grossly misrepresented both his interpretations and also the glowing beauty of sound and homogeneous balances for which he and the orchestra became so famous. The primitive acoustic recording horn's seriously limited frequency range could indeed only preserve a meagre hint of orchestral sonority, but despite that it is in fact possible to detect two elements in the playing that have traditionally remained right up to the present: pliant rhythmic flexibility and blending inner parts. That is a generalisation, as any orchestra's performance is of course affected by varying repertory and different conductors. Nevertheless, notwithstanding Toscanini's important comments, the very inadequate recordings of Nikisch and the Berlin Philharmonic Orchestra do in their extremely limited way intimate at the existence of stylistic and sonic traits that were to be such a notable feature of the orchestra's playing throughout the twentieth century.

Nikisch enlarged the orchestra's repertory significantly, particularly promoting the music of Bruckner, Tchaikovsky, Berlioz and Liszt and the avant-garde works of Strauss and Mahler. He also engaged many very prestigious soloists such as Ferruccio Busoni, Alfred Cortot, Carl Flesch, Bronislav Huberman, Jascha Heifetz, Pablo Casals, Maria Ivogün and Heinrich Schlusnus. When he died in 1922 the Berlin Philharmonic had become one of the world's most famous and highly regarded orchestras with a strong artistic identity of its own. It was also already the pride and honour of the city in which it resided. Berlin and in fact Germany regarded the

Berlin Philharmonic Orchestra, consisting mostly (though not exclusively) of German players, as a symbol of the Teutonic excellence and eminence in classical music that had arisen during the nineteenth century. The post of Music Director after Arthur Nikisch would only be considered for someone with exceptional qualities as a musician and performer. The orchestra's choice of Wilhelm Furtwängler for that position was to prove a remarkable stroke of judgement.

Furtwängler's era with the Berlin Philharmonic brought the orchestra unprecedented international prowess. In the first place his approach to both orchestral sonority and interpretation was closely related to that of Arthur Nikisch. Both conductors were strongly influenced by Wagner's conducting ethos, which was that performances should always ebb and flow, like a river running through a constantly changing landscape, although always with subtle and graded alterations of speeds and dynamics. For them, the printed notes of the score were only a limited guide and it was the performer's responsibility to find meanings behind them, which necessitated taking spontaneous liberties with the exact written notation if necessary. Furtwängler's conducting reflected Nikisch's improvisatory and sometimes emotionally impetuous qualities; however, his deeply philosophical preoccupation could also communicate a remarkable aura of concentrated stillness and create playing of great mystery. It was with the Berlin Philharmonic that Furtwängler felt he could most perfectly achieve his ideals of expression and atmosphere, and with intensive rehearsals the orchestra became especially famous for its warm, expressive power, deep resonant tone and organically blending balances, all held up by a powerfully fortifying bass line. These qualities, especially the vibrato espressivo of the strings, and a supple elasticity imparted from Furtwängler's fundamental rhythmic flexibility, became celebrated distinctive elements of the Berlin Philharmonic Orchestra that continued beyond Furtwängler's tenure up to the present time, albeit after his time there were very considerable changes in other respects.

It was particularly in German romantic repertory, especially the music of Beethoven, Schubert, Weber, Brahms, Wagner and Bruckner, that the Berlin Philharmonic became so celebrated in Furtwängler's era. Although he did programme some contemporary music, notably works by Hindemith, Prokofiev, Stravinsky and Schoenberg, the orchestra's strongest identity was in the output of the former composers, with whom Furtwängler felt such a deep and close affinity. The powerful and long-lasting bond between Furtwängler and the Berlin Philharmonic strongly affected the orchestra's entire style and sound for the best part of thirty-two years. Except for the period between 1945 and 1947 when he had to endure investigations at the Nuremberg trials because of his position with the orchestra in Nazi Germany, Furtwängler was the Berlin Philharmonic's Music Director from 1922 to 1954. During that protracted time he and they became deeply immersed in each other's psyches to a powerfully telepathic degree. At the same time, though, the orchestra was very responsive to distinguished guest conductors whose styles were notably different from Furtwängler's. During his tenure it also played with Erich Kleiber, Richard Strauss, Bruno Walter, Sir Thomas Beecham, Herbert von Karajan (on only a few occasions) and Victor de Sabata, amongst others. A striking example of how different the Berlin Philharmonic could sound, stylistically and sonorously, from how it was with Furtwängler can be heard by comparing recordings of the orchestra playing Brahms's Fourth Symphony with Furtwängler and de Sabata, dating from only four years apart (de Sabata, 1939 – Pearl GEMS 0054; Furtwängler, 1943 – Music and Arts CD804).

During the immediate post-war period when Furtwängler was not allowed to conduct the Berlin Philharmonic, the orchestra continued to flourish despite having to exist in the all but destroyed Berlin of 1945. Remarkably, only a few weeks after the end of the war it was giving concerts under Leo Borchard, whose tenure was fitful – he was shot not long after taking over. It was then that the orchestra engaged as his replacement a relatively unknown conductor who was soon to become one of the famous and controversial musicians of the next half century – Sergiu Celibidache, a fanatical and extrovert artist with a very different temperament from Furtwängler. His dynamic presence was of great importance in re-establishing the orchestra's international position after its years of control by the Nazi regime.

But even during Furtwängler's absence, his enormous influence remained. When he returned, it was like a homecoming. The rapport between him and the Berlin Philharmonic Orchestra can be heard in copious audio recordings from archive tapes of public performances, the majority issued after his death. However, the most striking evidence of their communication can be seen and heard in film footage of rehearsals and performances that were issued on *The Art of Conducting*. The films vividly illustrate the intense level of concentration between conductor and players and they reveal how in painstaking rehearsal and in his very unconventional baton technique Furtwängler conveyed the ebb and flow of movement and the warm, burnished sound he sought. For him a sharply predictable beat produced too harsh a sonority, as he usually wanted the sounds of chords to grow and evolve organically, and so players had to feel their way with him rather than take conventionally clear indications. This necessitated playing after rather than exactly on Furtwängler's beat, which helped influence the orchestra's warm and resonant sound and blending textures. The slightly delayed response to the beat was to be a notable feature of the Berlin Philharmonic's style after Furtwängler's death as it was also fundamental to the orchestra's relationship with Herbert von Karajan, his immensely powerful and influential successor. A measure of the further growth in the Berlin Philharmonic's status during Furtwängler's time was the municipal subsidy the conductor obtained for the orchestra from the city of Berlin. This was a vital step in the establishment of what in due course became one of the highest and most stable support incomes for any orchestra in history.

After Furtwängler's death in 1954, the members of the Berlin Philharmonic elected Herbert von Karajan to the post of Permanent Conductor and Artistic Director, and he took up his position in 1955. Once again the orchestra proved itself a remarkable judge of circumstance. For nearly thirty-four years Karajan exerted a level of international artistic and commercial influence that was probably unprecedented in orchestral history and, as with Furtwängler, it was in his capacity as conductor of the Berlin Philharmonic Orchestra that his power was most strongly felt. The era with Karajan maintained the orchestra's artistic prestige and brought it a new commercial status.

With Karajan the Berlin Philharmonic developed a distinctively opulent and voluptuous sonority which, particularly through the growing influence of recordings, became something of a yardstick for many international musicians, even though some were critical of what they felt was glamour in Karajan's interpretations. As the years went by he more and more wanted an intensely rich string vibrato, extreme contrasts of dynamics, and above all a seamless continuity of sound with mosaics of textures that were very precisely played but constantly blended as they came and went. During his tenure the orchestra's brass section, especially the trumpets, developed a characteristic sonority that was slightly slimmer than previously, but very brilliantly penetrating whilst also blending with the other sections. The standard of the orchestra's response to Karajan's demands brought it still wider fame and prestige, though of a different kind to its very high reputation in Furtwängler's time. With Karajan, whose interpretations were vastly different from Furtwängler's in approach and temperament, the expression was often less personal and, to many, more consciously sophisticated. During his era the orchestra's commercial image was also dramatically developed through his intense and remarkably resourceful publicity machine. A huge catalogue of audio recordings was built up followed by many pioneering video recordings that give a fascinating picture of the very powerful effect Karajan had on performers.

In many ways the Berlin Philharmonic's repertory during Karajan's time continued the emphasis of Furtwängler's era. Broadly speaking, it was most of all centred on the great European composers from Mozart to Shostakovich. Karajan himself rarely conducted later works unless, in general, they were composed in a more traditional language. However, in one very important area the Berlin Philharmonic enlarged its repertory during Karajan's era: opera. The orchestra played for many of his operatic recordings and appeared with him at a large number of his Easter and summer Salzburg Festival opera productions. It also played different repertory with its many distinguished guest conductors, such as Claudio Abbado, Karl Böhm, Rudolf Kempe and Seiji Ozawa, although even then the choice of music often tended to reflect Karajan's preferences.

During Karajan's tenure the Berlin Philharmonic's financial status and commercial prestige reached unprecedented levels in orchestral history. Apart from the fame and revenue brought by recordings, the subsidy from the city of Berlin was increased to a far higher figure than any other municipal or state budget for an orchestra in the Western world if not anywhere. The city's pride in its orchestra was, and to a large extent still is, an international example of outstanding arts support, and a telling affirmation in an era of generally increasing retrenchment. Also in Karajan's time, the orchestra at last obtained a new home to replace the Philharmonie Hall that had been bombed in 1944. Since 1963 they have rehearsed and performed in the Philharmonie on Kemperplatz, designed by Hans Scharoun. In 1987 a chamber music hall was added.

Despite Karajan's virtually unrivalled power and influence, some vital changes in the relationship between him as the Permanent Conductor and Artistic Director and the orchestra membership took place in his tenure. To understand them and their consequences for the orchestra, a short history of the Berlin Philharmonic's operational system is necessary. Since its foundation in 1882 the orchestra has basically been a self-governing body. Although employed by the city of Berlin, it has always had voting powers both for its personnel and its principal conductors – Furtwängler called it a 'free orchestral republic'. Although there was no formal legal procedure about this until 1989, Nikisch, Furtwängler and Karajan had been elected by the players and then their appointments were ratified by the Berlin Senate of Cultural Affairs, which however could exert a veto if it wished. Nevertheless artists of the stature of the Berlin Philharmonic's principal conductors inevitably exerted some substantial powers in certain areas, though in agreement with the orchestra's committees and the Berlin Senate. Karajan had asked the Berlin Senate for a life contract with the orchestra, which was initially refused, but by 1967 his success in Berlin was so remarkable that his wish was granted, and it inevitably increased his powers. By the 1980s the extent of Karajan's powers and the increasingly unilateral nature of his decision-making had begun to create conflicts with the orchestra. These particularly came to a head over recording contracts and personnel. Karajan had become unhappy that the orchestra was increasingly marketing itself independently. For instance, a troubled even if highly fruitful relationship existed between his private film company and the orchestra members' own media company, the

Berliner Philharmoniker, a wholly co-operative marketing organisation for audio and video recordings (the concert-giving orchestra financed by the city is the Berlin Philharmonisches Orchester). Separately, an acrimonious dispute arose over Karajan's autocratic method of imposing his choice of a new principal clarinet against the decision of the orchestra membership. He found a way of invoking his wish through a contractual loophole, although after a probationary year the player decided not to continue. These and other ensuing events were just some of the reasons that led to Karajan's resignation in 1989, whereupon a new formalised procedure for appointing his successor was initiated, including more precise definitions of the limits of the conductor's powers.

Such was the orchestra's status that some of the world's most internationally successful conductors let their interest in being named Karajan's successor be known. When the eclectic and internationally revered Claudio Abbado was eventually elected in 1989 as Karajan's successor, he was only the fifth Artistic Director in the Berlin Philharmonic Orchestra's history. He and the players felt very concerned for both preservation and change. Traditional characteristics of the Berlin Philharmonic's sound and style that had developed since Nikisch's time were maintained whilst at the same time Abbado introduced a wealth of new repertory that substantially broadened the orchestra's experience and outlook. In particular he programmed far more music of the twentieth century and included works by a number of contemporary avant-garde composers. He also introduced a new and ambitious genre of theme programming around literary subjects, placing the music the orchestra performed in a wide-ranging cultural context. These theme programmes have included extended series of concerts with titles such as Music inspired by the poetry of Hölderlin, *Faust*, The Greek Tragedy (*Oedipus, Elektra, Medea*), Shakespeare, Berg/Büchner, and *The Wanderer*. He also introduced regular concert performances of operas in the Berlin Philharmonie, the first time such an initiative had happened in the orchestra's history.

During Abbado's tenure, the Berlin Philharmonic Orchestra began to take into its ranks a new proportion of players from outside Germany. Previously the vast majority had been German born and reared, but within several years there were some players from other European countries and also continents. Both this factor and the less domineering presence of Abbado than his predecessor helped to create something of a new artistic flexibility in the orchestra. It had always been a highly flexible instrument in itself, but some people nevertheless felt that fundamentals of its style and sound had become almost permanently dominated by Karajan's influence. Many recordings of a wide range of repertory bear out the stylistic diversity and versatility during Abbado's tenure, which were enhanced by the orchestra's relationships with guest conductors such as James Levine, Pierre Boulez and Sir Simon Rattle.

In 1998 Claudio Abbado announced that he would not seek to extend his position with the Berlin Philharmonic beyond the 2001/2002 season. Once again some of the world's most prestigious conductors expressed their interest in being named the next Artistic Director and once again the members of the orchestra deliberated carefully before eventually making another astute choice. Continuing their wish for both preservation and change they decided on the meteorically successful and innovative Sir Simon Rattle, whose artistic and social vision for music is profoundly concerned with radical change whilst also deeply respecting long and powerfully established traditions. At the time of writing he has not yet begun his tenure, although he has already made some acclaimed recordings with the orchestra. He has also put forward an agenda for some challenging changes including a major reorganisation of the Berlin Philharmonic Orchestra's governmental constitution that will free it from the Senate's ultimate control and will help resolve conflicts between the players' co-operative Berliner Philharmoniker and the city. A new Berlin Philharmonic foundation will run the Philharmonie Hall, and the entire artistic and financial direction of the orchestra will be handled by its new board of directors. This will consist of management from the city-funded Berlin Philharmonisches Orchester, the players-run Berliner Philharmoniker, the playing chairman of the orchestra and the Artistic Director. This will be the Orchestra's most independent and also cohesive method of administration since its inception. Sir Simon has also been granted his need that players' salaries be raised and that there be an increase of about 12.5 per cent in the city funding of the orchestra, which has been starting at £8,000,000 a year.

2 St Petersburg Philharmonic Orchestra

The background to the St Petersburg Philharmonic Orchestra's birth and the history of its operations contrasts strongly with that of the Berlin Philharmonic. Before the Russian Revolution of 1917 there was only one permanent symphony orchestra in St Petersburg. It was the court orchestra, serving the Tsar and his aristocratic circles, and it had been founded in 1882. With the Russian Revolution the orchestra became state run and was later merged with a new orchestra, the Petrograd Philharmonic. This then became the Leningrad Philharmonic Orchestra in 1921 and it was strictly controlled and securely funded by the Soviet government. Unlike the Berlin Philharmonic, the members had no independent voting powers and the Music Director had supreme powers to determine personnel. The first Music Director was

Emil Cooper and he, like his successors in Soviet times, reported to the Ministry of Culture, which with him decided the orchestra's programming and schedules.

There was a strong socio-political agenda to the orchestra's activities as it was instructed to perform concerts in factories and other places of labour to enlighten the new work force of Russia. It also gave concerts in the former Assembly of the Nobility which later became known as the Leningrad Philharmonic Great Hall, which has been its home ever since. This hall possesses one of the finest acoustics in the world. The orchestra's repertory at this time was fairly eclectic, except for a degree of shunning of German music, and the programming was not yet influenced by the rigorous political controls that were later enforced during Joseph Stalin's regime. Leon Trotsky and Anatoly Lunacharsky, the Minister of Culture, decided not to interfere in the programming of music in Soviet Russia and in general the liberal attitudes of the Association for Contemporary Music (ACM) held greater sway than the nationalistic and reactionary assembly, the Russian Association of Proletarian Musicians (RAPM). That situation was to reverse dramatically by the 1930s when the Soviet Party gave its support to the RAPM and then disbanded it to set up a centralised, party-controlled composers' union to instigate tight controls for the maintenance of Socialist Realism in music. Back in the 1920s the Leningrad Philharmonic Orchestra played its relatively wide repertory with an impressive list of international conductors. It was guest conducted by distinguished Western European musicians such as Bruno Walter, Otto Klemperer, Erich Kleiber, Hans Knappertsbusch and Oskar Fried. Celebrated guest conductors from its own country included Alexander Glazunov and Serge Koussevitsky.

Emil Cooper left in 1923 and then from 1926 to 1929 the Music Director was Nicolai Malko, followed in 1930 by Alexander Gauk. They established reputations as fine craftsmen and technicians, and although there appears to be no recorded evidence of the orchestra's playing at this time, from reports it seems that the standard was high, certainly in the string departments. However, the subsequent illustrious fame of the Leningrad Philharmonic Orchestra as a virtuoso and meticulously disciplined ensemble of great brilliance and beauty of sound was still in the future. Meanwhile the influence of the musicologists Alexander Ossovsky and then Ivan Sollertinsky had by the beginning of the 1930s brought about an interest in the music of Mahler and Bruckner, which had now entered the orchestra's repertory.

In 1934 Fritz Stiedry was appointed Music Director, remaining for three difficult years. He did not make a very strong impression and also encountered increasing pressures from the Soviet Party about repertory. It was during his tenure that the abortive rehearsals for Shostakovich's Fourth Symphony took place: the work was withdrawn by Shostakovich just before the planned première in 1936, and ever since there has been speculation and debate as to whether this was for political or artistic reasons.

Fatefully though, the music of Shostakovich was very soon to be a catalyst in the dawn of a golden new era in the Leningrad Philharmonic. In 1937 a thirty-four-year-old guest conductor called Yevgeni Mravinsky, who had first worked with the orchestra in 1931, directed the world première of the composer's Fifth Symphony, and it materialised that the event was a double watershed. For Shostakovich, after suffering a dangerously scathing attack in Pravda the previous year for his opera *Lady Macbeth of Mtsensk*, this marked his rehabilitation by the Soviet Party, albeit a hollow one as it was to transpire. For the Leningrad Philharmonic Orchestra the concert was to prove a decisive factor in the appointment of Yevgeni Mravinsky as the new Music Director in 1938, and this marked the start of an extraordinary period of nearly fifty years during which the orchestra attained the highest international prestige. During this virtual half-century Yevgeni Mravinsky was its draconian, dictatorial tyrant who ruthlessly rehearsed in the greatest detail in his fanatical pursuit of artistic and technical perfection. His influence was all pervading: as a figure of authority within political circles he had absolute power over the players and his meticulous preparation, fearsome demands and tight technical control brought about a revolution in the orchestra's style, sonority and standard. Ironically, although Mravinsky's total personal control over the orchestra created serious fears for the players, the Leningrad Philharmonic became so prestigious during his era that the players were given high salaries and living conditions that almost rivalled those of ministers. Along with the Bolshoi Theatre it became Soviet Russia's cultural showpiece to demonstrate the Party's commitment to the arts, and in 1946 it was given the opportunity to be the first Soviet orchestra to tour outside Russia.

Amongst the large number of recordings that exist of Mravinsky and the Leningrad Philharmonic are a few invaluable audio and video documents of his rehearsals (for example, *Russian Disc* RDCD 10905). They illustrate his intensive industry for precision, balances, sonority and details, and his meticulous care for an intense but very controlled expressiveness. Members of the orchestra have related how Mravinsky always rehearsed in the greatest detail for very long hours, even when the repertory was extremely familiar. Under the force of his leadership, a combination of brilliance, expressiveness, objectivity and discipline became the hallmarks of the Leningrad Philharmonic's style and sound, fulfilling his interpretations which were usually highly dramatic but notably unsentimental.

In particular with Mravinsky, the strings of the Leningrad Philharmonic played with a very great range of dynamics, expression and colours, including markedly different shades of vibrato. Mravinsky's demands and conducting technique produced the corporate results, but at the same time it must be recorded that the technical and artistic standard of the individual string players was extremely high, and there were many players of solo instrumental standard. The leading Russian conservatoires provided extremely intensive and prolonged instruction and training, and string players who did not reach a virtuoso standard were expelled. Unlike anywhere else, the yardsticks in the state funded and controlled Soviet music colleges were identical for solo and orchestral string studies, and there was immense competition at orchestral auditions. With the brass, woodwind and percussion there was also great brilliance and flexibility, notably the marcato articulation in the trumpets, although there was criticism in some international quarters of the way the horns, trumpets and trombones often played very powerfully with a marked and wide vibrato. That can be heard on recordings of most Russian orchestras until relatively recent times, as it can on earlier recordings of most French orchestras, although the timbre was often lighter there. There has long been debate as to when and how this distinctive style originated, and there is some doubt whether it was in existence before Soviet times. It seems to be absent on recordings of the Imperial Opera Orchestra accompanying singers in the first decade of the twentieth century, although it is hard to be sure from the sound quality of those primitively made discs (for example, Pearl GEMM CD 9106, Lenski's aria from *Eugene Onegin*, accompanying Dmitri Smirnov). At the same time, it seems that the extent of the vibrato varied: there is none at all in the recordings of the horn solo at the beginning of Weber's *Oberon* Overture conducted by Mravinsky (Melodiya 74321251902).

Despite Mravinsky's total dominance over the Leningrad Philharmonic Orchestra – a kind of situation that is now anachronistic – the orchestra did adapt flexibly to the wishes of other conductors. There is a striking example of this in recordings of Tchaikovsky's Fourth Symphony that the orchestra made with Mravinsky and with Kurt Sanderling, the Assistant Music Director of the time, within just three or so years of each other. Both recorded by the same company, Deutsche Grammophon, the differences in the style and character of the playing in the last movement are remarkably extreme. With Sanderling the balance is homogeneous with sections of the orchestra easily blending, the dynamics are relatively temperate, and the sonority is warm rather than brilliant. With Mravinsky taking a far faster tempo, the balance is sharply linear with sections individually illuminated, the dynamic contrasts are extreme, and the sonority is very brilliant with highly contrasting colours. The brilliance and colour are enhanced by the strings' articulating with an extremely precise and rhythmic spiccato, and the brass and percussion's attack with sharp impact and very tight ensemble. The Mravinsky performance typifies the orchestra's virtuosity during his tenure, and for all the differences between his and Sanderling's readings of the Tchaikovsky symphony, Mravinsky's very powerful and protracted influence did strongly affect the general style and sound of the orchestra throughout his era. Its tone-colours, styles of phrasing and dynamic shadings could often be heard when it was conducted by other Russian conductors who had associations with it, such as Gennadi Rozhdestvensky and Mariss Jansons. Certainly, there was a strongly identifiable character and sonority in the Leningrad Philharmonic that generally made it sound immediately different from the Berlin Philharmonic, for instance. Indeed elements of the style are still prevalent today, although there have been notable changes since Mravinsky's time, and now the differences between the orchestra and other great international orchestras are less marked, as has generally become the case with most orchestras in recent times. Mravinsky's repertory was wide, but increasingly from the 1960s he and his assistant music directors specialised in a large range of Russian works from Glinka to Shostakovich. The orchestra's repertory was generally more diverse when it was directed by distinguished guest conductors such as Leopold Stokowski, Charles Munch, André Cluytens, Igor Markevitch, Josef Krips, Zoltán Kodály and Benjamin Britten.

The plentiful state subsidy for the Leningrad Philharmonic and Mravinsky's high status within Soviet authority meant that he had virtually carte blanche to rehearse whenever he wanted and instigate changes in personnel as he wished. This and his aloof and remote personality created an atmosphere of fear within the orchestra that lasted until his death in 1988. However, by then the political controls in Russia were being relaxed with Mikhail Gorbachev's perestroika and the atmosphere in the country was changing radically. Yuri Temirkanov's appointment as Music Director brought a radical difference in approach. His method of rehearsal and entire style of directing favoured an interactive flexibility and creativity between conductor and players that was unimaginable in Mravinsky's time. This is not to imply in any way that under Mravinsky the orchestra played inflexibly – on the very contrary, as well as the extreme precision and discipline there was a highly subtle artistic individuality, but it was nevertheless all dictated by Mravinsky. With Temirkanov the orchestra began to be responsible itself for its flexibility, as this conductor likes to improvise and maintain a chamber music-like relationship with the orchestra. The appointment of Yuri Temirkanov in 1988 was the first instance in the Leningrad Philharmonic Orchestra's history when a Music Director was elected by a secret ballot of the players. Contrary to what has been said and written, the decision to appoint Temirkanov, who was not a Soviet Party member, was not made by the Ministry, although it was necessary for the Party to ratify the outcome of the election.

With the collapse of the Soviet Union in 1991 the Leningrad Philharmonic Orchestra changed its name to the St Petersburg Philharmonic Orchestra and became the responsibility of the new Russian Federation. With

almost overnight vast changes in the funding and structure of arts operations in Russia, suddenly the players had to face serious financial insecurity.
Large state subsidies for the arts were no longer available, and new staff
had to be engaged to raise sponsorship and market the orchestra. Despite
their efforts, the dramatic change so seriously stripped the orchestra of its
security that the players needed and still need extra alternative income to
survive. Some of them have had to take part-time work outside performing
or teaching. But for all these very difficult conditions, Yuri Temirkanov has
helped to maintain the orchestra's confidence, and the famous string style
and sonority have been retained to a considerable extent. Both the styles
and the sounds of the woodwind, brass and percussion have changed in
some ways, though, especially as newer players have joined and more modern instruments have come into use. There is generally not such a strident
vibrato in the brass and somewhat less intense impact from them and the
percussion, whilst the woodwind play with a mellow, blending refinement
that is typical of the best Western European and American orchestras. This
can be heard in many recordings the orchestra has made with conductors
Yuri Temirkanov, Mariss Jansons and Vladimir Ashkenazy. The presence of
artists of their calibre and reputation are vital for the St Petersburg Philharmonic Orchestra's survival as it now has to battle to raise funding in
extremely difficult conditions.

3 London Symphony Orchestra

The reasons for the origins of the London Symphony Orchestra are not
dissimilar to those for the Berlin Philharmonic, although, as will be seen, the
LSO's artistic and corporate operations then developed along very different
lines. It was because of a source of discontentment amongst players in Henry
Wood's Queen's Hall Orchestra that the London Symphony Orchestra came
into existence in 1904. At that time Henry Wood, as Music Director of the
Queen's Hall Orchestra, provided a considerable amount of employment
for his musicians, but this was by no means sufficient for an annual income.
His Promenade Concerts were a valuable but part-time source of earnings
and the Queen's Hall Orchestra members had to find many other casual
engagements if they were to survive round the year. They were entirely
dependent on freelance engagements as there was not a single full-time
orchestra in London. Indeed, in the entire United Kingdom, only the Hallé
Orchestra offered a degree of permanent employment, and even then the
players were not paid all the year round. As a consequence, it had been
common practice that players engaged for a series or season of concerts
with a particular orchestra would on occasion send deputy replacements
of their choice to rehearsals if they had been offered more lucrative or

extended engagements elsewhere with clashes of availability. Naturally this 'deputy system', as it was known, was fiercely opposed by conductors such as Henry Wood, but, understandably, it was fiercely upheld by players as absolutely necessary for their security.

Matters came to a head in the Queen's Hall Orchestra in 1904 when Henry Wood issued an ultimatum: deputies would not be accepted under any circumstances, and offending players sending them would be dismissed. Immediately, four members of the orchestra decided to call a meeting and very soon they had drawn up plans to form a co-operative new organisation, the London Symphony Orchestra, which was to be owned by the players, who would all be shareholders of the company. The company – the Orchestra – would be governed by a board of directors elected by the players. The Board would fundamentally consist of orchestra members. Quickly the four musicians attracted more than half the members of the Queen's Hall Orchestra and had no difficulty recruiting other players to make up a full symphony orchestra. A board of directors was elected and it took full responsibility for all the artistic, managerial and fiscal affairs: arranging concerts, engaging conductors and soloists, handling finances, determining personnel and, particularly significantly, securing the services of a highly distinguished musician, Hans Richter, as Principal Conductor. This was an unprecedented situation in orchestral history in Britain: for the first time, an orchestra had been formed by players who were managing it entirely and were engaging a Principal Conductor, as opposed to the traditional situation where the Music Director was a conductor who exerted managerial powers over the orchestra. There was some scepticism about the venture's future, but it succeeded remarkably quickly with a first year of prestigious concerts with artists that included conductors Arthur Nikisch, Eduard Colonne, Fritz Steinbach and Sir Edward Elgar and soloists Achille Rivarde, Johannes Wolff, Peter Rabb and Ada Crossley. By 1905 the London Symphony Orchestra was well established as a major orchestra in Britain, with a considerable amount of work. Its self-governing format has basically remained the same since then, although in recent decades its managerial structure and operations have had to become far more complex, as will be related further on.

Hans Richter remained the Principal Conductor until 1911, and for the following season his position was taken by Sir Edward Elgar. Although he only stayed in that post for a year, thereafter Elgar maintained a close and mutually valuable relationship with the orchestra right up to the early 1930s, giving many concerts and making important landmark recordings of many of his works. In 1912 the LSO obtained the extremely highly sought-after services of Artur Nikisch as its Principal Conductor for two seasons, a very prestigious appointment for the orchestra. That same year a very brilliant young Leopold Stokowski, just taking on his post in Philadelphia, conducted the LSO for the first time. During Nikisch's tenure there were two especially historic events: an ambitious tour to the United States in 1912, the first by any European orchestra, and the recording of the LSO's first discs, in 1913. As with the Berlin Philharmonic's first recordings with Nikisch, made only several months earlier, it is difficult to draw conclusions about technical standards from such primitively made discs. Only a proportion of the orchestra was engaged and cramped together in a tiny, dead-sounding studio, and only a very limited proportion of their sounds could be preserved with any semblance of accuracy. However, within those limitations, it does seem that the LSO had some outstanding players, especially the principals. Particularly interesting is the recording of Liszt's *First Hungarian Rhapsody* with Nikisch, which after sounding insecure in ensemble and intonation at the start becomes remarkably virtuoso later, with brilliant attack and articulation (Electrola deleted LP, 1 C 053-01466).

Inevitably the orchestra's activities were curtailed somewhat during the First World War, and with Nikisch's post in Berlin continuing he was no longer available as the LSO's Principal Conductor during the hostilities with Germany. From 1915 to 1917 Sir Thomas Beecham was engaged as Principal Conductor, followed by Albert Coates from 1919 to 1922. For the following eight years there was no Principal Conductor, but the orchestra did play with some very distinguished guest conductors including Richard Strauss, Bruno Walter, Felix Weingartner and Sir Thomas Beecham. An important event was the orchestra's series of recordings of some of Strauss's works conducted by the composer for Columbia in the early 1920s. The LSO was also engaged to play for the short seasons at the Covent Garden Opera where it accompanied world famous singers with highly distinguished conductors.

However, the Great War and the difficult conditions thereafter had taken a toll on the LSO as well as all musical activities in England. The orchestra's playing began to receive some criticism and generally the country's musical standards were unfavourably compared to those in Europe and America, where far greater subsidies were available to maintain better conditions and more regular employment for orchestras and opera companies. In particular, when the new electrical recordings of the Philadelphia Orchestra with Leopold Stokowski and the Boston Symphony Orchestra with Serge Koussevitsky appeared in the mid-1920s, there were unfavourable comparisons for the LSO. Indeed the sonority, ensemble and intonation on many of its recordings at that time, even with celebrated conductors such as Weingartner and Walter, were noticeably less impressive than on the Philadelphia and Boston Symphony recordings. Some people also felt that standards were suffering through the lack of a real Music Director with a regular and long-lasting presence, such as existed in Berlin with Furtwängler and in New York with Mengelberg and then Toscanini. Such critics easily overlooked a more crucial problem, which was the inability of the LSO to be a permanent orchestra with regular rehearsals and concerts, as no finance for such an organisation was available in London, let alone most of the United Kingdom. When this situation was rectified much later, the orchestra proved its corporate technical virtuosity and extremely high artistic standards with its Principal Conductors and the finest of its guest conductors, and today it is internationally acclaimed as one of the world's most artistic and brilliant of all ensembles. There are many reasons for this, which are listed later, but the far finer conditions that have increasingly been achieved for the orchestra in the last ten years have been vital for the growth of a new agenda that has enabled it to realise its highest artistic potential.

By 1930 there was a growing demand for a regular orchestra in London that could provide high-quality concerts for most of the year. Visits to London by the Berlin Philharmonic in 1927 and the New York Philharmonic in 1930 reinforced this desire. Consequently, in the early 1930s major developments took place that were fundamentally to change the course of orchestral life in England. In 1930 the BBC Symphony Orchestra was created as a full-time ensemble with salaried employment. Two years later Sir Thomas Beecham formed his London Philharmonic Orchestra with similar, though by no means identical, conditions. It was generally felt that these two new orchestras, consisting of experienced and many new young players, gave England revolutionary standards of orchestral performance that could be compared to the finest orchestras abroad. Contrary to what has often been claimed, these developments in fact adversely affected the perception of the LSO's reputation rather than its actual quality, and if anything they contributed positively to the fortunes of its sound and standard. The BBC Symphony and London Philharmonic Orchestras were indeed able to become regularly outstanding ensembles very quickly and their conditions and newly constituted personnel, especially the virtuoso principals, made them the finest in England at the time. However, the LSO indirectly benefited from this. The example these orchestras set and the significant rise in the numbers of technically excellent young players in the 1930s helped to bring about a noticeable rise in the standards of ensemble, intonation and range of sonority in the LSO during the 1930s. In fact, even back in 1930 the LSO's quality had already been importantly affected by its decision to engage the Concertgebouw Orchestra of Amsterdam's celebrated and feared orchestra trainer and virtuoso conductor Willem Mengelberg as its Principal Conductor in an effort to improve its reputation and self-esteem. He stayed for one season, reportedly an acrimonious one, but it seems that he exerted significant influence, as the orchestra's recordings thereafter often reveal a considerably tighter ensemble and, on the whole, finer intonation. In particular, the recordings of the LSO with Elgar conducting his symphonic study *Falstaff*, in 1931, and his Violin Concerto with Yehudi Menuhin, in 1932, illustrate these qualities.

In 1932 the London Symphony Orchestra appointed Sir Hamilton Harty as its Principal Conductor. For three seasons the orchestra benefited from his dynamic presence and imaginative interpretations of a wide repertory of music, including an important première in 1934 – the First Symphony of Sir William Walton, performed initially in its incomplete three-movement format. Harty's recording of the work with the LSO (Dutton CDAX 8003) illustrates the orchestra's discipline and cohesion at that time, as do the recordings of other repertory the LSO made with Weingartner and Walter in 1937 and 1938 (for example, Walter compilation on Dutton CDLX 7008). Two particular qualities on these recordings reflect the new traits of the 1930s in orchestral playing in England: there are far fewer wide portamenti in the strings than in earlier decades and the woodwind have more bloom and warmth.

With the outbreak of the Second World War, once again the LSO's activities were considerably curtailed, although they did continue to perform, including playing frequently at the Henry Wood Promenade Concerts, which were now organised by the BBC. However, when the war ended the orchestra's reputation was again eclipsed by radical new developments when the Philharmonia Orchestra and Royal Philharmonic Orchestra were founded in 1945 and 1946. In both cases the finest players in Britain were handpicked by Walter Legge and Sir Thomas Beecham, respectively, who were setting out to create virtuoso orchestras of their own with financial stability and lucrative recording contracts. Their orchestras set even higher standards of virtuosity and artistry than the pre-war BBC Symphony and London Philharmonic Orchestras, and from the late 1940s the Philharmonia regularly attracted many of the world's most highly sought-after conductors and soloists. It was therefore an important move for the LSO when they were able to engage the services of Josef Krips as Principal Conductor in 1951. A meticulous rehearser for detail, style and ensemble, for three years his presence had a particularly strong influence on the orchestra's sound and approach to the great German and Austrian classics, as can be heard on their (currently deleted) recordings of symphonies by Mozart, Schubert and Brahms. His tenure with the LSO ended in 1954 following an unfortunate misunderstanding, and there then followed a short period of instability that was the prelude to a major change in the orchestra's entire make-up and future existence.

In 1955 the Board of Directors – all members of the London Symphony Orchestra – decided to take a strong line with players who were sometimes not performing with the orchestra because they were accepting alternative engagements. The post-war era of expansion in arts activities and increased subsidies was helping the LSO to work more regularly now, and the Board were concerned about the orchestra's reputation and lack of stable attendance. Ironically, their stance against a similar practice to that which had contributed to the orchestra's creation in 1904 was to lead to a vital development in the LSO's fortunes. A dispute arose and the majority of the section principals and then some rank and file players left the orchestra. Within a year a substantial number of LSO members had been replaced by many extremely talented young players who soon brought the orchestra a new high reputation. By the late 1950s the LSO was becoming greatly admired for its brilliance and zest and it was regularly attracting major conductors of the calibre of Leopold Stokowski, who had conducted the orchestra in 1956 after a long absence, Pierre Monteux, Antal Dorati and Jascha Horenstein. The LSO's association with Antal Dorati was of particular importance, as he worked assiduously with them on a very wide repertory for a large number of recordings, and many of the players later spoke of the value of his rigorous demands for detail and discipline. This was a significant example of a successful, if sometimes stormy, relationship between an uncompromising conductor and the self-governing orchestra that was employing him.

An important driving force was Ernest Fleischmann, a radically imaginative manager (his title was General Secretary, responsible to the LSO Board of Directors), who played a vital role in creating favourable conditions to attract an ever-greater range of internationally renowned artists to perform with the orchestra. During his era, the appointment of the highly revered Pierre Monteux as the LSO's Principal Conductor in 1961 was a landmark for the orchestra that consolidated and sealed its new status as a major international ensemble. In the following three years the LSO rose to world fame, both for its playing, which became virtuoso with the finest conductors, and for its association with a new scale of acclaimed artists. Monteux's presence, the increasing number of celebrated guest conductors such as Colin Davis, Georg Solti, Gennadi Rozhdestvensky and Benjamin Britten, in addition to those already mentioned, and a cachet of some of the world's most highly sought-after guest soloists and singers, brought the orchestra unprecedented prestige.

The LSO's transformation into one of the world's finest and most admired orchestras took place, remarkably, in a relatively short space of time. It was allied to a very successful fundraising and sponsorship campaign, necessary to create the finances for its ambitious developments. That contrasts with the steady, long-term evolution of funding, quality and reputation of the Berlin Philharmonic and Leningrad Philharmonic Orchestras, which enjoyed so much more financial and professional stability in their very different ways. This is an important factor affecting the subsequent history of the LSO, which in due course addressed its funding, its membership and its programming in a completely new way and in doing so achieved another equally dramatic transformation.

The orchestra's reputation during the Monteux era was certainly maintained after his death in 1964, when István Kertész was appointed Principal Conductor, followed by eleven highly successful years with André Previn as his successor, from 1968 to 1979. Previn initiated an important series of television programmes – which he hosted – that were designed to be both recreational and educational, and they brought the LSO and indeed classical music to a new wide public in Britain. From the mid-1960s onwards the list of guest conductors expanded further to include Claudio Abbado, Leonard Bernstein and George Szell (he had previously conducted the Orchestra in 1962 but had not returned), and later the LSO regularly attracted Sergiu Celibidache, Karl Böhm and Seiji Ozawa. The range of guest soloists also increased to include Sir Clifford Curzon, Martha Argerich and Alfred Brendel in addition to Dietrich Fischer-Dieskau and Mstislav Rostropovich, who had appeared before. It was sometimes said that during the 1960s and 1970s the LSO's brilliant sonorities and notably attacking style excelled more in the music of composers such as Berlioz, Stravinsky, Dvořák, Bartók, Ravel and Copland than in the German and Austrian classics by Mozart, Beethoven, Schubert and Brahms (Mahler was an exception). In fact, though, it was a very versatile orchestra indeed, highly able to reflect the tastes of vastly different conductors. This can be heard in commercial recordings with Monteux, Kertész, Previn, Bernstein and Szell and archive-recordings of performances with Celibidache, Böhm and Ozawa (for example, Monteux's *Ravel* and *Debussy* on Philips 4425442 or Szell's *Mahler* on EMI CDM 5672362).

In 1979 Claudio Abbado was appointed Principal Conductor. During his eight-year tenure the LSO maintained its standards, whilst its reputation was particularly enhanced by Abbado's imaginative programming, introducing some series of concerts based on specific themes – historical, literary or with other connotations. This was a blueprint for a new approach to programming that was then adopted regularly by the LSO, influencing the future of general concert programming in London. The LSO made many recordings with Abbado in this period, and some particularly notable events with artists making very rare appearances were performances by Carlos Kleiber in 1981 and Arturo Benedetti Michelangeli in 1983, who was accompanied by Sergiu Celibidache.

In 1982 the Barbican Arts Centre opened and the LSO became the orchestra in residence, with the very first permanent rehearsal and performance home for a London orchestra. At the same time it entered a severe financial and public attendance crisis that was ironically to lead to the birth of a revolutionary new agenda in its life. In 1984 Clive Gillinson, a cellist in the orchestra since 1970, took over as Managing Director and during a long period strategically instigated novel concepts for funding, programming and membership that brought the LSO a new stability and an unprecedented level of consistent artistic success.

There were many kinds of innovations that all brought to the LSO a new and far higher level of funding from both the private and public sectors, enabling the orchestra to operate in far better conditions than before and pursue more ambitious artistic policies. Whereas previously to counteract the relative paucity of public funding the LSO had taken on much work of lesser artistic significance for financial reasons, now the Board accepted the new Managing Director's proposals to restructure its operations radically for high artistic consistency and new and increased funding. Over a period of time the LSO's life steadily changed. The orchestra was enlarged to include joint principals in all sections, theme programme series were extended to include in-depth overviews of various composers' works, and close and on-going relationships with selected guest conductors and soloists were forged, such as Pierre Boulez, Mstislav Rostropovich, Riccardo Chailly, Lorin Maazel, Maxim Vengerov and Anne-Sofie Mutter. A particularly important relationship was created with Mstislav Rostropovich in his capacity as conductor, with the orchestra making many recordings with him up to the present time. An annual series of concert performances of operas with some of the world's most sought-after singers was also introduced. Rehearsal times and conditions were improved so that the orchestra's general schedule was less crowded and more time could be devoted to the main concerts of the season. All this, and an intake of new players, some from overseas who were particularly attracted by the artistic conditions, brought about a new, consistently high standard of playing and, in the string sections, a deepening and enrichment of the sound. In recent years the orchestra has been widely and regularly acclaimed as being on the level of the world's very finest.

In 1987 Michael Tilson Thomas succeeded Claudio Abbado as Principal Conductor and attracted considerable interest in the eclecticism of his repertory, which included much unfamiliar American music and some original wide-ranging theme programme series. Some of this repertory was included amongst his many recordings with the orchestra. After Michael Tilson Thomas, Sir Colin Davis was appointed Principal Conductor, and during his era the orchestra has achieved its highest plaudits for the range of sonority, corporate discipline, and artistic individuality in its playing. Ambitious concert series have included a cycle of all Berlioz's orchestral and operatic works, most of which have been recorded from actual performances and released on the LSO's new CD label, LSO Live.

An important part of the LSO's operations is its sophisticated educational agenda, the LSO Discovery programme, in which the players and leading

7.1 The London Symphony Orchestra at the Barbican Centre, London. Photo: Keith Saunders

conductors take part in a wide variety of events, including talks, workshops, illustrated rehearsals and many creative composing sessions at schools.

4 New York Philharmonic Orchestra

Like the LSO, the New York Philharmonic Orchestra was also formed as a self governing co-operative, but for very different reasons, and its constitution and operations subsequently developed in markedly different ways. Unlike the case of the Berlin Philharmonic and London Symphony Orchestras, which were formed by players who desired independence from existing privately run orchestras, the New York Philharmonic was created by a group of musicians who wished to provide the city of New York with its first permanent orchestra. In 1842 the conductor Ureli Corelli Hill called a meeting of locally well-known and influential names of the time, who included Anthony Rief jr, Vincent Wallace, George Loder jr, Alfred Boucher, Edward Hodges and William Scharfenberg. They formed the Philharmonic Symphony Society of New York, and funds from wealthy patrons were raised to assemble sixty-three players for the first concert of the New York Philharmonic Orchestra that December. Hill conducted and the programme included Beethoven's 5th Symphony, which had received its American première under Hill at another society's concert the previous year. The concert was a success, but the Philharmonic Symphony Society soon found that the practicality of financing and organising a full-time orchestra was a daunting challenge. The orchestra did continue; however, in effect it was a part-time ensemble for many decades, as indeed at that time were most of the world's musical organisations that were not owned or funded by monarchies and courts. Only a few concerts a year were given, and the conductors were frequently drawn from the orchestra's membership. Nevertheless there were Principal Conductors who assumed the role of Music Director – Ureli Hill up to 1847, followed by Theodore Eisfeld, then Carl Bergmann in 1855.

In 1867 the New York Philharmonic's membership increased to 100 and the orchestra acquired new, larger premises at the Academy of Music. In 1876 Leopold Damrosch was the Principal Conductor for a season, and then the following year a highly respected American conductor, Theodore Thomas, took over the position, raising the orchestra's profile significantly. He was succeeded in 1891 by a conductor of international repute, the Hungarian Anton Seidl. The same year the Carnegie Hall opened and in 1892 the orchestra gave its first concert in that venue, which was to be its main centre until 1963. Seidl remained as Principal Conductor until his death in 1898, and that year his position was taken by Emil Paur, who was succeeded by Walter Damrosch for a season in 1902. By now the number of concerts per year had begun to increase and the Philharmonic Symphony Society had gathered increasing respect, although its finances were still drawn from a relatively small number of donors. The repertory throughout this period had often been dominated by German music, reflecting the musical backgrounds of many of the conductors, and indeed some of the members of the orchestra were of German and occasionally other European origin. It appears that the standard of playing was often good, although it seems that the orchestra did not have the kind of reputation that leading European orchestras, such as the Berlin Philharmonic and the Concertgebouw of Amsterdam, were gaining. This may have been linked to the comparatively limited amount of public and financial support for the New York Philharmonic Orchestra at this time, a situation that was, before long, to change dramatically.

In 1906 Wassily Safonoff, a leading international conductor of the day, became the New York Philharmonic Orchestra's Principal Conductor for three years. Accounts of the time speak of the strong impression the orchestra's performances with him made, notably in the music of Beethoven and Tchaikovsky. However, the significance of his tenure was eclipsed by the short, stormy but greatly important era that began in 1909 when Gustav

Mahler was appointed to the new post of Music Director. The arrival of Mahler with an international reputation as one of the most demanding and revered conductors in memory coincided with the reorganisation of the orchestra as a more permanent ensemble under the management of a group of financial guarantors. They injected substantial new subsidies into the orchestra's Society, which was now renamed the Philharmonic Society of New York. After more than half a century as a basically part-time organisation running its own affairs, the New York Philharmonic was now effectively taken over by a controlling board of funding and sponsoring directors that sought regular concerts and gave the Music Director virtually unilateral powers over the orchestra personnel. The numbers of concerts were considerably increased, and the repertory was enlarged to include a wider representation of international music and more contemporary works, even though Mahler, and indeed also his successors, often encountered great resistance against particularly innovative programming ideas.

Although opinions about his interpretations and his personality were often very divided, the impact of Mahler's tenure with the New York Philharmonic Orchestra on music in America as well as Europe cannot be overestimated. In many ways he revolutionised public awareness of the symphony orchestra and its potential. With his fanatical pursuit of technical and stylistic standards, the New York Philharmonic's reputation rose dramatically. This is borne out in a series of invaluable interviews that were recorded in the early 1960s with many musicians who recalled playing with Mahler. The conversations were compiled into a series of radio programmes called 'I Remember Mahler' which was presented and produced by the recorder of the interviews, William Malloch, for KPFK Radio in America in 1964. The complete series of programmes may be heard at the Music Performance Research Centre in the Barbican Library in London (catalogue no. BCT FEA 0513). Some extracts from the original programmes were subsequently commercially issued on LP and then on CD (Pickwick GLRS 101).

Gustav Mahler's two-year tenure with the New York Philharmonic Orchestra was followed by something of an anti-climax when Joseph Stransky became the next Music Director, remaining until 1923. Although he was popular with the orchestra's patrons, the new sophisticated audiences who had been so stimulated by Mahler's innovations were critical of Stransky's unadventurous conservatism. Nevertheless the standard of the New York Philharmonic's playing remained high, as can be heard on the earliest recorded evidence of the orchestra, with Stransky conducting, in 1917. If these primitively made acoustic process recordings are to be believed, the corporate discipline and intonation of the entire orchestra was very good on the whole. Only some wide and slow portamenti in the strings sound untidy.

Only a few years later the New York Philharmonic's playing became virtuoso and the orchestra's reputation soared. In 1922 the flamboyant Willem Mengelberg was appointed co-principal conductor and the next year he became sole Music Director. His notoriously intensive and fanatical rehearsing must have been profitable for the orchestra, because on the evidence of the recordings he made with it from 1924 to 1930 there was a new brilliance, virtuosity and flexibility which put it on a par with the coveted Philadelphia and Boston Symphony Orchestras. Increasing numbers of very gifted young American players joined the orchestra, and the New York Philharmonic formed its distinctive style and sound that were to remain for some decades, and which still exist to an extent today. There was extremely tight cohesion and exemplary intonation, and the overall sonority was brilliant and bright but also rich. The brass had a cutting edge and played very incisively and with sharp articulation. The woodwind were very agile, not always as mellow as the best French and soon to come English players (in particular the flutes played with a very fast, quivering vibrato), but very flexible nevertheless. The timpani and percussion were played with notable neatness, accuracy and colour. The strings played most expressively and sonorously with bold tones and yet gossamer textures too. String portamento was used, especially as Mengelberg favoured it, but it was generally subtle, swift and expressive, as opposed to just being a technical means of sliding between notes. The New York Philharmonic's discipline, intonation, brilliance and flexibility can be especially tellingly heard on its recordings with Mengelberg that were reissued by the Pearl Company for the orchestra's 150th anniversary, even though Mengelberg was dissatisfied with the dry-sounding recording quality (Pearl GEMM CDS 9922).

By 1928 the New York Philharmonic's reputation was so high that Arturo Toscanini, who had first guest conducted the orchestra in 1926, one year after Wilhelm Furtwängler's guest début, accepted the Philharmonic Society's invitation to share the principal direction with Mengelberg. A condition was an enlargement of the membership, and so the Philharmonic now absorbed the New York Symphony Orchestra and became known as the New York Philharmonic Symphony Orchestra, remaining thus until 1958 when it reverted to its original title of New York Philharmonic Orchestra. There were also now increasingly more outstanding young American players available, and the combination of this and the direction of Toscanini and Mengelberg made the New York Philharmonic of the time one of the most outstanding and admired orchestras in memory. Its prestige was so high that funding, nearly all from the private sector, was found to enlarge the season to twenty-eight weeks each year. More and more outstanding guest conductors and soloists appeared with the New York Philharmonic, and a notable event was the simultaneous US début of Sir Thomas Beecham and Vladimir Horowitz at the Carnegie Hall in 1928.

In 1930 Toscanini assumed sole music directorship of the orchestra, and during his tenure for the next six years the New York Philharmonic enjoyed an exceptionally prestigious reputation. Toscanini's zealous insistence on accuracy and precision of ensemble, his meticulous care for details and dynamics, and his vehement demands for expression and colour gave the already outstanding New York Philharmonic an even greater degree of virtuosity and refinement, as can be heard on the celebrated recordings of the time. The string sound became yet warmer, less voluptuous than with Mengelberg, but intensely expressive and luminous in a cantabile style that was fundamental to Toscanini's music-making. If anything, the woodwind became more mellow in tone during this period, as was happening in many orchestras now (although nowhere to the extent that it was in the London Philharmonic Orchestra, where Léon Goossens and Reginald Kell were introducing the most striking innovations). The New York Philharmonic Orchestra's fame was also enhanced by Toscanini's influence and reputation as a revolutionary interpreter who rigorously pursued the utmost objectivity and fidelity to the letter of the composer's score. Altogether his presence gave the orchestra an unprecedented status, and as well as regular guest appearances by highly revered conductors such as Bruno Walter and Erich Kleiber there were frequent visits from some of the very most sought-after solo instrumentalists and singers.

When Arturo Toscanini retired from the New York Philharmonic in 1936 the orchestra was at the height of its fame. The daunting task of succeeding him was undertaken by the thirty-six-year-old John Barbirolli, who after encountering undeserved hostility from some of the press at first then won great popularity with his romantic and volatile interpretations which were played with brilliance and discipline by the orchestra. After his tenure Artur Rodzinski was Music Director from 1943 to 1947. He was a meticulous rehearser and obtained fiery and highly disciplined results. He introduced much contemporary and neglected repertory that somewhat divided his audiences, and his sometimes explosive and uncompromising personality made him enemies in the Society and also the orchestra. His very important contribution should not be overlooked, though, and he played a vital role in bringing a young Leonard Bernstein to the public's attention for the first time by selecting him as his assistant conductor. When Bruno Walter fell ill one day in 1943, Bernstein was the twenty-five-year-old stand-in for him with the Philharmonic at just a day's notice, and his extraordinary success shot him to overnight fame immediately. Walter was one of a very impressive list of guest conductors who appeared with the orchestra during the

1940s – it also included Fritz Reiner, Fritz Busch, Sir Thomas Beecham, Serge Koussevitsky, Leopold Stokowski, Charles Munch, George Szell, Victor de Sabata, Igor Stravinsky and Pierre Monteux.

In 1947 the greatly revered Bruno Walter became the New York Philharmonic's Music Director, continuing the orchestra's high prestige for two years, and notably bringing performances of Mahler to New York, as indeed did his celebrated virtuoso successor, Leopold Stokowski, during his brief one-season tenure. They and several other distinguished conductors of the orchestra, including Fritz Reiner and Artur Rodzinski, can be seen in the 1947 film *Carnegie Hall*, which also includes some of the outstanding soloists who were the orchestra's guests at this time, such as Jascha Heifetz, Artur Rubinstein and Gregor Piatigorsky.

In 1950 Stokowski was succeeded by Dimitri Mitropoulos, an unconventional and controversial conductor of rare brilliance and flair, who enterprisingly introduced a plethora of contemporary and unusual repertory to the orchestra's audiences. His eight-year tenure, though, was unfortunately marred by a decline in the corporate discipline of the orchestra, which many attributed to Mitropoulos's unpredictable manner of conducting and his relative lack of concern for fine precision in the standard classics. The orchestra's most notable performances with him were often of exotic and avant-garde scores, to which he brought extra special colour, sparkle and clarity, even if the ensemble was not always perfect. Amongst some important recordings he made with the orchestra of contemporary music of the time, his Western première disc of Shostakovich's 10th Symphony, released soon after the work's world première, particularly well illustrates the dynamism, abandon and colour in his performances (Sony MPK 45698).

At the time of Mitropoulos's death in 1958 the New York Philharmonic Orchestra felt demoralised through the decline in its reputation and the lack of cohesive balance and ensemble it was suffering in classical repertory. It was being particularly unfavourably compared to the Cleveland and Chicago Symphony Orchestras which had risen to pre-eminence as exceptionally brilliant, artistic and virtuoso ensembles of the highest discipline under George Szell and Fritz Reiner, respectively. The Philharmonic Society's choice for a successor to Mitropoulos now brought the orchestra the most dramatic possible reversal of its fortunes and, within a short time, its greatest prestige since the days of Toscanini. The charismatic and flamboyant Leonard Bernstein took over as Music Director and during his eleven-year tenure the orchestra became one of the world's most illustrious, dynamic and versatile ensembles.

Bernstein's glamour and emotionalism could not have been further afield from Toscanini's draconian and intensely disciplined objectivity, but nevertheless he was greatly demanding for detail, nuance, colour and expression and also insisted on great finesse and control when necessary. The orchestra again played with cohesion, virtuosity, flexibility and, usually, discipline, even though there were some criticisms that Bernstein's interpretations could be excessively expressive with contrasts of tempi and dynamics that sometimes exceeded the letter of the composer's score. He gave the orchestra a very wide range of European and American repertory with some contemporary music, though relatively little of the most experimental avant-garde. In particular, he continued its famous Mahler tradition with important performance and recording cycles, which played an important role in the new interest in Mahler's music in the 1960s. He also brought the New York Philharmonic an unprecedented level of commercial success and worldwide fame through his regular series of innovative television programmes introducing a wide repertory of classical and also jazz-inspired music to huge new numbers of people. Many of these programmes have now been issued on videograms, adding to the extremely large numbers of recordings that have been released of the New York Philharmonic with Bernstein. On many of these recordings it can be heard how some younger new players were contributing to the growth of a more mellow sound in the woodwind and brass sections, as was becoming more customary in many parts of Europe and America.

The Bernstein era of the New York Philharmonic also witnessed the transfer of its home to the new Avery Fisher Hall in the purpose-built Lincoln Center and the extension of the orchestra's season to throughout the year with the members' first full-time contracts. Increasing funding from corporate and private donors, foundations and sponsors gave the Philharmonic its most stable existence to that date. Relatively little money was available from the State, as has usually been the case in the US, and so the governing power was very much in the hands of the board of directors who were answerable to, and sometimes included, the patrons, as had been the case since 1909. Similarly since then, the Music Director retained his powers of employment over the orchestra personnel. These conditions still exist today.

In 1971 Pierre Boulez began his tenure as Music Director of the New York Philharmonic Orchestra. This was a bold but very successful decision. There could have been no greater contrast to Bernstein's personality, repertory and interpretations than those of Boulez, who was celebrated for his objectivity, meticulous rehearsal for precision of minute details, and powerful advocacy of the latest avant-garde music. For six years he convinced patrons and audiences of his very ambitious programming and won over a following for a notably new repertory with the orchestra. During this time he also gained in stature as an interpreter of the more standard classical repertory and the orchestra's playing in this and also contemporary music was widely admired and praised.

In 1978 Zubin Mehta succeeded Pierre Boulez as Music Director and began a very successful thirteen-year period with the New York Philharmonic, during which the orchestra's high status and quality were maintained. Mehta brought a very wide repertory with a mix of European classics, American works and contemporary music, including avant-garde compositions, all receiving carefully rehearsed performances with impressively integrated playing, as can be heard on many recordings. The Philharmonic also benefited from his close associations with some of the most sought-after solo instrumentalists such as Isaac Stern, Itzhak Perlman, Daniel Barenboim, and Yo Yo Ma, who especially liked to come and perform with him and the orchestra.

In 1991 the Philharmonic Society appointed Kurt Masur as Music Director, and once again an astute decision brought the New York Philharmonic a highly successful and very different kind of era. During Masur's ten-year tenure the orchestra particularly greatly benefited from his long-established renown as a distinguished and searching interpreter of the great German and Austrian classics, whilst Masur surprised his audiences by developing his new taste and flair for much American music, including jazz-related works. His directorship has seen the orchestra's status ride especially high as a greatly admired ensemble of versatility, warmth and discipline, with excellence of intonation and ensemble, great brilliance and outstanding integration, borne out on numerous recordings. At the time of writing (2001) Lorin Maazel has just been named as his successor. For the Millennium the New York Philharmonic Orchestra issued a 10 CD set of previously unreleased recordings of broadcasts of some of its most important concerts from 1922 to the present day. It gives a very telling overview of the orchestra's remarkable history (New York Philharmonic Orchestra EY5 9701).

8 The revival of historical instruments

COLIN LAWSON

Introduction

During the past thirty years or so, historical performance in theory and practice has truly established itself as a vibrant part of the orchestral scene. Period instruments are routinely encountered in the concert hall from San Francisco to Budapest and from Toronto to Rio de Janeiro; indeed, they have become virtually obligatory in substantial areas of the orchestral repertory. There is now a widespread interest in recreating the original sounds and styles of a composer's own time and in acquiring appropriate instruments and technique. Meanwhile, the entire focus of such endeavours has been subject to stimulating discussion and argument. It cannot be denied that artistic life today makes demands which are decidedly unhistorical; for example, the microphone introduces a set of parameters which would have been unthinkable in previous generations. Furthermore, air travel has wrought such changes that we do not have the option to turn back the clock. Nevertheless, examination of a variety of primary sources, complementing tradition and intuition, enables earlier styles of performance to be explored; for, as Roger Norrington has remarked, 'a relationship with the past needs to be founded on truth as well as sympathy, concern as well as exploitation, information as well as guesswork'.[1]

Historical awareness in performance has a long and fascinating pedigree, which has been traced in some detail by Harry Haskell and others. In the late nineteenth century there finally sprang a growing desire to investigate instruments and performing styles that were contemporary with and appropriate to earlier music. At this time of great technological development, there was lively discussion as to whether orchestral instruments had been improving or had merely changed. For example, Wagner was in no doubt that in Beethoven's symphonies valved trumpets and horns should be used rather than their natural precursors; he rewrote their parts to remove any supposed limitations. On the other hand, Berlioz described the use of valves for stopped notes in Beethoven as a dangerous abuse; this is of special significance in the context of his general enthusiasm for the latest developments, such as Adolphe Sax's recent improvements to the clarinet and the newly devised Boehm flute.[2] At a similar period Gleich claimed that the use of valves in Weber and Beethoven was a 'Vandalismus'.[3] The first edition of

Grove's Dictionary reckoned that increased mechanism had impaired the true tone-quality of woodwind instruments such as the oboe and bassoon, an issue that was widely debated elsewhere.

In 1884 the violinist Joseph Joachim directed a Bach festival at Eisenach, where Bach's B minor Mass was performed, with some care taken towards the recreation of the composer's original instruments. Joachim and his associate Andreas Moser also signalled a seminal change in performing attitudes with some far-sighted advice in their *Violinschule* of 1905:

> In order to do justice to the piece which he is about to perform, the player must first acquaint himself with the conditions under which it originated. For a work by Bach or Tartini demands a different style of delivery from one by Mendelssohn or Spohr. The space of a century that divides the two first mentioned from the last two means in the historical development of our art not only a great difference in regard to form, but even a greater with respect to musical expression.[4]

Joachim's historical approach to Bach or Tartini must have been very different from today's and certainly did not involve a change of violin or bow. But one of the remarkable achievements of the following hundred years was to be the probing investigation of musical styles and eras, with stimulating and often surprising results. The great pioneer Arnold Dolmetsch once characteristically remarked that he wanted his pupils to learn principles rather than pieces, so that they could do their own thinking.[5] Dolmetsch set out his philosophy of historical performance in *The Interpretation of Music of the XVII and XVIII Centuries* (London, 1915) and put it into practice at his centre at Haslemere for the study and recreation of the traditions of performance of early music.[6] His great gift was indeed that he had both the imagination and the musicianship to take a work which had become a museum piece and make it speak to the people of his own time. His comments on period instruments are full of insight, arguing for example that the one-keyed flute *can* be played in tune, but that this 'requires constant watchfulness of the ear, which thus becomes more and more sensitive to faults of intonation'.[7]

Dolmetsch's special status in the history of period performance is justified by the wisdom of his book rather than the eccentricities of his career. It is significant that in the very year of the publication of his book, Saint-Saëns surveyed the principal issues of style, technique and equipment in a lecture in San Francisco.[8] In Germany a key figure was Christian Döbereiner, co-founder in 1905 of the Munich-based Deutsche Vereinigung für alte Musik. He was largely responsible for widespread use of historical instruments in the Bach festivals that proliferated in Germany in the early 1900s under the impetus of the Bach Gesellschaft. The crusade was continued by the scholars Robert Haas and Joachim-pupil Arnold Schering, both of whom published influential studies.[9] Dolmetsch's pupil Robert Donington produced some indispensable reference works involving the decoding and clarification of notational conventions and ambiguities within established musical and historical contexts. These conventions will always remain for us a foreign language, but such source studies can furnish us with the necessary grammar, vocabulary and knowledge to communicate freely and expressively as musicians. In England, Thurston Dart and Denis Stevens were among those who gave early music a renewed impetus through inspired teaching, performances and scholarship, encouraging David Munrow and especially Christopher Hogwood to put theory into practice and act as a catalyst for a wide range of period instrumentalists.

There had already been a long tradition of early music at Basle when the gambist August Wenzinger co-founded the Schola Cantorum Basiliensis in 1933. Established as a teaching and research institute for the study of music from the Middle Ages to Mozart, it gave a new prominence to instrumental music, though retaining a sacred and secular vocal syllabus. Its avowed intention was that early music should become an integral part of everyday life, whilst aspiring to professional standards rather than those of the dilettante. Nikolaus Harnoncourt founded his Concentus Musicus in 1953 and he has subsequently been a seminal figure as writer and scholar. The violinist Franzjosef Maier's Collegium Aureum was established in 1962, pioneering the recording of classical repertory on original instruments well in advance of such major figures as Christopher Hogwood and Roger Norrington.

Members of the Leonhardt family were also highly influential, especially in the Netherlands, which in the 1950s and 1960s became one of the world centres of the early music movement. The Kuijken brothers, Frans Brüggen and Anner Bylsma were among those who established a Dutch school which Laurence Dreyfus has described as 'strikingly speech-like by mimicking ever-shifting patterns of thought'.[10] Leonhardt remarked that we have gradually begun to see that Baroque music is, if anything, *more* expressive than Romantic music, but in detail rather than large lines. The eminent recorder player Frans Brüggen soon brought his own distinctive expressive style to a variety of later music with his Orchestra of the Eighteenth Century.

The espousal of period performance by record companies provided a major commercial impetus to the early music movement as long ago as the 1930s. In the post-war period much Baroque music was recorded on period instruments, often for record labels especially created for the purpose. In 1954 Wenzinger co-directed the Capella Coloniensis, a period-instrument chamber orchestra formed by Westdeutscher Rundfunk to record and tour worldwide. The following year Wenzinger's performance of Monteverdi's *Orfeo* was a notable success; other milestones included Harnoncourt's

Brandenburg Concertos for Telefunken in 1964. By 1972 Leonhardt and Harnoncourt were embarking on a monumental Bach cantata series, contemporary with the foundation of English ensembles by Gardiner, Hogwood, Norrington and Pinnock. At this time the explosion in the recording industry attracted an increasing number of converts to historical performance; among other star performers were Reinhard Goebel, William Christie, Ton Koopman, Arnold Ostman and Jordi Savall. Significantly, the most prominent early music ensembles of the 1970s and 1980s were not collegium-type groups or small consorts but full orchestras of period instruments, such as the Amsterdam Baroque Orchestra and Les Arts Florissants.

Decca's complete cycle of Mozart's symphonies by Hogwood, Jaap Schröder and the Academy of Ancient Music under the scholarly eye of Neal Zaslaw proved a significant turning point, after which performers and scholars began to work together on various projects, including opera. As Robin Stowell has observed, 'Both factions recognised the irrationality of Bach being played as if it were Beethoven, and Mozart as if it were Wagner, and the 'performance practice' movement began truly to blossom'.[11] Period Beethoven cycles continued apace, whilst Berlioz, Mendelssohn, Schumann, Brahms, Wagner and Verdi also proved ripe for treatment, with Britain's self-governing Orchestra of the Age of Enlightenment playing an especially prominent role in this later repertory. Several groups, notably the New Queen's Hall Orchestra, have specialised in the period performance of early modern music. So historical awareness has eventually overlapped with the era of early recordings, bringing a further perspective to its aspirations and limitations.

The changed profile of the recording industry at the start of the new millennium has wrought some profound alterations to the world of historical performance. Whilst the development of the compact disc was timed nicely to give the early music revival a vital boost in the 1980s, the downturn some twenty years later reflected the difficulty of selling classical recordings in a glutted market. Many companies abolished their separate early music imprints, prompting some period orchestras to found their own labels. The satellite ensembles equipped to tackle baroque and early classical repertory which John Eliot Gardiner was urging upon orchestral managers ten years ago never came into being.[12] But in today's climate, a new flexibility within early music discredits the idea that there is a single historical style to which everyone must conform, while profoundly influencing unexpected areas of the mainstream, including the Berlin Philharmonic, the Philharmonia and the London Symphony Orchestra.

Kenyon has remarked that the early music movement has, in the view of some, left too many wounded and injured in its path. Yet Andras Schiff and Murray Perahia are among those to have collaborated with modern-instrument orchestras to play Bach concertos on the piano, while Haydn and Mozart are slowly finding their way back into symphony orchestra schedules. Charles Mackerras has been notably successful in introducing natural horns and trumpets and period timpani into the modern-instrument Scottish Chamber Orchestra, for classical repertory. Meanwhile, distinctive Brahms symphony cycles by Harnoncourt and Mackerras have benefited from the insights of a considered historical perspective. This rapprochement of styles testifies to the true value and potential of historical awareness.

The value of historical performance

In 1983 Laurence Dreyfus offered a comparison of the dominant social codes of early music and the mainstream.[13] At that time he asserted that early music was attempting to hold musicians' envious desires in check by negating every sign of social difference. The heavy price for this was an enforced routine and a uniform mediocrity. Early music was characterised by its banishment of the conductor, the equality and versatility of its ensemble members, implicit discouragement of virtuosity, mediocre technical professional standards, identification of audience with performers (and repertory), dull and homogeneous programmes, and critical reports of instruments, composers and pieces, rather than performer and interpretation. The scene described here could perhaps be applied to some of the post-war medieval, Renaissance and baroque groups but clearly pre-dates the era of those star directors whose orchestras took on board a varying degree of characteristics from the mainstream. Indeed, the presence of a conductor in repertory such as Mozart's piano concertos has been clearly motivated by some other force than historical fidelity, since these pieces were originally directed by the soloist.

Some of the most trenchant criticisms of historical performance predate the recent rise in technical standards. Dreyfus found an unprecedented attack on the infamy of early music in the work of the French surgeon and self-proclaimed sexologist Gérard Zwang, a tirade which he attributes to 'a process of musical defamiliarisation which has robbed him of prized possessions'. Zwang's 1977 book *A Contre-Bruit* speaks of worthless antiquarianism, anti-art and of 'those old buggies which they have the effrontery to call musical instruments'.[14] The comments by virtuoso violinist Pinchas Zukerman have already acquired a certain notoriety: historical performance is 'asinine stuff ... a complete and absolute farce ... nobody wants to hear that stuff. I don't.'[15] Orchestral conductors have remained as divided as ever, with fierce criticism from such diverse characters as Pierre Boulez, Colin Davis and Neville Marriner counterbalanced by enthusiastic espousal by such notable figures as Mark Elder, Charles Mackerras and Simon Rattle.[16]

Most conductors of an earlier generation were sceptical. Leopold Stokowski, for example, contrasted the written and literal aspects of music with its importance in our imagination and its constant evolution; in this belief in musical progress, which he defended until his death in 1974, he was a true child of the nineteenth century. On the other hand, Arturo Toscanini believed passionately in a literal respect for the score, a position fraught with difficulty in (for example) Baroque repertory, where conventions of notation were subject to substantial change. In an article of 1932 Wilhelm Furtwängler was highly critical of the trend towards small-scale performances of Baroque music, for which chamber orchestras were soon to arise; as for historical performance, he dismissed its practical relevance.

Some forceful counter-arguments have been adduced by protagonists, fortepianist Malcolm Bilson memorably remarking: 'One of the things that is missing in most modern playing is that there are not enough ingredients in it.'[17] The art of rhetoric was continually emphasised in the eighteenth century and an over-standardised approach to articulation has increasingly been seen to fail to emulate what is implied by the evidence. It has been acknowledged that a revival of interest in the subtleties of continuo accompaniment, which differed according to period, genre, nationality and even locality, has greatly enhanced recent baroque performance. On stringed instruments, it has been realised that vibrato was normally employed selectively as an expressive ornament until the late nineteenth century and became continuous only at the beginning of the twentieth. Distinctive national styles and preferences, extending from compositional idiom to instrument manufacture and playing techniques, have been taken into account in varying degrees.[18] Tempo flexibility was always a vital element in music-making of earlier times and has been one of the most difficult features to recreate, since neither notation nor words can accurately delineate it. This area illustrates the importance of interpreting historical evidence in the spirit of its own time; little of it is unambiguous, as shown by the vast range of approaches cultivated by period performers of the present day.

An important development during the past fifty years has been the realisation that music after 1750 could benefit from historical awareness. In 1955 H. C. Robbins Landon remarked in his otherwise far-sighted book on Haydn's symphonies that 'no-one will want to perform Haydn's music with natural trumpets and ancient woodwind when our modern counterparts are in most cases superior in every way', a viewpoint which held sway for some considerable time.[19] In 1969 a well-known dictionary made a clear distinction between baroque and classical styles: 'In the period after Bach the problems of performance practice largely disappear, owing to the more specific directions of composers for clearly indicating their intentions.'[20] Even in 1980 the article 'Performing practice' in *The New Grove* claimed that in contrast to music written before 1750 'there has been no severance of contact with post-Baroque music as a whole, nor with the instruments used in performing it'. Subsequent musical revelations proved this argument untenable; in the event, performance practice from Brahms's time was shown to be fraught with ambiguities that are in some ways as challenging as those relating to earlier periods. *The New Grove* appeared just at the time when later repertories were about to be explored on period instruments. Howard Mayer Brown's observation that 'the practical difficulties of assembling and equipping such an orchestra [for Beethoven symphonies] are almost insuperable' was soon overtaken by events. Norrington's spectacular Beethoven cycle in the 1980s was revelatory by any standards, beginning with a remarkable recording of the Second and Eighth Symphonies. Just a decade later classical and romantic performing performance was the subject of a meticulously researched 662-page book.[21] Significantly, *The New Grove II* (London, 2001) described early music as 'a term once applied to music of the Baroque and earlier periods, but now commonly used to denote any music for which a historically appropriate style of performance must be reconstructed on the basis of surviving scores'.

As already noted, the reduction of music from all periods to a standard style and instrumentation (as was happening in the mainstream from the 1960s) had inevitably become a cause for concern, as at least one world-class violinist admitted at that time.[22] Harnoncourt dates the origins of such an approach to the simplification of music and its confinement to the emotional sphere at the time of the French Revolution. The newly founded Paris Conservatoire initiated the trend for drilling performance techniques rather than teaching music as a language. Wagner was a great admirer of this new performance aesthetic, replacing verbal elements of interpretation with the pictorial. Today's reversal of this in the name of historical performance may be as characteristic of our own time as of earlier periods, as Richard Taruskin has famously argued:

> I am convinced that 'historical' performance today is not really historical; that a thin veneer of historicism clothes a performance style that is completely of our own time, and is in fact the most modern style around; and that the historical hardware has won its wide acceptance, and above all its commercial viability precisely by virtues of its novelty, not its antiquity.[23]

But as another writer has put it, no one can doubt that historical – or at any rate historically informed – performance has unquestionably become the dominant musical ideology of our time.

Taruskin proposes that the ambience of emotional detachment is the hardest to justify on historical grounds, claiming that an equation with freedom from error or anachronism constitutes texts rather than acts. The evidence of recordings from the early twentieth century supports this argument. Robert Philip has remarked that such performances give a vivid sense of being projected spontaneously and that the balance of priorities has since shifted towards clarity and accuracy. If pre-war recordings resemble live performance, many of today's concerts show a palpable influence of the recording session, with control and detail an overriding priority.[24] Norrington surely underestimates the value of early recordings for recreating Brahms, when he writes, 'In seeking for a historical viewpoint, we can only hope for limited help from them.'[25]

Musical expression

The degree of expression appropriate in the context of 'early music' was an important issue throughout the twentieth century. Dart concluded his book with the observation, 'The written text must never be regarded as a dead laboratory specimen; it is only sleeping, though both love and time will be needed to awaken it. But love and time will be wasted without a sense of tradition and of historical continuity . . . .'[26] Dart was critical of Dolmetsch's waywardness and reliance on hunches, but nevertheless his comment reflects the older man's rejection of the idea that 'expression in music is a modern thing, and that the old music requires nothing beyond mechanical precision'.[27] Later scholars were keen to lay down rules of interpretation. But the art of music remained more difficult to quantify than the craft, a point signalled in Türk's *Clavierschule* of 1789, which lays out various stylistic precepts but finally admits that some aspects of musicianship cannot be taught and that all one can do is simply listen to the best singers.[28]

The widespread aversion to 'interpretation' has been linked with Stravinskian neo-classicism, as performers shied away, not just from virtuosity and exhibitionism, but from interventionism of any kind. When artists were thanked for their voluntary restraint in recreating an atmosphere of tranquillity appropriate for early music, authenticity was bound to get a bad name, making the term 'scholarly' when applied to performance synonymous with dull and unimaginative. Meanwhile, the critic Theodor Adorno wrote of 'impotent nostalgia' during the course of one of his celebrated articles.[29] Adorno was especially critical of Hindemith, who in fact showed himself well aware of the inevitable subjectivity of interpretation, whilst eloquently defining the value of a historical approach in his book *A Composer's World* of 1952.

Some thirty years later Laurence Dreyfus could justifiably remark upon the conspiracy of silence surrounding the cultural phenomenon of 'Early Music'. He argued that the 'authentic' musician acted willingly in the service of the composer, denying any form of self-expression, but attained this by following the textbook rules for 'scientific method' with a strictly empirical programme to verify historical practices. These, when all is said and done, are magically transformed into the composer's intentions. Dreyfus highlights the irony that the puritan has implanted the civilised ban on the uninhibited expression of feelings directly into the art form whose purpose it was, in the first place, to sublimate it. He concluded that the real advances were by 1983 not in the outward signs of historicity, such as original instruments, verifiable performing forces or text-critical editions, but in the revised operations in the minds of the players. The question of musical expression was notoriously brought into focus in a 1984 review of Hogwood's Mozart Symphonies, which praised them for being 'not merely under-interpreted but uninterpreted', thereby offering 'potentially an experience of unequalled authenticity, using that word in a sense as much existential as musicological'.[30]

Practical expediency versus historical accuracy

It is strange that prior to 1980 no coherent opposition was ever launched to the very idea of period instruments and the notion of historical authenticity. The strong and detailed attack on its whole philosophical basis that might have been expected never materialised. At that time questionable technical standards were allied to musical mannerisms – 'thin whiney string sounds with exaggerated "bulges", dodgy intonation, woodwind squawks and squeaks of the most painful kind'.[31] The prevailing air of supreme confidence and exclusivity among certain period players might well have provoked such a formal outburst, reflecting the verbal denunciation among players which was then common.

In 1984 Hans Keller could bluntly assert that 'most of the authentic boys just aren't good enough as players to make their way without musicological crutches'.[32] A year later Joseph Kerman complained of the toleration of relaxed standards of instrumental and vocal technique, as well as of interpretation.[33] As the 'early music movement' developed from a radical fringe activity into a major part of international musical life, its original pioneering spirit was all too easily eclipsed by the requirements of a post-modern technical proficiency. No one can doubt that mastery of an instrument is invaluable, provided that it is nourished by continuing stylistic awareness. In any event, the image of the early musician as an eccentric counterculture figure is now thoroughly outdated, with period orchestras retaining administrative staff to handle promotion, tours, recording and fundraising.

Some former claims to authenticity or even historical accuracy now seem over-stated, if not embarrassing. Expressions such as 'the most original Beethoven yet recorded'[34] have become ever more scarce. During the heady days of recording activity in 1992 Clive Brown issued a timely warning that the characteristics of some of the instruments employed in Beethoven cycles by The Hanover Band, Hogwood and Norrington would certainly not have been familiar to the musicians in Beethoven's Vienna, and that the situation with regard to playing techniques was even more complicated. He claimed with some justification that the commercially motivated race to push period performance ever more rapidly into the nineteenth century did not offer much hope that the musicians, even if they obtained the appropriate instruments, would have the opportunity to find or consolidate appropriate styles of playing them. He rightly notes that there is infinitely more to historically sensitive performance than merely employing the right equipment, and that the public is in danger of being offered attractively packaged but unripe fruit.[35] It is true that each period orchestral musician occupies an individual position within a spectrum ranging from historical awareness to practical expediency, often with insufficient consciousness of his own or his colleagues' stance. For the general public the phrase 'on original instruments' does literally cover a multitude of varying practices.

Earlier players used new instruments and this alone might be thought sufficient justification for commissioning replicas, many of which involve some element of compromise. For example, modern methods of making gut strings constitute an inevitable improvement on the past. Regrettably, weights of bows and some of their characteristics have sometimes been attuned to the tastes of players in modern symphony orchestras who dabble in period performance. Furthermore, some contemporary makers have been guilty of beefing up their reproduction instruments to make their sound more acceptable to modern ears, for example by adding extra keys to woodwinds.[36] In this respect, the lack of organological interest among period conductors has offered little incentive for change.

By way of example, a new species of vented trumpet designed for today's conditions has been described in detail by Robert Barclay:

> The natural trumpet is the one instrument not yet fully revived for use in the performance of Baroque music . . . . Most current players have taken to using machine-made instruments with as many as four finger-holes placed in their tubing near to pressure nodes, so that the so-called 'out-of-tune harmonics' of the natural series . . . will not be unpleasant to modern sensitivity. The vented instruments that have resulted from this recent 'invention of tradition' are often equipped with so many anachronistic

8.1 The Hanover Band directed by Roy Goodman at London's Banqueting House. Photo © Alex von Koettlitz

features that the result is a trumpet which resembles its baroque counterpart only superficially, whose playing technique is quite different, and whose timbre is far removed from that expected for Baroque music.[37]

Reproduction instruments tend to be standardised in all kinds of unhistorical ways. For example, relatively few original woodwinds are being copied in relation to the rapidly increasing number of players. The use of an electronic tuner to impose equal temperament can be misguided. Furthermore, pitch has been unrealistically restricted in recent historical performance, with an almost exclusive focus upon $a'=415$ (baroque), $a'=430$ (classical) and $a'=435$ or 440 (romantic). This is no more than a conventional and over-simplified response to the evidence, even though the degree of acceptable compromise will vary according to musical context. Ironically, Quantz in 1752 lamented the lack of a uniform pitch, which he reckoned was detrimental to his work as a flautist and also to music in general; he expressed the hope that a universal standard would soon find favour. Significantly, a wind manufacturer's advertisement in the *Wiener Zeitung* of 25 February 1789 contained a request that prospective foreign clients should specify the

8.2 Colin Lawson playing Mozart's Clarinet Concerto on a basset clarinet recreated by the Cambridge maker Daniel Bangham. Photo © Bill Cooper

required pitch, 'whether Vienna pitch, *Kammerton,* or even French pitch, or send him a tuning fork . . . '[38]

Original wind instruments survive in a variety of conditions; the finest are eminently playable, but internal bore measurements are especially susceptible to change and there may sometimes be evidence of attempts to alter the pitch. Nevertheless, antiques have a special value for the amount of historical information they can impart and can also have an investment value in accordance with the laws of supply and demand. An old wooden instrument can be particularly prone to cracking when subjected to the changes in atmospheric conditions associated with central heating or air travel; curators of collections world-wide vary widely in their attitude to conservation, some allowing instruments to be borrowed, others promoting policies closer to a museum culture.

Orchestral achievements and aspirations

No amount of research into musical conditions and practices can give an unambiguous indication of the original effect. Written descriptions of concert standards are notoriously difficult to interpret. A famous example is Burney's account of the Mannheim orchestra as 'an army of generals, equally fit to plan a battle, as to fight it'; for he qualified his enthusiasm of the wind tuning, whose sourness was reckoned by him to be a universal orchestral problem.[39] In fact, it has become normal to interpret selectively some of the more wayward portrayals of musical standards in aiming to recreate the best of what has gone before. An oft-quoted example is the celebrated account of the Lyons orchestra in 1785–6, whose problems were surely not unique. It is reported that the leader had neither intelligence nor an accurate style of performance and that there were unauthorised absences among his colleagues for reasons which we should now regard as paltry.[40] At this period most concerts (unlike opera) could usually count on only one rehearsal and sometimes there were none.

The historical evidence of original concert venues is nowadays often ignored for commercial reasons. By 1700 spaces whose grand architecture was politically inspired contrasted with smaller arenas whose character was motivated by artistic considerations. Here the proximity of performers and audience encouraged a subtle, articulated delivery, by comparison with the larger-scale Romantic approach. Only in the nineteenth century were the grand civic halls built to house the new philharmonic societies and the large-scale music-making they represented. In recent years original concert programmes have been increasingly subject to scrutiny, though rarely have they been recreated. Variety and novelty were often important, comprising a mixture of solo, chamber, orchestral and vocal music; the solo recital is a comparatively recent development.

In the first half of the eighteenth century orchestral size and make-up depended as much on circumstance as on the demands of the work to be performed. Available players and size of hall were important factors, and so a surviving score might not necessarily indicate how a work was originally performed. Bach's aspirations of a 'well-appointed church music', stated in his famous memorandum of 23 August 1730 to the Leipzig Council, amounted to a mere 18–20 players; it seems clear that he lacked even what resources he deemed necessary.[41] Many musicians (including Bach) regarded orchestral layout as of the utmost importance, and it was far from standardised.[42] As with musical direction and conducting, such historical evidence has not always been carefully adhered to. Brahms conducted orchestras of varying sizes; his close association with the Meiningen orchestra, which was less than fifty-strong, has led some scholars to conclude that he actually preferred smaller ensembles. There is no firm evidence for this; it was surely rather the disciplined training of the conductor Hans von Bülow which attracted Brahms to Meiningen. In any event it has only recently been acknowledged that Brahms's music suffers from an interpretation that applies the Wagnerian ideal of an endless, long-line melody and the heavy sound and texture appropriate for Bayreuth. His favourite seating plans have been recently reconstituted with some success, notably a division of the violins and placement of cellos and basses on each wing.

Earlier styles of orchestral playing have been recreated with reference to a variety of primary source materials, ranging from instrumental and theoretical treatises to surviving instruments, iconography, archives, journals, newspaper reports, letters and diaries. This list could also be extended to include aspects of other art forms such as dance, some steps of which may have important implications for musical tempo. Instrumental and vocal treatises have offered the most direct access to fundamental technical instruction, interpretation and more general matters such as notation, musical history, expression, taste and aesthetics. As they usually present the fruits of many years of thought, experience and observation, their instructions may lag behind actual contemporary practice. It has been justifiably claimed that treatises cannot be used safely without assessment of the personality, background, knowledge, status and influence of the writer, the credibility, reliability and consistency of both the treatise's textual content and the musical style and aesthetic it propounds, the readership to whom it is addressed, its relationship to other sources, its geographical and temporal limitations, and its relationship to the repertory (and the composers) to which it is applicable.[43]

The assimilation of such historical information enables earlier performances to be recreated rather than merely reproduced. In a world of few certainties, Gustav Leonhardt has recently summarised the historical performer's best aspirations: 'When one is a student one does things consciously, but when one is more experienced one does not play intellectually any more. One doesn't *think*; one has *thought* . . . things are done automatically, depending on what you intend to say.'[44] For many musicians, the artistic results speak for themselves; meanwhile, some leading practitioners have moved from studying treatises to writing their own, material which will undoubtedly be studied years from now as evidence of how today's performers approached historical performance. Times may at present be harder in purely commercial terms, yet as Nicholas Kenyon has recently claimed, there is no worthwhile, thoughtful, intellectually stimulating and musically adventurous performance going on today that has not been touched by the period instrument movement. This may yet turn out to be its greatest legacy.

9 Recording the orchestra

JOHN RUSHBY-SMITH

'Will the Oracle in the Cave of Harmony please speak?' According to legend, the conductor Sir Thomas Beecham would utter these words on completing a recording take. 'The Cave of Harmony' was the recording booth. 'The Oracle' was the recording engineer.

If Beecham's sarcastic wit endeared him to his champions, it probably upset some of his collaborators. Working (literally) at the cutting edge, his engineers, like today's, would have been doing their best to capture his performances in their full glory, but for most of Beecham's lifetime they were constrained by an inadequate medium. Not only was the sound quality deficient, but the performances themselves were also compromised. The maximum time that could be recorded on one side of a 78 rpm shellac disc was about five minutes. Domestic listeners to extended classical works were obliged to change record sides at frequent intervals, which impaired concentration, and broadcasters had to resort to multiple copies and deft changeover procedures in order to present a recorded work in uninterrupted form. Moreover, conductors were obliged to choose tempi that matched side changes to natural musical junctions, so when, for example, we hear Gustav Holst conducting 'Mars' from his own *Planets* suite in a very fast five minutes, it is unwise to deduce that this reveals the definitive tempo.

Despite the early limitations, recording has transformed musical appreciation. It is through recordings that we can still appreciate the drama of Callas or the virtuosity of Heifetz. As Robert Philip demonstrates in chapter 12, the huge canon of recorded material accumulated over the last century means that scholars no longer need to speculate over such matters as whether the strings played with vibrato or portamento or how much rubato pianists used. The evidence is there for all to hear. Had recording been available in the eighteenth century, the endless current debates about authenticity could be resolved at the drop of a needle. Imagine the impact on present-day interpretation if some contemporary engineer had been able to record, say, Bach's orchestra at the Court of Brandenburg or the world première of Mozart's *Don Giovanni*.

The hi-fi revolution

Recording really came of age with the advent of the high-fidelity long-playing microgroove record (LP) in the 1950s. This permitted accurate reproduction of the full range of audible frequencies and, being made from vinyl, the LP was largely free of the surface noise that bedevilled its shellac predecessor. Furthermore, up to thirty minutes could be recorded on one side of a disc. Stereo further enhanced the listening experience a few years later by adding a spatial dimension akin to that encountered in the live environment. VHF/FM transmission systems brought about a concurrent improvement in radio broadcasting quality.

Since then, improvements have mainly concerned the recording medium itself. The 1970s saw the introduction of noise reduction systems that attenuated the tape hiss inherent in analogue master recordings, and by the mid-1980s digital technology eliminated it altogether. Once encoded in digital form, recordings can be copied from one digital medium to another without degradation of quality. By the 1990s, digital CDs (Compact Discs) almost entirely supplanted the LP. Physically robust, CDs can hold seventy-five minutes or so of unbroken music and the sound quality is theoretically indistinguishable from that of a master recording. In its turn, the CD is now under threat from memory-based systems, accessible in cyber-space, and the future will doubtless see whole symphonies stored on microchips the size of a pinhead.

Acoustics

A good recording naturally depends upon many factors beyond the merely technical. Musical excellence, achieved most obviously through the choice of performers, is a *sine qua non*. Then comes the performing environment. This includes mundane considerations such as heating, lighting and lack of extraneous noise, but the paramount requirement is a helpful acoustic. Put a virtuoso violinist with a priceless Stradivarius in the middle of a field and the sound will be thin and lifeless, however brilliantly he or she plays. Place the same artist in (say) Carnegie Hall and the sound will bloom. What the hall adds is reverberation, which blends the 'raw' sound with reflections off surrounding surfaces.

Reverberation adds fullness and drama to a sound, but it must be the right sort. Too much causes the sound to become confused and 'muddy', whereas too little produces a lifeless quality. Too much treble reverberation makes the sound shrill or harsh; too much bass reverberation makes it boomy. Over-long reverberation times and specific echoes can blur clarity, as anyone old enough to have experienced London's Royal Albert Hall before the installation of the 'flying saucers'[1] will remember. As Beecham quipped, 'British composers should all endeavour to have their works performed in this hall; they will thus be assured of at least two performances.'[2]

Achieving the optimum reverberation characteristics is the prime objective of modern auditorium design. In pursuit of this end, an even diffusion of reflections is crucial. Halls such as Symphony Hall in Birmingham, England, or the Meyerson Symphony Center in Dallas, Texas, have huge reflectors suspended from the ceiling. Canberra's Llewellyn Hall in Australia uses massive vertical panels to great effect. In Berlin's Philharmonie, Leipzig's Gewandhaus, Tokyo's Suntory Hall and Cardiff's St David's Hall (among others), the audience sits in 'vineyard' blocks, whose concrete fascias form a complex arrangement of reflectors, designed to distribute the sound evenly around the auditorium.

Absorption

In a large hall, much of the reflected sound reaches a listener significantly later than the direct sound. This helps the ear to distinguish between attack and reverberation. In small halls or recording studios, however, reflected and direct sounds arrive almost, but not quite, simultaneously. This can blur attack and impede precision. The sound may also become saturated and uncomfortably loud – no joke for players who often spend many hours in such surroundings. To control such problems some sound absorption may be necessary. Wooden membranes with air gaps behind them and cavities within the walls themselves can be tuned to resonate at, and hence absorb, lower and middle frequencies, while foam padding and fabric drapes can absorb unwanted high-frequency reflections.

In all auditoria, some absorption is inevitable. Soft materials damp sound and in acoustic terms people are soft, as are the seats they sit on. Modern practice gives empty seats the same absorption coefficient as occupied ones, thereby achieving minimal acoustical variation between rehearsals in an empty hall and performances in a full house.

Myths and mishaps

Many misconceptions surround acoustics. One of the most prevalent ascribes almost magical properties to wood. Visually wood is perceived as warm, and since to some extent what you see can affect what you hear, many people presume that wood gives a 'warm' sound. However, unless they are dense and rigid, wooden structures will tend to resonate and, as described above, will absorb valuable sound energy. In practice, most of the world's best halls are either concrete or plaster over brick – materials that reflect sound.

Another popular myth is the notion that modern science is inferior to empirical instinct. Famous nineteenth-century halls such as the Grosser Musikvereinsaal in Vienna or Amsterdam's Concertgebouw are cited to back this view and it is indeed likely that their excellent acoustics arose from inspired guesswork, helped by the fortuitous functions of a 'shoe-box' shape, which produces strong lateral reflections, and ornate plasterwork, which diffuses reflections evenly. Conveniently ignored are the same period's numerous poor halls, whose acoustics bear witness to naïve theories more often inspired, one suspects, by the dynamics of the ear trumpet than by an understanding of physics. In contrast, Richard Wagner's Festspielhaus in Bayreuth (1876) reveals an astute awareness of acoustical performance, and the much-vaunted Symphony Hall in Boston, Massachusetts, built in 1900, is the product of assiduous acoustical research applied by Wallace Sabine, a professor of physics at Harvard University and a founding father of modern auditorium design.

It took another sixty years for musical acoustics to evolve into the refined art it is today. Meanwhile, ambitious predictions published before auditoria were completed exposed acousticians to attack. The opening in 1951 of London's Royal Festival Hall coincided with the rise of hi-fi. Clarity was a prime objective but although the sound was clear, it lacked dynamic impact. When the conductor Ernest Ansermet was told that in the Festival Hall you could hear a pin drop, he reputedly remarked: 'But I don't want to hear a pin drop; I want to hear an orchestra.' The shortcoming was not entirely the fault of the acousticians. To save on structural costs, the density of the plaster ceiling was reduced, so it acted more like a resonating absorber than as a reflector. Eventually electronic 'assisted resonance' was installed. A somewhat desperate measure, this involved a system of microphones and loudspeakers disposed all over the ceiling.

A similar fate befell the Philharmonic Hall in New York's Lincoln Center a decade later. Optimistic expectations were confounded by reality and the hall was radically refurbished in 1972 at great expense, eventually taking the name of its enabling benefactor, Avery Fisher.

The present

Nowadays there is a consensus regarding what makes for good musical acoustics. Modern acoustic designers seek to combine a flattering acoustic profile with even distribution of sound throughout the auditorium. Players need to hear each other clearly, so great care is taken with platform design. Size is important too. Sound can saturate a small space uncomfortably and can lose impact in a very large one, so the optimal capacity has settled at between 2,000 and 3,000 seats, with an overall volume of around eight cubic metres per seat. Today's acousticians use scale models and/or computer simulation to predict acoustical performance and in recent years have achieved highly successful results. Many splendid modern halls around the world now meet the highest criteria and the concomitant improvement in the orchestral environment has had a noteworthy effect on performance standards. If a hall is rewarding to play in, musicians will automatically play better.

Following the best acoustical practice is not always easy. Acousticians may have to accommodate the sculptural ambitions of architects or the economically determined, but acoustically incompatible, demands of symphony concert on the one hand and corporate convention on the other. Meeting these demands has given rise to the multi-purpose hall and although some very clever systems for varying acoustic response have been devised, very few such halls have proved wholly successful for orchestral music.

Microphone techniques and stereo

Let us assume a top orchestra and soloist have been engaged to record a piano concerto in a fine hall. The work will be recorded digitally in stereo.

In principle, the sound a listener hears in the centre of the hall should be close to the ideal. Theoretically, all that is needed is to place a microphone in a similar position and record its signal on a digital recorder. To achieve stereo, however, there must be two discrete signals. Stereo is an illusion. We hear the sound of two loudspeakers, but when both produce an identical sound each of our ears hears an identical sound and we perceive it as emanating from a point midway between the two sources. Comparing sounds between two ears is how we locate sound in nature and our brains are capable of interpreting minute differences in amplitude, time, phase and frequency.

Instead of a single microphone, therefore, we must use two. A favoured method is the 'Blumlein'[3] or 'coincident' pair. This consists of two microphones mounted close together on a common bracket, or sometimes contained within a common case. The microphones must be directional, which means that they are more sensitive to sound on their axes than from their sides. They are arranged so that one faces towards the left and the other to the right. An angle of forty-five degrees each way is usual and will normally ensure that the violins are louder on the left microphone and the cellos and basses louder on the right-hand one. Instruments in the middle, such as the violas, woodwind and piano, will be equally loud on both microphones.

Typically, the recording equipment will be installed in a 'control room', acoustically isolated from the main hall. The sound will be 'monitored' over a pair of loudspeakers, each reproducing the sound of its respective microphone. All being well, the spread of sound in the control room will resemble that in the hall: the violins will appear to the left, the cellos and basses to the right and the violas, woodwind and piano will occupy the middle.

Balance

Besides a clear stereo image, three other elements must be considered: Perspective, Proportion and Quality. Perspective is the apparent distance of the performers from us, the listeners. Proportion is the relative balance between performers. Quality defines whether performers sound as they should sound or, more subtly, as they hope they sound.

In our hypothetical control room, the sound may seem more diffuse than it does in the hall. This is because some of the reflected sound, including that from behind the microphones, is picked up by the same microphones and added to the frontal sound emanating from the loudspeakers. To rectify this *perspective* error the ratio of direct to reflected sound must be increased by moving the microphones closer to the orchestra. However, this means they are now *proportionally* much closer to the piano than they are to the woodwind, and the piano may sound too strong.

To correct this, the microphones may be raised so that they 'look' over the piano, but this can impair the piano's sound *quality*. Pianos are designed so that sound reflects off the lid, and placing microphones above the soundboard and hammers can make the instrument sound hard-edged. It may therefore be preferable to leave the main pair *in situ* and install an additional pair of microphones above the woodwind. It is now possible that the strings will sound weak, so two separate microphones may be installed a few metres either side of the main stereo pair. As no more than two microphones can be connected directly to a two-channel recorder, a 'mixer' must now be used. Each microphone is accorded its own volume, tone and panning (left/right balance) controls, making it possible to adjust how much of each ingredient is put into the 'mix', to modify its sound (if necessary) and to control where it is placed in the stereo image.

Alternative methods

The above example is an amalgam of two methods. In the 1930s, pioneering essays into stereophony took different routes in Europe and the USA. While the Europeans pursued Blumlein's method, Dr Harvey Fletcher of Bell

Laboratories in the USA was experimenting with 'spaced' microphones. This technique uses two omni-directional microphones spaced some distance apart and, unlike the Blumlein method, which is amplitude-dependent, it exploits time differences. Being nearer to them, the left-hand microphone will 'hear' the violins a split second before the right-hand one does. Spaced omnidirectional microphones tend to give a fuller sound but the stereo effect can be unfocused, with the sound forming two distinct pools. To overcome this, later developments increased the number of microphones to three or more, with their outputs being 'panned' to appropriate positions in the stereo image.

A system developed in Germany combines the amplitude and time elements of both techniques and adds phase and frequency factors. It involves the insertion of microphones into the ears of a *Kunstkopf* – a dummy head, made from polystyrene. This acts as a baffle that attenuates high frequency sounds coming from the opposite side, while the physical separation of the microphones introduces differences in phase and time. Impaled upon a stand, the *Kunstkopf* surveys hapless musicians with all the inscrutability of a rather ghoulish critic. 'Binaural' stereo is a distillation of this technique that replaces the *Kunstkopf* with a simple – and less intimidating – Perspex disc.

In pursuit of realism, forays have also been made into quadraphony, but none of the commercially viable systems proved compatible with good stereo presentation and limited demand saw its early demise in all but a few specialist markets.

Extended techniques

Matters may be complicated by many factors. Vocal soloists usually need their own microphones, as their voices rarely penetrate the orchestral texture to sufficient degree, especially in a recording, where the listener is 'blind'. By dint of their position behind the orchestra, choruses may also need separate microphone cover, particularly to assist word clarity. Some orchestral layouts call for the addition of 'spot' microphones to help instruments that would otherwise be overwhelmed.

In some halls and studios, the acoustics may be too 'dry' and may dictate judicious use of artificial reverberation. In early days, mainly for effects in radio drama productions, 'reverb' was added using an echo room. The output of a microphone was sent to a loudspeaker placed in a bare room with hard walls and another microphone in the room picked up the resulting sound and fed it back into the mix. Later devices were electro-mechanical. Instead of a room they involved a coiled spring, a steel plate or a sheet of gold foil, energised at one end by the appropriate sound with the resulting 'twang' being picked up at the other. They could be surprisingly effective

9.1 Pierre Boulez recording with the BBC Symphony Orchestra in the BBC's Maida Vale studio (1980s). Note the absorption panels on the walls and the stereo microphones suspended behind the conductor and over the centre of the orchestra. Photo: Alex von Koettlitz

but have now been supplanted by elaborate digital reverberators that can synthesise almost any desired acoustic.

Whichever tools are used, judging balance calls for musical awareness and an aptitude for aural analysis. The best recording engineers earn their reputations through aural and artistic acuity, rather than through technical dexterity.

Production and editing

Most recording sessions are directed by a producer. Called a *Tonmeister* in Germany or *directeur artistique* in France, the producer works closely with the performers and engineer. Free from the encumbrances of playing, singing, conducting or manipulating knobs, the producer is able to concentrate wholly on the minutiae of performance. The best will also use their experience to advise on matters of interpretation, and must be able to combine tact with authority. Producers are also responsible for running sessions, making sure that everything is recorded within the time available and that mistakes, technical or musical, are corrected.

It is common practice to record a short passage and invite the principal artists to hear a playback before committing to a balance. Once agreement has been reached and the conductor has regained his podium, recording can begin in earnest. Over a talkback system the producer asks for silence in the hall, the recorders are started (usually recordings are made in duplicate for safety's sake) and a red light is switched on as a signal to begin. Ideally, an entire movement would be recorded in one go, or 'take', but let us suppose that there were some noticeable lapses in ensemble between the soloist and orchestra at bar X, and the brass were too loud at bar Y. In Beecham's day this would have meant either ignoring the flaws or recording the whole movement again. Fortunately, the advent of tape recording made it possible to cut and splice, enabling the relevant passages to be re-recorded on their own for insertion at a subsequent editing session.

Physically cutting and joining analogue tape has to be very precise and there is always a risk of damaging or losing the original material. Many an editing session has seen editors rummaging around on the cutting-room floor looking for a few centimetres of tape. Today's editing is done digitally using a computer – much like cutting and pasting on a word-processor but with added facilities that enable blending across the joins and, *in extremis*, the adjustment of tempo and even pitch. Since digital editing is non-destructive, edits can be reworked until they are perfect.

Recording is not the same as concert-giving. They are separate media and have their own disciplines and objectives. The live concert is intended to give immediate satisfaction. Blemishes are heard once and are generally forgotten by the time the final bars have sounded. Recordings are heard repeatedly and the smallest flaw is multiplied by the number of times the recording is played, so the quest must be for a level of perfection rarely attainable in live performance.

Economics

The most expensive element in most orchestral recordings is the musicians' time. A typical modern recording session will produce about fifteen minutes of music after editing. Most producers would relish the extravagance of having all the participants on hand throughout all the sessions and recording everything in its correct sequence, but for large-scale works, especially oratorios or operas involving multiple soloists and choruses, this presumes a generous budget and diaries free of other engagements – rare among top-rank performers. It is much more economical to split large works into separate sections and to plan a schedule that makes the best use of the artists' time and stamina. For complex recordings using multiple microphones and the spatial effects that are common in operatic recordings, balancing the sound can be a time-consuming and, for the performers, tedious procedure. For this reason many record companies use multi-track. Each microphone is allocated a separate track on a multi-track recorder and these tracks are mixed later in a post-production studio. In extreme cases, such as can arise through accident or illness, it is possible to record individual soloists on their own, when they will be required to synchronise their performances to pre-recorded accompaniments – a technique that has also been used by unscrupulous commercial interests to make stars out of musical nonentities.

The total process thus has some similarity to film making, where the finished performance only exists after final compilation. As with film making, rigorous attention must be paid to continuity. Tempo and balance must be matched and the appropriate dramatic mood must be sustained. Atmospheric noise levels (e.g. from air-conditioning systems) must be consistent – trying to join takes when the atmosphere doesn't match is a frustrating procedure. If there is an *a capella* element, pitch must be checked carefully, as correcting it retrospectively is extremely difficult, if possible at all.

A disciplined approach to planning and pacing is essential. In the United Kingdom the standard session length is three hours. This normally includes a twenty-minute break half way through – essential, as concentration levels are extremely high. Overrunning a session can invoke considerable bills for overtime, and having to re-book performers to complete a recording or to correct things that cannot be made to work in the editing suite is even more expensive.

The final objective

Provided that musical flow and a sense of performance are not disrupted by over-zealous nit-picking, discontinuous recording sessions can have a liberating effect. They can be paced to avoid overtaxing singers' vocal cords or wind players' lips, performers are less likely to spend hours 'waiting in the wings', and the workshop spirit can stimulate constructive discourse. Moreover, the possibility of retakes enables artists to take risks they would never dare take on the concert platform, often with breathtaking results.

On the technical side, there are those who would never countenance any other *modus operandi* beyond the 'pure' Blumlein method outlined earlier. Such a stringent standpoint presumes ideal circumstances, artistic and physical, and has precluded the recording of many a major work, as is often apparent when browsing through adherents' catalogues. It also assumes, incorrectly, that the chosen method is unimpeachable and fails to recognise that a recording is an artistic artefact. In any art, rigid adherence to strict formulas stultifies creativity and tends to indicate insecure aesthetic judgement. When the purist's approach dictates awkward orchestral layouts that hamper rapport between players, the tail of dogma can end up wagging the dog of performance.

Recordings capture the ephemeral and enable us to play with time itself. They can make or break reputations and can shape the musical taste of a generation. No matter how cherished the recording technique, it is the musicians' role that is the most fragile and it is their skills that face the closest scrutiny. In the Cave of Harmony, it is the function of producers and engineers to present them, and allow them to present themselves, in the best possible light.

10 Training the orchestral musician

SIMON CHANNING

Recent history

Conservatoire training for orchestral musicians has changed dramatically during the past fifteen years. This change has been reflected in a much more intensive and detailed curriculum, particularly at postgraduate level, designed to produce students who are fully prepared for the various demands of a rapidly changing profession.

When I attended the Guildhall School of Music and Drama in London as a postgraduate student on the 'orchestral training' course, there was comparatively little on offer by way of officially organised training. The principal study lesson was the main focus, lasting an hour a week. As my teacher, Peter Lloyd, was principal flute with the LSO, I naturally learned a great deal about orchestral playing as well as attending LSO rehearsals at his invitation. As far as the syllabus was concerned, however, there was no official requirement to learn orchestral repertory and no formal assessment. Apart from my flute lessons, I played in the Symphony Orchestra three times during the year: Berlioz *Symphonie fantastique*, Sibelius Symphony No. 2 and the concerto competition finals as well as accompanying the opera. For the rest of my time, I was free to practise and to use this relative freedom to make music with my fellow students. At the end of the course I left, the proud recipient of a 'Certificate of Advanced Studies' in 'orchestral training', and I still look back at the year as having been pivotal in my development, in spite of – or perhaps because of – the lack of institutional rigour. Such courses were typical of all music colleges in the UK at the time. Students were left to pick up certain skills by osmosis, and their readiness for entering the profession was, to a very large degree, dependent on the work done with the principal study professor. In that respect, I was simply lucky.

The situation now is very different. Throughout the world both conservatoires and orchestras have had to change radically in response to the dictates of the market and to fundamental cultural changes. The status quo of fifteen years ago was built on a belief that the high arts were of indisputable value and their permanence assured. Today, such a belief looks either touchingly naïve, nostalgic even, or simply complacent. Now both the arts and education have to justify themselves every step of the way. Training is increasingly being tailored to the 'changing profession'. This is a phrase used daily in discussions and the changes in question have made conservatoires rethink the range of skills which they are teaching their students. Orchestras now are more and more seen as a resource for the community at large, and whilst concert-giving is still the main focus, the range of activities surrounding these concerts is widening and increasing in number.

These changes reflect deeper cultural trends. Orchestras are expected to undertake more varied forms of music-making and to play a major role in music education, partly because central governments are reducing core funding in this area. As noted by several of my fellow authors elsewhere in this book, there are even suggestions that orchestras will become looser confederations of players ready and willing to undertake an ever-increasing variety of work. What is certain is that as society becomes less willing to accept as a 'given' the relevance of the cultural norms of previous generations, so orchestras will have to meet the same challenges if they are to survive and remain relevant.

These changes have profound significance for orchestral training. When we ask ourselves what skills our students need the answers are very different from even five years ago. Certainly the core skills have changed little. The gateway to joining an orchestra is still the audition, often followed by the lengthy trial period described in chapter 11. For this, students will need to be highly proficient instrumentalists with a thorough knowledge of the standard repertory. Even here, however, the horizons have widened. Orchestral players now need to understand the fundamentals of period performance and to be conversant in the recondite requirements of contemporary instrumental techniques. Such are the 'needs' or requirements for joining an orchestra; but conservatoires must also nurture students who will be able to contribute to the wider development of the ensemble.

One of the most profound symptoms of the recent cultural changes has been a change in attitude to authority. A generation brought up to accept a society which was planned, static and organised has given way to one less accepting of the status quo. Orchestras are by their nature authoritarian – the conductor is the final arbiter – and in any history of the great orchestras in the twentieth century the music director almost always baulks larger than the ensemble. This was often a recipe for wonderful music-making, but it surely took its toll on the psyche of the musician whose subservience was only compounded by the narrow work pattern and limited opportunity for career development and personal growth. Today the music director is still of crucial importance, and players will submit to his authority, but an orchestra's concert-giving is increasingly surrounded by a hinterland which offers players autonomy and freedom to make both personal and artistic choices. If the orchestral profession is to change and develop, conservatoires must train students who will revel in these opportunities and for whom joining an orchestra is the start of a journey rather than a final refuge.

A constant theme throughout this book is the range of skills increasingly demanded of orchestral players, including the ability to lead a team, to introduce concerts, to improvise in education workshops and to manage projects. All of this requires a curiosity to welcome change and variety, within which orchestral life can be potentially hugely fulfilling. The challenge facing conservatoires is to reflect the increasing breadth required of today's musicians without compromising the delivery of basic instrumental skills. Two recent reports demonstrate just how difficult this balance is to achieve. In 'The British Conservatoires' BMus (Hons) award, Current Attributes and Key Directions for the Future',[1] British conservatoires were asked which general skills they felt their students acquired before graduation. There was a very positive response in such areas as the ability to work in a team, ability to be self-critical, ability to solve problems, to gather appropriate information and to be self-motivating. Where there was less confidence was in areas such as: ability to lead a team, ability to be self-confident, to manage projects, to be entrepreneurial, and to learn new skills quickly. This suggests that conservatoires are producing students able to fit into a team and to lead fulfilled lives within that team. But when it comes to nurturing individuals who will actively lead the process of change and act as a galvanising influence within an organisation, the response is less confident.

These findings are reinforced by a report by the UK Musicians' Union: 'Research into the training needs of orchestral musicians'.[2] A questionnaire was sent to all orchestral musicians in the UK asking them to comment on their own experiences of conservatoire training and on recent changes in the pattern of orchestral work. The responses to the latter vary, but two consistent viewpoints emerge. First, that many players are perplexed by, and hostile to, the recent changes: 'There is a real danger that the present vogue for education and outreach work is becoming a major distraction and that a disproportionate amount of funding and sponsorship is being allocated to it. Our orchestras must concentrate on the real task of giving high quality concerts.' The other response is more positive, although still concerned that players need to be properly trained for the demands of education and outreach work: 'Being an experienced workshop leader and project planner, I would be interested in taking part/observing very experienced workshop leaders. . . A certain amount of training is already available to us – but the more opportunities the better!'

From this initial general survey, it can be seen that the subject of 'training the orchestral musician' resonates far beyond the conservatoires. All over the world, the role of orchestras is changing and conservatoires need to provide a broad general musical education that will equip musicians for a variety of possible careers. It is also true that, in spite of the difficulty in finding work on leaving music college, students are thinking more and more of alternative careers: the best string players, in particular, will often combine work in a freelance chamber orchestra with teaching and perhaps chamber music, rather than joining a symphony orchestra.

Orchestras and the conservatoire curriculum

Although conservatoires are increasingly trying to broaden their range of activities, the orchestra's place in the life of the institution is still paramount all over the world. The way a music college's orchestra plays is seen as a barometer for the health of the whole institution. The reasons for this are clear: orchestral playing is communal music-making at its most inclusive and the quality and morale of its orchestras reflects the standards across the whole institution.

A brief look at the Juilliard School prospectus, for instance, reveals the huge influence of orchestral playing in the running of its programmes. In the very first paragraph introducing the music faculty, the prospectus claims that 'numerous faculty members are drawn from the New York Philharmonic and the Metropolitan Opera Orchestra. Many have appeared as soloists with the orchestra'. It is only in the second paragraph that we are told 'members of the voice faculty have appeared as principals in productions

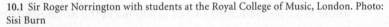

10.1 Sir Roger Norrington with students at the Royal College of Music, London. Photo: Sisi Burn

of the Metropolitan Opera'. The Manhattan School of Music in its own prospectus places 'Positions in Professional Orchestras won this year' above 'Recent Competition winners'. Incidentally, the number of positions won for the year 1999–2000 was ten, including the concertmaster of the Berlin Philharmonic – Guy Braunstein, a pupil on Pinchas Zukerman's course at the School. Similarly, Frank Caputo, Assistant to the President at the Cleveland Institute for Music, whilst recognising that many students are increasingly looking to a varied career including chamber music and teaching, is still quick to add that over 30 per cent of the Cleveland Orchestra are CIM alumni.

In London, all the music colleges place great emphasis on their orchestral training and have attracted an impressive list of guest conductors. Recent visitors have included Boulez, Sir Colin Davis, Michael Tilson Thomas, Haitink, Maazel, Masur, Norrington, János Fürst, Gardiner and Andrew Litton. Sometimes their appearances are relatively brief – a single open rehearsal for example; on other occasions substantial projects have been undertaken, including Sir Colin Davis appearing at the Proms with the Guildhall School in Berlioz's *Requiem*, and Bernard Haitink visiting the Royal College of Music for a week leading to a performance of Shostakovich Symphony No. 8. Such visits are evidence that these great conductors are keen to nurture young talent and that the colleges are aspiring to the highest standards of orchestral education.

In today's conservatoires there are many facets of orchestral training, with different orchestral projects catering for different educational needs. The traditional weekly repertoire orchestra rehearsal used to form the backbone of orchestral training in many colleges – in the UK, most famously under Maurice Handford's strict discipline at the Royal Academy of Music. The number of successful players to have emerged from this training is remarkable: there is a famous photograph of one such session in which three future leaders of London orchestras are all playing in the first violin section. Although a great deal of repertory was covered, Handford's skill and discipline ensured that these were far more than mere 'note bashing sessions', as he somehow managed to cover a large amount of music in depth. Colleges nowadays operate a much more 'mixed economy' in an attempt to tailor different projects to specific needs. The 'rep orchestra' will always have its place, because it teaches students to play instinctively and to learn quickly, encouraging them to fix problems – of balance, intonation – on the spot, but without the pressure of preparing for a public performance. It must also be remembered that many students, particularly in their early years at music college, suffer from nerve problems – joining a conservatoire is a daunting step for many of them – and the relative informality of the repertoire orchestra is absolutely right for their needs.

Such a pattern is capable of interesting variation. For instance, when Simon Rattle visited the Curtis Institute to conduct Dvořák's Carnival overture, he treated the three-hour rehearsal like a London recording session, rehearsing for two hours before recording the work in a single 'take'. This was then played back to the orchestra on the stage, with Rattle discussing the performance in a form of critique.

Given too much prominence, however, there is a danger that the repertoire orchestra will lead to students not seriously grappling with more complex technical and musical problems and for this reason many colleges have introduced different levels of preparation. The Royal Academy of Music has a series of lunchtime orchestral concerts that are prepared intensively for just two days. This involves three hours of sectional rehearsals leading to six hours of tutti rehearsals before the concert. Such projects are easily placed within the timetable and replicate the amount of rehearsal which is often the norm for freelance orchestras in London. Yet these concerts are by no means under-rehearsed, and recent guest conductors have included Sir Colin Davis, Sir Charles Mackerras and Elgar Howarth.

The final level on this ladder of progression is the intensively prepared, high-profile Symphony Orchestra concert, often conducted by a distinguished visitor. When Sir Colin Davis conducted the Guildhall School Symphony Orchestra at the Proms, the students had been thoroughly prepared in sectional rehearsals before Sir Colin arrived for the final week of rehearsals. For Haitink's visit to the RCM to conduct Shostakovich Symphony No. 8, the preparations were equally thorough. Students were sent the instrumental parts during the summer holidays and were required to play sections of the work for their orchestral auditions at the beginning of the new academic year. Before Haitink arrived for the final week, each student had taken part in a full tutti run-through with a student conductor, individual instrumental sectional rehearsals (flutes, oboes etc. separately) leading to full woodwind, brass and string rehearsals. Such intensive preparation is obviously worthwhile on its own terms, giving plenty of scope for going into great detail so that string players can discuss different bowings, and the wind and brass can work on balance, rhythm, tuning and articulation, and when Haitink arrived, he was able to work immediately on the highest level.

Sometimes these high-profile concerts provide a focal point for a project or festival which features all the faculties in a conservatoire. A typical example of this is the 'focus' festival at the Juilliard School – an annual week-long festival of twentieth-century music, involving more than 200 students, which frequently incorporates collaborations between music, dance and drama. Such projects are also a good example of the current trend towards greater collaboration and synthesis in the arts and in education.

Whilst the pattern of full symphony orchestra rehearsals and concerts represents the most visible area of orchestral training, much important teaching happens less visibly within the general curriculum. The basis for this training involves the teaching of core skills, some of which will be purely musical, whilst others will include more general qualities such as a wide knowledge of cultural history, the ability to communicate in writing and in speech and the ability to use IT equipment. These skills are just as relevant to the orchestral musician as they are to the chamber musician or soloist.

All undergraduate students at conservatoires throughout the world receive a basic musical training which includes the teaching of history, aural and keyboard skills. Some students are able to take up liberal arts options as well. Increasingly, students are being encouraged to understand how skills can be transferred from one situation to another. For instance, a requirement that chamber groups and soloists must introduce their own concerts prepares them for public speaking and encourages them to make use of library facilities to research their introductions. Later in their careers, they may have to stand up in front of a violin section to explain and demonstrate a musical point. Many fine players find this a difficult skill to learn later in their career. But by adopting such customs and practices in their formative years, students learn them as an integrated part of their musical education, whilst being taught to express themselves and to be creative. Some conservatoires have taken this a stage further. The Cleveland Institute, for instance, requires all string chamber groups to play at least one concert in the local community each term. Such demands may seem far removed from traditional orchestral skills, but they are extremely relevant today when, for instance, 80 per cent of the LSO are regularly taking part in such education and outreach projects.

The core instrumental skills are learned in the principal study lesson. Whilst there are many specific skills which the orchestral musician must learn, none of them is of any real value unless students reach a high level of competence on their instruments. Indeed, it is the relatively unglamorous fundamentals of technique that are of greatest importance in orchestral playing. Many of the top orchestral players have an ambivalent attitude towards some soloists, for whom, for instance, a lack of control at extremes of dynamic may be less noticeable or critical than for the orchestral player.

For woodwind, brass and percussion players, the principal study teacher is very often an eminent orchestral player, and much of the tuition will inevitably be aimed at developing orchestral skills. At Juilliard, for instance, all wind and brass applicants for both undergraduate and postgraduate study are required to play orchestral excerpts at their entrance auditions as well as at exams throughout their course. With string players the emphasis is different. Whilst many of them will follow an orchestral career, there is very often a lack of specific orchestral training within the faculty. Also, most of the pre-eminent string teachers are not orchestral players. String players auditioning for Juilliard are asked to play an advanced Caprice in place of the orchestral excerpts. This difference of emphasis between faculties can lead to string-playing students being rather reluctant to participate in orchestral activities – an attitude often fostered by an unrealistic expectation on the students' part that they are destined to become soloists. It is interesting to note, in this context, that Bob Fitzpatrick, Dean of the Curtis Institute, says that even this pre-eminent conservatoire, which offers places to only 7 per cent of applicants, has produced just three international soloists during the past ten years: Hilary Hahn, Pamela Frank and Leila Josefowicz.

In addition to the principal study lesson, all music students are offered coaching in chamber music as part of the curriculum. It is here that they start to learn the basics of ensemble playing. For string players this will include detailed discussions of bowings, fingerings and vibrato as well as more general matters of interpretation. It is also through playing chamber music that string players can learn the skills needed for leading an orchestral section. Indeed, at the Royal College of Music there are quartet classes, taught by Gordan Nikolitch (leader of the LSO), which are specifically for training future leaders. Professional orchestras are increasingly asking applicants to play chamber music as part of the selection process, where they can find out about their personal characteristics – whether they can take criticism, or make decisions as part of a team – as well as their musical ones.

For wind players, the disciplines of playing in a small chamber group are also very much a part of their orchestral training. Here they learn how to blend the different timbres of the instruments, to balance and tune chords, to bring out solos and to accompany each other by turn. It is also relevant that with orchestras being seen more and more as a resource – Boulez's 'ensemble of possibilities' – there are increasing opportunities for players to work as chamber musicians under the banner of their orchestra. The London Symphony Orchestra, for instance, frequently includes chamber recitals within its own promotions, as well as concerts by its own string and brass ensembles.

The next step up in size from the chamber groups is to the larger faculty ensembles. Here students' skills are developed on a broader scale than in the smaller chamber ensembles, but with an attention to detail which it is not always possible to achieve in the context of a full symphony orchestra. String ensembles, for example, can concentrate on the disciplines needed to play in a section. Similarly, brass players learn the large-scale orchestral challenges in a particularly detailed way, by playing in a wind orchestra, usually under the expert guidance of a fellow brass player. The Royal Northern College of Music in Manchester has a renowned wind orchestra which has made a number of acclaimed CDs, many of them featuring highly complex contemporary repertory, with opportunities for students to play challenging solo parts. Even such specialist ensembles as the big band are important training grounds for orchestral musicians, helping to create adaptable, instinctive players, and preparing them for film session work and the ever-increasing number of 'crossover' concerts in which symphony orchestras partner such artists as Lalo Shiffrin, Dave Brubeck and Wynton Marsalis.

We have seen, therefore, that the different levels of full orchestral projects – from repertoire orchestra to fully prepared concert – are balanced by the instrumental provision available to students from the one-to-one lesson through chamber coaching to the larger ensembles, and that this latter category is a vital part of orchestral training. But even this is only part of the full picture. If a prospective orchestral player leaving music college only possesses instrumental and ensemble skills, then they will not be fully prepared for orchestral life. Just as doctors are expected to have a basic knowledge of all branches of medicine before specialising, so any musician must have a broad range of skills and knowledge, whatever their speciality.

Postgraduate orchestral courses

Whilst orchestral training is an integral part of the curriculum for all students learning orchestral instruments, many conservatoires have also developed specialist postgraduate courses which have transformed the teaching of orchestral musicians. According to its website, the Manhattan School of Music's course was 'the first accredited degree programme of its kind, and was founded on the belief that a career as a member of a Symphony orchestra is as desirable and artistically rewarding as a career as a solo performer'. The general aim of the programme is the training of students 'in both performance and other non-musical aspects of life in the modern orchestra, such as orchestra governance, artistic planning, community outreach, and audience development'. This is an ambitious statement, both for the course itself and for the combination of skills we are expecting of the orchestral player of the future. Accompanying the course description, there is an impressive list of thirty-one former students who have won places in professional orchestras – eleven of them in orchestras outside the US.

All the music colleges in the UK have developed similar courses. The two-year orchestral pathway at the Royal College of Music, for instance, introduces students to all the musical and non-musical aspects described in the Manhattan prospectus, although the emphasis is perhaps more on the purely musical training. As well as the one-to-one principal study lesson, students attend regular classes focusing on orchestral repertory. There are tutti wind and brass repertory classes, including side-by-side sessions with both the RPO and LSO, in which each student section is joined by a professional player. The repertory is varied, but tends to be large scale, and often linked to public performance. Over the past year, the sessions have focussed on Berlioz *Symphonie fantastique* and Janáček *Sinfonietta* with the LSO, and Mahler Symphony No. 5 and Bartók *Concerto for Orchestra* with the Royal Philharmonic. These projects are of great value to the students, who are often surprised by the sheer volume of sound that is required in the profession and by the fact that there are occasions when ensemble playing involves latching on to other players in the section at the expense of following the conductor. A highlight of the scheme for the students is an invitation for them to sit on stage in a full professional orchestral rehearsal.

The course also requires instrumental students to work with student composers, and there are classes devoted to the teaching of contemporary instrumental techniques. Students are also invited to join education projects run by the RPO and Philharmonia Orchestra, which often involve working with schoolchildren. Students also receive guidance in the writing of CVs, as well as attending a series of workshops on more general matters, including orchestral management, public funding of the arts, licensing, royalties and copyright, tax and personal finance, how to put on a concert, and coping with nerves. Students are assessed in short solo recitals, in education work, and in an orchestral context, when LSO players act as examiners by sitting within the body of a specially convened orchestra for an exam which involves a three-hour rehearsal followed by a short performance. At the end of the second year of the course, students take a 'mock audition'. This is treated exactly like a professional audition, beginning with a concerto movement, followed by a number of prepared excerpts, and finishing with sight-reading. Students also have to present a CV at the audition for which the panel always includes an external specialist from one of the London orchestras. Preparation for the exam includes audition seminars which build on the work done in the orchestral repertory sessions.

Links between conservatoires and professional orchestras

Closely related to the development of specific orchestral courses is an ever-stronger association between professional orchestras and conservatoires. As well as running their side-by-side sessions, the LSO has a highly successful scheme, 'The LSO String Experience', designed to attract the best conservatoire string players to play in symphony orchestras. Students audition to join the scheme, having first been nominated by their conservatoire. The successful ones are invited to play in LSO rehearsals, with some progressing to full concerts.

In the US, many such schemes exist. The Philadelphia Orchestra regularly auditions students at Curtis for its 'sub-list'. On a recent tour to Europe, seven out of the twenty-nine violinists in the orchestra were current students or recent graduates from the scheme. At Eastman, all third-year undergraduates audition for the Rochester Philharmonic, with feedback being given on the spot, and string students are invited to play with the orchestra, for which scholarships are awarded in lieu of payment. These initiatives have a number of benefits: they encourage the most talented students to sample symphony orchestra playing at its best, they help students bridge the sometimes daunting rite of passage between conservatoire life and the profession, and they put some money in the pockets of students who are facing ever-increasing financial burdens.

Youth orchestras

In spite of the drastic cutbacks in music provision in schools both in Europe and the US, the last decade has also seen a dramatic increase in the number of youth orchestras all over the world. Perhaps this is not surprising. Indeed, many of these youth orchestras see it as part of their mission to compensate for these cutbacks in public funding. For instance, the Chicago Youth Symphony Orchestra on its website specifically describes its artistic policy as being a 'response' to the '1988 budget cuts, which nearly eliminated the study of music from the Chicago public school curriculum'. Many youth orchestras have been set up by professional symphony orchestras, both as a training ground for future players – the Chicago Youth Symphony has provided thirteen members for the parent orchestra – and as a resource for their community and outreach programme. There are no better advocates for classical music than enthusiastic children. Apart from Chicago, other orchestras to have started their own youth orchestras include Cleveland, St Louis, San Francisco and the London Philharmonic.

The age range of the orchestras varies, some concentrating solely on students who are still at school, others offering additional training – usually in the holidays – to students of conservatoire age. The San Francisco Symphony Youth Orchestra is an example of the former. As well as giving concerts as part of the parent orchestra's subscription season, the youth orchestra frequently tours, most recently performing to packed houses in Moscow, St Petersburg, Vilnius, Cork and Dublin in programmes which included Prokofiev Symphony No. 5, Tchaikovsky Symphony No. 5, Copland

Appalachian Spring and John Adams *Lowapalooza*. John Adams has also accepted a commission to write a work for the orchestra. Alasdair Neale, the orchestra's Music Director, is also Michael Tilson Thomas's assistant with the San Francisco Symphony and artistic advisor to the San Francisco Conservatory. Some 20 per cent of the orchestral members will go on to follow a career in music, the rest becoming enthusiastic amateurs and strong advocates for orchestral music in the community.

The National Youth Orchestra of Great Britain is also specifically for non-conservatoire students, meeting in the school holidays and performing regularly with such conductors as Rattle, Boulez, Norrington and Yan Pascal Tortelier. The orchestra has proved a very fertile training ground for professional orchestras in the UK. Four of the current LSO principal wind players were members, as well as the principal cello, principal second violin and principal percussion. The standards of discipline in the NYO are legendary: before each tutti rehearsal, every wind and brass player takes a solo A from their section principal whilst the rest of the orchestra sits in complete silence. This takes twenty-five minutes. Then the orchestra sits in silence for a further five minutes before the conductor arrives, by which time the sense of expectation is palpable.

The European Union Youth Orchestra, by contrast, offers places to students of any age, many of whom are studying at conservatoires. The orchestra, which was founded by Claudio Abbado, achieves extraordinarily high standards, playing at all the major European festivals, and providing a stream of players filling principal positions in orchestras throughout Europe. The Chamber Orchestra of Europe was founded by a dedicated and talented group of players from the EUYO's earliest years.

An orchestra which fits into neither of the above categories is the New World Symphony. Founded by Michael Tilson Thomas in 1987 and based in Miami, the orchestra is made up of the cream of recent conservatoire graduates. It is in effect a full-time orchestral finishing school, with a consistent personnel, many of whom will soon move on to prestigious positions in professional orchestras. The average age of the players, who are paid for their services, is twenty-five. The orchestra undertakes a full programme of concerts and education and outreach work, with each concert being preceded by eighteen hours of tutti rehearsal as well as additional sectional rehearsals. At the start of each season, members of the Cleveland Orchestra are invited to coach for a week, and on one occasion, members of the Vienna Philharmonic helped to prepare an all-Brahms programme, conducted by Tilson Thomas. There is certainly a place for such orchestras in helping players to bridge the gap between full-time education and entry into the profession. Perhaps the huge success of the New World Symphony will lead to other orchestras being set up, although a similar venture, the National Centre for Orchestra Studies in London, failed for lack of financial support.

Repertory

Attitudes towards repertory have changed markedly over the past decade, characterised particularly by an ever-greater interest in both period performance and contemporary music. It is still a matter of fierce debate as to how relevant authentic performance is to the modern symphony orchestra. Certainly, many orchestras in the US seem not to have responded to the challenge. In Europe, however, the influence of the period movement is much more pervasive. In the 2001 Royal Philharmonic Society Lecture in London, Nicholas Kenyon argued that, with pioneering conductors such as Norrington, Gardiner and Harnoncourt now regularly working with Europe's major orchestras, aspects of period performance have been subsumed in the general approach to this repertory.

Conservatoires in Europe have been eager to reflect these developments. Norrington, Gardiner and Pinnock have all conducted at the London colleges, and the RAM in particular has two classical/baroque orchestras: one on period instruments playing at a′ = 415, and one on modern instruments playing at a′ = 440. At the Royal Scottish Academy of Music and Drama, all BMus students in their second year are required to have lessons in authentic performance, for which tuition is free.

Contemporary music is also an important component of the curriculum. Students are taught the fundamentals of contemporary instrumental techniques and there is ever-increasing collaboration between student composers and their instrumental colleagues. Many of these new compositions are for unusual configurations of instruments rather than for the traditional symphony orchestra. James Undercofler, Director at the Eastman School of Music, notes that the trend is a dramatic one, with over 70 per cent of all performances at the school involving repertory written after 1900.

It is surprising that in spite of these developments, the notion of what constitutes standard repertory has changed little over the past decade. Although students must have a knowledge of contemporary techniques – playing harmonics, quarter tones and chords, as well as understanding such compositional conventions as aleatoric writing, such as is found in Lutoslawski's *Livre pour orchestre* – the list of orchestral repertory students are expected to know includes no works written in the past twenty years. This is not because conservatoires are simply living up to the limitations implied by their very name. Michael Tilson Thomas is at the forefront as an advocate for contemporary music, yet the list of excerpts set as audition repertory for the New World Symphony would have been no different fifteen years ago. Horn players, for instance are asked to prepare:

(All 1st horn unless noted):
Beethoven: Symphony No. 9 (3rd mvt, 4th horn solo)
Beethoven: Symphony No. 3 (3rd mvt, 1st and 2nd horn)
Brahms: Symphony No. 3
Mahler: Symphony No. 1 (3rd mvt)
Mahler: Symphony No. 5
Mendelssohn: *A Midsummer Night's Dream*
Mussorgsky–Ravel: *Pictures at an Exhibition*
Ravel: Piano Concerto in G
Shostakovich: Symphony No. 5
Strauss: *Ein Heldenleben*
Strauss: *Till Eulenspiegel*
Wagner: *Siegfried* (short call)

Conclusion

There have been some dire predictions recently about the future of classical music in general, and particularly about the future of orchestras. Some of these are discussed by Stephen Cottrell later in this book. Serious questions have been raised about orchestras' relevance in the world today. However, they have an extraordinary capacity for survival and renewal, and the changes that have been described here are evidence that orchestras are gradually repositioning themselves as a vital resource for the whole community. The challenge for those who train orchestral musicians is to reflect these developments in the range of skills taught without compromising the learning of basic instrumental techniques, and to balance specialisation with a broader understanding of the musical and cultural issues which face everybody working in the arts.

11 The life of an orchestral musician

CLIVE GILLINSON AND JONATHAN VAUGHAN

Introduction

The life of an orchestral musician can be highly rewarding, challenging and exciting, but is just as likely to be frustrating, exhausting and unfulfilling. Between these two extremes there are many different realities. In order to understand and determine at which end of the spectrum a player's life might fall, one must understand not only the individual's particular circumstances and attitude towards his or her position, but also the artistic, financial and political background in which he or she operates. It is also important to appreciate that most people take up music professionally because they have artistic aspirations, whereas their orchestral role is largely that of an artisan. Artistic creativity lies primarily with conductors and soloists, although there is significant creative input from principal players. Many orchestral musicians understand and accept this role and are able to find great fulfilment and enjoyment, as well as camaraderie, in their work. Those who fail to develop creative outlets often find that the inherent tension of an artist working primarily as an artisan leads to frustration and a lack of personal growth and creativity.

The orchestra as a community

An orchestra is a microcosm of society and a cross-section of people from all kinds of social backgrounds, working together in close proximity. As with any social system, there are many ways of organising its internal political structures, a topic that forms part of the discussion in chapter 15 of this book. As noted by Simon Channing in the previous chapter, orchestras have become ever more consultative throughout the second half of the twentieth century, so that the musical director is no longer a dictator, as was often the case in the past.

The orchestra as employees

In orchestras where the players are employees, a feeling of 'them and us' often develops between the players and the music director and/or the management. The players frequently assume that the management is trying to exploit them whenever a new idea is put forward. This may lead to an over-unionised mentality that becomes far more concerned with fighting for the 'rights' and 'benefits' of the individual, rather than looking after the best interests of the music.

If players feel that they do not have a voice or that their views are disregarded, they will often start to treat the job simply as a nine-to-five one and, in the most extreme cases, will only put in the minimum of commitment necessary to do the job. This of course completely undermines the artistic integrity of an orchestra. In most successful and happy orchestras, players are kept well informed of developments, both internally and externally, so that their attitudes are driven by broader values than just those of pay and conditions. Players' representatives or committees have real input into the vision, strategy and major decisions of these orchestras and the whole system is relatively harmonious. One of the advantages of this system, when it works, is that a management team can be much more efficient and effective at decision-making than a more democratic system sometimes is.

The self-governing orchestra

Self-governing orchestras are usually owned by the players who are normally the only shareholders in their company. The players elect a board of directors from the orchestral membership and these directors are the ultimate decision-makers in relation to strategy, direction and policies of the company. At worst this system can be a total failure if it leads to decisions being made with the short-term self-interests of the players coming before the music. It can be rather like removing all the teachers from a school and expecting the students to take control. This can result in petty squabbling and political cliques within an orchestra, making for power struggles and all manner of mischief. However, when this system works well it is probably the best. With a good management team and a well-informed, responsible and committed board, the players have genuine input and empowerment in their orchestra. There is a sense of pride and ownership and a real opportunity to consider the health of the music as a priority. This in turn leads to an ability to implement changes for the long-term good of the orchestra rather than the short-term financial gain of the individual player.

Conductors

The conductor has a major impact on the players' feelings about their own music-making. The success or failure of this partnership depends on the aptitude and attitude of both parties. If either the conductor or the orchestra views the other as not good enough or discourteous in any way, then the relationship will very quickly deteriorate. A really successful artistic relationship relies on mutual respect and a sense of partnership. Some conductors have a reputation for being tyrannical, but this will usually be forgiven by the players if the end result is a great concert. It is only the conductors who are tyrannical and not talented who lose the respect of the orchestral musician! Equally, orchestras can have bad reputations for being intolerant towards conductors. This is ultimately the orchestra's loss because great conductors will not want to work with them and, whether they like it or not, orchestras need great conductors.

Appointment procedures

Appointment procedures differ greatly from orchestra to orchestra. The audition alone can take many forms. It may be played to any number of people, from a single music director to a select panel or the entire orchestra. Sometimes auditions are played behind screens and some American orchestras even go to the extreme lengths of asking candidates to take off their shoes so that the panel cannot determine the candidate's sex from the sound of their footfall. There are sometimes two rounds of auditions where candidates may be asked to play a short five-minute audition in order to qualify for a second more rigorous one. Every orchestra has a different idea of what should be played at an audition. Some stipulate specific pieces and give prepared orchestral excerpts; some ask candidates to prepare a previously unseen piece in as little time as fifteen minutes; others ask for sight-reading of well-known or not so well-known repertory. Auditions can last for anything from three minutes to half an hour.

After successfully passing an audition candidates will in some cases then become a member of an orchestra (albeit usually on probation), whilst in other cases they will be subject to a trial period in the orchestra. A trial can last from one week to two years. The trialist is booked on a freelance basis during this period. Most orchestras that have trial periods also like to see a trialist in a touring situation. In the words of Mark Twain, 'I have found that there ain't no surer way to find out whether you like people or hate them, than travel with them.' This may sound a rather spurious test, but the social aspect of orchestral life is extremely important. Players often spend more time with each other than they do with their families. Anyone who does not fit in musically and socially is likely to create problems later when it comes to the very high level of team co-operation required of orchestral players. A candidate is often in competition with two or three other trialists for a single vacancy, so there is no guarantee of getting a job at the end of this process.

Working practices

Pay and conditions are a crucial part of a player's well being. Many orchestras pay salaries which include pensions as well as sickness and maternity allowances, while other orchestras pay on a fee-per-call basis. Again, there are many combinations and variations of these two models. The intensity of work can vary dramatically too. Some orchestras in London work much harder than their counterparts in America and Europe. Within orchestras there is usually quite a significant pay differential between principal and section players. There is also a huge diversity in the flexibility and lifestyles in different positions around the world. A number of orchestras have very rigid regimes where the members have little opportunity to do anything other than their own orchestra's work whilst in others there are opportunities for solo, chamber and education work, away from the main symphonic activities of the orchestra.

Some orchestras pay everyone equally, some pay equally for the same level of musical responsibility and others negotiate fees individually with each player. In this situation players of a similar rank and position, with broadly similar jobs, may have considerable disparities between their fees. This can create a great deal of resentment when players realise they are earning less than some of their colleagues in a similar position. Once a system like this exists, it is very difficult to return to a strictly structured system based purely on rank, because either the higher paid players have to take considerable cuts in their fees (very rarely a realistic option) or all the players have to be paid at the highest prevailing rate for each position in the orchestra (a very expensive answer that would bankrupt many orchestras).

Touring is an important part of most orchestras' work. This can be anything from a short regional tour of a few days, to a full-blown month-long trip to a different continent playing in many cities. However well tours are arranged, they are normally very tiring for the players. After a long-haul flight, most orchestras will give their players at least one day off to recover. However, because of the huge costs associated with touring (travel, hotels, per diems etc.) there are relatively few free days once the tour is under way. Most orchestras need to perform as many concerts as possible in order to maximise revenues towards meeting the costs of touring. There are a few exceptions, mainly the major North American orchestras, which are able to cross-subsidise from large endowments or obtain major sponsors in order to make touring a little easier by giving a little more free time to the players.

A much more satisfactory way to tour is to create residencies. This means that the orchestra can stay in the same city for several days and present several different programmes. The most coherent way to do this is a festival, where the programmes are built around a concept or theme. Festivals are a very successful concept for touring because they capitalise on something that the orchestra has already performed in its hometown; they can be transported to any number of other cities either in their entirety or in part; they give an audience a much broader experience and can be used as a central theme around which to build any number of other events, a process which generates further interest in and profile of the concert series. Regional and national tours are also an important ingredient in the life of most orchestras, although national touring is usually dependent on many of the same resourcing issues as international touring. Most orchestras consider that it is important to develop a national profile to complement their home city and international roles. A typical day for a player on a major tour might be something like this:

7.00am	Coaches to airport
8.00am	Check-in
9.00am	Flight
10.40am	Coaches to new hotel
11.00am	Arrive at new hotel, where rooms are often not ready
11.10am	Leave suitcases with Bell Captain and go for lunch
5.00pm	Coach to hall
5.45 – 6.30pm	Seating rehearsal (for those orchestras that do this)
7.30pm	Concert

This timetable is typical of a day on a European tour and for most orchestras this basic blueprint would be repeated for five or six days a week for a trip lasting anything from one week upwards. Most orchestras limit tours to three weeks to avoid the musicians becoming jaded. As well as this arduous schedule there may also be problems with jet lag and time zone changes which all add to the very substantial demands that most players experience on tour.

A number of orchestras work extensively in the studio and this gives musicians a completely different outlook on life. In recent years the market for new classical recordings has contracted very significantly. There is now a very large number of recordings available on compact disc, a virtually indestructible carrier. If one wants to purchase a recording of a Beethoven symphony, for example, there is an enormous choice of both modern and archive recordings available, so that producing yet another recording is rarely economically viable. The consequence of this is that most orchestras are doing far less recording work than they used to do and this has generally reduced players' incomes.

One of the few areas of growth in the current recording industry is the 'own label live' recording. This concept has grown out of the drastic reduction in orchestral recording and the need for orchestras to preserve and disseminate their most important artistic work. As well as creating a practical financial solution to the substantial costs of recording, it also offers the consumer a different product. Two orchestras in the UK, the London Symphony Orchestra and the Royal Liverpool Philharmonic Orchestra, have both recently formed their own CD labels and are making recordings 'live' from concerts. It is normal practice for there to be a short patching within this process to edit out any serious audience noise or small errors in performance. It has only been possible to establish the 'own label' recording concept because the players, conductors and soloists have agreed to receive no initial recording fees, but share in the revenues once the start-up costs have been covered. A model of this type is only possible if players and unions fully understand and accept the real issues now facing orchestras in the market-place for recordings and are willing to see the health of the orchestra and the performers' own long-term interests as one. Some orchestras also supplement their incomes by doing light music and film music. In most countries both light and film music are paid at a higher rate than classical recordings.

There are several different techniques involved in recording, some of which are much more interesting than others from a player's point of view. Record producers tend to be perfectionist by nature and some are happy to retake continually very small excerpts of the music and then edit them all together to make a flawless recording. From a playing point of view this can be soul-destroying for the conductor and the players. To sit in a studio retaking each bar numerous times is very tough and can be extremely boring. It also gives no sense of the overall structure of the piece and very often a record which is produced in this way lacks the spirit of performance. Most conductors will intercede and insist that the producer records longer takes or even whole movements. Any corrections then have to be handled with a very few small patches. This approach is much more satisfying for all the performers and much more meaningful and representative of a real performance.

The techniques used for light and film work are quite different from those used for classical recording. The music is usually recorded to a click track, in a specially designed studio. Particularly in the case of films, the music must fit exactly to the action and so a computerised 'click track' is sometimes played through headphones to each musician. The click must be loud enough to be audible to the musicians but not so loud that there is leakage into the studio where it will be picked up by the microphones. Even with a click track the orchestra will still be conducted, to ensure that it is clear which beat of the bar relates to which click.

Some composers and conductors find that this method of recording makes the end result too stilted and metronomic. An alternative is to use a system of 'ribbons and punches'. These are visual cues which are put on to the film in the early stages of production and which coincide with key moments in the film's action. A ribbon is a white vertical strip which moves across the screen from left to right. When the ribbon reaches the right-hand side of the screen the conductor knows that he must have reached a certain point in the music to fit with the on-screen action. A punch is a circular disc, usually with a number inside it, very similar to the count-down on old newsreels, which again is used as a visual cue prompt. The conductor is then able to manage his tempi in order to synchronise with the film. From a playing point of view this method is less rigid than the click track, but relies on the skill of the conductor. It usually requires several takes to achieve perfect synchronisation with the film. Studio musicians often quote the phrase 'bored to death or scared to death', meaning that either the music is so straightforward that it becomes dull or that their part is so exposed and difficult that it is terrifying. Session players give the impression that there are few shades of grey between these two extremes.

In a world where the arts are often accused of élitism, one of the key challenges facing orchestras is the question of accessibility. Education aimed at all ages and areas of society has a key role to play in this respect; in chapter 14 of this book Sue Knussen discusses the range and scope of education programmes currently being developed. Times have changed since the days of the 'This is a flute, Beethoven was deaf!' approach; education programmes are nowadays not only beneficial and fulfilling for concert-goers and communities, but can be tremendously rewarding for the musicians. They give players the opportunity to put something back into the community and bring them much more closely in touch with their audience as well as giving them a role as an individual, not just as a team member.

Stress and anxiety

The music profession has always had a reputation of being stressful. The demands of delivering incredibly high standards of performance coupled with anti-social hours, long periods away from home, and in some countries poor pay and conditions all go to make this a very demanding and high-pressure profession. The stakes also seem to be getting higher as the marketplace becomes ever more competitive and funders demand increasing levels of accountability. With many orchestras now developing from relatively narrowly defined businesses into major, more diversified and much more complex ones, the demands upon players for increasingly higher standards of performance and professionalism are growing.

The main area of stress on musicians is peer pressure. Musicians who are susceptible to stress always say that it is what their immediate neighbours and colleagues on the platform think of them, rather than their audience, that makes them suffer from nerves or stage fright. If an orchestra is in a period of ascendancy, where standards of playing get higher and higher, this pressure increases. Some players turn to prescribed drugs such as beta blockers (a group of drugs used in the treatment of heart conditions) for help. However, intolerance of the old traditions (for example, drinking before concerts) is growing. Many orchestras now have zero tolerance of drinking and anyone found to be under the influence of alcohol during working hours can be summarily dismissed. Some players do, of course, choose healthier alternatives to combat stress. Jogging, working-out, yoga, meditation, Alexander Technique and relaxation therapy all have their place for today's musicians in combating the stresses and strains of the job.

Health and Safety is another area of concern for orchestral players. There have been several studies recently which have demonstrated that various places within the orchestra are subject to unacceptably high noise levels. Players who constantly sit in front of the timpani or brass sections either have to wear earplugs or have a specially designed Perspex screen placed between them and the offending section. The effect of being exposed to this kind of noise should not be underestimated. It is usual for the wind and brass sections to sit on raised platforms in order to be able to see the conductor and this can alleviate some of the noise problems. However, many recording engineers actually prefer the orchestra to sit on a flat floor so that the brass players are playing directly into the back of the string players, because this absorbs some of the brass sound and makes for a better recording.

Conclusion

One of the most frequently asked questions from the public of orchestral musicians is 'What do you do for a living?' Whilst some part-time and amateur players certainly do have other employment, most major orchestras work on a full-time basis. However, both the orchestras' activities and the individual members' lifestyles can be quite diverse. The concerts and rehearsals that are the central part of most orchestral musicians' lives can vary enormously from a single concert with relatively limited rehearsal time, to a series which is part of a festival, to a subscription series where each concert is repeated several times. In addition, the repertory developed for an orchestra's home-base concert series then forms the basis for most of the rest of its work: touring, education and recording.

As new partnerships emerge between communities, technology and orchestras, so the role of the orchestral musician will change. As remarked upon elsewhere in this book, the beginning of the twenty-first century is a time of great change for both orchestras and audiences alike. Players will need to gain a much broader base of expertise in areas such as educational responsibilities; social skills will be increasingly called upon for the cultivation of sponsors and supporters, who tend to value opportunities to meet performers. This flexibility and diversity will not only guarantee their professional survival but should also enhance the quality of their lives. It is in the interests of musicians and their unions to renegotiate their existing media agreements to give the public far greater access to their performances. Orchestras will need to gain a much broader audience base for their activities if they are to survive and prosper.

12 Historical recordings of orchestras

ROBERT PHILIP

Introduction

As late as the 1970s historical recordings of orchestral music were virtually ignored. A few enthusiasts stored collections of 78 rpm records in their attics, and spoke reverently of the pre-war Vienna Philharmonic Orchestra, as a motoring enthusiast would talk of the red RR on an early Rolls-Royce. But almost no old orchestral recordings were available in transfers to LP, apart from a few concerto recordings valued almost exclusively for their soloists. The sixteen-year-old Yehudi Menuhin's 1932 recording of Elgar's Violin Concerto, conducted by the composer, was rightly regarded as extraordinary. But its value was taken to lie exclusively in the beautiful playing of the miraculous teenager. The fact that it was conducted by Elgar was of little more than sentimental interest. And as for the orchestral playing, the predominant view was that it was something of a mess, and demonstrated how much orchestral standards in Britain had improved since the 1930s.

By the early twenty-first century, reactions to orchestral playing of that period have become more complex and less dismissive. We have become accustomed to the sounds of early twentieth-century orchestras through the thousands of reissues now available on CD. Only thirty years ago the rare speaker who wanted to play a pre-war orchestral recording on BBC Radio 3 would have to find the original 78 rpm records in the BBC library or in a private collection. Now hardly a day goes by without a historical orchestral recording being played on Radio 3, and it is almost always taken from a CD reissue. Music shops are full of them, and they have become so widely accepted that in many shops they are not restricted to a separate 'historical' section, but mixed up with the latest digital recordings, often at the same price. The past is ever-present.

Styles, tastes and standards

Aspects of Elgar's 1932 recording of his Violin Concerto still sound somewhat chaotic to a modern audience. The composer is not always good at following the soloist, and sometimes has to catch up. Rhythmic details in the orchestra often seem hurried or unclear. The wind tuning is unreliable. The portamento of the strings seems loose and haphazard. None of this has changed since the 1970s. But what has changed is the way these features are now regarded. We have begun to learn the obvious truth that what sounds messy or undisciplined to us did not necessarily sound like that to musicians and audiences of the past, and that there is no clear distinction to be made between what we think of as rising standards, and what we have come to acknowledge as changing style.

There is a danger of letting the pendulum swing too far. Whereas old orchestral recordings used to seem slapdash and incompetent, now everything can easily be accepted as stylistic or 'historical'. But realistically, although almost everything can be seen as an aspect of style, it cannot be denied that orchestral playing has improved in obvious ways over the last eighty years. The world-wide standards of playing to be heard on modern recordings are surely higher than at any time in history. Not just the famous orchestras, but comparatively obscure bodies from around the world, are almost always well in tune, accurate in ensemble, and well blended. To realise the truth of this, one only has to compare the performances now available on a thousand low-price CDs with the rough-and-ready performances which used to appear on low-price LPs in the 1960s and 1970s. Such comparisons have to be edged with caution, however. Not everything to be heard on a modern CD was actually achieved in the recording studio. Microphone placings, mixing equipment, and multi-track recording and editing techniques are now highly sophisticated. Much of the editing that is routinely carried out today was impossible in the days of reel-to-reel tape recorders, and on 78 rpm records there was no editing in the early years, and even in the 1940s editing possibilities were very crude and rarely used. A movement issued on a modern CD may well contain a hundred edits or more. These range from the correction of errors to choices made for reasons of artistic judgement, and they mean that results are achieved on CD which would be unattainable in the concert hall. Nevertheless in public performance too standards are very high. By contrast, almost all recordings of orchestras from the early decades of the twentieth century contain passages which would not be acceptable in modern performance.

Early conditions and achievements

When listening to the earliest 'orchestral' recordings, it is important to be aware of the conditions in which they were made. The pre-electric recording studio (that is, pre-1925) required all the musicians to be within close range of the recording horn in order to be audible. In practice, this usually meant a reduced number of players, perhaps thirty, crowded into a confined space, and with the scoring of large works drastically reduced.[1] An article in *The Gramophone* in December 1928 looks back at the days of 'acoustic' recording, and lists a typical string section of a recording orchestra as follows: 4 first violins, 2 Stroh second violins, 1 or 2 Stroh violas plus 1 clarinet, 1 cello plus 1 bassoon, 1 contrabassoon plus 1 tuba (the 'Stroh' violin was a specially constructed violin amplified by a horn). It is the tuba replacing the double basses which gives the 'oom-pah' character to many early recordings of opera arias, providing a sad contrast between the vividness of the voice and the dullness of the group accompanying it. Presumably a Nikisch or a Toscanini would not have tolerated a Stroh violin, and the ensemble described in *The Gramophone* was essentially an accompanying orchestra. But the quality of the playing on such recordings is also very variable. Much depended on the skill of the conductor. Experienced opera conductors, such as Landon Ronald and Percy Pitt, could achieve reasonable precision and point even under such conditions. The anonymous conductors who directed many of the early opera recordings presided over lamentable performances, ill-tuned and rhythmically leaden.

There were much more sophisticated attempts at early recording of orchestras without resort to such drastic re-scorings. What could be achieved in the early studio is demonstrated by the first recording session of the Boston Symphony Orchestra, conducted by Karl Muck, at which they played the Prelude to Act 3 of Wagner's *Lohengrin*. Subsidiary recording horns were set up outside the main studio, and wind soloists had to move to them to play their solos. The result is impressive. Probably the most substantial single achievement among pre-electrical orchestral recordings was the first recording of a Mahler symphony – No. 2 – played by the Orchestra of the Berlin State Opera under Oskar Fried in 1923/4. Despite the small orchestra and the cramped conditions, most of the symphony is rhythmically well disciplined and remarkably successful (though the choral ending is quite beyond the technology of the time). Nikisch's famous 1913 recording of Beethoven's Fifth Symphony, already mentioned by Jon Tolansky, is perhaps the most famous pre-electric orchestral recording. It conveys little of the power of the reduced Berlin Philharmonic, though it does give some idea of the drama of his fluctuating tempi (though both Boult and Toscanini said that it was not at all like Nikisch's concert performances).

Elgar and Richard Strauss were the first major composers to take recordings seriously, and both of them conducted pre-electric recordings of a number of their works. Elgar went to great efforts to re-score his works for the limited technology, and to decide on cuts to fit them on to the limited number of discs considered saleable. One result was his first recording of the Violin Concerto with Marie Hall as soloist, for which he wrote a new harp part to fill in the quiet textures, and cut each movement to a fraction of its original length to fit on one side.[2]

The quality of early orchestral recordings is therefore hit-and-miss, and needs to be judged with great caution. Their limitations generally made them less satisfactory than recordings of singers and chamber music, and few of them conveyed anything of the impression of a full orchestra in a concert hall. When, at the end of the period of acoustic recording, *The Gramophone* in October 1925 published a list of the most popular records as voted for by their readers, very few orchestral recordings were included. This was despite the fact that many orchestral recordings were by then available, including all of Beethoven's symphonies. When a similar survey of the most popular electrical recordings was published after only three years of electrical recording in April 1928, two thirds of them were orchestral, including seven of the ten most popular.[3]

Distinctive orchestral palettes

From the late 1920s the new electrical process led to a flood of orchestral recordings, covering a wide repertory, and they make it possible for us to assess realistically, though within limitations, the qualities of the world's major orchestras. Made in the days when international travel was difficult, and different countries still preserved their traditional ways of doing things, they reveal a variety of approaches, styles and standards that are unknown in today's 'globalised' environment.

Orchestras in different countries, and even in different cities within the same country, still had distinct sounds and styles. This was partly to do with differences in the instruments that were used. Some of the instruments that have become almost universal in later years were still only used in certain countries, whereas instruments that are now almost obsolete in the conventional modern orchestra were much more widespread then.

In the early decades of the twentieth century, the wooden flute was still predominant in Britain, Germany and Eastern Europe, and it was usually played with little or no vibrato. Even when the metal flute was used in these countries, it was generally played in the old manner. This old 'straight' style of flute-playing can be heard in many pre-war recordings of British and middle-European orchestras, such as the Vienna Philharmonic, Berlin Philharmonic and Czech Philharmonic. By contrast, the French school founded by Paul Taffanel (1844–1908) developed the use of a brilliant, expressive, and vibrant style on the metal flute, and it was this style which, in varied forms, came to dominate the world in the second half of the twentieth century. Taffanel's pupils Philippe Gaubert, Marcel Moyse and

Georges Barrère taught a new generation of flautists in France and America. The very fast vibrato of Barrère's pupil William Kincaid, principal of the Philadelphia Orchestra from 1921 to 1960, was particularly influential on later generations of American flautists. The metal flute and the French style were increasingly, though not exclusively, taken up by British players from the 1930s onwards, notably by Geoffrey Gilbert, principal flute in Beecham's London Philharmonic Orchestra, whose subtle playing of Debussy's *Prélude à l'après-midi d'un faune* in 1939 is one of the most beautiful on record.

Similar contrasts applied to bassoon-playing, though in this case it was the French who adhered longest to the more traditional instrument. The French bassoon in France was played, at its best, with a warm, vibrant tone and subtle phrasing. On the other hand, just how ill-tuned and crude a French bassoon could sound is demonstrated by early English recordings, and some French. The German bassoon, easier to play in tune, broader and fuller in tone, was already well established in Germany and Austria by 1900, and was played, like the flute in those countries, with little or no vibrato. The conductor of the Hallé Orchestra, Hans Richter, brought two Viennese bassoonists to Manchester in the early years of the century, and their use of the German bassoon spread, via Archie Camden (principal bassoon in the Hallé from 1914 and the BBC Symphony Orchestra from 1933), to other British players during the 1930s. In America the French bassoon is occasionally heard on recordings from the 1920s (played most beautifully in a *c.* 1926 recording of Ravel's *Mother Goose* Suite by the New York Symphony Orchestra under Damrosch). The German instrument predominated, but was often played with vibrato and with more flexible phrasing than was usual in Europe (for example in the Philadelphia Orchestra by Walter Guetter from 1922 and Sol Schoenbach from 1937).

There were also differences in the oboes and clarinets used in different countries, in the dimensions and shape of the bore, in the systems of key-work, and, most important, in the shape and style of reed. But as with flutes and bassoons, the broad trend over the twentieth century was towards greater flexibility of tone and phrasing, the increasing use of vibrato (though less widely on the clarinet than on the oboe and flute), and improved tuning. The developments in oboe style were led by the French, particularly by pupils of Georges Gillet, who occupied several of the principal positions in American orchestras. Prominent among these was Marcel Tabuteau in the Philadelphia Orchestra, whose flexibility of phrasing and delicate, fast vibrato influenced many American players of later generations. In England, Léon Goossens, the oboist with the most flexible phrasing and vibrato of any player before World War II, acknowledged the influence of the Belgian Henri de Busscher, who played in the Queen's Hall Orchestra from 1904, and whom Goossens succeeded as principal in 1913. But although many British oboists played on French instruments early in the twentieth century, the predominant style was powerful rather than subtle, largely without vibrato or nuances, and unreliable in tuning. Elements of this old English style continued into the 1930s, but by the 1940s almost all players had adopted the more refined and flexible style. Meanwhile in the orchestras of central Europe, the Berlin Philharmonic, the Vienna Philharmonic, the Dresden Staatskapelle and the Czech Philharmonic, the tradition of playing the oboe without vibrato persisted into the 1940s, though the style of phrasing was broader and smoother than in Britain, the predominant tone darker and mellower, and the tuning generally better (though by no means as reliable as in modern orchestras).

Charles Draper and his pupil Frederick Thurston, the most famous British clarinettists of the early twentieth century, played with a particularly clear and bright tone, broad phrasing, and with no vibrato at all. Reginald Kell was the first notable British clarinettist to adopt vibrato, and, like his colleagues in the London Philharmonic Orchestra Léon Goossens and Geoffrey Gilbert, he influenced a number of later players. But the two traditions continued to co-exist in Britain, some clarinettists playing with, others without, vibrato. When vibrato was used from the 1940s onwards, it was almost invariably quite slow and subtle. By contrast, some French clarinettists were already playing with a rapid tremor as early as the 1920s, and with a thinner and reedier tone than British players. Despite the influence of French woodwind in America, vibrato on the clarinet was rare in American orchestral recordings before World War II, and as in Britain many American clarinettists continued to play without vibrato into the twenty-first century (though some prominent soloists, such as Richard Stoltzman, do now play with vibrato). This reluctance to adopt vibrato in America is in contrast to pre-war jazz players, such as Benny Goodman, and it is perhaps because of the association with jazz that orchestral clarinettists in America remained so resistant to the vibrato of their oboist and flautist colleagues. Like the flute, oboe, and bassoon, the clarinet in central Europe was played without vibrato and with broad phrasing, and this remains the predominant style to this day despite the vibrato of oboists and flautists. The old Austro-German style was epitomised by Leopold Wlach, principal of the Vienna Philharmonic Orchestra from 1930 to 1953, whose creamy tone and broad, subtly nuanced phrasing stand at the opposite extreme from the bright and tremulous reediness of his contemporaries in France.

Listening to recordings of the woodwind section as a whole, it is most striking how the trend over the last hundred years has been towards smooth homogeneity of tone and ensemble. In general the modern woodwind section across the world blends together in a manner that was unknown in the great majority of orchestras in the early twentieth century. It was only in some American orchestras, particularly Toscanini's New York Philharmonic Symphony Orchestra, that a modern standard of woodwind ensemble was heard as early as the 1930s. Admittedly, at its best the central European woodwind of the 1930s could achieve an organ-like steadiness and breadth of tone, but the blend and tuning were not like those of the twenty-first century. This lack of blend was particularly marked in French orchestras, in which individual instruments tended to be quite distinct from each other in tone-colour. Stravinsky's own recordings of his ballet scores, and of *The Soldier's Tale* and the Octet, illustrate the point vividly. His Paris recordings made between 1928 and 1932, rhythmically nervous, and pungent in tone-colours, are quite different in character from his later American recordings, in which a more comfortable rhythmic stability is combined with a smoother, more blended ensemble.

The brass instruments also contribute to the changing tone-colours of Stravinsky's recordings. The pungent tone of French trumpets and cornets is distinct from the broader and bigger tone of later Americans, with their more confident vibrato. Horn-playing varied in style from one country to another. A delicate vibrato was often used in France, as well as in the Czech Philharmonic Orchestra. Narrow-bore French horns remained in general use in the 1930s in France and Britain, notably in the fine playing of Aubrey Brain and his son Dennis. The wider-bore German horn, and its American variants, already in use in Germany and America, came to dominate in the second half of the century. The general trend towards wider-bore brass instruments tended to produce a more massive brass section. The narrower-bore instruments in general use in the early years of the twentieth century were less inclined to overwhelm the strings with sheer weight of sound.

The general effect of this trend towards a heavier, wider-bore brass section has sometimes been exaggerated. Skilful players under a wise conductor could still create transparency of texture even with the instruments of the late twentieth century, as, for example, in Rudolf Kempe's wonderfully subtle performances and recordings of the works of Richard Strauss. If one compares the playing of Dennis Brain before and after he changed from the French to the German horn, it is striking how slight the difference is. It is probably true that the average brass section *c.* 1900 was less inclined to swamp the strings than the average brass section *c.* 2000, but this had at least as much to do with the demands of conductors and the habits of players as it had to do with the designs of instruments. And the comparison cannot fairly be made by recordings. Even in electrical recordings from the late 1920s onwards, the balance between the different sections of the orchestra cannot really be judged, because fortissimos tend to be congested and distorted, and what one is hearing is what was caught by microphones in particular positions, not what the audience would have heard in the concert hall. Recording levels on 78 rpm records had to be kept within a narrow dynamic range to avoid 'blasting', so the brass section on orchestral recordings is often rather distant, with the balance favouring the strings much more than in the concert hall.

In any case, as the brass have increased in power, so have the strings. Stringed instruments in the early twentieth century were predominantly strung with gut. Steel E-strings on the violin, though available from the 1890s, were still controversial through the 1920s and 1930s. Many players still favoured not only gut strings, but also the older, less assertive styles of bowing characteristic of Joachim, Piatti and other nineteenth-century teachers, together with their restrained approach to vibrato. High-powered soloists, notably Heifetz, and teachers such as Carl Flesch, encouraged the trend towards force, power, and vibrancy and one can hear the influence of this style particularly on the orchestras of America: Toscanini's New York Philharmonic Symphony Orchestra, Koussevitsky's Boston Symphony Orchestra, and Stokowski's Philadelphia Orchestra. By contrast, until World War II the Vienna Philharmonic Orchestra was still led by Arnold Rosé, a player brought up in the 1870s who had led concerts under Brahms and Mahler. The string style of the orchestra was sparing of vibrato, and the bowing and articulation much less assertive and high-powered than in the modern Vienna Philharmonic.

Of the orchestras recording in England in the late 1920s, the Hallé Orchestra in Manchester, conducted by Hamilton Harty, and the (New) Queen's Hall Orchestra in London, conducted by Henry Wood, were more regular in their membership that most of the London orchestras which still tolerated the 'deputy system'. Wood discouraged the very heavy portamento to be heard in many British recordings of the period, and the string-playing of his orchestra is therefore unusually 'clean'. Harty's Hallé played with heavier portamento, but the rhythmic discipline of his orchestra was more impressive than that of London orchestras. Harty's recording of the 'Enigma' variations is often tighter in rhythm and more incisive in ensemble than Elgar's own with the Royal Albert Hall Orchestra. Wood's recording of Elgar's Violin Concerto, with Albert Sammons, is better co-ordinated than Elgar's with the London Symphony Orchestra and Menuhin. Neither Harty nor Wood, however, gets from his orchestra that combination of energy and flexibility of nuance that Elgar achieved with more informal ensembles.

London orchestras produced huge quantities of recordings in the late 1920s. Because of the combination of irregular membership and shortage of rehearsal, the standard was often low (as it was in Paris, for the same reasons). Some of the best recordings were made by the orchestra of the Royal Philharmonic Society, which, though no more regular than other orchestras, assembled for the recording studio a team of strings which often

12.1 Adrian Boult and the BBC Symphony Orchestra leaving Euston Station in London for a concert at the Free Trade Hall, Manchester, 5 December 1934

show quite a subtle approach to portamento (notably in Delius recordings conducted by Beecham) and woodwind led by oboist Léon Goossens, whose flexibility of phrasing and use of vibrato were quite exceptional in Britain at that time.

Orchestral standards in London took a great leap forward with the establishment of two new regularly rehearsed orchestras in the early 1930s: the BBC Symphony Orchestra (founded 1930) conducted by Boult, and the London Philharmonic Orchestra (founded 1932) conducted by Beecham. Recordings show that they achieved a quality of ensemble, and refinement of sonority and phrasing, that were unknown in Britain in the 1920s. The LPO's woodwind were particularly distinguished. Several of Beecham's finest Sibelius and Delius recordings date from this period, including Sibelius's Fourth Symphony, the Prelude to Delius's *Irmelin*, with its beautiful string phrasing, and *La Calinda*, showing the subtlety of Léon Goossens's rubato. Boult's BBC orchestra was notable for more Germanic virtues of blend, firmness, and accuracy of ensemble. The brass were particularly fine, with the horns led by Aubrey Brain (who insisted on the use of the narrow-bore French horn in F), and the trumpets by Ernest Hall. The quality of the new BBC orchestra was such that Toscanini, visiting in 1935, cancelled some of the scheduled rehearsals. His recordings with them, of Beethoven's Symphonies Nos. 1, 4 and 6, have much of the intensity and precision of his American recordings, and Boult's of the Symphony No. 8 is remarkably similar in quality. The London Philharmonic Orchestra made some particularly distinguished concerto recordings in the 1930s: Brahms, Beethoven and Mendelssohn with Kreisler, Sibelius with Heifetz, Beethoven Nos. 2, 3 and 4 with Schnabel, Schumann and Franck (*Variations Symphoniques*) with Cortot. (Of these, only the Sibelius was conducted by Beecham, the others by Barbirolli, Sargent and Ronald.)

Influential conductors and orchestral discipline

The distinctiveness of early twentieth-century orchestras was partly to do with regional playing styles, but in some cases also to do with the demands of highly individual conductors. It is not for nothing that record labels often carried the wording 'Mengelberg's Concertgebouw Orchestra' or 'Stokowski's Philadelphia Orchestra'. Each of these orchestras had a highly individual string style encouraged by their conductors. Both used portamento much more heavily through the 1930s than other orchestras did by this time, the Philadelphia tending towards languorous swooping (as in Stokowski's famous Bach transcriptions), the Concertgebouw towards the use of the slide as a sentimental accent, often in surprising places. The Philadelphia sliding often sounds like an exaggerated form of the widespread habit of the 1920s, whereas the Concertgebouw sliding often sounds like a carefully rehearsed effect.

Toscanini's orchestras were noted for their extraordinary precision, ferocity of attack, and expressive intensity. In his recordings with the New York Philharmonic Symphony Orchestra in the late 1920s and early 1930s there is also great finesse and delicacy in both strings and woodwind, notably in his famous recording of Beethoven's Seventh Symphony (1936). With his last orchestra of the 1940s and 1950s, the NBC Symphony Orchestra, the attack could become somewhat brutal, particularly in the dry radio studio in which many of their recordings were made. The woodwind blend was not as subtle as in the New York Philharmonic Orchestra, and the oboe tone was more pungent than in other American orchestras. Often Toscanini's recordings are most impressive when he is visiting other orchestras. The recordings that he made during his season with the Philadelphia Orchestra are exceptionally fine, combining the grandeur and warmth of the orchestra trained under Stokowski (and more recently by Ormandy) with a new rhythmic focus and intensity. Their recording of Tchaikovsky's 'Pathétique' Symphony (1942) is perhaps the most remarkable of the series of recordings they made together.

By the late 1940s, the trend towards what now seems modern orchestral discipline and style was to be heard on recordings from all countries. The Philadelphia Orchestra under Ormandy, and the Concertgebouw under Van

Beinum, had refined their approach to portamento while retaining other aspects of their pre-war characters – breadth and richness of tone in Philadelphia, rhythmic force, and an exciting 'edge' to the brass, in Amsterdam.
French wind-playing tended towards a smoother blend than in pre-war
recordings, though there could still be sour tuning (as, to an astonishing
extent, in Oubradous's recording of Mozart's Serenade K361 for thirteen instruments, recorded in 1941). A wider vibrato in brass-playing than in the
1930s was to be heard in French orchestras, the Czech Philharmonic, and
in the Russian recordings that were now becoming available. The Vienna
Philharmonic and Berlin Philharmonic continued to play with little vibrato
in the woodwind until the 1950s; but the Vienna Philharmonic had lost
that characteristic 'straight' string sound and audible shifting of its pre-war
recordings, as the old guard led by Arnold Rosé was replaced by players with
a more modern approach to vibrato, portamento and bowing. In Britain
too, the string style was by the late 1940s free of prominent portamento,
and all oboists and flautists, and an increasing number of clarinettists and
bassoonists, played with vibrato. Two new orchestras again had the effect of
raising orchestral standards in Britain, as the BBC Symphony Orchestra and
London Philharmonic Orchestra had done in the early 1930s. These were the
Philharmonia Orchestra, founded specifically as a recording orchestra by the
producer/impresario Walter Legge, and the Royal Philharmonic Orchestra,
established by that compulsive orchestra-founder Beecham, following his
departure from the London Philharmonic.

The archive of orchestral recordings allows vivid comparisons to be
made. A difficult test piece, such as the scherzo from Mendelssohn's
Incidental Music for *A Midsummer Night's Dream*, brings the contrasts
into stark relief. Toscanini's recording with the Philharmonic Symphony
Orchestra of New York in 1929 is marvellously light and easy; his 1926
recording with the same orchestra is more clumsy, and his later recording with the NBC Symphony Orchestra (1946) is more tightly disciplined
than either of the earlier versions, though with an almost military edge
which takes away from the lightness. By comparison, the London Symphony
Orchestra under Beecham (*c.* 1926) barely gets through it. The rhythm is
not under control, and the players scramble in their attempt to keep together. This is a strong candidate for Beecham's worst ever recording. The
Royal Albert Hall Orchestra under Landon Ronald (*c.* 1926) is only slightly
more under control, confirming that what could be achieved with under-
rehearsed orchestras of irregular membership was strictly limited.

On the other hand, improvements in British orchestras in the 1930s are
equally clear from recordings. Elgar's two recordings of *Cockaigne* make a
typical comparison. With the Royal Albert Hall Orchestra (1926) rhythmic
details are often a little hasty and unclear. They are noticeably firmer and

more tightly controlled with the BBC Symphony Orchestra (1933). It is arguable how much of this is a stylistic shift: Elgar himself was satisfied with the RAH recording, and wondered why HMV wanted to record the work again. (Modern recordings of this work show yet more insistence on clarity of detail: would Elgar have found this pedantic?) Beecham's London Philharmonic Orchestra recordings from the 1930s show a similar tightening up of detail compared with London orchestras in the 1920s. Beecham made some good recordings of Mozart with the Royal Philharmonic Society's orchestra in the 1920s, but none is as refined in discipline and phrasing as the famous recordings of Mozart that he made with the London Philharmonic in the 1930s. Their 1938/9 recording of Mozart's 'Haffner' Symphony is as well disciplined as Toscanini's with the New York Philharmonic Symphony Orchestra (1928).

Of European orchestras Mengelberg's Concertgebouw Orchestra was the most highly disciplined during the 1920s and 1930s, bearing comparison with the finest American playing of the time. Their performance of Tchaikovsky's *Romeo and Juliet* (1930) is as well disciplined as that of Koussevitzky's Boston Symphony Orchestra (1936), though the weight and panache of the latter has even more impact (admittedly in a later and better recording). Though their co-ordination was not as strictly controlled, the Vienna Philharmonic Orchestra demonstrated impressive rhythmic grip (in Brahms and Mahler under Walter), and an easy rhythmic poise (as in their Mozart recordings, such as the overture to *The Marriage of Figaro* under Krauss). The Berlin Philharmonic Orchestra developed under Furtwängler a particularly impressive depth of string tone, combined with flexibility and breadth of phrasing. Comparison between live and studio recordings shows that Furtwängler and his orchestra in the concert hall sometimes played with greater flexibility of tempo, and particularly with broader tempi in slow sections, than in the studio, where records were made one side at a time.

The spread of uniformity

With the exception of Eastern European orchestras, which had developed a power and vibrancy all their own, the trend from the 1930s onwards was towards greater uniformity of style and standards across the world. By the end of the twentieth century it was often difficult to tell the difference between orchestras from across the world, and even the Eastern Europeans began to tone down their style to conform with this general picture. The easy availability of recordings meant that a generation of players had grown up with the sounds of all the world's musicians in their ears. Unlike musicians of the early twentieth century and earlier periods, they could pick and choose the styles on which to model their own playing. So an oboist in Britain might well sound like a blend of French, German and American styles. National differences in approach to string-playing became much more difficult to detect, as the generation for whom Russian, Franco-Belgian and German string-playing were distinct approaches gradually died out, giving way to a generation for whom style had largely become globalised.

This applies as much to 'period' orchestras as to others. The difference in basic style between period orchestras in America, Canada, Britain, Holland and Germany in the twenty-first century is slight – far slighter than the differences between orchestras in different countries must have been in the eighteenth and nineteenth centuries, the periods supposedly being recreated.

The value of recorded evidence

Where will all this lead? This is really a subject for other chapters, but the trends preserved on the recordings of the last hundred years do give some indications. In the fields of solo and chamber music, musicians of the highest quality will always find ways of asserting their individuality, despite globalisation. But the prospects for orchestral individuality are less certain. In the modern world, with its demand for reliability, the universal availability of 'perfect' recordings, and the financial requirement that flawless results should be achieved quickly, it is all too easy for orchestras to become bland and faceless bodies, able to produce efficient and musically impeccable performances, but galvanised into something more meaningful only by a conductor of commanding stature. And since conductors, like orchestras, have themselves tended in recent years to become less and less distinct from each other, and have travelled more and more from orchestra to orchestra rather than developing a deep rapport with one ensemble, this is an increasingly rare occurrence.

As already noted by Colin Lawson, period-instrument orchestras have recently reached the repertory that overlaps with the early years of recording. From Brahms and Mahler, just out of reach of recordings, period instrumentalists have tackled Elgar, who himself recorded most of his own works. One orchestra, the New Queen's Hall Orchestra (named, somewhat cheekily, after Henry Wood's orchestra), is dedicated specifically to the performance of late nineteenth- and early twentieth-century repertory, using the woodwind, brass and percussion instruments appropriate to the period (wooden flutes, French bassoons, narrow-bore brass, kettledrums with vellum covers). The stringed instruments are strung with gut.

Do experiments of this kind produce something like the sounds we hear on early twentieth-century recordings? It is either a relief or a disappointment, depending on one's point of view, to find that they do not. Not surprisingly, it proves very difficult for players who spend most of their time in conventional modern performance to break away from the styles and habits of their own day and step back a hundred years when playing familiar orchestral repertory. The positive side of this is that they play better in tune, and with more accurate co-ordination, than anything heard on early twentieth-century recordings. But this level of accuracy, as in so much modern playing, is bought at the expense of those freedoms and expressive flexibilities that are so characteristic of early twentieth-century playing. A modern body of orchestral string players cannot begin to think like a body of the early twentieth century. The orchestras of London, Amsterdam and Vienna were distinct in style, but what they had in common was an approach to phrasing which is utterly at loggerheads with modern neatness. Mengelberg's encouragement of portamento in the Concertgebouw Orchestra was perhaps extravagant. The fastidious Viennese tended to slide just audibly enough to prevent the listener forgetting that string-playing is a physical activity, in which hands move up and down fingerboards. The Royal Albert Hall Orchestra (with which Elgar recorded the 'Enigma' variations) were more lavish than the Viennese in their portamento and less disciplined in its application than the Concertgebouw. But with all three orchestras the sense of individuals 'doing their own thing', and more or less co-ordinating it, is very far from any modern ideas of orchestral ensemble. They lack the modern unanimity of execution, but at their best, they convey an extraordinary sense of unanimity of purpose. One cannot listen to the famous Viennese live performances of Mahler's *Das Lied von der Erde* and Ninth Symphony under Bruno Walter without feeling a powerful impression of individuals striving to put the music across together. Modern, highly polished performances of these works convey much less sense of individuals struggling to combine. They are, by comparison, immaculate and impersonal, because so much of the sense of the physical effort and presence of the musician has been removed from modern playing, particularly after it has been further refined in the recording studio and the editing channel.

The evidence of early recordings is surely the most important bridge we have back into the styles of the nineteenth century, in orchestral as in all other areas of musical performance. When we listen to the Vienna Philharmonic Orchestra recorded in the 1930s, we are hearing something which must be quite close to their sound and style when they played under Mahler and Brahms. However slapdash we may think the Royal Albert Hall Orchestra and the London Symphony Orchestra under Elgar, they are nevertheless the musicians with whom he worked, and whom he accepted as his colleagues and interpreters. The pungent sounds of French woodwind and brass are what Fauré, Debussy and Ravel expected (and in the case of Ravel, worked with on recordings).

But this evidence is not as convenient as many modern enthusiasts might like it to be. Many of the features of early recordings go quite against modern notions of style, ensemble, and competence, and anyone who listens to early recordings with open ears will realise that an attempt to reproduce what is heard would be pointless in the modern world, with its very different priorities and experience.

There are nevertheless important lessons to learn from them. The fact that orchestral music-making used to be so diverse, and is now, by comparison, so uniform, is surely not a trend to celebrate. The fact that orchestras were often imprecise is not necessarily something we would now wish to aspire to. But the fact that precision of ensemble used not to be the first priority in music-making, and that the taking of risks was much more a part of a musician's life than it is today, might make one regret that the priorities have shifted as far as they have. The technology of modern recording has exaggerated this trend: any imperfections caused by risk-taking in the studio are meticulously edited out. Thank goodness that there are still musicians who take risks in the concert hall, though perhaps not to the extent that they did back in the 1920s.

We are the first generation that can actually hear what musicians of seventy or eighty years ago actually sounded like. What should we do with this evidence? In practice, what happens when musicians study these recordings is that the elements of style that are compatible with modern notions of neatness get absorbed, or in some cases, imitated, but the elements that go against modern taste are discarded. That is probably inevitable in the short term. But in the longer term it would be nice to think that early recordings might help us to re-examine our obsession with precision, control, and uniformity, and to rediscover some of the freedom and diversity of the past.

13 The orchestral composer

ROBERT SAXTON

The composer and the orchestra today

'Though the standard orchestra is not yet an anachronism, perhaps, it can no longer be used standardly except by anachronistic composers.'[1] Stravinsky's statement, made in the late 1950s, undoubtedly carries weight: first, from a historical angle and secondly, on account of the aesthetic/technical issues raised by such a succinct, yet perceptive, remark.

The purely musical is unavoidably bound up with practical, cultural and social issues whenever a composer writes an orchestral piece. If the creative spark has been kindled by a commission, the terms of the contract are usually clear, those who manage both chamber and symphony orchestras being primarily concerned with financial survival and, intertwined with such a concern, audience numbers. In short, money and ratings matter. As a result, outside the quasi-Utopian realm of public service broadcasting, an orchestra is a business whose very existence depends on pleasing the public, with all that this implies. Composers today cannot rely on the seriousness of mind displayed by Frederick the Great towards Bach (what contemporary monarch or arts administrator could set a composer a fugue subject?), nor can they expect the average listener to be versed in a particularly wide-ranging repertory at any level other than the most superficial. An orchestral concert is, historically, as well as by nature and intention, a public event, albeit the nature and scope of the 'public' having changed over the course of three centuries. There is no doubt that Haydn's late symphonies parade their virtues in a way in which his mature quartets do not; the brushstrokes are broader. The respective functions of the genres were different, a distinct dividing line existing between the connoisseur player/listener and the wider audience. Consciously or unconsciously, a composer cannot avoid such a historical viewpoint, because the issues in question are inherited. When writing a commissioned piece for orchestra, a composer is aware of what constitutes either a 'standard' symphony or chamber orchestra and this affects the approach with regard to character, gesture and scale. It is not that one intentionally writes either 'historical' or 'public' music (what does this mean or entail?), but technical solutions to compositional problems must be found which relate directly to the orchestra as it is conventionally constituted, re-seating the orchestra, for example, being a serious time-management problem for most orchestras. Rehearsal schedules are of concern in a way which does not apply to the string quartet; 'anachronistic' medium though the latter may also be, it is not at the mercy of bureaucracy and under continual threat of financial extinction. There is a world of difference between a body of players assembled as an orchestra in an 'ideal' society and the reality of orchestras run as businesses, with their management structures, marketing departments and promotion of 'star' performers. The composer certainly has a role as part of an orchestra's education programme, but such an important aspect of building an audience for the future is rarely viewed as a vital element in the continuing existence of the orchestra as a business. If a composer ignores such matters and writes an uncommissioned orchestral work, then he/she embraces artistic freedom, but is such 'freedom' illusory and what does it mean in practice?

Despite the fact that the word 'orchestra', in both its Graeco-Roman and subsequent Renaissance usage, was a definition of place, not of the constituent parts of a whole, a composer writing for the conventionally seated orchestra in the early twenty-first century is faced with a more-or-less standardised playing body and, consequently, must pour new wine into an old bottle. However we consider these issues, we are inevitably faced with the nature of the orchestra as an 'instrument' which, in the final analysis, was developed to play homophonic music of the Common Practice harmonic era. The use of the orchestra in serious compositional practice is inseparable from the musical thought of a composer, the notable and important exception being in the realm of commercial music, where an orchestrator realises a composer's detailed draft. Brahms's textures, for example, with their frequently keyboard-derived arpeggiated motives and accompaniment figures, rhythmic subtlety and smooth voice-leading required a different conception of the orchestra from that of his older contemporary Bruckner, whose blocks of orchestral sonority delineate the architectural argument and sheer weight of sound in a specific and idiosyncratic fashion. The harmonic spectrum, from bass to treble, remained intact as the basis of the music, regardless of manner or style, and this applied equally to composers from outside the Austro-German tradition as within it.

Instrumentation as a manifestation of compositional thought

One has only to compare the slow introductions of Mozart's 'Prague' Symphony and Beethoven's Symphony No. 1 to see and hear not dissimilar expressive and structural intentions realised very differently within a style (the style here being the Classical Style, as opposed to 'manner', which I take

Ex. 13.1 From Elgar, Symphony No. 1

to refer to each composer's personal traits within the general style). Musical thought and instrumentation, in the hands of the greatest composers of the period, were one. Outside the realm of Austro-German practice the situation was somewhat different, a view cogently expressed by Boulez: 'If we are thinking in terms of characteristics rather than of tradition, then one of the constant features of French musical expression since the eighteenth century ... has been a preoccupation with sound itself.'[2] With the advent of the *Märchen* world of German Romanticism and its manifestation in

Ex. 13.1 (cont.)

the theatre, particularly in the hands of Weber, orchestral colour and effect began to take on a life of their own; indeed, in the case of later composers, it can fairly be said that many listeners can recognise works by Elgar,
Mahler, Richard Strauss and Sibelius from the individuality of their orchestral sound alone; one thinks of these contemporaries as primarily orchestral
thinkers, high watermarks of the great age of the symphony orchestra. A
detailed comparison between the third movement of Mahler's Ninth Symphony, Rondo-Burleske (1908–10) and the second movement (Scherzo) from

Ex. 13.2 From Mahler, Symphony No. 9

Elgar's First Symphony (1908) repays close study. Both pieces begin with abrupt gestures and 'scurrying' strings, the latter in both cases presenting material which will be used organically (Ex. 13.1: Elgar Symphony No. 1 in A♭, Op. 55, Novello, p. 64; Ex. 13.2: Mahler Symphony No. 9, U.E. (Philharmonia), p. 106). At rehearsal number 71 in the Elgar, we find the initial counterpoint in a lower register and spanning a narrower range than at first, functioning as a rhythmically dynamic accompaniment to the woodwind *Hauptstimme*. Mahler, similarly, uses his thematic fragments contrapuntally from bar 311, but as part of a sparer texture (horns, cellos and basses) over a relatively long span; this is then developed in a highly contrapuntal manner, its hard-edged linearity creating a world very different from that of Elgar's more kaleidoscopic, undulating aural landscape. For the past ninety years or so, composers have had to recreate the orchestra in their own image, the reasons for this being syntactical/grammatic. Once a functioning bass is no longer present (that is, one comprised of true tonal roots, not modal notes which happen to appear in the bass register), the constitution of the orchestra comes into question with respect to its constituent parts and their function.

The relationship between conception, ideas and their realisation

Ex. 13.3 shows the opening bars of Bach's Orchestral Suite No. 3 and it is plain that, limitations of brass and timpani aside, the 'orchestral' thinking is not far removed from organ registration. Of course, Bach was capable

Ex. 13.3 From Bach, Orchestral Suite No. 3

Ex. 13.4 From Haydn, Symphony No. 44, 'Trauer'

of extraordinarily virtuosic instrumentation, but this extract illustrates a general point with regard to the layered nature of the Baroque orchestra.

If there is a need to articulate quick changes of texture, mood and pacing in conjunction with a non-contrapuntal surface and at the service of musical drama, then a different 'instrument' must be developed, as was the case with the advent of the Classical Style. To a great extent, the end dictated the means and there exist countless examples, ranging from Haydn's highly original horn pairings and 'structural' use of wind instruments onwards. In *Sonata Forms*,[3] Rosen illustrates the sophisticated integration of compositional thought with structural/orchestral logic by citing the first horn's sounding f#′ (notated d″) in the seventeenth bar of the first-movement exposition of Haydn's Symphony No. 44 in E minor, the 'Trauer' (Ex. 13.4).

This note is isolated for one crotchet only; this is vital, in that it not only highlights the leading-note of G, the relative major towards which the music is directed, but throws a spotlight on a solo instrument which, until now, has merely supported the string harmony. The horn breaks through, uniting gesture, architectural thought and instrumental colour at a stroke. At the seventeenth bar of the slow movement of his Piano Concerto in F Major, K459 (Ex. 13.5), Mozart emphasises the flat supertonic by isolating the flute an octave above the first violins, reducing the dynamic level from forte to piano instantly. This creates not only 'local' drama, but also structural tension by delaying the cadence in the tonic for the entrance of the soloist. A finer example of structural-expressive-orchestral synthesis is hard to find, not only because of its musical logic (Haydn has this), but because of its unforced inevitability.

Ex. **13.5** From Mozart, Piano Concerto in F K459

It is known that Brahms was in awe of this quality in Mozart's work and it is instructive to examine the opening of his Symphony No. 4 in E minor in order to understand how he tried to recreate on his own terms such musical coherence and ease of utterance. Exx. 13.6a, b and c give the passage in question in a piano reduction.

Ex. 13.6 From Brahms, Symphony No. 4 (reductions by Robert Saxton)

In the case of Ex. 6a, the accompaniment is faithful in outline to the orchestral score; Ex. 6b goes a stage further, showing the accompaniment in a more generalised form which, from both a voice-leading and 'organic' angle, is no longer contextually specific; Ex. 6c takes generalisation to the extreme, displaying, by means of figuring, the harmonic changes over the tonic pedal. It is clear from the above that both the arpeggiated melody and the accompaniments are pianistic, but Brahms's orchestral conception is made manifest in a subtle and profound structural manner (Ex. 13.7).

As Schoenberg clarified in *Fundamentals of Musical Composition*,[4] the melodic line is a chain of descending and ascending thirds, the descent forming the antecedent and the ascent the consequent of the eight-bar statement. This is 'analysed' before our very ears in the woodwind, who play dyads in thirds over three octaves (later, sixths and two perfect fifths in the bassoons for 'bass' harmonic reasons). Vertical and linear are elements of a unified field and, although identical in terms of musical 'DNA', complement one another in terms of orchestral presentation. The sonority of first and second violins in octaves, and the binding two-part horn writing, assist in giving the texture its 'glow' (in the absence of a sustaining pedal), whilst the accompanying rising arpeggios reveal their own subtleties; note that Brahms places the double basses' E in the same sounding register as the initial E in the cellos, not an octave lower. This not only avoids the dangers of a low open string, but also leaves room for textural expansion later; the four repetitions

Ex. 13.7 From Brahms, Symphony No. 4

of the E unobtrusively 'point' the pedal note and the first stress of each bar, aiding the anacrusis of the upper melodic line. The arpeggios are spaced so that the cellos initially anticipate the divided violas' starting notes, emphasising the structural importance of the third. A less imaginative or thorough composer might simply have written ascending arpeggios 'in note order' (see example 13.6b), thereby losing this organic, lower-registral reflection of the third-saturated woodwind and violins. From rehearsal letter A, bar 19, it is the cellos and basses, in octave unison now, who herald the textural expansion, playing the weak-beat pattern heard at the beginning in the woodwind; this is not merely structurally cohesive on account of its origin, but also because its textural and functional source is that of the principle of invertible counterpoint. Whilst this occurs, Brahms introduces inter-family melodic doubling; this has been reserved until the altered first-subject restatement and 'develops' the use of the orchestra in conjunction with the musical argument's 'developing variation' principle.

Such richness of detail illustrates the potential inherent in conceiving of musical material and the use of orchestral families as mutually indispensable elements of a musical discourse. Since harmonic rhythm in the Common Practice era followed the 'natural' laws of the structure of the harmonic series, with the rate-of-change controlled by the bass moving more slowly than the upper voices, the standard orchestral families had developed 'naturally'. One could describe the 'standard' orchestral universe as a closed mechanism, which might both historically, and in practice, be compared with the 'closed' Newtonian model of the universe. It is, perhaps, not far-fetched to pinpoint the fundamental shift away from this 'safe' world as being contemporary with Einstein's *Special Theory of Relativity* in 1905. Schoenberg's Chamber Symphony No. 1, written the following year, was not the result of a commission for reduced forces, but a piece born out of compositional necessity. In no way a forerunner of later 'Back to Bach' neo-classicism, it demonstrated a resurgence of contrapuntal writing at the deepest level of need and musical thought. The title itself tells us this; mass effect (as opposed to the use of tutti passages) is irrelevant here and, from the social/cultural to the technical/aesthetic, the conception is evolutionary, not revolutionary. We are confronted with a symphony which is neither 'public' art, nor 'orchestral' in a received sense; the evolutionary aspect lies first in the combination of the renewal of contrapuntal thought inherent in the 'late' chamber music of Haydn, Mozart and Beethoven, secondly in the unbroken formal unity chiefly propounded by Liszt and, finally, in a need to redefine the medium in line with compositional requirements.

Possibly the most significant issue which emerged for path-breaking composers as different as Schoenberg, Ives and Varèse was the matter of doubling, the mainstay of the relationship between orchestral families in the 'blended' romantic orchestra. In the third of Schoenberg's Five Pieces for Orchestra, Op. 16, the initial slowly changing colours and harmony appear, at first, to be simply a textural idea, but when analysed, an intervallic canon is revealed, demonstrating once more the intertwining of compositional logic and sound; in one sense, there is no orchestration, a phrase frequently used by Sir Peter Maxwell Davies when describing his own orchestral writing. Where early serial practice was concerned, the avoidance of octave doubling was a serious problem, a taboo which highlighted the growing gap between thought and practice; octave doubling is 'logical' in homophonic music emanating from post-Baroque harmonic practice because of the logarithmic structure of the harmonic series, but in the case of a central horizontal axis of control, as in an isorhythmic motet, becomes redundant. As Hindemith stated in the second volume of *Traditional Harmony*,[5] '[I]t is just the music of the period before 1500 . . . that represents for the musician of today an inexhaustible source of stimulation and enlightenment, at least as important as the music of the eighteenth and nineteenth centuries, and in many respects more so.' Whether or not one considers Hindemith's mid-twentieth-century viewpoint relevant where current compositional issues are concerned, it should stimulate any composer to serious thought when approaching orchestral composition.

Truly contrapuntal music (as opposed to homophonic music which is then 'dissolved' contrapuntally) needs inter-familial doublings only to clarify and balance, as in the case of the finale of Mozart's 'Jupiter' Symphony and, brilliant though Elgar, Schoenberg and Stokowski proved to be when arranging organ music by Bach for symphony orchestra, it has to be admitted that the music does not require such treatment. All that is added are weight and density, not of thought, but of sound. On a cultural/historic/social level, even Webern's 'analytic' orchestration of the six-part Ricercare from Bach's *Musical Offering*, whilst being aesthetically serious, is evidence of an attempt to make public an essentially private musical experience. Herein lies the reasoning behind Stravinsky's remark with which this chapter began.

In the twentieth century, there appeared composers whose musical syntax/grammar and ideas broke new ground from conception to realisation and who, as a result, tended to require radical rethinking of the use of the medium. Obvious examples are Bartók's Piano Concerto No. 2 in which the whole orchestra is only used in the final movement, Stravinsky's *Symphonies of Wind Instruments*, in which ethos and means cohere, and Webern's Symphony Op. 21 which, without double basses and with its 'centric' use of the harp, both defines and unites formal issues, the medium employed and, above all, intervallic and contrapuntal space in an aural orbit concerned with a horizontal axis of symmetry.

Debussy and Ravel had a profound effect on the use of the orchestra as conventionally constituted; the opening bars of the former's *La Mer* and the latter's *La Valse* both present emerging sound, rather than motives. Whilst it is possible to trace such a conception back to the start of Beethoven's Ninth Symphony, later French composers were concerned, as Boulez has said, with the quality and nature of (orchestral) sound itself. The orchestra is no longer a layering of families articulating a tonal/thematic argument, but has been transformed into an instrument of continually changing shades of colour and density, which is required to recreate the speed of figuration and rapidly changing textures of piano music based on the arabesque. Describing *Jeux*, Debussy said that he wanted to achieve an orchestral sound 'sans pieds' – a profound statement whose implications go beyond mere instrumentation and which says much about early twentieth-century harmonic 'freedom'.

Amongst others, Mahler, Nielsen, Sibelius and Prokofiev, committed to the continuation of symphonic thought in the new century (and I emphasise *symphonic thought* here, as opposed to the mere designation *symphony*), remained faithful to the 'conventional' orchestra, albeit with additions and variations, although, as always, such categorisation is not water-tight. Mahler's later orchestral polyphony and heterophony are different in intention and realisation from Nielsen's orchestral counterpoint and layering and, in the case of Sibelius, linear counterpoint (as distinct from background structural voice-leading) is virtually non-existent; in each case, the use of the orchestra is unique to each composer from background to foreground. Whilst the Second Viennese School continued the Austro-German ethos of unity and *Durchführung* without producing a body of works entitled 'symphony', Shostakovich, a supposed traditionalist, reconstituted the orchestra for his 14th Symphony, an orchestral song-cycle without wind or brass. So, even broad categories make us wary of defining the constitution of the orchestra and the variety of demands made on it across three centuries by composers, when considering the nature of the generating idea for a specific work and its realisation.

Composers of the period of Common Practice wrote in conjunction with an *a priori* background, but this has clearly not been the general case since the late nineteenth century, a situation which has impinged directly on the use of the orchestra since and which is made manifest if we take as an example the operatic vocal score. A comparison between two vocal-score editions of the opening of the Prelude to Wagner's *Lohengrin* and a passage from the vocal score of Berg's *Wozzeck* makes the point. In the case of the first extract, from Sullivan and Pittman's late nineteenth-century Boosey edition, Wagner's quiet and ethereal string texture, in which violins divided into four parts are echoed by four solo violins one octave higher, is realised non-literally (Ex. 13.8: Wagner, *Lohengrin*, full score (Dover Publications Inc., New York, 1982), p. 1, bars 1 and 2; Ex. 13.9: Wagner, *Lohengrin*, vocal score by Sullivan and Pittman (Boosey and Co., 1872), p. 1, bars 1 and 2).

In his 1913 Schott edition, Karl Klindworth, in the same spirit as Sullivan and Pittman, places the pianissimo flute and oboe chord on the third beat of bar one but, in trying to 'absorb' the string triad in order to reflect Wagner's textural dovetailing, he respaces the chord (Ex. 13.10: Wagner, *Lohengrin*, vocal score by Klindworth, Schott and Co., 1913, p. 1, bars 1 and 2).

Where the Boosey edition starts with the chord in the correct octave and with Wagner's spacing, the Schott version, whilst placing the fifth of the triad, e″ uppermost, as does the orchestral score, shows it an octave lower. This is done in order to enable the repetiteur to play the opening chord with the right hand, the left being free to take the next root position triad, placed one octave higher; the latter transposition brings the note into the correct octave, e‴, the second bar reaching the next octave, as in the original, but with the third, c♯‴, a minor third beneath the e‴, filling in the perfect fifth where Wagner does not. Klindworth has done this for a practical 'pianistic' reason and has, as a result, been marginally less faithful to the original than Sullivan and Pittman. However, both editions recreate the music's character and expressive intentions. Alterations on the music's surface do not affect

Ex. 13.8 Wagner, *Lohengrin* (Dover full score), bars 1-9

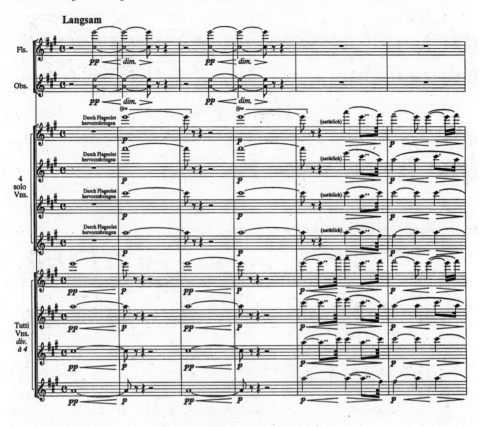

Ex. 13.9 Wagner, *Lohengrin* (Boosey & Co. piano reduction), bars 1-9

Ex. 13.10 Wagner, *Lohengrin* (Schott & Co. piano reduction), bars 1-9

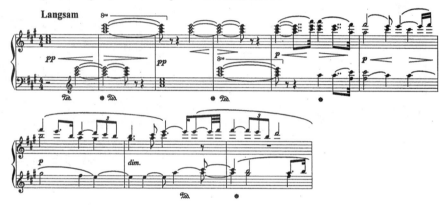

its essence. Importantly, where the audience hears a ceaseless musical flow towards the Prelude's climax and subsequent return to the opening harmony and texture, Wagner uses the orchestra highly structurally and systematically. The entry of the woodwind at bar 20 coincides with the first statement of the principal thematic material in the dominant, the entry of the horn quartet doubled by violas and cellos in bar 36 heralding the return of the tonic (if one allows that the music has ever truly departed from it). The heavy brass and timpani join the argument as climactic reinforcement, the *Hohepunkt* omitting the strings, their reappearance being elided with the fading brass and percussion and restoring the opening texture and triadic purity.

Not only have we seen how the foreground of the music may be realised in more than one way, on account of its *a priori* and generalised background (in terms of tonal and analytic theory), but we have also observed how Wagner's 'structural' scoring articulates the apparent seamless musical architecture; sophisticated doubling aside, the music is devoid of decoration. When we

Ex. 13.11 From Berg, *Wozzeck* (U.E. full score)

examine the extract from *Wozzeck*, the lack of a generalised *a priori* starting point has far-reaching consequences with regard to the entire musical
fabric and its instrumentation. In the eighth bar of the opening scene, Fritz
Heinrich Klein's vocal score is intentionally 'inaccurate' for pianistic reasons; although this does not alter the expressive world of the drama, the
internal changes reveal a wider issue compositionally. Where Berg, on the
third quaver of the bar in the full score, writes parallel motion between
oboe and clarinet, heard as a unit sounding in oblique motion against the
sustained c′ in the cor anglais and in contrary motion to the rising bassoon
figure (for the last two demisemiquavers), Klein's piano reduction includes
the linear motion as part of left-hand chords, the demisemiquaver flute
line being retained as one-voice right-hand melodic figuration; this is not
a question of merely omitting a detail within a triadic world but, however
briefly, alters the basic structure of the counterpoint, intervallic quality and
perception of the musical space. In addition, the left-hand triads (which are
not presented as simultaneities orchestrally) are prolonged for one quaver
each, which is not a feature of the woodwind sonority. Finally, Klein resorts
to showing the 'true' cor anglais and bassoon counterpoint on an extra stave
(Ex. 13.11: Berg, *Wozzeck*, full score, U.E., 1926/1955, p. 6, bar 8; Ex. 13.12:
Berg, *Wozzeck*, vocal score by Klein, U.E. 1931/1958, p. 9, bar 8).

   With the absence of a controlling background, even such an apparently insignificant adjustment as absorbing a lower contrapuntal voice into
a passing vertical aggregation alters the quality of the musical syntax in a
manner far more radical than the differences of detail displayed for practical
purposes in the Wagner examples given above. The role of motivic counterpoint in the absence of a pre-compositional harmonic premise demands a

Ex. 13.12 From Berg, *Wozzeck* (U.E. piano reduction)

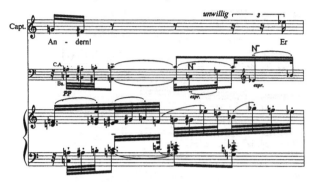

radical review of the use of the orchestra; whether or not subsequent analysis reveals a cohesive and consistent background is not, strictly, a compositional issue. In the case of 'real' tonal music[6] as we have seen in the Brahms examples, the background can be generalised, as Schenker revealed, a theoretical goal to which scientists and mathematicians aspire in their respective fields. Despite Allen Forte's outstanding attempt to find a general theory for pre-serial non-tonal music in *The Structure of Atonal Music*, for a composer the foreground/background problem manifest in the Berg extract acts as both a warning and an inspiration with regard to the use of the orchestra.

The composer and the commissioner: what price artistic freedom?

A composer stores ideas continually. As in the case of a painter or writer, a commission usually brings one of these into focus, so that the issue is not what to do 'out of nothing', but how to realise what is in one's imagination in relation to what is required, rather than expected, any artist hoping, at one level, not to offer the obvious. On receiving a commission to write a chamber-orchestral work for a tour including classical works without clarinets, a composer may have in mind a specific piece which has no connection technically with 'classical' orchestral practice. Whilst remaining faithful to the initial idea, the task is to (re)create the sound-world heard with the 'inner ear' for a woodwind section consisting of only one flute and pairs of oboes and bassoons. Use of the paired horns in conjunction with the woodwind has to be thought about in a fresh light, as does overall balance and the relationship between orchestral families, with regard to both individual instruments as well as 'tuttis'. Without trumpets, timpani will also be unavailable and, with only two double basses, it is necessary to invent ways of creating a sonorous whole. 'Binding' the whole without the hierarchy implied by a functional bass becomes an inspiring problem to be solved. Not only is this inseparable from the character and quality of musical material, but it also stimulates the creative juices and the path to solutions frequently brings forth further ideas.

Regarding writing for the 'standard' symphony orchestra, conception, idea and eventual realisation may entail novel solutions, with the composer gaining 'the upper hand' over the usual practical and financial issues. Two outstanding examples stemming, significantly, from the middle years of the twentieth century, when a spirit of questioning and adventure was rife, illustrate far-reaching relationships between surface, content and intention. What is noticeable in the case of both works is the use of layers of activity in order to achieve richness and variety in conjunction with new ideas about the passing and nature of musical time. Both use the medium as an essential ingredient in the argument, much as colour for Kandinsky, Klee or Matisse was far more than merely 'clothing' a line drawing. Boulez illustrates the point:

> I have compared the sketches for *La Mer* with the finished score, and it is
> quite plain that there are a whole host of small figurations and motifs that
> were added to the instrumentation at the last minute. This is not just a
> matter of preparing an orchestral version from a score that is already
> completely defined, as happens with Ravel; the difference is that in
> Debussy's case the sketches, though complete from the compositional
> point of view, still need the illumination of the orchestra before the work
> acquires its real dimensions and true relief.[7]

Stockhausen's *Gruppen* (1957) displays multi-layered relationships across the spectrum by taking serial organisation to a conceptually, colouristically and architecturally unified stage. (The aged Otto Klemperer is supposed to have been delighted at a rehearsal of the work, a salutary reminder of the creative mental vigour and forward-looking vision of a man who had been a repetiteur for Mahler nearly half a century earlier and whose musical/orchestral interests went beyond a museum mentality.) The linking of the harmonic series with serial ordering of texture, register, rhythm and duration required the use of three orchestras and three conductors, in order to realise Stockhausen's compositional intentions. From a practical point of view, the work is not as fearsome to programme as some may think, the three groups called for being subdivisions of one orchestra consisting of 109 players. Stockhausen made clear his new orchestral thinking by redefining the difference between tutti and non-tutti passages respectively as statistical and soloistic, an indication that the music's unifying principle was no longer related to an exclusive harmonic system.

With his *Concerto for Orchestra* (1968), Elliott Carter fulfilled a commission to celebrate the 125th anniversary of the New York Philharmonic, finding an ingenious and original way of producing a display piece which, simultaneously, continued his deepest compositional concerns. The result is an intertwining of the traditional and the inventive, also serving as an illustration of a composer's dichotomy in an artistically 100 per cent 'privatised' society. The music, in four continuous movements, is never still, the source of inspiration being lines from St. John Perse's poem *Vents* which, according to David Schiff, 'describes winds blowing over the American plains destroying old, dried-up forms and sweeping in the new – a vision particularly relevant to the turbulent America of the late '60s'.[8] So, at the most immediate level, Carter provides an easily graspable programme, but deeper strata reveal another solution to the 'anachronistic' orchestra and more recent aesthetic and technical matters. Schiff continues: 'Like Debussy, Carter sought to achieve an orchestral sonority not based on the string choir . . . he wanted to use the orchestra in a very full manner, as opposed to the spare orchestration of Stravinsky.'

The opening of the work builds to a tutti, in which a twelve-note aggregate is partitioned into what will become 'characteristic' intervals and which, simultaneously, introduces unconventionally placed orchestral groups, each group playing allotted notes and intervals in specific structural registers. The orchestra is, in fact, regrouped according to instrumental range and sonority. For example, bassoons, wooden percussion, harp and cellos are seated together, their musical material defining the characteristic sound, gesture and tempo of the first movement. As a result, whenever this material is played, the listener in the hall will hear it sounding from a specific area on the platform, the quadrophonic placing of the groups realising the cross-cutting technique of Carter's structural plan; there is no dichotomy between means and ends. The integration of conception and means is described by Schiff as follows: 'The harmonic resources of the Concerto . . . are vast . . . the expanded possibilities for harmony opened up by the use of the thirty-eight five-note chords (and their seven-note complements) can be put into perspective if we recall that, in tonal harmony, only two such chords, the major and minor dominant ninths, are officially sanctioned.' Carter, having rethought the orchestral layout in line with his architectural goal, invents methods of organising musical Space and Time. However, in the 'real' world of orchestras and so-called repertory, such a work is impractical. Carter has himself said that possibly the best performances of his *Concerto for Orchestra* have been given by youth orchestras, or orchestras at Summer Music Schools, where rehearsal time is relatively generous and he is not confronted by ingrained attitudes of various kinds. There is no doubt that there remains a difference between an American composer and his/her

European counterpart, the latter, particularly in the immediate post-war era, having at his/her disposal orchestras and choirs funded by public service broadcasting stations, the former writing in a completely 'privatised' society in which orchestras are at the mercy of conservative subscribers, but the gap is closing increasingly quickly, particularly in Britain. Many other examples could of course be given, in order to illustrate the ways in which composers in the last century faced the challenge of realising their ideas orchestrally, but it is the wider issue of message/medium with which we are concerned.

Composers and the orchestra: the past, the 'repertoire' and the future

The concept of a repertoire is recent in relation to the history of Western music. One has only to glance at a complete list of Mozart's orchestral works to see how few of them are truly regular visitors to the concert hall. After all, when Mozart travelled, he usually wrote new works for his concert appearances, untroubled by the 'second performance' syndrome. Fashions also dictate relatively rapid alterations to 'the canon'; some forty years ago, Franck's D minor Symphony still held its place on concert programmes, at a time when Mahler's symphonies were a rarity; the situation from the perspective of the early twenty-first century could hardly be more different. This matters with regard to composers working today, because a composer has to decide whether or not to be practical at all costs (in itself no guarantee of inclusion in any repertoire), or to obey the creative spirit regardless.

Granted, there are those who occasionally achieve both. In an age when commercial factors are paramount and mass communication has meant a change from 'popular' to 'populism', a composer writing for the 'anachronistic' orchestra must ride a tight-rope between artistic and imaginative/ conceptual aims and the realities of the current climate of concert-giving. Few composers have achieved the balance as cleverly as Lutoslawski in his orchestral works between 1960 and the late 1980s and it is of interest to observe that, with his layered orchestral writing, we find familial separation which comes close to the earlier eighteenth-century conception of an orchestra. Thus does the wheel come full circle.

In the United States there is no question that there exist composers who, on account of the present set-up, are prepared to serve up old wine in the 'orchestral museum bottle'; the work becomes a product, aiming to satisfy an audience very different from that which heard Haydn's mature symphonies and a far cry from the post-Beethovenian symphonic orchestral work as a living cultural force. Still less is it a vehicle for research and imaginative leaps in the deepest and best sense. Whether, indeed, orchestras will survive financially is a moot point, but should they do so, it seems inevitable that they will be suppliers of a relatively small repertoire, primarily dictated by subscribers.

The relationship between medium and message has a long and complex history, from the Council of Trent's pronouncement concerning ecclesiastical polyphony versus audibility of text in the sixteenth century to Schoenberg's *Moses and Aaron* and beyond. The orchestra is a challenging and rich 'instrument' and there are, today, many composers who write for it imaginatively and with flair; if there is a problem, it lies with the need of orchestras to survive financially in a climate which is competitive in a way unknown before the 'communication explosion'. In many respects, recording and broadcasting, with all that follows, have given orchestras a new lease of life and composers certainly have a role in the new environment, as Composers-in-Association, with some responsibility for orchestras' education programmes, an area not to be underestimated. Two issues lie at the root of any future relationship between orchestras (as businesses) and composers. One is the matter of 'artistic faith' and trust, the issue being one of commitment on the part of orchestral managements and players to creative artists; composers must play their part in this too, but while to some extent keeping their part of whatever bargain may be struck, they should not have to suffer the 'difficulty versus rehearsal time' problem which is all too prevalent. I speak here not of orchestras playing the correct notes, but achieving a real performance, and, in the case of a new work, this should be paramount. The other issue is the even more serious one of whether or not those responsible for programming, from management to conductors, are prepared to be bold and supportive. The United States is ahead of Europe in this regard; due to the subscription system (and despite the conservatism of most subscribers), an American orchestra usually plays a new work two or three times in one week, the conductor, players and composer finding themselves in a relationship akin to that between a theatre director, actors and a writer. This approach, combined with Composer-in-Association and education projects, may bode well for a non-anachronistic orchestral future.

14 Educational programmes

SUE KNUSSEN

Introduction

Think 'symphony orchestra' and a number of images come to mind: beautiful music; concert halls with chandeliers and gilded balconies; a hundred musicians, mainly men, elegantly dressed in tails. All of this may in fact exist, especially in the older capital cities of Europe, but even when the concert halls are dark, there is a lot more happening in the world of the symphony orchestra and the chamber orchestra, especially in the UK and the US. Administratively, there is a welter of fundraising, publicity, marketing and accounting activities, but there is another sphere that works symbiotically with the artistic and administrative areas of the orchestra. In the early twenty-first century, most professional orchestras have Education Departments specifically dedicated to the provision of a range of programmes for their subscribers and for the greater community.

Education programmes are not new: specially designated children's concerts have existed since the early twentieth century, when there was an enthusiastic audience of adults who regarded these concerts as an important supplement to children's general education and as an element in the continuation of family tradition. Nearly a hundred years later, most professional orchestras continue to consider children's concerts as the flagships of their education departments. Nowadays, however, these concerts constitute only a part of a wide array of programmes, serving all segments of the community.

Educational need

Education departments in orchestras grew significantly during the last two decades of the twentieth century. During that time, orchestras faced new challenges brought on by profound changes, over the last half of the century, in the social, intellectual and cultural landscape. This transformation was a result of a number of factors, not the least being the proliferation of pop culture, through ever-prevalent means of mass communication. First there was radio, then television, and the internet, all pumping out a constant stream of manufactured 'art' or 'culture'. In addition, the population itself has changed considerably. Patterns of immigration have shifted, so that

Western cultures have been broadened and enriched by large groups of people from other parts of the world – Asia, Africa, Latin America – for whom traditional Western art forms have no intrinsic resonance. Also, the focus of public (state) primary and secondary education moved away from the European, classically inspired curriculum towards more practically driven, sociologically motivated subject areas. Therefore, orchestral music, with its European roots and associations, became more and more marginalised in the education world.

In spite of the good intentions which motivated the changes in British and American education, the 1990s brought the realisation, in the US as well as the UK, that education in general was in trouble. Fixing it was a necessary plank in any political party's platform. With national economies on the upswing, education became the natural recipient of both Foundation grants and individual philanthropy. However, the abysmal standards prevalent in public education caused authorities to decree a strong emphasis on the 'basics', or the three Rs. Priority and money were immediately directed towards addressing those areas. There could be no argument about the fact that standards of literacy had to be improved, but this did not necessarily benefit arts education. In fact, many of the remaining programmes in music and the other arts were squeezed out, as school schedules increased the emphasis on instruction in the basics.

The devolution of classical culture was not quite as rapid in the UK as in the US, partly because Britain had a musical tradition which, while limited in comparison with some of the countries on the Continent, went back to the Renaissance. Nevertheless, the conditions with which orchestras in the UK had to deal were similar to those in the US. The waves of immigration were balanced differently, but similar groups arrived on its shores. Ethnic groups, whose cultural interests had previously been fulfilled within their own communities, were developing a stronger presence in the mainstream arts, and government departments and committees insisted on funding them from the meagre available pot, leaving less money for the 'classical' arts. Popular culture was also becoming more and more dominant.

As the education cuts of the Reagan and Thatcher eras began to take their toll, arts education was amongst the major casualties. Music, in particular, was targeted because of the expense involved in providing instruments and, in those systems which offered it, individual instruction. Also, prior to these draconian cuts, there was a growth in liberal approaches to art and education, militating against the discipline-based teaching required for developing real skills on musical instruments. During the 1990s, numerous academic studies established that work in the arts, and especially the active playing of musical instruments, has a positive effect on learning and produces measurable increases in standardised test scores. At the time of the cuts, however, the arts were seen as 'frills', or luxuries, which could easily be sacrificed.

The orchestras' point of view

These conditions caused considerable concern amongst those who believed that the arts are essential to a civilised life, and many orchestras recognised a void which they believed they could fill. However, orchestras embraced educational activities with varying degrees of enthusiasm. Money was always an issue: who would pay for these programmes? Would their costs eat into already stretched budgets? Would the money be recouped, and perhaps even augmented, through increased revenue from ticket sales? Then came further questions: of what would these programmes consist? What was appropriate? How, if at all, would they relate to public (state) school curricula? What impact would they have? How would this impact be assessed? What about adult education? It is easy to see why there may have been hesitation on the part of orchestras and their managements to take on this challenge.

However, there were three very strong inducements: a crying need, sometimes a demand, from the community; a passionate wish on the part of some (but decidedly not all) of the musicians to take action; and, perhaps most urgently, a fear that if the situation in education continued along the path it was treading, there would be no audiences in the future.

One reality which orchestras had to accept very early in the process was that educational activities were not going to generate appreciable revenue. Ticket sales for regular subscription concerts, even in the case of sold-out concerts, have not covered the cost of mounting the events. Education concerts, with their shorter lengths and audiences consisting of large numbers of young people, were hardly going to justify high ticket prices, so they would bring in even less revenue. Nevertheless, there was also a sense that, whatever the drawbacks, getting seriously involved in education was 'the right thing to do'.

Audience numbers were another cause for concern. Demographics, with the changing ethnic and national origins of a majority of the population in general, had a significant effect on these numbers. When orchestras first proliferated in the US, their ranks, as well as their audiences, included large numbers of musicians who were European émigrés, for whom, in their home cultures, concert-going and music-making were essential elements of life. For these people, subscribing to the local orchestra (especially if it was one with the high musical and technical standards of the then-called 'Big Five') was a way of staying culturally close to 'home'. However, as the children and grandchildren of these European immigrants assimilated and became more American or British, they became more and more influenced by popular culture. On the one hand, orchestra music and concert-going did not have the emotional draw that it did for their parents; on the other hand, they were influenced (some would say brainwashed) by peer groups obsessed with popular art forms rather than the 'classical' arts.

Concurrently with all of this (but surely no coincidence), the core audience for symphony orchestras was shrinking, often ageing. Audiences often included members of metropolitan 'aristocracies' (for example, Boston Brahmins) – often the 'old money' of the region. These aristocratic segments of the audience were not necessarily replenished with new generations of assimilated immigrants. Therefore, there was (and continues to be in some circles) deep concern for the future of orchestras, with real questions as to who their audiences would be.

All of these factors combined to raise serious worries about the survival of the symphony orchestra as a cultural presence. It seemed clear that there was not an assured continuity of interest, because music was disappearing from private family culture at the same time it was being eradicated from school curricula. If children were not exposed to music at school or at home, what could possibly induce them to become subscribers, or even occasional ticket-buyers, to orchestras?

Institutional self-interest aside, there was a strong case to be made, as the effects of the cuts began to be evident, for the importance of educating the whole person. This was particularly true in urban areas, where the deterioration of traditional values manifested itself, at its worst, in gang violence, and where huge numbers of children were lacking the parental support for engaging seriously in their educational activities.

Action

It was time for action in both countries. Children needed to be informed about and, most importantly, engaged in the arts, and orchestras needed to ensure their future audiences. Orchestras began to take up the slack with a commitment to providing ever-stronger education programmes, and they had the motivation in three significant areas: the potential erosion of their own audience base, the education crisis in the greater community, and the documented advantage of exposure to and participation in music. Now there was a double case for being proactive: not only did music, with its charms to heal the human heart, have spiritual value; it also raised the level of academic performance.

All of the above conditions motivated orchestras on both sides of the Atlantic to develop their education programmes. Given these considerations,

14.1 An educational project with The Hanover Band.

orchestras could not deny the contribution they could make to the young people of the community as well as to the upper crust. The ubiquitous Children's Concerts remained a flagship of most orchestras' education programmes, but they became just one facet of a burgeoning collection of educational activities offered by orchestras. The two largest areas of growth were in-school programmmes and those which reached out into the community. Many orchestras also had activities (youth orchestras, competitions, festivals, side-by-side performances) to enhance the performance opportunities for young musicians who already played instruments. Most stepped up their adult education offerings, and many developed programmmes designed for pre-school-aged children.

Children's Concerts

Children's concerts, youth concerts, family concerts – these are the terms variously used to describe what has long been the mainstay of orchestras' educational activities. They pre-date the late twentieth century's preoccupations and come from a time when a background in the arts was considered mandatory and desirable. However, when most of us think about these concerts today, we still tend to associate them with what is now considered a golden era of Leonard Bernstein and the New York Philharmonic's Young People's Concerts. These concerts, which are now, over a decade after Bernstein's death, commercially available on video, were notable for their vibrant combination of entertainment and strong musical content. The irrepressible enthusiasm of the maestro was quite contagious, and he talked easily about great works in a manner that was truly engaging to all, often drawing on analogies to contemporary culture. One notable example was his analysis of a Beatles song, still relatively fresh and not yet deemed artistically 'great', but the work of the most popular performers on the planet at the time. Bernstein's apparent spontaneity was genuine, but it was also a result of intensive planning and careful scripting, with editorial input from a crack team of advisors and employees. Of course, this amount of preparation was necessitated by the fact that the concerts were being broadcast on network television, and is rarely available for today's children's concerts. Bernstein's infectious enthusiasm, extraordinary ability to communicate, prodigious musicality, and probing intelligence, all in the service of a mission to teach, were inimitable. Ever since he stopped doing the Young People's Concerts, the industry has been seeking an heir, and while a number of people do these concerts well, Leonard Bernstein was unique.

Of course, even if Bernstein were alive and presenting Children's Concerts today, he would undoubtedly have to make some alterations to their verbal content. The young audiences for whom Bernstein performed still had some music in their general educations and will have been at least aware of the names of a few composers – 'the three Bs' (Bach, Beethoven, Brahms) was a phrase almost as universally understood as 'the three Rs'. By the end of the twentieth century, however, these composers, even as names, and symphony orchestras, were not even on the radar screens of the general youth population. So the challenge is not only to find 'the next Leonard Bernstein', but also to find ways to prepare young audiences for the experience of hearing a symphony orchestra.

As the twentieth century neared its close, questions of all kinds began to be asked about Children's Concerts and their relevance to their target audiences of young people. These concerts remain, however, a staple of orchestral education programmes and, when well-planned, presented, and performed, provide an entertaining and stimulating introduction to the enthralling sound-world of live orchestral music. There are still people who report the 'thunderbolt' experience of hearing a great musical work – perhaps *The Young Person's Guide to the Orchestra*, or the 'Ride of the Valkyries', or *Peter and the Wolf* – for the first time at one of these concerts and then becoming 'hooked'. After all, music really *can* change people's lives.

There are, however, limits to the effectiveness of these concerts as educational activities. First of all, they are not necessarily part of an educational continuum: in the current educational environment, there is not necessarily adequate preparation for or follow-up to these concerts, relegating them, at best, to the realm of 'entertainment' for many children and, at worst, to boring weekend events, endured as part of a family outing, with the promise of a post-concert trip to a fast-food restaurant to sugar the pill. (On the upside, these concerts do provide an opportunity for a shared experience across the generations, with parents or grandparents sharing their own passions with their young relatives, or learning with them.)

Additionally, because the concert experience is not part of the larger cultural landscape for most children, the rituals and requirements of the occasion – sitting quietly in rows, applauding only at specific times – can be intimidating or alienating. Orchestras have been variously addressing these issues by incorporating other elements (e.g. story-telling or dance) into the mix; having masters or mistresses of ceremonies to guide the audience through the experience (conductors vary in their effectiveness as public speakers); dressing more informally – sometimes even in T-shirts (sometimes colour-coded to identify the instrument families – strings in red, woodwinds in blue, etc.); borrowing from the pop world and projecting the onstage activities on to large screens so that children can actually see a featured instrument, helping them to focus their listening. In today's visually biased world, the hope is that attracting the eye will sharpen the ear.

Another criticism made of children's concerts is that they are passive occasions, with the audience merely observing, rather than participating in the festivities. Many orchestras have been actively addressing this issue, creating presentations which include the audience. The audience may be invited to sing along, taught to conduct patterns of 2, 3, and 4, or to engage in call-and-response activities.

The success of these initiatives is dependent on a mixture of creative thinking and planning, collaboration, and rehearsal. The production of the children's concert series is one of the major responsibilities of orchestral education departments, who must initiate and facilitate much of the above as well as creating engaging print materials for the concerts. When the concerts are for school groups (as opposed to ticket-buying audiences of subscribers), extensive preparatory materials are provided so that classroom teachers, if they can find the time, might prepare the children for the occasion.

Another enhancement to these concerts has been the introduction of pre-concert activities, usually held in the lobbies of concert halls. These consist of several kinds of hands-on exhibits, ranging from 'instrument petting zoos' to interdisciplinary activities – dance workshops, for instance, or perhaps science experiments demonstrating acoustical principles, or the construction of their own hand-made instruments. Considerable time, effort, and expense are devoted to these activities, which, especially for younger children, become an incentive to attend the actual concert. When members of the orchestra itself participate in this pre-concert phase, the connection is enhanced, and the children often feel that they have a relationship with what happens onstage.

The musicians' role

Orchestral musicians, in fact, have often been passionate advocates of and participants in their institutions' education programmes. While some more conservative players want to play their concerts and leave the educating to others, large numbers have become extremely active in the education area. There are a number of reasons, both professional and personal, for their interest. In some cases, they have noticed a change in the audiences and are concerned about the possible erosion of the audience base. At the most practical level, the musicians' livelihoods could be at stake if new generations fail to replenish current audiences. More importantly, the musicians want to share their music with the widest possible range of the community. They have worked hard to refine and develop their talents, and they care passionately about music, so of course they want to pass it on. Also, they feel a personal responsibility to help close the gap left by decades of educational abandonment of the arts. These players, many of whom are mothers and fathers of school-age children themselves, have increased motivation to act. Therefore, more and more often, orchestral musicians, either individually or in small ensembles, are going into schools and undertaking a range of activities with the students: coaching sectional rehearsals of the school orchestra or band; giving lecture-demonstrations on their instruments; coaching chamber music; or sometimes just talking with students about their lives as musicians. These programmes are most successful when they are structured so that a real relationship develops between the musicians and the students. Some orchestras have Adopt-a-Player programmes, in which schools adopt a specific musician who, in addition to their in-school visits, hosts the students at rehearsals or concerts, greeting them, and perhaps taking them backstage so that they get a special, behind-the-scenes view of orchestral life. The students then have a friend to watch in performance, thus making personal what would have been an anonymous group of adults. This personal attention to the young people helps to forge a real connection, encouraging the students to feel that the orchestra is for *them*, and that they are welcome in its concerts. It also augments the work of the classroom teachers and the music specialist teachers, helping students see the making of music as a human activity in which real people engage.

There is also considerable payback for the professionals. Life in a symphony orchestra, while artistically enriching and relatively lucrative, can have its drawbacks for talented instrumentalists. As students, they worked hard to perfect their art, receiving suitable recognition for their gifts and for their work. When they become part of a symphony orchestra, however, they enter a society of equals, but one in which it can be difficult, especially for string players and for players in second or third chair positions in the wind and brass and percussion sections, to shine. They sometimes begin to feel like cogs in a complex machine in which the real recognition is reserved for the principal players and, even more, for the conductor. After all the years of training and countless hours of practice, they can sometimes feel invisible. When they go out into the schools, however, they often rediscover their musical individuality and find a new artistic and communicative outlet.

Out of this commitment, some extraordinarily creative work has emerged in programmes which have been created with the goal of giving students active participation in music-making. The UK has been at the forefront of this movement, with a number of musicians dedicating themselves to programmes which involve students in active music-making, in both performance and composition. Composers team up with performers to craft projects which often involve improvisation, as well as more traditional singing and playing. The result is an enthusiastic engagement on the part of the students, based on the benefits of active participation. They are doing something which had previously seemed remote, composing their own musical works and experiencing the exhilaration that goes with real creative activity.

The quantity of these activities, however, is limited by a number of factors: the time available in the schools' schedules, which are often packed with required classes necessitated by the proliferation of standardised testing; the sometimes limited interest and confidence of the school teachers – after all, many of them were themselves deprived of education in the arts; and the availability of the professional musicians. The large American orchestras work to the terms of delicately negotiated contracts, and their rehearsal times often conflict with the available time slots in the school days. Smaller orchestras, with shorter seasons and fewer rehearsals and concerts, provide more flexibility for the musicians. It is also economically more attractive to the musicians of the smaller orchestras, who are paid considerably less than those in the large metropolitan institutions. Therefore, in the United States, some of the most interesting work in education is being done by the less prominent organisations.

As the primary musical organisations in their communities, most symphony orchestras feel a commitment to providing experiences to enrich the musical lives of talented young musicians, who have already reached relatively advanced levels of achievement on their instruments. These activities include coaching sessions, competitions, youth orchestras, and side-by-side rehearsals and concerts. These side-by-sides are particularly effective, and they provide an opportunity which is, in any given community, unique to the symphony orchestra. For these activities, the students sit amongst the orchestra, each partnered with one of the professionals. For the student musicians, these events often represent a life-changing opportunity to share a music-making experience with their role models. The students, sitting and playing next to their professional counterparts, learn by example, improving their performance and learning subtleties of playing in a way that an individual lesson cannot provide. They also get the added bonus of playing under the baton of, and being inspired by, professional conductors, sometimes of world class. For the professionals, the events provide an opportunity for real connection with students, some of whom will one day be their colleagues, and for real mentorship. It is a time when they can be true role models through their high standard of playing, their subtlety of interpretations, and their serious commitment to the art they practise. Along with all of this comes the knowledge that they contributed to an experience which the young musicians will remember for the rest of their lives.

Adult education

Education does not, of course, end with the end of school, college, or university, and symphony orchestras are, more and more, entering the field of adult education. Many of them regularly offer pre-concert talks, in which eminent musicians, musicologists, or other relevant experts prepare concert-goers for the impending programme. They might illuminate the historical content of the works in the concert, the relationship of the music to other art works of the time, or any other subject which might shed light on the repertory to be heard, thus preparing interested patrons for the concert. These pre-concert events tend to be extremely well attended, and those people who make the effort to arrive early are enthusiastic, and seem to feel that it's well worth their time. This seems to be true amongst the musically literate as well as the novices.

Expanding upon the pre-concert lecture experience, some orchestras present seminars and study days, usually focused on a particular concert or group of concerts which are unusual or celebratory, such as a mini-festival of works by a particular composer, or concerts which are part of a thematic strand in the orchestra's season. These days might include talks, performances of chamber music, screenings of relevant films, or discussions or performances of other art forms, all designed to enrich the audience's appreciation and understanding of the music and its place in a broader context.

A specialised type of study day is for the professional development of teachers. Many of today's classroom teachers were themselves educated during the time when, due to drastic budget cuts, arts education had been virtually eradicated from the curriculum. The result for them has been a limited knowledge of music and a lack of confidence, bordering on intimidation, about dealing with 'serious' music in the classroom. Professional development days, therefore, provide an opportunity to increase the teachers' knowledge of music and to build their confidence in including it in the curriculum. The bonus here is that the teachers receive significant enrichment to their own education, resulting in an enthusiasm which they may then pass on to their students. In addition to segments about repertory they might be hearing in that evening's concert, a professional development day might include sessions about a particular musical element, such as rhythm or harmony. There might also be presentations about the integration of music across the curriculum, showing its connection to dance, painting, architecture, literature, history or science. An example of this growing area of arts education might be an explanation of the principles of acoustics, demonstrating the way instruments produce their various musical sounds and pitches, thus making a connection between music and science.

Community programmes

Many of the education programmes discussed above involve audiences who go to concert halls in order to hear the music, but there is another large area of activity which involves the orchestra, or groups of musicians from it, going out into the community. This area is generally referred to as 'outreach', and in some orchestras, these outreach activities are classified as 'community programmes', as distinct from education programmes. However, it would be difficult to argue against their having an educational purpose. After all, outreach usually implies reaching out to segments of the community whose citizens do not normally attend orchestra concerts. The venues visited might be churches, community centres, day centres for the elderly, hospices or prisons. The programmes tend to be specifically designed to appeal to those particular audiences.

In addition to, and undoubtedly more significant than, outreach concerts, some extremely effective creative work is being done, especially in the UK, in prisons, centres for the elderly, hospices, and other community venues, in which the residents work with individual musicians and composers, under the aegis of orchestras. They work on projects, often related to concert performances they will hear, and creating works of their own, under the guidance of the professionals. This work provides an opportunity for deep connection with music as an emotional and creative outlet for people who never considered musical engagement to be relevant to their lives. It has been anecdotally reported that this work has an extraordinary effect on the people to whom it is offered, whether they are people facing terminal illness or hard-bitten criminals serving life sentences. The effect on the professional musicians is equally profound, as they use their art to change the lives of people whom they would be highly unlikely to encounter under any other circumstances.

As the twenty-first century begins to unfold in ways we could never have imagined, it becomes more and more evident that people in the Western world have a great need for the arts in general and music in particular. In its abstraction and its ability to address issues of the human spirit that cannot be articulated, music attends to the soul in ways that transcend theology. It addresses the full range of emotions, from joy to sorrow, from violence to peace. While the music speaks for itself, its effects can often be strengthened by professional guidance which can, through a range of activities, attune the ears and open the minds of its listeners. Through the wide range of educational programmes which they offer, orchestras can and do supply that guidance, and thus make a significant contribution to the lives of their recipients, and there is potential to do even more. When arguing about the relevance of orchestras in today's world, the decision-makers should never forget that this potential is vast. By integrating education programmes ever more significantly into their activities, orchestras can become more and more essential to their communities and, it is hoped, thus secure their place in cultural life well into the twenty-first century.

15 The future of the orchestra

STEPHEN COTTRELL

Introduction

The symphony orchestra is undoubtedly one of the great cultural achievements of European civilisation. It is also one of Europe's most significant cultural exports. What began as relatively small collections of musicians in the courts of central Europe in the seventeenth century has not only grown in size but also achieved a wide geographical spread. Indeed, the orchestra is now a truly world-wide phenomenon, and such globalisation can largely be explained as a result of two significant factors. First, European expatriation in the nineteenth and early twentieth centuries, whereby migrant communities from various European countries settled elsewhere, inevitably resulted in the transplantation of numerous aspects of European culture; Western art music and its most significant ensemble, the symphony orchestra, were invariably part of this process. Second, as Western culture generally and its music in particular became more widely disseminated, helped later by the growth of the recording industry and the global domination of a small number of Western record companies, Western art music achieved a degree of popularity – and sometimes cultural ascendancy – in areas where it was not part of the indigenous culture. Along with Western-style institutions of music education (conservatoires and exam boards, for example) the symphony orchestra became seen as an acceptable, even desirable, organisation, for rather complex and variable reasons relating to local cultural and political aspirations.

Yet after this period of expansion and popularity, many orchestras since the Second World War have found the social climate in which they operate rather more challenging, and (as discussed in chapter 11 and elsewhere) they have struggled to stay afloat financially and to retain audiences. In this chapter I shall review the present position of the symphony orchestra as an institution in the West, and consider some of the strategies proposed by both musicians and administrators as they seek to face the challenges of the future. I shall also contrast the situation of Western orchestras with their newer counterparts in the East, which perhaps have different agendas and thus face slightly different challenges.

The symphony orchestra in the West today

As observed elsewhere in this book, the symphony orchestra as an institution appears to be in difficulties in many parts of Europe and America. Orchestras all too frequently suffer from a perceived lack of support from local or national funding bodies, with diminishing subsidies or other income often in stark contrast to the huge fees demanded by star conductors and soloists. Musicians find themselves increasingly stressed, even within the context of what is by nature a stressful occupation, with expanding workloads, long foreign tours and unsociable hours. And often this is in the context of dwindling audience numbers, leading to questions from the press and politicians as to why public money should be used to support this 'minority' art form.

Some explanation of the funding mechanisms which underpin orchestras will illustrate these dilemmas. Most orchestras in the West are organised according to one of three possible models. In the first, the orchestra is financially supported by a civic authority or other body – the BBC in London is an obvious example, Berlin City Council is another – and the musicians are employed by that authority; they are technically civil servants or staff members. Although theoretically under the control of their employers, in practice they do have considerable input into the way the orchestra is run. This is the model that prevails in much of continental Europe and occasionally in Britain. In the second model, more common in the United States, the orchestra is run by an independent non-profit organisation, with a non-professional board overseeing professional managers who run the day-to-day affairs of the orchestra; the New York Philharmonic or Manchester's Hallé Orchestra provide examples. In these cases government agencies may contribute modest amounts, but the orchestras are also dependent on private benefactors, trusts, and foundations. The third model, less common but found in some orchestras in London and others such as the Vienna and Israeli Philharmonics, is where the players form a co-operative. Thus the orchestra is both owned and organised by the players themselves, although usually with professional managerial assistance. Government agencies frequently provide financial support, but these orchestras are often more reliant than others on earned income in order to survive.

None of these models provides complete security, however. Civic authorities or other employers may institute budget cutbacks which affect orchestras and the musicians in them. Charitable foundations or private donors may redistribute their largesse elsewhere. Government subsidies can be notoriously fickle, as well as being dependent on macro-economic cycles against which the orchestras have little protection.

As an example of financial miscalculation, we might consider the case of the Oakland Symphony Orchestra, a regional orchestra in North California. In 1986 this organisation went bankrupt after a series of difficulties with endowments, the purchase and renovation of a performance space, the sudden death of the artistic director, etc. Yet during these troubled times the orchestra found it difficult to gain the public support necessary for it to continue. As Marcia Herndon has pointed out,[1] although the people of Oakland *said* that the symphony orchestra was important, in fact considerably more pride – and economic support – was actually invested in the local football team. This illustrates the difficulties orchestras have in competing with other organisations for the limited amounts of public sympathy (and finance) available, further compounding the economic difficulties they sometimes experience. However, in the case of the Oakland orchestra, it should be noted that it was later reconstituted into the present 'Oakland East Bay Symphony', which perhaps reveals something of the underlying resilience of the musicians in such situations.

London provides another example of the challenging financial climate in which orchestras have to operate, since particular circumstances prevail there which make life for the city's orchestras especially demanding. London has five major symphony orchestras, four of which are established on the co-operative model outlined above. They are obliged to compete with one another for shared use of a limited number of performance spaces, since none has its own venue in which to create a significant identity for itself, unlike, for example, the Berlin Philharmonic or the Amsterdam Concertgebouw. This is coupled with a funding system which is not only based on short-term cycles – that is, the orchestras can never be sure how much subsidy they are going to receive more than one year in advance – but is also considerably less generous than some European equivalents.

Clearly, the economic foundations underpinning many orchestras are problematic. Even in cities which were previously notably generous, such as Berlin, significant cutbacks have recently been instituted. For the foreseeable future many orchestras are resigned to the fact that they will continue to survive through a complex mixture of state support, endowments, grants, benefactors, and commercial income. Although this uncertainty would alarm other businesses of a similar size, orchestras and their managers have become highly adept at dealing with such vicissitudes, and there is no reason to believe that, in most cases, they will not continue to do so. However, they have given considerable thought to the ways in which they might transform one of their most important income streams, the live orchestral concert.

The changing face of the orchestral concert in the West

Orchestras are only too aware that they often struggle to fill seats in their concert halls, and that audiences comprise a disproportionate number of the over-forties. Stagnant repertory can readily contribute to a 'living museum' culture. In part, such attitudes arise from the ritualised format of orchestral concerts themselves. People unfamiliar with such events frequently have a misguided perception as to their exact nature. Indeed, an orchestral violist once remarked, only partly in jest, that 'some people think we still wear wigs!'. While this may be an extreme view, it does illustrate the difficulties orchestras have in persuading certain sections of Western society that there is something of interest for them at an orchestral concert. The perceived 'stuffiness' of these concerts no doubt relates to the formal dress worn by the orchestra (a hangover from the nineteenth century). Together with other patterns of behaviour (such as being relatively silent during performance, having specific points for polite applause, the conductor turning his back to the audience, etc.), this all generates what is often seen as a forbiddingly formal environment for those unfamiliar with such practices.

Orchestras are sensitive to these difficulties, however, and have at various times suggested strategies to overcome them. Initiatives by London's Royal Philharmonic Orchestra in the mid-1990s were heralded as follows:

> Concert going is about to change. The Royal Philharmonic has big plans, which include training a camera on individual musicians and the conductor's face to magnify their images on to a screen; taking the orchestra out of evening dress for some concerts; holding concerts in the round, and as a spokesman says, 'have drama, lasers and maybe a camera right down the clarinet'.[2]

The clarinettist's response to this last idea is not recorded, and little of what was proposed actually came to pass. Nevertheless, orchestras are at least considering how to break down the relatively static ritual inherent within their performance events. At some concerts the conductor or an invited guest will introduce the works from the platform, developing the relationship between the audience and those on stage. On other occasions musicians will change into less formal attire, particularly for early evening or afternoon concerts, or in concerts which are deliberately conceived to attract a new, often younger, audience. Concerts may occur outside of the traditional setting – in parks, amphitheatres or other open-air venues – and these again may help to reduce the formality traditionally associated with the event.

But the difficulty for orchestras contemplating such innovations is that there is a balance to be struck between tradition and change. Some people attend orchestral concerts precisely *because* they feel comfortable with hearing music they know, under circumstances which are both familiar and comfortable. They may be put off by too many innovations in style or content, and there is little point in attracting new audiences if the strategies employed simply alienate existing ones.

Such difficulties become particularly crystallised in relation to contemporary repertory (largely post-1945) and new music. Here many orchestras find themselves attempting to resolve an irreducible paradox. On the one hand much contemporary art music is unpopular, and does not attract paying audiences; indeed it often has quite the opposite effect. While there are some composers who may generate good box-office returns – such as John Adams, Henryk Gorecki or Michael Nyman – many programmes that feature contemporary music, particularly of the more 'difficult' kind, do very badly at the box office. Furthermore, orchestras are themselves often rather traditional in their outlook, and orchestral musicians can be deeply ambivalent about the contemporary pieces put before them. In contrast, many of the funding authorities which subsidise orchestras make it a condition of their support that the orchestra is committed to playing new music, either by introducing unfamiliar works into their programmes or by commissioning new works from living composers. Often orchestras prefer the latter course because of the additional kudos it brings with the funding authorities, plus the possibility of attracting the attention of newspaper critics and the publicity this generates.

Although this paradox has no simple solution it has prompted many orchestras to develop various strategies to accommodate contemporary music in their programmes. Pre-concert talks, where the composer and possibly the conductor or other significant figures discuss the work to be performed, have become more common. Such talks are usually free to ticket holders for the main concert, and have both an educational value, in that they seek to inform the audience about the structure and context of the new work, as well as perhaps making the composer and the performers rather less 'anonymous' or remote than might otherwise be the case. Similarly, shorter chamber concerts immediately before the main evening event have also been used to introduce unfamiliar works and composers to interested concert-goers. Certain conductors, such as Simon Rattle, Esa Pekka Salonen and Michael Tilson Thomas, have become well known for their commitment to new music. With careful programming and/or judicious use of the subscription series, audiences feel they can develop a relationship with a particular conductor. This brings about the kind of trust that allows a conductor to make decisions about contemporary music on an audience's behalf, as already signalled by Clive Gillinson and Jonathan Vaughan elsewhere in this book. Another ploy has been to appoint a composer-in-residence, more closely identifying the orchestra with the work of that particular composer.

All these innovations attempt to develop better relationships between musicians, composers, and audiences, and to alleviate some of the difficulties associated with the integration of contemporary music into the standard orchestral repertory. Clearly, if the tradition of symphonic orchestral music is to move forward, it cannot rely on a relatively small number of works endlessly reconstituted for a devoted but diminishing audience. Although the performance of unfamiliar pieces presents many challenges to orchestras and their managers, these are challenges which are being met, and must continue to be met, if they are to face the future with confidence.

A further paradox is that in order to preserve their status as arts organisations, orchestras cannot be seen to be simply providing the most popular pieces in 'lowest common denominator' programmes. An endless diet of all-Tchaikovsky or all-Mozart concerts might be easier to sell, but it would be unlikely to satisfy the funding criteria for many of those organisations, public or private, which support orchestras; it would certainly become tedious for the musicians involved, and would ultimately be self-defeating by failing to attract new audiences. Yet many orchestras have developed either particular concerts or series of concerts which concentrate on 'the popular classics' at the expense of more challenging programming. Some, following on from the success of the Boston Pops Orchestra, have actually marketed themselves under a slightly different name, to distinguish this particular facet of their corporate image. Their defence would be that the income generated is a useful part of the complex financial equation they must resolve in order to support themselves; few if any would wish this to be the main focus of their work.

In a further attempt to appeal to new audiences concerts have also been revitalised through the introduction of musical styles and/or instruments not traditionally associated with standard Western art music repertory. Thus jazz composers and performers, and occasionally even pop and rock musicians, have been enticed on to the concert platform, either to write for or perform with an orchestra. Although such collaborations do not always appeal to traditionalists, and have on occasion drawn sharp words from critics, they do succeed in drawing popular attention to the work of orchestras, and can generate widespread publicity that might otherwise be hard to achieve. Paul McCartney's *Liverpool Oratorio*, Mark Anthony Turnage's work with the jazz drummer Peter Erskine, and the San Francisco Orchestra's sessions with Metallica and the Grateful Dead, to take just three of many possible examples, have all taken traditional orchestral work into new territories.

In the last thirty years or so, like other small to medium-sized companies before them, orchestras have learned that diversification is the key to sustaining their position in the market-place. New strategies have been developed to compete with the many other attractions – film and video, theatre, television, jazz and pop concerts, etc. – which their potential audience has as a means to occupy its leisure time. Such innovation and imagination in the use of orchestral resources will doubtless continue to be important through the coming century. The days have passed when orchestras in the West could survive simply by giving concerts of standard repertory, supplemented by film and recording fees. They must now be much more proactive in generating work for themselves at home and abroad, in attracting new audiences, and in presenting and promoting themselves as vigorously and resourcefully as possible. It is no coincidence that most orchestras now have full-time employees with particular responsibility for marketing and promoting the orchestra's work. Orchestras know that audiences will no longer simply come looking for them, but need to be enticed into the concert hall.

The issues surrounding both the presentation and the musical content of concert programmes will continue to be at the centre of debates among orchestras and their managers for the foreseeable future. As urban Western culture continues its increasing reliance on digital technology and the rapid communications it allows; when visual and aural stimuli can be consumed with ease from numerous sources – CDs, DVDs, video, TV and radio, the internet, etc.; when three-minute pop songs and televised soundbites make ever-reducing demands on concentration spans; and when individuals can exert such enormous and immediate control over their personal listening environment, the orchestra is in danger of appearing an anachronistic throwback to a previous age, bound up in ritualised practices which many in the present generations feel has no relevance for them. Orchestral musicians and those who work with them are clearly aware of these dilemmas, and many have put forward bold and imaginative solutions which will become increasingly widespread as the century progresses.

The future for the orchestral musician

The future of any orchestra is inevitably bound up with the aspirations of the individuals within it, at least to the extent of their influence upon the orchestra's activities. As observed elsewhere in this book, Western art music training has tended to concentrate on developing individual skills and interpretation, and to emphasise the importance of individual musicality. Yet the symphony orchestra requires of the individual musician that many of their own musical ideas must be subsumed to the will of the conductor, or at least moderated to complement those of the other musicians around them. The extent to which musicians feel genuinely recognised as individuals within orchestras can be variable, particularly if one considers the collective requirements of, for example, any of the large string sections.

These issues were neatly summed up by a clarinettist in a British television documentary on the Philharmonia Orchestra, who remarked:

> The whole nature of being an orchestra musician is that you basically subjugate your whole person, all your own personal ideas, you have to just completely throw them away. Just say, right, I don't matter. The guy on the box, on the podium, he's the guy that matters, and you have to give them what they want.[3]

It is fortuitous, therefore, that the diversification of orchestral practice outlined previously has often also allowed individuals within the orchestra to have more prominence in the work they undertake. Performing smaller-scale concerts before the main evening event, for example, whether of mainstream or contemporary repertory, usually involves the musicians in chamber ensembles, work which many of them find a satisfying contrast to the symphonic repertory. Indeed, groups put together for such events sometimes continue as active ensembles themselves, when the orchestral schedule permits. This is particularly common among wind instrumentalists, who may form quintets or octets to perform music written for these combinations. Yet, even the entire cello section of the Berlin Philharmonic Orchestra, for example, gives concerts separately from main orchestral engagements, allowing the spotlight to fall on them in a rather different way than when they perform as part of the orchestra. The educational work described by Sue Knussen in chapter 14 is another area where musicians can develop skills and interests which build on their central role as orchestral performers.

While orchestras will continue to provide the major musical events which are the cornerstones of their work, they can no longer be viewed as cultural monoliths whose only raison d'être is the performance of late eighteenth- and nineteenth-century masterpieces. Rather, they should perhaps be seen as a resource centre, a collection of highly skilled musicians whose talents can be put to use in a variety of contexts. Such views are becoming increasingly common in the West, and they have been particularly well articulated by Ernest Fleischmann, a highly respected orchestral administrator who has managed major orchestras on both sides of the Atlantic. In an address given at the Cleveland Institute of Music in 1987, Fleischmann put forward in uncompromising fashion some of the difficulties facing orchestral musicians:

> For the musicians, life even in some of the great orchestras [is]
> increasingly frustrating: repetitive or boring repertoire, loss of musical
> identity, particularly for string players, incompetent conductors, bad halls,
> not enough money, much stress. No life for a real musician this, with little
> opportunity to develop as an artist, let alone as a human being.
> Dissatisfaction, frustration, antagonism, boredom – all these still exist
> among musicians in orchestras everywhere... Why the hell should anyone
> then contemplate an orchestral career?[4]

As a potential solution to these difficulties Fleischmann advocated abolishing the concept of orchestras entirely (in fact he suggested burning them!), and replacing them instead with 'Communities of Musicians'. These would comprise some 140–150 musicians, who could then be employed in a variety of situations often covered by several different ensembles at present.

Integrating them into one large group would allow more cross-fertilisation between the various performance genres than is often achieved within any given orchestra. Those normally confined only to symphonic repertory would get much more opportunity to play chamber music; the contemporary specialists would be given their own programmes but with more rehearsal time, and would also be used in other areas as the situation demanded; a similar approach would be taken towards early music specialists; musicians particularly predisposed towards educational work would lead residential projects, but all the various ensembles within the community would be available to schools and other institutions for concerts directed towards younger audiences. As yet Fleischmann's proposals have not been implemented in full anywhere, but they provide an imaginative blueprint for a model which would tackle many of the problems the orchestras face in the immediate future.

Fleischmann's views are resonant with those of Basil Tschaikov, another influential administrator, who in the 1980s was the director of the National Centre for Orchestral Studies in London, a training institution for musicians hoping to embark on an orchestral career. Tschaikov also felt it was important to enlarge the role of the orchestra, distribute its resources in other ways, and present fresh horizons for the orchestral musician:

> Dividing the orchestras into a number of smaller groups and ensembles creates many problems, especially for older players. But those preparing to be musicians who will serve audiences well into the twenty-first century, must have broader aspirations than their parents ... Our best players should be doing some teaching in the schools ... And they should play in the schools too, sometimes in small ensembles, sometimes in larger ones ... Musicians have a special place in societies where either unemployment or the shorter working week gives many people much more leisure time. Here they have a role as animateurs, as well as performers.[5]

Elsewhere he writes of his concern for what he describes as the rather 'abstract' nature of orchestral concerts, which, he suggests, is 'clearly no longer economically, socially or musically suited to the requirements of the future'.[6]

Evidently there is a consensus emerging that if the symphony orchestra as an institution is to survive for another century, then both the orchestras themselves and the players within them will need to be as flexible and adaptable as possible. And orchestral managers will need to show considerably more imagination, both in how resources are deployed and in the ways in which their concerts are presented, than might have been necessary for orchestras in the past.

A view from the East: orchestras in east Asia

If the perspective offered above is slightly negative – the symphony orchestra in the West in a gentle but continuous decline from its heyday of the late nineteenth and early twentieth centuries – this is in notable contrast to the situation in certain parts of east Asia, particularly in the second half of the twentieth century. As signalled in the opening chapter of this book, there has been a growing interest in certain types of symphonic Western art music – largely the nineteenth-century romantic tradition – which has in turn provided the impetus for the establishing of numerous orchestras to recreate the masterworks of this tradition.

There are a number of related reasons for this. The twentieth century has, in some of these Asian countries, seen the rise of a middle-class urban population in a similar fashion to that which arose in many areas of Europe during the nineteenth century. Richard Kraus has suggested that, in the case of China at least, 'the artistic preferences of the Chinese middle class flow also from the social implications which are embedded within this [Western] musical culture'.[7]

Although a sociologist might reasonably ask just *how* these social implications come to be 'embedded' in a symphony by Beethoven or Brahms, the parallel affinities within the two different contexts deserve to be noted. Furthermore, the migration of European citizens to various parts of Asia laid the foundations for tours by numerous European and American orchestras during the early twentieth century, in which they reconstituted the great nineteenth-century symphonies for the émigrés, as well as introducing them to particular sectors of the indigenous population. This in turn meant that, as Western art music and the instruments associated with it became more popular, many instrumentalists and composers from Asia came to Europe to learn the associated compositional and performance techniques. On their return they sought not only more performance opportunities with local orchestras, but also to establish a music education system of conservatoires and competitions which again paralleled that in the West. Moreover, the widespread availability of commercial recordings, allied to radio broadcasting, also contributed to the extensive dissemination of Western art music.

All of this led to a vigorous expansion of Western-style orchestral music in this part of the globe, and the creation of a surprisingly large number of ensembles in a relatively short period of time. The following list gives some flavour of this: in Japan the New Symphony Orchestra was founded in Tokyo in 1926, and after a period as the Japan Symphony Orchestra became the house orchestra of the broadcaster NHK in 1951; Tokyo alone now has numerous orchestras of various descriptions, with others in different Japanese cities. The Central Philharmonic Orchestra was established in

Beijing, China, in 1951, and, having only just survived Chairman Mao's profoundly nationalist 'Great Leap Forward' from 1958–61, today finds itself
one of the longest established of the many orchestras now resident in China's
major cities; a Chinese radio orchestra was briefly established in 1949,
before being disbanded and then re-established in the 1970s. Across the
Taiwan Strait the Taipei City Symphony Orchestra was founded in 1969.
In Korea the Seoul Philharmonic dates back to 1945, to be followed by the
Korean Broadcasting Service's own orchestra in 1956. Hong Kong, notwithstanding its colonial history, only established its Philharmonic Orchestra on
a professional basis in 1974.

This hotbed of activity suggests that orchestral music-making is in a
healthy and vibrant state on Asia's eastern shores. But this analysis glosses
over some important differences, as well as some significant similarities,
with orchestras in the West. For example, east Asian audiences for orchestral
music, perhaps even more than their Western counterparts, are rather conservative in their expectations of orchestral programming; the major works
of the late-eighteenth and nineteenth centuries account for by far the greatest proportion of works played, with little interest in modern works nor in
the music of earlier periods. Again the essentially static nature of the repertory may be off-putting to younger audiences, particularly as orchestral
music now has to compete with a considerable amount of locally produced
popular music. It is noticeable that, as in the West, audiences for classical
music have been declining in recent years.

One area of repertory development that has been explored in an attempt to combat this is the use by local composers of traditional Asian
instruments in the orchestral context. Such instruments have not found a
permanent place in the orchestra, but are occasional visitors, rather like the
saxophone or the guitar in the West. Although the incorporation of these instruments has not been universally successful, they do provide a particularly
Asian dimension to the evolution of orchestral music. Certain works, such
as those by the Chinese-born but now American-based composer Tan Dun,
have proved successful enough to have received performances in other parts
of the world. These meetings between traditional local musics and Western
symphonic forces remain potentially interesting areas for exploration, although whether the results of such fusions become widely accepted by the
listening public, either at home or abroad, is another matter.

Orchestras in the Far East have also suffered by often not being able to
secure major recording contracts in the way that many of their Western
counterparts have done. Whereas Western orchestras have (at least until
recently) buttressed the insecurities of their performance activities with
often lucrative session work, either by recording standard repertory for
global distribution by the major record companies or through film scores

and other commercial work, this option has been less available to the newer orchestras in the East. There are a number of complex reasons for this. Partly it is because the more established orchestras of the West have been better connected with both the record companies themselves and the conductors who play such an important role in the provision of these contracts. Equally, it has taken some time for any east Asian orchestra to achieve the technical standards that have long been common among the top Western orchestras. But there is also perhaps an implicit assumption in certain quarters that Western musicians simply play Western music better, because it is somehow more 'their' tradition. For all these reasons, east Asian orchestras have not had the same exposure from the major record companies as their Western counterparts. Although the situation is changing slowly, it will be some time yet before any of these orchestras manages to establish itself in the way that, for example, the Berlin Philharmonic or the Philharmonia Orchestra has done, on the back of a large catalogue of significant recordings.

The lives of individual orchestral musicians have also in part begun to parallel those in the West. Just as an orchestral career now makes considerable and varied demands on Western musicians, with basic funding insecure and diversification inevitable, so similar situations are beginning to arise in the East. Kraus notes that under recent Chinese reforms, for example, financial stability has been eroded:

> Arts ensembles have been urged to become financially self-sufficient...
> The Central Philharmonic has had to record film soundtracks for income,
> at the expense of rehearsal time for the music it wants to play. The
> Shanghai Symphony must divide into 'light music groups' which provide
> background music in hotels and restaurants ... Individual musicians also
> supplement their low incomes by moonlighting as teachers and pop
> performers.[8]

While such specific difficulties may not apply in every case, it seems clear that, despite their apparent industriousness and vitality, east Asian orchestras and the musicians within them face many of the problems shared by their Western counterparts. They may also in future need to consider some of the solutions presently being adopted in the West, if they are to secure their positions both at home and abroad.

Conclusions

Much of what has been written here has concentrated on the larger symphonic orchestra, and while the picture of eighty or so musicians wearing full evening dress is undoubtedly the image which springs to many minds when the word 'orchestra' is mentioned, it is important to observe that from the early twentieth century onwards other types of ensemble might equally have been connoted. In particular, the rise of the chamber orchestra has been especially significant. Such groups are smaller, cheaper and often more flexible than their larger siblings, and thus go some way towards mitigating both the economic and repertory difficulties discussed earlier. Some of these have carved a niche for themselves through specialising in particular repertories such as contemporary music (for example, Ensemble Intercontemporain in France or the London Sinfonietta), or through period performance (The Hanover Band or the Amsterdam Baroque Orchestra). Other such ensembles have proved to be rather transient, often put together by a particular conductor or composer to provide a platform for that individual's skills; yet some, such as the St. Pauls Chamber Orchestra in Minnesota or the Basle Chamber Orchestra, have achieved a permanence and longevity comparable to some major symphony orchestras, with a deserved reputation to match.

Being relatively recently established, many of these smaller ensembles have felt less encumbered by the traditions underpinning the older symphonic orchestras. But the adventurousness they have shown, not only in terms of their programming but also in how they have marketed themselves and generated new audiences, may provide some inspiration for their larger cousins as the latter seek to overcome the difficulties for their own future. In the twenty-first century marketing and corporate image-making are as important to orchestras as they are to any other medium-sized business; the symphony orchestra of today is akin to a small corporation, with a profile, employee numbers and a turnover to match, and both musicians and their managers have learned through painful experience that they must be as professional in their attitude to the business side of their operations as they are in their attitude towards their music-making. New media and information technology are at the heart of this business revolution. Orchestras are already making use of email distribution lists, websites and similar marketing ploys, as well as using more creative images and other artwork sometimes influenced by popular culture, in order to promote themselves both as widely and as cost effectively as possible.

Information technology presents other opportunities for the orchestras' future, particularly in relation to recorded music. Traditionally orchestras have recorded for large record companies, who have generally paid the orchestra, recording, production and distribution costs, and have then retained any profits (or borne any losses) that the disc might make. This is still the model that prevails in most situations, particularly with the major record labels. But there are now alternatives. Recording and production costs are lower than in the past, and the internet presents significant opportunities for the dissemination of orchestral recordings, either as a means simply to sell pre-recorded CDs as at present, or, conceivably, as soundfiles (mp3, for example) direct to the consumer. As noted in chapter 11, a few orchestras have already set up their own record labels to market and distribute their recordings, and adept use of the internet could boost this trend quite significantly. Potentially, orchestras could target niche markets for contemporary music, early music, or works by less well-known composers, without the need for expensive mass marketing. Recordings could be made available on a subscription basis, whereby a fixed number of subscribers to a soundfile would ensure that the recording was made, and it could then be transmitted direct to the subscriber's home. Or, for a small additional fee, recordings of concerts could be subsequently transmitted into the homes of those who attended the concert. Such things may seem far-fetched at present, but the digital revolution has transformed so many aspects of global culture so quickly that it is difficult to foresee how orchestras may be harnessing its benefits in fifty years' time.

The social and cultural contexts in which orchestras work have evolved beyond all recognition since the seventeenth century, and particularly in the last few decades. For many years orchestras stood still while the world around them moved on, and for some people the orchestra remains a relic from a previous age. This need not be the case, and there are many musicians and administrators who are showing great imagination, flexibility and commitment as they lead the orchestra into the twenty-first century. But if this great cultural institution is to survive into the twenty-second century, such approaches must become the norm, not the exception. The orchestra is too important to be allowed to subside into a cultural antiquity for an ever-diminishing group of interested historians.

Notes

Preface
1 Henry Pleasants, *Serious Music and All That Jazz* (London, 1969), pp. 78–9.

1 The history of the orchestra
1 It is interesting to note that this division between orchestras specialising in 'light' and 'serious' music survives up to the present day. For example, the BBC employs two orchestras in London – the Concert Orchestra performs the lighter repertory which is normally avoided by the Symphony Orchestra.
2 William Weber, 'The Rise of the Classical Repertoire in Nineteenth-Century Orchestral Concerts', in J. Peyser (ed.), *The Orchestra: Origins and Transformations* (New York, 1986), p. 372.
3 Daniel J. Koury, *Orchestral Performance Practices in the Nineteenth Century: Size, Proportion and Seating* (Ann Arbor, 1986), pp. 299–301.
4 Julia Allmendinger and J. Richard Hackman, 'The More, the Better? A Four-Nation Study of the Inclusion of Women in Symphony Orchestras'. *Social Forces* 74 (1995), pp. 423–60.
5 In the twenty-first century, it is even possible to talk of two distinctive orchestral repertories, one designed for the concert hall, the other conceived for the record enthusiast.

2 The development of musical instruments: national trends and musical implications
1 Herbert Spencer's assertion that 'Music must take rank as one of the highest of the fine arts' ('On the origin and function of music', *Fraser's Magazine* 56, 334 (1857), p. 408) is clear indication of the position of musical composition in the social scale.
2 Philipp Spitta, *Johann Sebastian Bach*, trans. Clara Bell and J. A. Fuller-Maitland (London, 1889), vol. II, p. 44.
3 Reinhard Beuth, 'Playing on a Stradivarius: an Interview with Anne-Sophie Mutter', *Encounter* 70 (May 1988), pp. 71–5.
4 Laurence Libin, 'Progress, Adaptation and the Evolution of Musical Instruments', *Journal of the American Musical Instrument Society* 26 (2000), pp. 187–213.

5 Stewart Carter, 'Georges Kastner on Brass Instruments', in S. Carter (ed.), *Perspectives in Brass Scholarship* (New York, 1997), p. 191.
6 The element of change comes from a move from a direct vendor–purchaser relationship to what Trevor Herbert describes as a 'process culture' in which the process of making, selling, buying, dispensing, etc. obtains its own motion that is independent of the type of direct negotiation that took place in the previous period. In essence, the market replaces the individual.
7 Many of these innovations in brass instruments are illustrated by Arnold Myers in 'Design, Technology and Manufacture since 1800', in T. Herbert and J. Wallace (eds.), *The Cambridge Companion to Brass Instruments* (Cambridge, 1997), pp. 115–30.
8 This subject is dealt with by this author in 'A New Species of Instrument: the vented trumpet in context', *Historic Brass Society Journal* 10 (1998), pp. 1–13.
9 Michael Praetorius, *Syntagma Musicum, Vol. II, De Organographia* (Wolffenbüttel, 1619), p. 48. 'Und demnach dieselbige jedermanniglichen bestandt ist darvon . . . etwas mehr anzudeuten und zu schreiben unnotig.'
10 Although published over 40 years ago, Anthony Baines's *Woodwind Instruments and Their History* (London, 1957, 3rd edn 1967) still provides an excellent introduction.
11 See note 8 and pp. 164–5.
12 Donald Boalch, *Makers of the Harpsichord and Clavichord, 1440–1840*, ed. Charles Mould (Oxford, 3rd edn, 1995).
13 Grant O'Brien, 'Ioannes and Andreas Ruckers', *Early Music* 7 (1979), pp. 453–66.
14 Baines, *Woodwind Instruments*, pp. 297–302.
15 This spelling of Leichamschneider is taken from L. G. Langwill, *Index of Musical Wind Instrument Makers* (Edinburgh, 5th edn, 1972).
16 The phenomenon of the 'invention of tradition' is covered in a series of essays under this title edited by Eric Hobsbawm and Terence Ranger: *The Invention of Tradition* (Cambridge, 1984).
17 This violin, known as *Le Messie*, is part of the Hill Collection in the Ashmolean Museum, Oxford.

18 This complex subject is discussed very thoroughly by James Beament in *The Violin Explained* (Oxford, 1997), p. 236. The early 20th-century research of J. Chenantais, *Le violoniste et le violon* (Nantes, 1927), is also essential to a well-rounded understanding.

19 Baines, *Woodwind Instruments*, p. 94.

20 Museum of London, accession number 61.20, on loan from HM The Queen.

21 Musikinstrumenten-museum der Karl-Marx-Universität, Leipzig, #1835.

22 Ralph Dudgeon, 'Keyed Brass', in Herbert and Wallace (eds.), *The Cambridge Companion to Brass Instruments*, pp. 140–2.

23 Arnold Myers illustrates this in 'Design, technology and manufacture since 1800', ibid., p. 121.

24 Clifford Bevan, 'The Low Brass', ibid., p. 148.

25 Haine, Malou, *Adolphe Sax: sa vie, son oeuvre, ses instruments de musique* (Brussels, 1980).

26 Babcock's patent is illustrated in J. Parakilas et al., *Piano Roles* (New Haven and London, 1999), p. 59. This series of essays provides a good overview of piano development.

27 Simon Wills, 'Brass in the Modern Orchestra', in Herbert and Wallace (eds.), *The Cambridge Companion to Brass Instruments*, p. 157.

28 Gayle Young, *The Sackbut Blues: Hugh Le Caine, Pioneer in Electronic Music* (Ottawa, 1989).

29 Baines, *Woodwind Instruments*, p. 321.

30 Jaap Frank, Michael Cox and Hélène La Rue, 'The Louis Lot Debate', *Pan* 14/3 (September 1996), pp. 35–6.

31 Baines, *Woodwind Instruments*, pp. 49–51.

32 Horn player Richard Seraphinoff observes that 'the double horn is a device invented to preserve the player's sanity, and to help insure job security in orchestras where the works of Richard Strauss are often played'.

33 Baines, *Woodwind Instruments*, pp. 239–41.

34 Ibid., p. 239.

3 The orchestral repertory

1 See John Spitzer and Neal Zaslaw, 'Orchestra', in Sadie and J. Tyrrell (eds.), *The New Grove Dictionary of Music and Musicians*, (2nd rev. edn, London, 2001), vol. XVIII, p. 531. See also the early part of chapter 1 of this book.

2 Jan LaRue, *A Catalogue of 18th-Century Symphonies.* Vol. I: Thematic Identifier (Bloomington, IN, 1988).

3 The best study of this gigantic repertory is by Stefan Kunze, *Die Sinfonie im 18. Jahrhundert: Von der Opernsinfonie zur Konzertsinfonie* (Laaber, 1993).

4 A large number of these works are available for study in Barry S. Brook (ed.), *The Symphony 1720–1840: A comprehensive collection of full scores in sixty volumes* (New York, 1979–85).

5 On Stamitz see Eugene K. Wolf, *The Symphonies of Johann Stamitz: A Study in the Formation of the Classical Style* (Utrecht, 1981).

6 On C. P. E. Bach's symphonies, see G. Wagner, *Die Sinfonien Carl Philipp Emanuel Bachs: Werdende Gattung und Originalgenie* (Stuttgart and Weimar, 1994).

7 The definitive study of Haydn's symphonies is still the *magnum opus* of H. C. Robbins Landon, *The Symphonies of Joseph Haydn* (London, 1955).

8 The standard work on Mozart's symphonies is Neal Zaslaw, *Mozart's Symphonies: Context, Performance Practice, Reception* (Oxford, 1989).

9 Of the enormous literature on Beethoven, a fine general treatment of the symphonies may be found in Antony Hopkins, *The Nine Symphonies of Beethoven* (London, 1981).

10 Brian Newbould's *Schubert and the Symphony: A New Perspective* (London, 1992) is a comprehensive treatment of its subject. See also L. Michael Griffel's article 'Schubert's Orchestral Music: "striving after the highest in art"', in Christopher H. Gibbs (ed.), *The Cambridge Companion to Schubert* (Cambridge, 1997), pp. 193–206.

11 Berlioz's symphonies and concert overtures have recently been discussed by Jeffrey Langford and Diana Binckley, respectively, in Peter Bloom (ed.), *The Cambridge Companion to Berlioz* (Cambridge, 2000), pp. 53–68 and 69–80.

12 R. Larry Todd contributed a useful overview of Mendelssohn's symphonic works to D. Kern Holoman (ed.), *The Nineteenth-Century Symphony* (New York, 1997).

13 For a good summary introduction to Schumann's symphonies, see Linda Correll Roesner, 'Schumann', ibid., pp. 43–77.

14 In his programme to the *Symphonie fantastique*, Berlioz emphasises: 'The composer's intention has been to develop, *insofar as they contain musical possibilities,* various situations in the life of an artist.' (Translation from the Norton Critical Score edited by Edward T. Cone (New York, 1971), p. 21 (author's emphasis).)

15   The Liszt essay in Holoman (ed.),
Nineteenth-Century Symphony, pp. 142–62, by
Kenneth Hamilton, also covers the symphonic
poems.
16   A good concise introduction to
Bruckner's symphonies is Philip Barford's
volume, entitled *Bruckner Symphonies*, in the
BBC Music Guides series (London, 1978).
17   Raymond Knapp's *Brahms and the
Challenge of the Symphony* (Stuyvestant, NY,
1997) is an interesting new study of Brahms's
orchestral music.
18   The numbering of Dvořák's symphonies
follows Jarmil Burghauser's catalogue, which
was the first to establish their correct
chronology.
19   The Tchaikovsky and Dvořák chapters in
Holoman (ed.), *Nineteenth-Century Symphony*,
pp. 299–326 and 273–98 (by Joseph Straus
and Michael Beckerman, respectively),
provide a good start for the study of the two
composers' works.
20   Strauss also wrote two early symphonies,
both before the age of twenty.
21   The most comprehensive work on
Richard Strauss's music is Norman Del Mar,
Richard Strauss (London, 1962–72, repr.
1978).
22   At the beginning of his *Mahler
Remembered* (London, 1987), Norman
Lebrecht offers an interesting chart about the
chain of influences that started with Mahler.
Of the enormous literature on the composer,
the most comprehensive analysis of the
orchestral works may be found in Donald
Mitchell's *Mahler: the Wunderhorn Years* and
*Gustav Mahler: Songs and Symphonies of Life and
Death* (London, 1985).
23   The seminal monograph on Sibelius is
Erik Tawaststjerna, *Sibelius*, tr. Robert Layton
(London, 1976–97).
24   On Elgar, see R. Anderson, *Elgar*
(London, 1993).
25   On Nielsen, see M. Miller (ed.), *The
Nielsen Companion* (London, 1994).
26   Each one of Ravel's works is discussed in
Arbie Orenstein, *Ravel: Man and Musician*
(London, 1975).
27   On Vaughan Williams, see Michael
Kennedy, *The Works of Ralph Vaughan Williams*
(London, 1964, rev. 1980).
28   On Bartók's orchestral music see David
Cooper, 'Bartók's orchestral music and the
modern world', in Amanda Bayley (ed.), *The
Cambridge Companion to Bartók* (Cambridge,
2001), pp. 45–61.
29   Paul Griffiths's *Stravinsky* (London, 1992)
is an excellent one-volume introduction to
the composer's life and works.

30   Phillip Huscher, programme note for the
Chicago Symphony, 15 October 1997. On
Berg's music, see Anthony Pople (ed.), *The
Cambridge Companion to Berg* (Cambridge,
1997).
31   There are many new works on Webern,
but none as comprehensive as Hans
Moldenhauer's *Anton von Webern: A Chronicle
of his Life and Works* (London, 1978).
32   On Prokofiev, see Harlow Robinson:
Sergey Prokofiev: A Biography (New York, 1988).
33   Lest this aspect of Shostakovich be
considered exclusively from a political point
of view, it should be remembered that Mahler,
too, had created a similar ambiguity in the
finale of his Seventh Symphony, among other
places.
34   See Neil Butterworth, *The American
Symphony* (Aldershot, 1998).
35   The most up-to-date introduction to
Messiaen is Peter Hill (ed.), *The Messiaen
Companion* (London, 1994).
36   On Carter, see David Schiff, *The Music of
Elliott Carter* (Ithaca, 2nd edn, 1998).
37   On Lutoslawski, see Charles Bodman
Rae, *The Music of Lutoslawski* (London, 3rd
edn, 1999).
38   Dominique Jameux's *Pierre Boulez* (tr.
Susan Bradshaw, Cambridge, MA, 1991)
contains an overview of the works written up
to 1986, and offers individual commentaries
on them.
39   Iannis Xenakis, *Formalized Music: Thought
and Mathematics in Composition* (Bloomington,
IN, 1971), p. 237.
40   See Friedrich Spangemacher, 'Punk und
Muttermilch. Ein Gespräch mit dem
finnischen Komponisten Magnus Lindberg',
Neue Zeitschrift für Musik (1991/1),
pp. 25–8.

4   From notation to sound
1   But see below, concerning Ex. 4.6.
2   This point is made by Gordon Jacob,
Orchestral Technique (London, 1931, 2nd edn
1940), p. 62. Jacob's book is, incidentally, a
very useful handbook for score-readers,
although it was written for composers.
3   I use 'bar-lined' here not to mean simply
'barred' but more specifically 'barred through
one or more staves in the system to
distinguish instrumental family or other
groupings'.
4   In dealing with percussion instruments,
especially, many music-lovers are confused by
the instrumental names in the various
languages. There is a useful table of names in
Jacob, *Orchestral Technique*, pp. 4–5.

5 Until well into the twentieth century horns were conventionally written an octave lower than expected, therefore transposing upwards, when in the bass clef. For a fuller account of transposition conventions, including a discussion of transposing instruments, see Richard Rastall, *The Notation of Western Music* (London, 1983, rev. 2nd edn Leeds, 1998), pp. 236–40.

6 Jacob, *Orchestral Technique*; Hector Berlioz, *Grand traité d'instrumentation et d'orchestration modernes* (Paris, 1843, Eng. tr. 1856); Cecil Forsyth, *Orchestration* (London, 1914); Walter Piston, *Orchestration* (New York, 1955); N. Rimsky-Korsakov, *Principles of Orchestration* (St Petersburg, 1913; London, 1922, 2nd edn 1964).

7 Further on this, see the article 'Harmonics' in S. Sadie and J. Tyrrell (eds.), *The New Grove Dictionary of Music and Musicians* (rev. 2nd edn, London, 2001), vol. X, pp. 854–6.

8 For more detail on mutes, including a list of brass mutes, see the article 'Mute' in ibid., vol. XVII, especially pp. 559–61.

9 There are of course many other effects possible in the orchestra. The reader will find the less common ones gradually by studying scores and listening to the music while following the notation.

10 For a very good brief explanation of the harp's working see Jacob, *Orchestral Technique*, pp. 74–8.

11 'Pitch-class' refers to all the notes of a particular name – thus all the C♯s form a pitch-class, as do all the G♯s, and so on.

5 The art of orchestration

1 Various authors, 'Instrumentation and orchestration', in S. Sadie and J. Tyrrell (eds.), *The New Grove Dictionary of Music and Musicians* (rev. 2nd edn, London, 2001). Prior to *The New Grove* (1980), all editions except the second (1906) deal with the subject under the heading 'Orchestration'.

2 H. Berlioz, *Grand traité d'instrumentation et d'orchestration modernes* (Paris, 1843, Eng. tr. 1856). H. Macdonald, *Berlioz's Orchestration Treatise: a Translation and Commentary* (Cambridge, 2002) includes many supplementary notes and a valuable summary of treatises before Berlioz.

3 'F.C.', 'Instrumentation', in J. A. Fuller-Maitland (ed.), *Grove's Dictionary of Music and Musicians* (London, 2nd edn, 1906), vol. II, pp. 473–84; F. Corder, *The Orchestra and How to Write for it: a Practical Guide* (London, 1896).

4 H. Riemann, *Katechismus der Orchestrierung (Anleitung zum Instrumentieren)* (Leipzig,

1902); R. Strauss, *Instrumentationslehre von Hector Berlioz* (Leipzig, 1905).

5 A. Reicha, *Traité de haute composition musicale* (Paris, 1824–6).

6 C.-M. Widor, *Technique de l'orchestre moderne* (Paris, 1904).

7 Igor Stravinsky and Robert Craft, *Conversations with Igor Stravinsky* (London, 1959), p. 31.

8 Gluck began this practice in Vienna, with *Orfeo ed Euridice* (1762). By the mid-1770s, the keyboard instrument was excluded from many orchestral locations, including the Paris Opéra. While in the 1790s Haydn in London presided over performances at the keyboard, actually playing the instrument was seldom obligatory. Some operatic traditions, however, retained a keyboard to accompany simple recitatives well into the 19th century, although there was no necessity for the keyboard to play elsewhere.

9 F.-A. Gevaert, *Nouveau traité d'instrumentation* (Paris, 1885) methodically covers the capabilities of the instruments, while his *Cours méthodique d'orchestration* (Paris, 1890) treats the ensemble as a whole.

10 An earlier instance of timpani playing a tritone appears in an opera, *La grotta di Trofonio*, by one of Beethoven's teachers, Salieri.

11 Music for ophicleide can be found in Mendelssohn, Overture *A Midsummer Night's Dream* (1826) and Berlioz, *Symphonie fantastique* (1830).

12 C. Dahlhaus, *Schoenberg and the New Music*, tr. D. Puffett and A. Clayton (Cambridge, 1987), p. 41.

13 H. Macdonald, 'Berlioz's Orchestration: Human or Divine?', *The Musical Times* 110 (1969), p. 256. C. Forsyth, *Orchestration* (London, 1914), pp. 135–6; Norman Del Mar, *Conducting Berlioz* (Oxford, 1997), p. 202.

14 Strauss, *Instrumentationslehre*. In the introduction Strauss states that Wagner represents the only progress in instrumentation since Berlioz.

15 Rimsky-Korsakov's *Principles of Orchestration* (St Petersburg, 1913) was unfinished at the composer's death and eventually published by his son-in-law, the composer Maximilian Steinberg.

16 M. Russ, *Musorgsky: Pictures in an Exhibition* (Cambridge University Press, 1992).

6 The history of direction and conducting

1 Carl Flesch, *Memoirs*, tr. Hans Keller (London, 1957), quoted in Harold Schonberg *The Great Conductors* (New York, 1967), p. 15.

2 Quoted in ibid.

3 Oscar Levant, *A Smattering of Ignorance* (New York, 1942), quoted in Nat Shapiro, *An Encyclopedia of Quotations About Music* (New York, 1978), p. 76.

4 Adam Carse, *The Orchestra from Beethoven to Berlioz* (Cambridge, 1948), p. 339.

5 Ornithoparchus (Andreas Vogelhofer), *Musicae activae micrologus* (Leipzig, 1517), quoted in Schonberg, *Great Conductors*, p. 27.

6 Thomas Morley, *A Plain and Easy Introduction to Practical Music* (London, 1597, repr. London, 1963), p. 19.

7 Johann Matthias Gesner, in his edition of Quintilian's *Institutio oratoria* (Göttingen, 1738), quoted in Schonberg, *Great Conductors*, p. 39.

8 François Raguenet, *A Comparison between the French and Italian Musick and Operas* (Paris, 1702, Eng. tr. London, 1709), quoted in ibid., p. 82.

9 Georg Sievers, quoted in ibid., p. 72.

10 *The Musical World*, London, 29 March 1840, quoted in Carse, *Beethoven to Berlioz*, p. 330.

11 Felix Weingartner, quoted in ibid., p. 353.

12 Richard Wagner, quoted in Schonberg, *Great Conductors*, p. 108.

13 *The Musical World*, London, 5 August 1836, quoted in Adam Carse, *The Life of Jullien* (Cambridge, 1951), p. 131.

14 *The Courier and Enquirer*, New York, 1853, quoted in Schonberg, *Great Conductors*, p. 154.

15 John Reynolds, quoted in Carse, *Life of Jullien*, p. 131.

8 The revival of historical instruments

1 In Clive Brown, *Classical and Romantic Performance Practice 1750–1900* (Oxford, 1999), Preface, p. vii.

2 H. Berlioz, *Grand traité d'instrumentation et d'orchestration modernes* (Eng. tr. London, 1856), pp. 115, 116, 141.

3 F. Gleich, *Handbuch der modernen Instrumentirung für Orchester und Militärmusikcorps* (Leipzig, 1853), p. 37.

4 J. Joachim and A. Moser, *Violinschule* (3 vols., Berlin, 1902–5), vol. III, p. 5.

5 Robert Donington in E. Blom (ed.), *Grove's Dictionary of Music and Musicians* (London, 5th edn, 1954), cited by Margaret Campbell in S. Sadie (ed.), *The New Grove Dictionary of Music and Musicians* (20 vols., London, 1980), vol. V, p. 530, art. 'Dolmetsch, Arnold'.

6 See Robert Donington, *The Work and Ideas of Arnold Dolmetsch* (Haslemere, 1932); Margaret Campbell, *Dolmetsch: the Man and his Work* (London, 1975).

7 Dolmetsch, *Interpretation*, p. 458.

8 C. Saint-Saëns, 'The Execution of Classical Works: Notably Those of the Older Masters', *Musical Times* 56 (1915), pp. 474–8, reprinted in *MT* 138 (1997), pp. 31–5. This is the text of a lecture delivered on 1 June 1915 before the Salon de la Pensée Française at the San Francisco Exposition and first published in the local French newspaper, *Le Franco-Californien*. Saint-Saëns was honorary president of the Société des Instruments Anciens, which had been founded by Henri Casadesus in 1901.

9 Robert Haas, *Aufführungspraxis der Musik* (Wildpark-Potsdam, 1931), and Arnold Schering, *Aufführungspraxis alter Musik* (Leipzig, 1931).

10 Laurence Dreyfus, 'The Early Music debate', *Journal of Musicology* 10 (Winter 1992), p. 115.

11 Robin Stowell, *The Early Violin and Viola* (Cambridge, 2001), p. 3.

12 John Eliot Gardiner, 'Stand and Deliver', *BBC Music Magazine* (May, 1998), pp. 42–5. For Ernest Fleischmann's comments on the same subject, see p. 258.

13 Laurence Dreyfus, 'Early Music Defended Against its Devotees: a Theory of Historical Performance in the Twentieth Century', *Musical Quarterly* 49 (1983), pp. 297–322.

14 Ibid., p. 210.

15 D. K. Nelson, 'An Interview with Pinchas Zukerman', *Fanfare* 13 (March/April 1990), p. 38.

16 Neville Marriner played an important part in accustoming audiences to a leaner, crisper sound in classical repertory, but his Academy of St Martin-in-the-Fields, like Camerata Bern or I Musici, was effectively ousted by the period revival within his specialist area.

17 B. Sherman, *Inside Early Music: Conversations with Performers* (Oxford, 1997), p. 310.

18 I have suggested elsewhere that recent period recordings of Beethoven, Cherubini and Rossini have failed to illustrate these differences, especially in the area of playing technique.

19 H. C. Robbins Landon, *The Symphonies of Joseph Haydn* (London, 1955), p. 110.

20 W. Apel (ed.), *Harvard Dictionary of Music* (Cambridge, MA, 2nd edn, 1969).

21 C. Brown, *Classical and Romantic Performing Practice* (Oxford, 1999).

22 Joseph Szigeti, *A Violinist's Notebook* (London, 1969), p. 134: '[we produce] a big and somewhat undifferentiated tone; we neglect many bowing subtleties ... we

articulate with less character than even a few decades ago'.

23 Richard Taruskin, *Text and Act* (Oxford, 1995), p. 102.

24 See Robert Philip, *Early Recordings and Musical Style: Changing Tastes in Instrumental Performance 1900–1950* (Cambridge, 1992).

25 Booklet note to EMI CDC 7 54286 2, Brahms Symphony No. 1 (1991).

26 R. T. Dart, *The Interpretation of Music* (London, 1954), p. 165.

27 Dolmetsch, *Interpretation*, p. vii.

28 D. G. Türk, *Clavierschule, oder Anweisung zum Clavierspielen* (Leipzig and Halle, 1789); tr. by Raymond H. Haggh as *School of Clavier Playing* (Lincoln, NE and London, 1982), p. 337.

29 T. Adorno, 'Bach Defended Against His Devotees', in *Prisms*, tr. S. and S. Weber (London, 1967), pp. 133–46: 'At times one can hardly avoid the suspicion that the sole concern of today's devotees is to see that no inauthentic dynamics, modifications of tempo, oversize choirs and orchestras creep in; they seem to wait with potential fury lest any more humane impulse become audible in the rendition.'

30 *Early Music* 12 (1984), p. 519.

31 Gardiner, 'Stand and Deliver', p. 42.

32 In Dominic Gill (ed.), *The Book of the Violin* (Oxford, 1984), p. 154.

33 J. Kerman, *Musicology* (London, 1985), p. 208. Nicholas Kenyon has recently offered the more sympathetic observation that in order to develop the old techniques, players were taking big risks in cutting themselves off from the mainstream of orchestral life. John Eliot Gardiner has written of the lonely periods of trial and error and the brave experimentation under the scrutiny of a critical and sometimes sceptical public.

34 Sleeve-note to The Hanover Band recording of Beethoven's First Symphony and First Piano Concerto, Nimbus 5003 (1982).

35 C. Brown, 'Historical Performance, Metronome Marks and Tempo in Beethoven Symphonies', *Early Music* 19 (1992), pp. 247–58.

36 As John Solum has suggested in relation to the flute, the greatest antiques may have tonal superiorities to the best modern replicas, but the degree of difference is not as much as generally exists between old and new stringed instruments.

37 Robert Barclay, 'A New Species of Instrument: the Vented Trumpet in Context', *Historic Brass Journal* 10 (1998), p. 1.

38 R. Maunder, 'Viennese Wind-instrument Makers, 1700–1800', *The Galpin Society Journal* 51 (1998), p. 185.

39 Charles Burney, *The Present State of Music in Germany the Netherlands and United Provinces* (London, 1773), pp. 95–7.

40 L. Vallas, *Un siècle de musique et de théâtre à Lyon 1688–1789* (Lyons, 1932), p. 432. Neal Zaslaw ('Toward the Revival of the Classical Orchestra', *Proceedings of the Royal Musical Association* 103 (1976–7), p. 167) notes that this was not a satire, but a sober bureaucratic report, written at the request of the sponsoring organisation's board of directors.

41 See H. T. David and A. Mendel (eds.), *The Bach Reader: A Life of Johann Sebastian Bach in Letters and Documents* (New York, 1945, repr. 1966), pp. 120–4.

42 For illustrations and discussion of orchestral layout, see C. Lawson and R. Stowell, *The Historical Performance of Music: an Introduction* (Cambridge, 1999), pp. 95, 96, 134, 135, 141.

43 Ibid., p. 23.

44 Ibid., p. 1.

9 Recording the orchestra

1 Circular acoustic panels suspended below the dome and installed under BBC guidance. Reflective on their undersides and absorbent on their upper surfaces, they largely eliminate the formerly notorious double echo.

2 H. Atkins and A. Newman, *Beecham Stories* (London, 1978), p. 65.

3 The method was invented by the EMI sound engineer and pioneer of stereo, Alan Dower Blumlein (1903–42).

10 Training the orchestral musician

1 A. Pearce, 'The British Conservatoires' BMus (Hons) award; Current Attributes and Key Directions for the Future', *The Tacit Curriculum*, Birmingham Conservatoire, University of Central England (1997).

2 'Musicians' Union Research into the Training Needs of Orchestral Musicians' (London, 2000).

12 Historical recordings of orchestras

1 Conditions were not quite as cramped as some of the photographs of sessions suggest. A famous photograph taken in the studio after Elgar's first recording session in January 1914 is sometimes taken to show the players in their performing positions (most recently in the article on 'Recorded Sound' in *The New Grove II*). But most of the players have no music stands and no instruments, and have

clearly been grouped closely together in order to bring them within the field of view of the camera.

2   Details of this recording session and its preparations are given in Jerrold Northrop Moore, *Elgar on Record* (Oxford, 1974), pp. 19–21.

3   The range of orchestral recordings made by the old acoustic process is shown in Claude Graveley Arnold, *The Orchestra on Record, 1896–1926: An Encyclopedia of Orchestral Recordings made by the Acoustic Process* (Westport, CT and London, 1997).

13 The orchestral composer

1   Igor Stravinsky and Robert Craft, *Conversations with Igor Stravinsky* (London, 1959), pp. 29–30. See also Julian Rushton's observations in chapter 5.

2   Pierre Boulez, *Conversations with Celestin Deliege* (London, 1976), pp. 20–1.

3   Charles Rosen, *Sonata Forms* (New York and London, 1980, revd. 1988), footnote p. 105.

4   Arnold Schoenberg, *Fundamentals of Musical Composition*, ed. G. Strang and L. Stein (London, 1967), p. 11.

5   Paul Hindemith, *Traditional Harmony* (New York, 1953), p. 13.

6   It is beyond the scope of this article to delve deeper into post-tonal modality and its possible background/foreground, as attempted by Felix Salzer in *Structural Hearing: Tonal Coherence in Music* (New York, 1952, repr. 1962), particularly in relation to orchestral usage.

7   Boulez, *Conversations*, p. 20.

8   David Schiff, *The Music of Elliott Carter* (New York, 1983), pp. 247–8.

15 The future of the orchestra

1   Marcia Herndon, 'Cultural Engagement: The Case of the Oakland Symphony Orchestra', *Yearbook for Traditional Music* 20 (1988), pp. 134–45.

2   *The Independent*, 8 August 1994, p. 14.

3   *The Phil*, part 1. Channel 4 television, 24 January 1999.

4   Ernest Fleischmann, 'The Orchestra is Dead. Long Live the Community of Musicians', address given at the commencement exercises of the Cleveland Institute of Music, 16 May 1987, p. 2.

5   Basil N. Tschaikov, 'Preparation for the Orchestral Profession: which kind of symphony orchestra will we have in 2000?', *International Journal of Music Education* 9 (1987), p. 6.

6   Ibid.

7   Richard Kurt Kraus, *Pianos and Politics in China* (Oxford, 1989), p. 8.

8   Ibid., p. 186.

Appendix 1

The constitution of selected orchestras, 1670–1865

Note: Given the *ad hoc* nature of instrumental groupings in the early and mid Baroque period, attempting such an overview would serve scant purpose. For the period up to 1800, at least, statistics such as these must be treated with caution: they variously rely on haphazard sources, do not always take account of possible doublings or additional players, and sometimes tend to reflect extraordinary events. For this period, too, a 'continuo' group should be assumed even if it is not specified.

		Strings					Woodwind					Brass			Other				
Date	Place	Vn 1	Vn 2	Va	Vc	Cb	Fl	Ob	Cl	Bn	Hn	Tpt	Trbn	Tuba	Hp	Timp	Perc	Additional instruments	Notes
1670s–80s	Paris	6		12	6		2	2		1		2				1		1 hpd	For Lully operas, violas in various sizes
1708	Rome, Palazzo Bonelli	23		4	6	6		4				2	1					1 va da gamba; 1 hpd	For Handel, *La Resurrezione*
1712	Berlin, Royal Chapel	6	5	2	5		3	4		3	3							Court trumpeters and drummers	Same players on fl and hn
1713	Paris, Opéra	12		7	8	2		8									1		Violas in various sizes
1728	London, King's Theatre	22		2	3	2	2	2		3	2							2 hpd; 1 theorbo	
1730	Leipzig, Thomaskirche	6		4	2	1		3		2		3				1		2 kbd	
1738	Hamburg, Opera	8		3	2	2	5	5		5	4	6				1		various flutes; 2 ob d'amore; 2 chalumeaux; 2 cornetts; va d'amore; va da gamba	

Date	Place	Strings					Woodwind				Brass				Hp	Other		Additional instruments	Notes
		Vn 1	Vn 2	Va	Vc	Cb	Fl	Ob	Cl	Bn	Hn	Tpt	Trbn	Tuba	Hp	Timp	Perc		
1740s–50s	Naples, Teatro S. Carlo	28		5	2	4		4		2		4				1		2 hpd	
1751	Paris, Opéra	16	16	6	10		2	3		3–4		1–2				1		2 va da gamba; 1 hpd	
1754	London, Foundling Hospital	14	14	5	3	2		4		4		2				1		1 kbd	For Handel, *Messiah*
1771	Milan, Regio Ducal Teatro	14	14	6	2	6	2	4		2	4	2				?1		2 hpd	For Mozart, *Mitridate, re di Ponto*
1773	Paris, Concert spirituel	13	11	4	10	4		3	2	4	2	2				1			
1777	Mannheim, Court Orch.	10–11	10–11	4	4	4	2	2	2	4	2	?2				?1			
1781	Leipzig, Gewandhaus-Orch.	6	6	3	4		2	2		3	2	2				1			
1781	Vienna	40	40	10	8	10	4	4	4	6	4	4				1			Society of Musicians benefit concert, including a Mozart symphony
1781	Vienna, Burgtheater	6	6	4	3	3	2	2	2	2	4	2				1		1 kbd	
1783	Eszterháza	6	5	2	2	2	2	2	2	2	2								
1784	London	48	47	26	21	15	6	26		26	12	12	6			2	?	1 double-bn; 1 org	For Handel Commemoration
1791	London, Salomon Concerts	12–16		4	3	4	2	2	?2	2	2	2				1			
1805	Dresden, Hof-Orch.	17		4	4	4	3	3	2	4	4	x				x	x		
1810	Paris, Opéra	12	12	8	12	6	2	4	2	5	4	4	3			x	x	1 hpd	
1811	Berlin, Hofoper	11	11	5	11	5	4	4	4	4	7	2	3			x	x		
1814	Vienna, Redouten-Saal	18	18	14	12	17	2	2	2	2	2	2	2			x	x		For Beethoven concert
1818	London, King's Theatre	10	9	4	4	5	2	2	2	2	2	2	1			x	x		

(cont.)

Date	Place	Strings					Woodwind				Brass				Other			Additional instruments	Notes
		Vn 1	Vn 2	Va	Vc	Cb	Fl	Ob	Cl	Bn	Hn	Tpt	Trbn	Tuba	Hp	Timp	Perc		
1823	Dresden, Königlich-Sächsische Kapelle	18		4	5	5	5	5	5	5	6	2				1		2 Org	
1828	Paris, Société des Concerts	15	15	8	12	8	4	3	4	4	4	2	3			1		1 ophicleide	
1831	Leipzig, Gewandhaus - Orch.	8	8	4	3	3	2	2	2	2	2	2				1	X		
1837	London, Philharmonic Society	14	14	8	8	6	2	2	2	2	4	2	3			X			
1841	Paris, Pasdeloup Concerts	15	12	10	13	11	4	3	2	4	4	4	3			X			
1842	Vienna, Philharmonic Orch.	10	10	7	4	5	3	3	4	3	6	4	4		2	2	2		
1844	Munich, Hof Orchestra	26		3	8	6	7	6	7	4	5	5				2	x		
1850	Dresden, Hofoper	18	11	5	5	5	4	4	3	4	5	8	3		x	1	1		
1855	Paris, Opéra	11		8	10	8	3	3	3	4	5	4	4	1	2	1	4		
1858	London, Philharmonic Society	14	14	8	9	8	2	2	2	2	4	2	3			1			
1859	Paris, Conservatoire Orch.	15	14	10	12	9	4	2	2	4	4	2	3		1	1	1	1 cornet	
1865	Leipzig, Gewandhaus - Orch.	16	14	8	9	5	2	2	2	2	2	4	3			1		1 ophicleide	

Sources (adapted): Stanley Sadie (ed.), *The New Grove Dictionary of Music and Musicians* (London, 1980), vol. xiii, p. 690 (table compiled by Eleanor Selfridge-Field and Neal Zaslaw); Ludwig Finscher et al. (eds.), *Die Musik in Geschichte und Gegenwart* (Kassel, 2nd edn, 1996–), 'Sachteil', vol. vii, cols. 835–52 (table compiled by Christoph-Hellmut Mahling); Daniel J. Koury, *Orchestral Performance Practices in the Nineteenth Century: Size, Proportion and Seating* (Ann Arbor, 1986).

Appendix 2
Orchestras founded in the nineteenth century

The following selective list is limited to orchestras that have survived into the twentieth century.

1808	City Opera and Museum Orchestra of Frankfurt am Main
1815	Handel and Haydn Society, Boston (reconstituted 1986 as period-instrument orchestra)
1828	Hamburg Philharmonic Society
	Paris Conservatoire Orchestra
1833	Chemnitz City Orchestra (now known as the Robert Schumann Philharmonic)
1840	Gürzenich Orchestra, Cologne
	Royal Liverpool Philharmonic Orchestra
1841	Mozarteum Orchestra, Salzburg
1842	New York Philharmonic Orchestra
	Vienna Philharmonic Orchestra
1849	Wuppertal Symphony Orchestra
1850	Saint Caecilia Orchestra, Bordeaux
1853	Budapest Philharmonic Orchestra
1855	Strasbourg Philharmonic Orchestra
1856	Monte-Carlo Philharmonic Orchestra
1858	Hallé Orchestra, Manchester
1861	Pasdeloup Orchestra (Paris)
1864	Düsseldorf Symphony Orchestra
1868	Tonhalle Orchestra, Zurich
1870	Dresden Philharmonic Orchestra
1871	Zagreb Philharmonic Orchestra
1873	Concerts Colonne, Paris
1875	Winterthur Symphony Orchestra
1877	Berne Symphony Orchestra
	St. Louis Symphony Orchestra
1881	Boston Symphony Orchestra
	Lamoureux Orchestra, Paris
	Pecs Symphony Orchestra, Hungary
1882	Berlin Philharmonic Orchestra
	Helsinki Philharmonic Orchestra
	St Petersburg Philharmonic Orchestra
1884	Orchestre Symphonique et Lyrique de Nancy
1887	Detroit Symphony Orchestra
	Dortmund Philharmonic Orchestra

1888	Concertgebouw Orchestra, Amsterdam
1889	Arnhem Philharmonic Orchestra
1891	Chicago Symphony Orchestra
1893	Bournemouth Symphony Orchestra
	Munich Philharmonic Orchestra
1894	Cincinnati Symphony Orchestra
	Györ Philharmonic Orchestra, Hungary
1895	Pittsburgh Symphony Orchestra
1899	Essen Philharmonic Orchestra

Appendix 3
Orchestras founded in the twentieth century

Period-instrument orchestras are indicated in bold.

1900	Dallas Symphony Orchestra
	Honolulu Symphony Orchestra
	Philadelphia Orchestra
1901	Czech Philharmonic Orchestra
	Minnesota Orchestra
	Warsaw Philharmonic Orchestra
1904	London Symphony Orchestra
	Residentie-Orkest, The Hague
1905	Gothenburg Symphony Orchestra
1906	Toronto Symphony Orchestra
1907	Beethovenhalle Orchestra, Bonn
	Orchestra of the National Academy of Santa Cecilia, Rome
1908	Slovenian Philharmonic Orchestra, Ljubljana
1911	Austin Symphony Orchestra
	San Francisco Symphony Orchestra
	Tokyo Philharmonic Orchestra
1912	Helsingborg Symphony Orchestra
	Norrköping Symphony Orchestra
1914	Stockholm Philharmonic Orchestra
1916	Baltimore Symphony Orchestra
1918	Cleveland Orchestra
	Orchestre de la Suisse Romande
	Rotterdam Philharmonic Orchestra
	National Symphony Orchestra of Ukraine
1919	Bochum Symphony Orchestra
	Los Angeles Philharmonic Orchestra
	Oslo Philharmonic Orchestra
	Staatsphilharmonie Rheinland-Pfalz
1920	City of Birmingham Symphony Orchestra
1922	Lucerne Symphony Orchestra
	Vienna Symphony Orchestra
1923	Belgrade Philharmonic Orchestra
	Cologne Chamber Orchestra
	Hungarian State Symphony Orchestra
	Sarajevo Philharmonic Orchestra
	Swedish Radio Orchestra (reconstituted 1967)

1924   Rundfunks Sinfonie Orchester, Berlin
       MDR Symphony Orchestra, Leipzig
       Stuttgart Philharmonic Orchestra
1925   Danish Radio Symphony Orchestra
       Malmö Symphony Orchestra
1926   Basle Chamber Orchestra
       NHK Symphony Orchestra, Tokyo
       Prague Radio Symphony Orchestra
1927   Finnish Radio Symphony Orchestra
       Turku Philharmonic Orchestra
1928   Orchestra del Maggio Musicale Fiorentino
       Romanian National Radio Orchestra
1929   Radio Symphony Orchestra, Frankfurt
       Slovak Radio Symphony Orchestra
       Xalapa Symphony Orchestra, Mexico
1930   BBC Symphony Orchestra
       Indianapolis Symphony Orchestra
       Tchaikovsky Symphony Orchestra of Moscow Radio
       Tampere Philharmonic Orchestra, Finland
1931   Armenian Philharmonic Orchestra
       National Symphony Orchestra, Washington DC
       Vancouver Symphony Orchestra
1932   London Philharmonic Orchestra
       Sydney Symphony Orchestra
1933   BBC Northern Orchestra (renamed BBC Philharmonic 1982)
       Orchestre Philharmonique de Luxembourg
1934   Orchestre Nationale de France
       Jena Philharmonic Orchestra
       Prague Symphony Orchestra
       Szeged Symphony Orchestra, Hungary
1935   Aarhus Symphony Orchestra
       BBC Scottish Symphony Orchestra
       BBC Welsh Orchestra (renamed BBC National Orchestra of Wales,
       1993)
       Flemish Radio Orchestra
       Montreal Symphony Orchestra
       Polish National Radio Symphony Orchestra, Katowice
       Tenerife Symphony Orchestra
1936   Belgian National Orchestra
       Israel Philharmonic Orchestra
       Jerusalem Symphony Orchestra
       Symphony Orchestra of the RAI, Rome
       USSR (now Russian State) Symphony Orchestra
1937   Orchestre Philharmonique de Radio France (reconstituted 1976)
       Oulu Symphony Orchestra, Finland
1938   CBC Radio Orchestra, Vancouver

1940	Symphony Orchestra of Brazil, Rio di Janeiro
	Société des Concerts du Conservatoire, Bordeaux
	Lausanne Chamber Orchestra
1941	Symphony Orchestra of Chile, Santiago
	National Symphony Orchestra of Costa Rica
	National Symphony Orchestra of Panama
1942	National Orchestra of Spain
1943	Aalborg Symphony Orchestra
	Valencia Orchestra
1944	Atlanta Symphony Orchestra
	Barcelona Symphony Orchestra
1945	Kraków Philharmonic Orchestra
	Gumma Symphony Orchestra, Japan
	Macedonian Philharmonic Orchestra
	Moravian Philharmonic Orchestra
	Munich Symphony Orchestra
	NDR Symphony Orchestra, Hamburg
	Netherlands Radio Philharmonic Orchestra
	Orchestra of Hungarian Radio and Television
	Orchestre Philharmonique de Bordeaux
	Philharmonia Orchestra, London
	Polish State Philharmonic Orchestra, Katowice
	Seoul Philharmonic (enlarged 1992)
	Staatsorchester Rheinische Philharmonie
	Symphony Orchestra of the Artur Rubinstein
	Philharmonic of Łodz
1946	Bamberg Symphony Orchestra
	Buenos Aires Philharmonic Orchestra
	New Zealand Symphony Orchestra
	Norwegian Radio Orchestra
	Odense Symphony Orchestra
	Philharmonische Staatsorchester, Halle
	RIAS Symphony Orchestra, Berlin – reconstituted as Berlin
	Radio Symphony Orchestra (1977) and Deutsches Sinfonie
	Orchester (1993)
	Royal Philharmonic Orchestra
	SWR Symphony Orchestra, Baden-Baden and Freiburg
1947	National Symphony Orchestra of Mexico
	Osaka Philharmonic Orchestra
	Queensland Symphony Orchestra
	Radio Telefis Eirreann Symphony Orchestra
	WDR Radio Symphony Orchestra, Cologne
	Winnipeg Symphony Orchestra
1948	Bavarian Radio Symphony Orchestra
	Tasmanian Symphony Orchestra

1949   National Symphony Orchestra of Argentina
Orquesta Sinfonica de Guayaquil, Ecuador
Lahti Symphony Orchestra, Finland
London Mozart Players
Slovak Philharmonic Orchestra

1950   Canberra Symphony Orchestra
Haifa Symphony Orchestra
Iceland Symphony Orchestra
Melbourne Symphony Orchestra
NDR Philharmonic Orchestra, Hanover
Nordwestdeutsche Philharmonie, Herford
Scottish National Orchestra

1951   I Musici
Prague Chamber Orchestra
SWR Radio Orchestra, Kaiserslautern
SWR Radio Symphony Orchestra, Stuttgart
Central Philharmonic Orchestra, Beijing

1953   *Concentus Musicus, Vienna*
Kyushu Symphony Orchestra
Moscow Philharmonic Orchestra
Zagreb Soloists

1954   Bialystock State Philharmonic Orchestra
Janáček Philharmonic Orchestra, Ostrava
Wroclaw Philharmonic Orchestra

1955   Moscow Chamber Orchestra
Jyväsklä City Orchestra, Finland
Orchestra della Radio Svizzera Italiana, Lugano
Slovenian Radio Symphony Orchestra

1956   Gulbenkian Orchestra, Lisbon
Japan Philharmonic Symphony Orchestra
Kyoto Philharmonic Orchestra
KBS Symphony Orchestra, South Korea
Novosibirsk Philharmonic Orchestra
Puerto Rico Symphony Orchestra
Transylvanian Philharmonic Orchestra, Cluj

1957   Hamburg Symphony Orchestra

1958   Northern Sinfonia of England

1959   Academy of St. Martin-in-the-Fields
Cairo Symphony Orchestra
Philharmonia Hungarica

1960   English Chamber Orchestra
Liège Philharmonic Orchestra

1961   Brazil National Symphony Orchestra
Danube Symphony Orchestra, Hungary
Württemberg Chamber Orchestra, Heilbronn

1962   *Collegium Aureum Cologne*
Savaria Symphony Orchestra, Hungary

Spanish Radio and Television Symphony Orchestra
Yomiuri Nippon Symphony Orchestra

1963 Orchestre Symphonique de Bordeaux
Orchestra of the Finnish National Opera

1965 Israel Chamber Orchestra
Sjaellands Symphony Orchestra, Copenhagen
Tokyo Metropolitan Symphony Orchestra

1966 Nagoya Philharmonic Orchestra
Ulster Orchestra

1967 National Arts Centre Orchestra, Ottawa
Orchestre de Paris
Orchestra of St. John's, Smith Square, London
Oregon Symphony Orchestra

1968 London Sinfonietta
Los Angeles Chamber Orchestra
Monteverdi Orchestra (renamed English Boroque Soloists, 1977)
Orchestre Nationale de Lyon
Slovak State Symphony Orchestra, Košice
Uppsala Chamber Orchestra

1969 Biel Symphony Orchestra, Switzerland
ORF Radio Symphony Orchestra, Vienna
Japan Shinsei Symphony Orchestra
Taipei City Symphony Orchestra

1970 Kanagawa Philharmonic Orchestra

1971 City of London Sinfonia
State Symphony Orchestra of Mexico
Orchestre Nationale des Pays de la Loire
Staatsorchester Frankfurt, Oder

1972 Hiroshima Symphony Orchestra
La Petite Bande
Les Musiciens du Louvre, Grenoble
New Japan Philharmonic Orchestra
Orchestre de Picardie
Polish Chamber Orchestra/Sinfonia Varsovia
Yamagata Symphony Orchestra

1973 ***Academy of Ancient Music***
The English Concert

1974 Hong Kong Philharmonic Orchestra
Orpheus Chamber Orchestra
Scottish Chamber Orchestra

1975 Australian Chamber Orchestra
Brandenburg Consort and Orchestra
Orchestra Sinfonica dell'Emiglia-Romagna 'Arturo Toscanini'
Tokyo City Philharmonic Orchestra

1976 L'Orchestre Nationale de Lille
Ensemble Intercontemporain, Paris
La Philharmonie de Lorraine

	Smithsonian Chamber Players and Orchestra
1977	**English Baroque Soloists**
	Geneva Symphony Orchestra
1978	Orchestre Philharmonique de la BRTN, Brussels
	English Northern Philharmonia
	London Classical Players
	Mexico City Philharmonic Orchestra
	Pacific Symphony Orchestra
	RTBF Symphony Orchestra, Brussels
1979	**Amsterdam Baroque Orchestra**
	Black Sea Philharmonic Orchestra, Romania
	Orchestre Philharmonique de Montpellier-Languedoc-Roussillon
	Singapore Symphony Orchestra
	Tafelmusik Baroque Orchestra, Canada
1980	Auckland Philharmonic Orchestra
	Basel Sinfonietta
	Das Kleine Konzert
	The Hanover Band
	The King's Consort
	Orchestre Nationale de Bordeaux-Aquitaine
	Orquesta Filarmonica de Gran Canaria
	Osaka Symphony Orchestra
1981	Chamber Orchestra of Europe
	Deutsche Kammerphilharmonie, Bremen
	Ensemble Modern, Frankfurt
	Failoni Orchestra, Hungary
	Orchestra of the Eighteenth Century
	Orchestre d'Auvergne
	Orchestre Nationale du Capitole de Toulouse
1982	Kansai Philharmonic Orchestra
	Orchestre Philharmonique de Nice
	Turin Philharmonic Orchestra
1983	Avanti! Chamber Orchestra, Finland
	Budapest Festival Orchestra
	Concerto Armonico, Budapest
	Orchestre de l'Opéra National de Lyon
	Santo Andre Symphony Orchestra, Brazil
	Symphony Nova Scotia
1984	Orchestre des Pays de Savoie
	Musica Alta Ripa, Hanover
1985	**Concerto Köln**
	Ensemble Baroque de Limoges
	European Community Baroque Orchestra
	Flanders Philharmonic Orchestra
	Haydn Sinfonietta, Vienna

Il Giardino Armonico, Milan

1986   Cologne Philharmonic Orchestra
       Frankfurt Baroque Orchestra
       Orchestra of the Age of Enlightenment
       Taiwan National Symphony Orchestra
       Freiburg Baroque Orchestra
1988   Lithuanian Symphony Orchestra
       Le Concert Spirituel, Paris
       La Stravaganza, Cologne
       Century Orchestra, Osaka
       Il Fondamento, Bruges
       L'Europa Galante, Rome
       Le Concert des Nations, Barcelona
       Moscow Symphony Orchestra
       Orchestre de Bretagne
       Ostrobothnian Chamber Orchestra, Finland
       Bach Collegium, Japan
       Finnish Chamber Orchestra
       National Symphony Orchestra of Ireland
       Orchestra van Wassenaer, The Hague
       Orchestre Révolutionnaire et Romantique
       Russian National Orchestra
       Seville Symphony Orchestra
       Tel-Aviv Symphony Orchestra
       Tokyo New City Orchestra
       Debrecen Philharmonic Orchestra
       Les Talens Lyriques, Paris
       L'Orchestre des Champs-Élysées
1992   Geneva Chamber Orchestra
1993   Malaysian National Symphony Orchestra
       Milan Symphony Orchestra
       Portuguese Symphony Orchestra
       Tblisi Symphony Orchestra
1994   Rome Symphony Orchestra
       Slovenian Chamber Orchestra
1996   Neue Philharmonie Westfalen
       Warsaw Symphony Orchestra
1997   Symphony Orchestra, Basle (created through a fusion of the Basle
       Symphony Orchestra and the Radio Symphony Orchestra, Basle)
       Venice Baroque Orchestra
1998   *Das Neue Orchester, Cologne*
2000   China Philharmonic Orchestra

Select bibliography

Allmendinger, J., and Hackman, J. R., 'Organizations in Changing Environments: the Case of East German Symphony Orchestras', *Administrative Science Quarterly* 40 (1996), pp. 337–69
'The More, the Better? A Four-Nation Study of the Inclusion of Women in Symphony Orchestras', *Social Forces* 74 (1995), pp. 423–60
Allmendinger, J., Hackman, J. R., and Lehman, E. V., 'Life and Work in Symphony Orchestras', *Musical Quarterly* 80 (1996), pp. 194–219
Andersen, A., *Practical Orchestration* (Boston and New York, 1929)
Arnold, C. G., *The Orchestra on Record, 1896–1926: An Encyclopedia of Orchestral Recordings made by the Acoustic Process* (Westport, CT and London, 1997)
Atkins, H., and Newman, A., *Beecham Stories* (London, 1978)
Baines, A., *Brass Instruments: their History and Development* (London, 1976)
Woodwind Instruments and Their History (London, 1957, 3rd edn 1967)
Bamberger, C. (ed.), *The Conductor's Art* (New York, 1965)
Barclay, R., 'A New Species of Instrument: the vented trumpet in context', *Historic Brass Society Journal* 10 (1998), pp. 1–13
The Art of the Trumpet-maker (Oxford, 1992)
Beament, J., *The Violin Explained* (Oxford, 1997)
Bekker, P., *The Story of the Orchestra* (New York, 1936)
Benoit, M., *Versailles et les musiciens du roi, 1661–1733* (Paris, 1971)
Beraneck, L., *Concert and Opera Halls: How they sound* (New York, 1996)
Music, Acoustics and Architecture (New York, 1962)
Berlioz, H., *Grand traité d'instrumentation et d'orchestration modernes* (Paris, 1843); tr. Mary Cowden Clarke as *A Treatise upon Modern Orchestration and Instrumentation* (London, 1856; rev. Joseph Bennett, 1882)
Beuth, R., 'Playing on a Stradivarius: an interview with Anne-Sophie Mutter', *Encounter* 70 (May 1988), pp. 71–5.
Bial, B., *Focus on the Philharmonic* (New York, 1992)
Bianconi, L., and Walker, T., 'Production, Consumption and Political Function of Seventeenth-Century Opera', *Early Music History* 4 (1984), pp. 209–96
Blandford, L., *The LSO: Scenes from Orchestral Life* (London, 1984)
Borris, S., *Die grossen Orchester: eine Kulturgeschichte* (Hamburg, 1969)
Boult, A., *A Handbook on the Art of Conducting* (Oxford and London, 1921, 7th edn 1949)
Thoughts on Conducting (London, 1963)
Bowles, E. A., *Musical Ensembles in Festival Books, 1500–1800: an Iconographical and Documentary Survey* (Ann Arbor, 1989)
Bowles, M., *The Art of Conducting* (New York, 1959)
Boyden, D., *The History of Violin Playing from its Origins to 1761* (London, 1965)

Brown, C., *Classical and Romantic Performance Practice 1750–1900* (Oxford, 1999)
  'The Orchestra in Beethoven's Vienna', *Early Music* 16 (1988), pp. 4–20
Brown, H. M., and Sadie, S. (eds.), *Performance Practice* (2 vols., London, 1989)
Brymer, J., *From Where I Sit* (London, 1979)
  In the Orchestra (London, 1987)
Cahn-Speyer, R., *Handbuch des Dirigierens* (Leipzig, 1909, 2nd edn 1919, repr. 1974)
Carse, A., *The History of Orchestration* (London, 1925)
  The Orchestra from Beethoven to Berlioz (Cambridge, 1948)
  The Orchestra in the Eighteenth Century (Cambridge, 1940)
  Orchestral Conducting (London, 1929)
Carter, S., 'Georges Kastner on Brass Instruments', in Carter, S. (ed.), *Perspectives in Brass Scholarship* (New York, 1997)
Chanan, M., *Musica Practica: The Social Practice of Western Music from Gregorian Chant to Postmodernism* (London, 1994)
Chenantais, J., *Le violoniste et le violon* (Nantes, 1927)
Clarke, J.-H., *Manual of Orchestration* (London, 1888)
Cooper, J., *The Rise of Instrumental Music and Concert Series in Paris, 1828–1871* (Ann Arbor, 1983)
Corder, F., *The Orchestra and How to Write for it: a Practical Guide* (London, 1896)
Craven, R. R. (ed.), *Symphony Orchestras of the United States: Selected Profiles* (New York, 1986)
Creuzburg, E., *Die Gewandhaus-Konzerte zu Leipzig, 1781–1931* (Leipzig, 1931)
Dandelot, A., *La société des concerts du Conservatoire de 1823 à 1897* (Paris, 1898)
Danziger, D., *The Orchestra: The Lives Behind the Music* (London, 1995)
Del Mar, N., *A Companion to the Orchestra* (London, 1987)
Dreyfus, L., 'Early Music Defended Against Its Devotees: a Theory of Historical Performance in the Twentieth Century', *Musical Quarterly* 49 (1983), pp. 297–322
Dupuis, X., *Les musiciens professionels d'orchestre: étude d'une profession artistique* (Paris, 1993)
Edge, D., 'Mozart's Viennese Orchestras', *Early Music* 20 (1992), pp. 64–88
Ehrlich, C., *First Philharmonic: a history of the Royal Philharmonic Society* (Oxford, 1995)
  The Music Profession in Britain since the Eighteenth Century (Oxford, 1985)
Eisen, C., 'Mozart's Salzburg Orchestras', *Early Music* 20 (1992), pp. 89–103
Elkin, R., *Queen's Hall 1893–1941* (London, 1944)
  Royal Philharmonic: the Annals of the Royal Philharmonic Society (London, 1947)
Elwart, A., *Histoire de la société des concerts du Conservatoire impériale de musique* (Paris, 1860, enlarged 2nd edn 1864)
  Histoire des concerts populaires de musique classique (Paris, 1864)
Enrico, E., *The Orchestra at San Petronio in the Baroque Era* (Washington, DC, 1976)
Eppelsheim, J., *Das Orchester in den Werken Jean-Baptiste Lullys* (Tutzing, 1961)
Erskine, J., *Philharmonic-Symphony Society of New York: its first hundred Years* (New York, 1943)
Evans, E., *Method of Instrumentation* (London, 1925–7)

Faulkner, R., 'Career Concerns and Mobility Motivations of Orchestral Musicians', *Sociological Quarterly* 14 (1973), 334–49

'Orchestra Interaction', *Sociological Quarterly* 14 (1973), 147–57

Fleischmann, E., 'The Orchestra Is Dead. Long Live the Community of Musicians', address given at the commencement exercises of the Cleveland Institute of Music, 16 May 1987

Forsyth, C., *Orchestration* (London, 1914, 2nd edn 1935)

Forsyth, M., *Auditoria – Designing for the Performing Arts* (London, 1987)

Buildings for Music (Cambridge, 1985)

Foss, H., and Goodwin, N., *London Symphony: Portrait of an Orchestra* (London, 1954)

Frank, J., Cox, M., and La Rue, H., 'The Louis Lot Debate', *Pan* 14/3 (September 1996), pp. 35–6

Galeazzi, F., *Elementi teorico-practici di musica* (Rome, 1791–6)

Gardner, H., *Intelligence Reframed: Multiple Intelligences for the 21st Century* (New York, 2000)

Gassner, F., *Dirigent und Ripienist* (Karlsruhe, 1844)

Gevaert, F.-A., *Cours méthodique d'orchestration* (Paris, 1890)

Nouveau traité d'instrumentation (Paris, 1885)

Traité général d'instrumentation (Ghent, 1863)

Grosbayne, B., *Techniques of Modern Orchestral Conducting* (Cambridge, MA, 1956, rev. 2nd edn 1973)

Hansell, S., 'Orchestral Practice at the Court of Cardinal Pietro Ottoboni', *Journal of the American Musicological Society* 19 (1966), pp. 398–403

Hanslick, E., *Geschichte des Concertwesens in Wien* (Vienna, 1869–70)

Harnoncourt, N., *Baroque Music Today: Music as Speech* (London, 1988)

Hart, P., *Orpheus in the New World: the Symphony Orchestra as an American Cultural Institution* (New York, 1973)

Haskell, H., *The Early Music Revival* (London, 1988)

Herndon, M., 'Cultural Engagement: The Case of the Oakland Symphony Orchestra', *Yearbook for Traditional Music* 20 (1988), pp. 134–45

Hills, O., and Thackeray, V., *Coming in from the Cold* (London, 1997)

Hindemith, P., *A Composer's World* (Cambridge, MA, 1952)

Hobsbawm, E., and Ranger, T., *The Invention of Tradition* (Cambridge, 1984)

Holman, P., *Four and Twenty Fiddlers: the Violin at the English Court, 1540–1690* (Oxford, 1993)

Howitt, B., *Life in a Penguin Suit* (Manchester, 1993)

Jacob, G., *Orchestral Technique* (London, 1931, 2nd edn 1940)

Jerger, W., *Die Wiener Philharmoniker: Erbe und Sendung* (Vienna, 1942, 2nd edn 1943)

John, E., 'Orchester ohne Dirigent', *Das Orchester* 45/2 (1997), pp. 15–20; 46/1 (1998), pp. 11–15

Johnson, R., 'The Acoustics of Concert Halls', The Royal Society, London, England, 1994

'Designing a Hall for the Orchestra', American Symphony Orchestra League 49th National Conference, Dallas, TX, 1994

Jordan, V. H., *Acoustical Design of Concert Halls* (London, 1980)

Judy, P. R., 'The Uniqueness and Commonality of American Symphony Orchestra Organizations, *Harmony* 1 (1995), pp. 11–36

Kastner, J.-G., *Cours d'instrumentation considéré sous les rapports poétiques et philosophiques de l'art* (Paris, 1839, 2nd edn 1839; supplement 1844)
Traité général d'instrumentation (Paris, 1837)

Kennedy, M., *The Hallé: 1858–1983* (Manchester, 1982)

Kenyon, N. (ed.), *Authenticity and Early Music* (London, 1988)

Keys, A. C., 'Names for an Orchestra', *Studies in Music* (Australia) 9 (1975), pp. 54–63

Kleefeld, W., 'Das Orchester der Hamburger Oper, 1678–1738', *Sammelbände der Internationalen Musik-Gesellschaft*, I (1899–1900), pp. 219–89

Klein, F., *Geschichte des Orchestervereins der Gesellschaft der Musikfreunde von 1859–1934* (Vienna, 1934)

Koechlin, C., *Traité de l'orchestration* (Paris, 1954–9)

Koury, D., *Orchestral Performance Practices in the Nineteenth century: Size, Proportion and Seating* (Ann Arbor, 1986)

Kralik, H. von, *Die Wiener Philharmoniker: Monographie eines Orchesters* (Vienna, 1938, 2nd edn 1957 as *Das grosse Orchester*)
Die Wiener Philharmoniker und ihre Dirigenten (Vienna, 1960)

Kraus, R. K., *Pianos and Politics in China* (Oxford, 1989)

Kufferath, M., *L'art de diriger l'orchestre* (Brussels, 1891, 3rd edn 1909)

Kupferberg, M., *Those Fabulous Philadelphians* (New York, 1969)

Langwill, L. G., *Index of Musical Wind Instrument Makers* (Edinburgh, 1960, rev. enlarged 6th edn 1980), rev. W. Waterhouse as *The New Langwill Index* (London, 1993)

Laurence, L., 'Progress, Adaptation and the Evolution of Musical Instruments', *Journal of the American Musical Instrument Society* 26 (2000), 187–213

Lavoix, H., *Histoire de l'instrumentation depuis le seizième siècle jusqu'à nos jours* (Paris, 1878)

Lawson, C., and Stowell, R., *The Historical Performance of Music: an Introduction* (Cambridge, 1999)

Leibowitz, R., and Maguire, J., *Thinking for Orchestra: Practical Exercises in Orchestration* (New York, 1960)

Maitlis, S., 'Decision Making in British Symphony Orchestras: formal structures, informal systems, and the role of players', *Harmony* 4 (1997), pp. 45–55

Malko, N., *The Conductor and his Baton* (Copenhagen, 1950)

Mark, D., *Zur Bestandaufnahme des Wiener Orchesterrepertoires* (Vienna, 1979)

Mattheson, J., *Der vollkommene Capellmeister* (Hamburg, 1739)

McVeigh, S., *Concert Life in London from Mozart to Haydn* (Cambridge, 1993)

Moore, J. N., *Elgar on Record* (Oxford, 1974)

Mueller, J. H., *The American Symphony Orchestra: a Social History of Musical Taste* (Bloomington, IN, 1951)

Mueller, K. H., *Twenty-Seven Major American Symphony Orchestras: a History and Analysis of their Repertoire 1842–43 through 1969–70* (Bloomington, IN, 1973)

Myers, A., 'Design, Technology and Manufacture Since 1800', in Herbert, T., and Wallace, J. (eds.), *The Cambridge Companion to Brass Instruments* (Cambridge, 1997), pp. 115–30

Nettel, R., *The Orchestra in England: a Social History* (London, 1946, 3rd edn 1956)

O'Brien, G., 'Ioannes and Andreas Ruckers', *Early Music* 7 (1979), pp. 453–66

Opperby, P., *Leopold Stokowski* (New York, 1982)

Palmer, C. K., *Teach Yourself Orchestration* (London, 1964)

Parakilas, J., et al., *Piano Roles* (New Haven and London, 1999)

Parkin, P. H., and Humphries, H. R., *Acoustics, Noise and Buildings* (London, 1958)

Pearton, M., *LSO at 70: a History of the Orchestra* (London, 1974)

Peyser, J. (ed.), *The Orchestra: Origins and Transformations* (New York, 1986)

Philip, R., *Early Recordings and Musical Style: Changing Tastes in Instrumental Performance 1900–1950* (Cambridge, 1992)
  'The Recordings of Edward Elgar (1857–1934): Authenticity and Performance Practice', *Early Music* 12 (1984), pp. 481–9

Pilotti, G., *Breve insegnamento teorico . . . di scrivere per tutti gli strumenti d'orchestra* (Milan, 1875)

Pincherle, M., *L'orchestre de chambre* (Paris, 1948)

Piston, W., *Orchestration* (New York, 1955)

Previn, A., *Orchestra* (London, 1979)

Prout, E., *A Course of Lectures on Orchestration* (London, 1905)
  Instrumentation (London, 1876)

Quantz, J. J., *Versuch einer Anweisung die Flöte traversiere zu spielen* (Berlin, 1752, 3rd edn 1789, repr. 1952; Eng. tr. London, 1966)

Quentin, A., *Musique – orchestration: traité d'instrumentation* (Paris, 1864)

Rastall, R., *The Notation of Western Music* (London, 1983, rev. 2nd edn Leeds, 1998)

Raynor, H., *The Orchestra* (London, 1978)

Read, G., *Music Notation* (London, 1974)
  Thesaurus of Orchestral Devices (New York, 1953)

Reicha, A., *Cours de composition musicale ou traité complet et raisonné d'harmonie pratique* (Paris, 1824–6)

Reichardt, J. F., *Über die Pflichten des ripien-Violinisten* (Berlin and Leipzig, 1776)

Riemann, H., *Katechismus der Orchestrierung (Anleitung zum Instrumentieren)* (Leipzig, 1902, 5th edn 1921 as *Handbuch der Orchestrierung*)

Riley, G. A. B., 'The Two Auditoria of Australia's National Capital', Tenth International Congress on Acoustics, Sydney, 1980

Rimsky-Korsakov, N., *Principles of Orchestration*, ed. Maximilian Steinberg (St Peterburg, 1913), tr. Edward Agate (London, 1922, 2nd edn 1964)

Robjohns, H., 'Stereo Lab – Stereo Microphone Techniques explained', *Sound On Sound Magazine* (February 1997) (internet: www.sospubs.co.uk)

Rodzinski, H., *Our Two Lives* (New York, 1976)

Rosen, C., *Sonata Forms* (New York and London, 1980, rev. 1988)

Rudolf, M., *The Grammar of Conducting* (New York, 1949)

Rushby-Smith, J., 'Broadcasting the Proms', *BBC Proms Prospectus*, 1982, repr. 1986
  'A Subjective Assessment of the Acoustical Properties of Concert Halls', *Proceedings of the Institute of Acoustics* 10/2 (1988), pp. 321–9

Russell, Thomas, *Philharmonic* (London, 1953)

Sadie, S. (ed.), *The New Grove Dictionary of Music and Musicians* (20 vols., London, 1980, rev. 2nd edn, 29 vols. ed. Sadie and Tyrell, J., 2001)

Scherchen, H., *Lehrbuch des Dirigierens* (Leipzig, 1929, 2nd edn 1956, Eng. tr. 1933)

Schoenberg, A., *Fundamentals of Musical Composition*, ed. G. Strang and L. Stein (London, 1967)

Schonberg, H., *The Great Conductors* (New York, 1968)

Schreiber, O., *Orchester und Orchesterpraxis in Deutschland zwischen 1780 und 1850* (Berlin, 1838)

Schubert, G., 'Zur Geschichte des Kammerorchesters im 20 Jahrhundert', in Beer, A., Pfarr, K., and Ruf, W. (eds.), *Festschrift Christoph-Hellmut Mahling* (Tutzing, 1997), pp. 1235–50

Schünemann, G., *Geschichte des Dirigierens* (Leipzig, 1913, repr. 1965)

Schulz, W., 'Analysis of a Symphony Orchestra: Sociological and Sociopsychological Aspects', in M. Pipereck (ed.), *Stress and Music: Medical, Psychological, Sociological and Legal Strain Factors in a Symphony-Orchestra Musician's Profession* (Vienna, 1981), pp. 35–56

Schwarz, S., 'The Economics of the Performing Arts: a Case Study of the Major Orchestras', in Kamerman, J. B., and Martorella, R. (eds.), *Performers & Performances: the Social Organization of Artistic Work* (New York, 1986), pp. 409–33

Selfridge-Field, E., *Venetian Instrumental Music from Gabrieli to Vivaldi* (London, 1975, 3rd edn 1994)

Shanet, H., *Philharmonic: a History of New York's Orchestra* (New York, 1975)

Sherman, B., *Inside Early Music: Conversations with Performers* (Oxford, 1997)

Small, C., *Musicking: the meanings of performing and listening* (Hanover and London, 1998)

  'Performance as Ritual: sketch for an enquiry into the true nature of a symphony concert', in White, A. L. (ed.), *Lost in Music: Culture, Style and the Musical Event* (London, 1987), pp. 6–32

Sonneck, O., *Early Concert-Life in America* (Leipzig, 1907)

Spitzer, J., 'The Birth of the Orchestra in Rome: an Iconographical Study', *Early Music* 19 (1991), pp. 9–28

  'Metaphors of the Orchestra: the Orchestra as Metaphor', *Musical Quarterly* 53 (1996), pp. 234–64

Spitzer, J., and Zaslaw, N., 'Improvised Ornamentation in Eighteenth-Century Orchestras', *Journal of the American Musicological Society* 39 (1986), pp. 524–77

Stephenson, K., *Hundert Jahre Philharmonische Gesellschaft in Hamburg* (Hamburg, 1928)

Stewart, A., *LSO at 90: from Queen's Hall to the Barbican Centre* (London, 1994)

Stoessel, A., *The Technique of the Baton* (New York, 1920, 2nd edn 1928)

Stowell, R., *The Early Violin and Viola* (Cambridge, 2001)

  'Good Execution and Other Necessary Skills: the role of the concertmaster in the late eighteenth century', *Early Music* 16 (1988), pp. 21–33

Stowell, R. (ed.), *Performing Beethoven* (Cambridge, 1994)

Strauss, R., *Instrumentationslehre von Hector Berlioz* (Leipzig, 1905)

Taubman, H., *The Symphony Orchestra Abroad* (Vienna, VA, 1970)

Terry, C. S., *Bach's Orchestra* (London, 1932, 2nd edn 1958)

Tschaikov, B. N., 'Preparation for the Orchestral Profession: which kind of symphony orchestra will we have in 2000?', *International Journal of Music Education* 9 (1987), pp. 3–6

Volbach, F., *Das moderne Orchester in seiner Entwicklung* (Leipzig, 1910, 2nd edn 1919)

Wagner, R., *Über das Dirigieren* (1869; Eng. tr. 1887, 4th edn 1940)

Weaver, R. L., 'The Orchestra in Early Italian Opera', *Journal of the American Musicological Society* 17 (1964), pp. 83–9

Weingartner, F., *Über das Dirigieren* (Leipzig, 1895, 5th edn 1913; Eng. tr. 1906, 2nd edn 1925)

Wellesz, E., *Die Neue Instrumentation* (Berlin, 1928–9)

Widor, C.-M., *Technique de l'orchestre moderne* (Paris, 1904, rev. 5th edn 1925)

Willener, A., *La pyramide symphonique: exécuter, créer? Une sociologie des instrumentistes d'orchestres* (Zurich, 1997)

Wood, H. J., *About Conducting* (London, 1945, rev. 1972)

Wooldridge, D., *Conductor's World* (London, 1970)

www.mindset.org/MIND2/research.html, University of California at Irvine, M.I.N.D. Institute

www.orchestranet.co.uk, Association of British Orchestras

www.symphony.org American Symphony Orchestra League links

Young, G., *The Sackbut Blues: Hugh Le Caine, Pioneer in Electronic Music* (Ottawa, 1989)

  'The Compleat Orchestral Musician', *Early Music* 7 (1979), pp. 46–57, 71–2

Zaslaw, N., *Mozart's Symphonies: Context, Performance Practice, Reception* (Oxford, 1989)

  'Three Notes on the Early History of the Orchestra', *Historical Performance* 1 (1988), pp. 63–7

  'Toward the Revival of the Classical Orchestra', *Proceedings of the Royal Musical Association* 103 (1976–7), p. 158

  'When is an Orchestra not an Orchestra?', *Early Music* 16 (1988), pp. 438–95

Index